THREE THOUSAND
YEARS OF HEBREW
VERSIFICATION

THREE THOUSAND YEARS OF HEBREW VERSIFICATION

Essays in Comparative Prosody

Benjamin Harshav

Yale
UNIVERSITY PRESS
New Haven & London

Published with assistance from the Louis Stern Memorial Fund.

Yale University Press books may be purchased in quantity for educational, business, or promotional use. For information, please e-mail sales.press@yale.edu (U.S. office) or sales@yaleup.co.uk (U.K. office).

Set in Minion by Alpha Design & Composition of Pittsfield, New Hampshire.
Printed in the United States of America.

Library of Congress Cataloging-in-Publication Data
Harshav, Benjamin, 1928–
Three thousand years of Hebrew versification : essays in comparative prosody / Benjamin Harshav.
pages cm
Includes bibliographical references and index.
ISBN 978-0-300-14487-1 (hardback)
1. Hebrew language—Versification.   2. Hebrew poetry—History and criticism
3. Hebrew language—Syllabication.   4. Hebrew language—Rhythm.   I. Title.
PJ4598.H37 2014
892.4'1009—dc23   2013044554

A catalogue record for this book is available from the British Library.

This paper meets the requirements of ANSI/NISO Z39.48-1992 (Permanence of Paper).

10 9 8 7 6 5 4 3 2 1

In memory of
Roman Jakobson

scholar linguist friend

CONTENTS

PRELUDE

Poetry is the language-mediated art of imagined
situations.
And it is the self-conscious art of the language
of art.

"Poetry is the rhythmic expression in rhythmic
language of rhythmic poetic emotions."

(B. Roland Lewis)

Poetry plays an indispensable role in every culture. In traditional, premod-
ernist societies, poetry was part of one cultural polyphony including national
myth, identity, and fictional literature. With Hegel, poetry was seen as the peak
of the cultural hierarchy. In the twentieth century, however, culture meant a
plurality of specialists' professions: poetry was carried by several segments of
society and communities of discourse. The culture as a whole incorporated
poetry-making and poetry-consuming groups and institutions on several
levels as autonomous branches of a language culture. Yet there was no longer
any necessary continuity between the high and the low, between rap lyrics and
T. S. Eliot, between Expressionism and Surrealism.

Versification was mandatory in many genres of verbal art. National epics
and romantic monologues, French neoclassical comedies and tragedies, poetic
narratives and anti-narratives (the Russian *poema*), lyrical poetry and popular
songs—all were transmitted to us in precise meters or obligatory meter-and-
rhyme. Language cultures—French, Italian, Spanish, German, English, Rus-
sian, etc.—were unthinkable without versification. In languages of the East,

such as Arabic, Persian, Georgian (*The Knight in the Panther's Skin*), for rhyme to encase strophic structures was equally obligatory.

The European classical heritage in Hebrew, Greek, and Latin had no rhyme, because rhyme as a device of composition was not yet invented when "classical" texts were written. As I shall show in Chapter 4, this extraordinary invention occurred in post-Biblical Hebrew poetry in the early centuries CE in Byzantine-ruled Palestine. On the continent of Europe, epic poetry was written in precise meters emphatically without rhyme: Milton's *Paradise Lost*, Klopstock's *Messiah*, Mickiewicz's *Pan Tadeusz*, the eighteenth-century Hebrew writer Naftali Wesseli's *Sublime Poems*. Poetry meant elevation of the sounds from the syntax and the meanings of words to form a structure of their own— which might then be applied again to represent meaning.

In English poetry, a compromise was achieved: most short and lyrical poems were rhymed (Donne, Marvell, Keats, Shelley, Wordsworth), while long narrative poems and poetic drama required meter alone (Shakespeare, Milton, Wordsworth's *Prelude*). On the continent, however, Dante's *Divine Comedy*, the plays of Molière and Corneille, Lope de Vega's work, Torquatto Tasso's *Liberated Jerusalem,* the Yiddish poet Elia Levita's *Bovo-bukh* (Padua-Venice, 1508/1509), Goethe's *Faust*, and Pushkin's *Eugene Onegin* were all consistently written in rhymed and predetermined strophic structures. Lord Byron belongs to the "continental" (Italian) option, imposing both rhyme and meter. However, his meter in *Don Juan* is the iambic pentameter of English narrative poetry and not the symmetrical four iambs of Pushkin or the ottava rima of Levita's *Bovo-bukh*.

In the first half of the twentieth century, scholars and philosophers wrote theories of poetry (or *Dichtung*—in Heidegger's German: from "density"), having in mind literature as a whole, or what we might call today the "literariness" of literature. Benedetto Croce, Lascelles Abercrombie, I. A. Richards, Martin Heidegger, Roman Jakobson, Yuri Tynjanov, Cleanth Brooks, Monroe Beardsley, Paul de Man, and many others wrote theories of poetry and the language of poetry—as opposed to both the language of prose and the language of science. For Croce, even the *Divine Comedy* was an anthology of mere "literature," studded with gems of poetry.

In all languages, writing poetry required adherence to rigorous rules of versification. Writing poetry without meter was like writing language without syntax. Meter was the grammar of the poetic text. In short, the quintessential aspect of literature was poetry, and the constitutive feature of poetry was regular versification.

In 1905, F. T. Marinetti launched an "international inquiry on free verse," published only with his Futurist Manifesto in 1909. The new spirit swept through young poets in many countries. Marinetti proclaimed "Words in Freedom," and several Russian Cubo-Futurists wrote a manifesto for "the word as such" (*samovitoe slovo*).

In 1910, Symbolism in Russia was pronounced dead. The young Russian Formalist Boris Eikhenbaum, in his book on Anna Akhmatova, distinguished between two options in modern poetry: evolution (Acmeism) and revolution (Futurism). "Free verse," a label attached to both, became a ubiquitous slogan.

In English, Ezra Pound included "free verse" in his relatively modest Imagist manifesto (1912) and changed the nature of English poetry. Today, hardly anybody writes poetry in English in regular meters (except for stubborn Richard Wilbur). To be sure, the movement for free verse started in Europe a little earlier (there are always precursors to any new phenomenon) with several minor French Symbolist poets in the late nineteenth century. An English precursor in the twentieth century was Amy Lowell's little journal *Poetry*. Still, free verse was one option of many in French Symbolist poetry. Some famous earlier poets—Novalis, Hölderlin, Whitman—were co-opted to the trend.

A similar wave, called Expressionism, emerged in Germany (see Michael Hamburger's essay "1912"). Almost overnight, free verse and other deviations from regular meters came to dominate modern poetry in all languages by all kinds of poets, from T. S. Eliot, who came "in and out of iambic pentameter," to the neoclassical Modernists Osip Mandelshtam, R. M. Rilke, and A. Sutzkever. Nevertheless, meters still echoed in the resonance chamber of creative poetry.

Contrary to some apologists for poetry and against widespread opinion, the arts evolved with their own dynamics, independently of history and not directly reflecting it. Most ideas of avant-garde movements appeared before World War I. But after the shock of the war, the "prescient" slogans of many marginal coteries moved from the periphery to the centers of culture. Marc Chagall said that Lenin stood Russia on its head, as in his paintings. The ISMs (El Lissitzky's term) and the avant-garde of the twentieth century had many typical and contradictory features, but the idea of free verse conquered all countries and languages.

A similar change occurred in the history of art, where the idea of non-figurative or "Object-less" (misleadingly translated as "Non-objective") art performed a revolution like the one free verse had achieved in poetry. If there could be poetry without meter, why not art without represented figures? It was a challenge to the whole history and the very institutions of poetry and art. Though the semantic and imagery aspects of the language of poetry (metaphor, allusion, paradox) may seem to us today more important and meaningful than versification, for many centuries versification was the constitutive aspect of poetry—what made a poem a poem and not necessarily a good poem.

An individual poem's meter may seem trite and redundant in interpreting a poem, it may not seem to contribute to its "meaning" and interpretation, but for the institutions of culture meter was a necessary scaffolding—indeed, the only mandatory structure for almost every poem in the language. The attempts at broadening out from the boundaries of verse showed how entrenched those institutions were.

What is the role of meter in poetry? Meter weaves a parallel thread underneath—and throughout—the verbal fabric. To use another metaphor, the text and its meter are two faces of a double helix, intertwined and interacting, mirroring and reinforcing each other at every spot and intersection. The units of verse and the units of language challenge and compete with each other step after step, word after word. They are the foundation of what has been described as semantic density and compactness of poetic language. Much as in popular songs, a few words in a poem suffice for the evocation of images, situations, ideas, and readers' emotions. The meter, rhyme, and sound orchestration of the text give weight to the words' meanings and authorize the text to be called poetry—and to be read as poetry: condensed and evocative. The content of a poem is not given as an outline of a story or a detailed description of a "world," as in a novel, but as an evocation of a situation that rhythmically participates, syllable after syllable, and grows in the rhythmical continuous texture.

It is almost impossible to describe the experience of meter in rational terms. Suggestive language may be more appropriate. Meter permeates all the cells of the text and creates a rhythmical impulse of words and sounds melted into one (as Emil Staiger insisted) and reenacted in the reader's mind. The "set toward the text itself" (in Jakobson's phrase: "set toward the message") calls up effects of what Paul de Man called "materiality": sound patterns, parallelism, repetition, and concrete images that appeal directly to the reader's sensibilities. The metrical structure (meter, rhyme, strophes) determines the size of the text and its subdivisions.

In a dichotomy of "content" and "form," meter provides "form" for a work of poetry. The form as elaborated in the verse is total, permeating and framing the whole text. Beyond that, there are partial forms made of the thematic material of the poem itself, which is sporadic in each poem and occasional in a body of poetry.

A work of poetry constitutes a bridge between the individual poem or the individual poet and the institutions of culture. The meter of a poem also indicates that this poem is part of the institution of poetry and, if there are pertinent genres, part of a genre as well. Meter is not simply one aspect of an individual poem, its "form," but representative of a system that covers all the poetry in its domain. Before meter was downplayed, poets were not free to write poetry outside that system unless they took part in its reformation.

For many centuries, working within a mandatory versification system was a sine qua non. There have been different versification systems in different languages and in different periods, however. Thus French and Italian poetry basically used a **syllabic meter:** the number of syllables in a verse line and in a hemistich is fixed in a syllabic meter, while the number and placement of language stresses is free, except for the last and/or penultimate syllable, which is regularly accented.

On the other hand, in **accentual meters**, in Old German, Old English, and Old Yiddish, the number of accents in a verse line, reinforced by alliteration, is fixed (in epic poetry, there are usually four major accents per line), while the number of syllables between any two accents is free.

In languages with a "free" stress, a new metrical system had developed since the Renaissance, one that took into account both the number of syllables per line and the number and placement of stresses. Those **accentual-syllabic** meters dominated English, German, Russian, Yiddish, and Hebrew verse for several centuries at the peak of the creative poetic achievements in those languages. In Polish, where stress is fixed on the penultimate syllable of each word, there are two metrical systems: *syllabism*—as in Romance languages—and *syllabotonism*, impressed by its neighbor languages Russian and German.

This book presents a family of interrelated studies of verse in language and verse in history. I explore the "deep structure" of changing versification systems, their dependence on the structure of language, and their place in multilingual history. I explore issues concerning the poetics of prosody, free verse and its constraints, and the importance of local rhythmical configurations.

As a prime case, I analyze the history of versification in the languages I have worked with, mainly the Hebrew and Yiddish of the past three thousand years (give or take half a millennium) and the past seven hundred years, respectively. Naturally, research in the Jewish languages contributes to our understanding of Jewish culture, yet it also contributes to the study of other languages and methodologies. This book is not an anthology of individual cases, however, but an integrated book with a unified theory and forays in several directions for illustrative purposes. The questions are general, the theory is transnational and comparative, and the concrete material is embedded in the history of culture.

Thus, the book has two horizons in mind: the general theory and poetics of versification (comparative prosody), on the one hand, and the history of Hebrew and Yiddish poetry, on the other. The very same material can be used in both directions. Hebrew poetry in the past three millennia and Yiddish poetry in the past seven hundred years were situated in the midst of languages not necessarily related, making them "comparative" literatures par excellence.

The Prelude sets the place of versification in general culture. Chapters 1 and 2, which map out the horizons of this book, discuss the relations of sound and meaning as examined in English verse. Other chapters may be of interest to students of comparative prosody. Chapter 1 outlines some basic notions about meter and rhythm to provide a level field for all the historical studies, and Chapter 2 offers a general theoretical discussion of the question Do sounds have meaning? I argue that the sound/meaning nexus—like other theoretical generalizations—is not an either/or question, and I propose four different classes, ranging from full onomatopoeia to "neutral" sound patterns, which fulfill a general "poetic function."

Chapter 3 investigates the rhythms of the Bible, which were subsequently echoed in texts of vernacular literatures. More specifically, Chapter 3 revisits the rhythms of a world classic—the Bible—in several genres (poetry, prophecy, prose), showing the differences between the original Hebrew and its English translation (the King James version). In addition to the accepted idea of horizontal multimedia parallelism, we observe also vertical parallels and the hierarchical structures of a prophetic grid.

Chapters 4 and 5 look at the two great discoveries of Jewish poetry: the invention of rhyme, not as embellishment, but with a compositional strophe-making function, and the discovery of accentual iambs in European poetry, as observed in the languages at hand: English, German, Russian, and Yiddish. To explore the first, Chapter 4 presents a sweeping survey of three thousand

years of Hebrew poetry, representing twelve different areas of Hebrew versi-
fication through history and analyzing the deep structures of those systems.
Chapter 5 follows the survey of Hebrew poetry with a multicultural study of
the conditions of transition from earlier verse systems to accentual-syllabic
meters (in English, German, Russian, Hebrew, and other languages). Beyond
that, in Chapters 6 and 7, I examine a body of free rhythms in folksongs and
in modern poetry in Yiddish, developing a new classification of free rhythms.

In all cases of the transition to accentual-syllabic meters, there was a conflu-
ence of a native accentual tradition (usually requiring four accents in a verse
line) and an imported syllabic norm (requiring a fixed number of syllables:
mainly eight or ten). The accentual source was mostly Germanic; the syllabic
source was mostly Italian. This study shows how the first to systematically
discover accentual iambs in Europe was the Hebrew and Yiddish poet and
"bachelor" Elia Levita (Eliahu Baḥur in Hebrew, Elye Bokher in Yiddish).

Was Levita that rare Jew, a bachelor and wandering scholar, or was he a
bachelor of arts? He was a polyglot and a versatile writer who taught Hebrew
and Kabbalah to prominent Christian Renaissance figures, including Cardinal
Viterbo in Rome (in whose house he lived), and published a Latin-German-
Yiddish-Hebrew dictionary. He wrote two epic romances in Yiddish in the
Italian ottava rima strophe, as well as satirical poems in Yiddish.

In writing his romances, he imposed the Italian syllabic requirement on the
Yiddish text, which was written in an accentual language, Germanic in origin.
While writing this rhymed romance, Levita gradually merged the two metric
principles—accent and syllable—and discovered the precise iambic verse line.
(I use the term "accentual iamb" to distinguish this meter from the Greek quan-
titative iamb.) Gradually, Levita invented rhymes in Yiddish to meet the Italian
requirements and whimsically developed an iambic tetrameter in the sextet
of an ottava rima strophe and an iambic pentameter in the closing couplet.

Levita's story is a microcosm of the great shift that occurred in European
poetry, which made possible the flexible language and subtle rhythmical varia-
tions of Shakespeare, Goethe, and Pushkin. I discuss this transition in several
literatures in a comparative perspective.

ACKNOWLEDGMENTS

Over the course of years, with changes in place, language, and technology, the essays here have had to be rewritten, rethought, and retyped several times, and a lot of technical work has had to be done. Several of my publications and books on prosody in Hebrew had not been translated into English, which also meant translation work.

I am grateful to Israel Carmel, my publisher in Jerusalem, and to Professor Avidov Lipsker and my friends at Bar-Ilan University Press in Israel. My special thanks go to Professor Ziva Ben-Porath, former director of the Porter Institute for Poetics and Semiotics at Tel Aviv University, and all my friends there for their help and conversation, especially Harai Golomb, Menakhem Perry, Itamar Even-Zohar, and Dmitry Segal. I am grateful for the support of my research provided by the research fund of Tel Aviv University and the Rifkind Fund at the Judaic Studies Program at Yale University.

Personal thanks are owed to the late linguist and Yiddish scholar Uriel Weinreich, with whom I had rich dialogues before his death in New York at the age of forty. To my friend the linguist Roman Jakobson at Harvard and MIT, in whose home I stayed on my visits to the United States and of whom I have warm memories. To Uri (Robert B.) Alter, who understood me so well, though working far from his field. To the late T. Carmi, who encouraged me to write on versification in his exquisite Hebrew poetry anthologies.

To my editors at Yale University Press who believed in this book, Jonathan Brent, Sarah Miller, and Mary Pasti. To Juan Cruz at Aberdeen University in Scotland for his first-class index. For my assistants at Yale University: Eyal Dotan, Yasha Klots, Kolya Borodulin, Roman Utkin, Josh Price, and Michal Herzberg.

To others at Yale University Press who have helped with this book, including John Palmer, Heather Gold, Meredith Phillips, Lindsey Voskowsky, and Aldo Cupo, and to all my friends at Yale University Press. To all scholars and students with goodwill and intelligence—my deepest gratitude and thanks to all.

At this moment I feel obliged to several towering figures in modern linguistics and poetics as well as in the study of Jewish poetry. The very solid linguist and Yiddish scholar Uriel Weinreich invited me at the age of twenty-five to write an essay for his first volume, *The Field of Yiddish, on the 200th Anniversary of Columbia University,* encompassing the whole body of Yiddish poetry and relating it to general theory and research. The study of Yiddish free rhythms was rewritten for this volume sixty years later, in Chapter 5. The Hebrew equivalent was published as a little book, *Rithmus Ha-rakhavut,* and reprinted in my book *The Art of Poetry.*

The stature and tradition of Roman Jakobson are hovering above this work. My friend Uri (Robert B.) Alter was a living example of integrating Jewish research with "general" topics and methods. How nice to have such standard-bearers in front of new adventures.

Ve-aḥron aḥaron Ḥaviv, my partner among books, Bobbi.

A Note to the Reader

This book is written in English with an English-speaking reader in mind. Most texts in other languages have been explained, and transcriptions and translations are provided when needed for the main argument, but the "argument" is the goal.

Several of the studies here were first published many years ago (since 1954; see the list of my publications on prosody at the end of the book). Because I myself moved on to other concerns, some references to research may look antiquated. Literary criticism in this period was preoccupied with interpreting the individual poem and, later, with addressing cultural and political questions. In preparing this book I augmented and thoroughly reedited these studies.

Furthermore, in my early years I accepted the prevalent view of "scientific" studies even in the humanities, as based on all the scholarship on the topic at hand. Many good ideas were buried in long footnotes or published in old collections or in abstruse journals. For this book I lifted much researched material from the footnotes and incorporated them into the text.

Primary texts are reproduced here in Hebrew, Yiddish, or English and, where appropriate, provided with transcriptions and transliterations. The emphasis is on general theory and historical and structural analysis. The direction of the metrical schemata is usually from left to right, as part of the English text, and is indicated by an arrow.

TRANSCRIPTIONS

This is not a philological treatise. The principle of explication is to be user-friendly and to provide the sound of a contemporary reading of the printed text. The same words were pronounced differently in different countries and periods; the previous pronunciation is not always clear to us today. I prefer today's pronunciation, familiar to the reader, to problematic attempts at restoring the sounds of the past.

HEBREW

The general direction of the pronunciation here is contemporary Israeli. In several respects there are similarities between the contemporary Israeli accent and that of other periods. Thus *qamats* (ָ) rhymes with *patah* (ַ), and both are pronounced *a* in the Byzantine Hebrew piyut, in Spain, and in Israeli Hebrew today.

SYMBOLS OF VERSIFICATION

—	metrical accent
∪	metrical slack (unaccented syllable)
|∪∪—|	foot boundaries
//	caesura
|∪—∪|	word boundaries
ó, x́	stressed syllable
ő	strongly stressed syllable
x	undecided accent or accent not assigned
0	absent syllable; missing accent

Three Thousand
Years of Hebrew
Versification

Basic Aspects
of Meter and Rhythm

WHAT IS METER?

In the Modern Hebrew and English traditions, meter can be seen as a regular pulse, as a wave of ups and downs, as a series of stressed and unstressed syllables.

Let us read aloud the first strophe of William Blake's poem "The Tyger."

> Tyger! Tyger! burning bright
> In the forests of the night,
> What immortal hand or eye
> Could frame thy fearful symmetry?

Most readers are drawn into it and convey the rhythmical beat smoothly but slow down or stumble in the fourth line. Why?

In this poem the first line has four words, each word has two syllables, and the first syllable is stressed $/- \cup / - \cup / - \cup / - 0 /$. The language itself provides a metrical line. There is a regular beat, starting with the first syllable (**ta**-ta **ta**-ta **ta**-ta **ta**). By *inertia,* the beat is continued in the next line, "**In** the **for**ests **of** the **night**." In this tradition of rhymed lyrical poems, the word "bright" in the rhyming position requires a response in the next line or lines. The reader is pulled forward to fulfill both requirements, of meter and of rhyme.

Yet, in the second line, only two words provide definitive stresses: "forests" and "night"; the other words may not be stressed at all in normal speech: "in the forests" is usually read as one word, although it can accept a secondary stress if the reader is swept up by the metrical impulse.

Meter is an abstract and regular pattern provided by the language of the text. It is abstract because it is imposed regardless of any concrete details about the language or degrees of stress; and it is regular because the same abstract unit, the foot /— ∪/, is repeated throughout the poem—in our case, four times in each line and four lines in a strophe. (Some critics would describe this metrical line as three and a half feet, but we use here the number of accents alone, leaving the number of syllables at the end of a line optional.)

Now, let us reread the first strophe in its entirety:

> Tyger! Tyger! burning bright
> In the forests of the night,
> What immortal hand or eye
> Could frame thy fearful symmetry?

If read emphasizing the four-beat meter of "What immortal hand or eye" (**ta**-ta **ta**-ta **ta**-ta **ta**), the last line should read, "**Could** frame **thy** fear**ful** symmetry?" This sounds grotesque. The poet added only one syllable in front of line 4, so we have to revise our whole reading of the poem. We turn the trochaic meter, going from the stress down /— ∪/, into an iambic meter, going upward /∪ —/, in a total reversal of the rhythmical move. We end up reading those words twice, slowing down, and evoking the "semantic density" of these lines. In adjusting to the deviant syllable, we come up with various solutions for the performance, for example, reading the last two lines as one uninterrupted unit, we get: "**What** immor**tal hand** or **eye** could **frame** thy fear**ful sym**metry?" / — ∪ / — ∪ / — ∪ / — ∪ / — ∪ / — ∪ / — /.

How much easier it would have been without the added syllable: "**frame** thy fear**ful sym**metry?" But Blake does it intentionally: all strophes of the poem have the same additional syllable at the beginning of their last lines; hence it is part of the poem's design. Only with a background of precise regularity in the system of poetry can such a reversal be effective.

In addition to the regular meter and rhyme, there are several free sound patterns (not alliterations). I have in mind clusters of two or more consonants: *BuRning BRight* enforced by the paradox of a burning tiger. Such clusters are *FoRests-FRame-FeaRFul* and *iMMoRTal-syMMeTRy*, where the last two clusters converge in the final formula of the strophe. Thus we have a box covered on three sides: the lower and upper verse and the right rhyme, where every word has a double.

This change of one syllable also indicates a period in English poetry. It is part of a "Romantic" tendency (not necessarily fully Romantic poetry) and not to be expected, for example, in a Shakespearean sonnet.

This device may serve as a marker to differentiate between two shades of English Romanticism represented by Wordsworth and Shelley. Wordsworth is more "classical"; the meter is subdued and automatic. He does not play with detailed variations, whereas Shelley pays a great deal of attention to formal details of the verse and strophic structures. Here is the first strophe in Shelley's "Stanzas Written in Dejection, Near Naples":

> The sun is warm, the sky is clear,
>> The waves are dancing fast and bright,
> Blue isles and snowy mountains wear
>> The purple noon's transparent might,
>> The breath of the moist earth is light,
> Around its unexpanded buds;
>> Like many a voice of one delight,
> The winds, the birds, the ocean floods,
> The City's voice itself, is soft like Solitude's.

Wordsworth would use the same pattern of a line throughout a poem, hence unobtrusively, almost automatically. The rhymes here are /abab/bcbc/c for two quatrains, while the second quatrain picks up a rhyme from the first (b), and the last rhyme of the second quatrain is repeated in a ninth-line closure (c). The graphic arrangement highlights the three rhymes in three levels of indentation. Some of the rhymes are precise, while others mix sound rhyme with "eye rhyme." In Blake's poem the rhyme *eye/symmetry* is a "sound rhyme." The reading *symme**try*** ("symme*try*") is forced by the meter. The rhyme *buds/floods/Solitude's* has an "ear rhyme," *buds/floods,* and then a pseudo–eye rhyme in another direction (*floods/Solitude's*). The last word rhymes by the sound in one direction and by the eye in another. The meter is four iambs per line in eight lines, but expands to ten syllables in the last line in Shelley's self-conscious art of composition. The closure line is reinforced by a pattern of eight sibilants in eighteen syllables.

Logically, there can be only five kinds of meters:

Binary meters	Ternary meters
iamb /∪ —/	anapest /∪ ∪ —/
trochee /— ∪/	amphibrach /∪ — ∪/
	dactyl /— ∪ ∪/

The length of the line is labeled in Greek terms: tetrameter (four feet), pentameter (five), and hexameter (six). Sometimes we use a larger foot of four syllables, a *paeon*. We mark the place of the stress with roman numbers—here, paeon III: /∪ ∪ — ∪ / ∪ ∪ —/ (*in the forests / of the night*). A paeon easily disintegrates into two iambs or two trochees. In Blake's poem, the reader is hovering between two readings: either four trochees or two paeons III. It is a matter of expressive reading: between a mechanical, monotone beat, on the one end, and the stresses of a content-oriented performance, on the other. We could also retain two levels of accents: *in the fOrests of the NIGHT* /— ∪ ⁻̈ ∪ / — ∪ ⁻̈ /. However, this precise matching of language stress and metrical accents in the first line of Blake's poem is rare in English poetry and is used for special rhythmical effects.

Here is another example, of the most widespread meter in English—iambic pentameter—which encompasses all traditional narrative and dramatic poetry, all sonnets, and many lyrical poems. The first sentence in Milton's *Paradise Lost* is spread out over sixteen lines of verse.

> Of man's first disobedience, and the fruit
> Of that forbidden tree whose mortal taste
> Brought death into the world, and all our woe,
> With loss of Eden, till one greater Man
> Restore us, and regain the blissful seat,
> Sing, Heavenly Muse, that, on the secret top
> Of Oreb, or of Sinai, didst inspire
> That shepherd who first taught the chosen seed
> In the beginning how the Heavens and Earth
> Rose out of Chaos: or, if Sion hill
> Delight thee more, and Siloa's brook that flowed
> Fast by the oracle of God, I thence
> Invoke thy aid to my adventurous song,
> That with no middle flight intends to soar
> Above th' Aonian mount, while it pursues
> Things unattempted yet in prose or rhyme.

Every line has ten syllables when read as intended. The first line reads: "Of man's first disobedience, and the fruit" |x x́|x́| x x x́ x|x x x́|. The syllables ending in a stress are 2-1-3-4. No regularity here. Observing these variegated words and stresses, some critics claimed that there is no iambic pentameter and that all there is are four accents, i.e. the same Old English "native" verse, without any regularity in the number of syllables.

Here, however, is the same line with exactly the same words and the same number of syllables (ten), but with the word "first" moved a few syllables forward: "Of man's disobedience, and the first fruit" /∪ — ∪ — ∪ — ∪ — ∪ —/. I only moved the word "first" a few syllables forward. True, Blake's version [1] may fulfill the four-accent requirement of Old English meters, and if we read it stressing only the four accents, we may feel no contradiction between the two versions. But if we read the line in five iambs, my "correction" does not work out. Concretely, this reading is correct:

Of **man's** first **disoBEdience, and** the **fruit** /∪ — ∪ — ∪ — ∪ — ∪ —/

And this reading is not. The line is unreadable:

Of **man's** dis**Obedience,** and **the** first **fruit** /∪ — ∪ — ∪ — ∪ — ∪ —/

I distinguish between language *stress* and metrical *accent*. For a verse line to have a certain meter, there must be a correlation between the language and the metrical matrix. The rules of this correlation are as follows. When a meter is applied to language, the feet must adapt to the text.

1) Some words use their stress for an accent (*man's*).
2) In some words the stress is used in a non-accented position (*first*).
3) If any metrical accents fall on a word, at least one of them must fall on the stressed syllable.

In fact, the third rule covers all three points and is the final rule of correlation between verse and language. In the word *disobedience* /— ∪ — ∪/, the stress falls on the syllable *be,* so one or more accents can be added: *dis-o-be-dience* /— ∪ — ∪/. On the other hand, in the incorrect version the stressed syllable *be* is not accented in the meter; there is a clash between language and meter: *disobedience* /∪ — ∪́ —/ has a stress with no accent and an accent without a stress.

In sum: the meter is not given as such in the language of the poem; it is a construct based in the traditional institution of verse. The last line reads: "Things **unattemp**ted yet in prose or rhyme" /∪ — ∪ — ∪ —/∪— ∪ —/. The long word "**un**attempted" has two accents, one of them falling on the stressed syllable "temp."

This correlation requirement is not as widely used in English as in Hebrew or Russian; because of the overwhelming amount of monosyllabic words in English, the emphasis shifts to phrase stress and the oscillation between the two, as in "To **be** or **not** to **be**, that **is** the **ques**tion" /∪ — ∪ — ∪ —/∪ — ∪ — ∪/. For the phrase stress, we may emphasize the "**is**"; for local stress, "**that** is." Here Shakespeare uses the word-stress rule. But he does not activate the phrase stress and does not emphasize the "is," so we may read "that **is** the question," "that is the **ques**tion" or "**that** is the question." The first line of *Paradise Lost* reads: "Of man's first disobedience, and the fruit" /∪ — ̆ ́ — ∪ — ̆ ∪ — ∪ — ́ /. "Man's" is accented (rule 1); "first" is not (rule 2); disobedience has two accents, and the second is stressed in the language (rule 3).

Saying that a verse line has a certain meter means that the text *can* be read by that meter (so-called "scanning"). The meter lies in the base of the poetic text; it is the infrastructure of any rhythmical reading. But the actual rhythmical pattern is woven out of the irregularities that permeate the whole body of the verse. The regular meter is the symmetrical warp, and the free local configurations make up the colorful woof.

This is a good example of verse ambiguity. The same line can enable a construct of an iambic pentameter or a four-accentual paeon. The decision of which to select depends on the literary system to which it belongs. In the first case, the rule of language/verse correlation must be observed. In the second case, the number of syllables between stresses is immaterial.

VERSE AND SYNTAX

A "natural" rhythmical unit is one that cannot divide into further regular groups—i.e. it consists of two or three subunits (see Chapter 3). The iambic pentameter has five subunits ("feet") and will normally divide into two asymmetrical subunits (2 + 3 feet or 3 + 2 feet). A key role is performed by the *colon*, the smallest syntactic-rhythmical unit. The first colon covers the first three iambs; then a second colon begins ("and the fruit"—two iambs). Clearly, this colon is interrupted. In general, the strongest divide between words in Milton's passage is not at the end of a line, but in its asymmetrical middle. Most lines here end close to the middle of a colon and require complementary grammatical parts of speech, or complementary objects in the fictional world, or both. This is not an individual case.

A tension is established between two forces: verse and grammar. As soon as the first colon is finished, the verse line pulls us forward to the completion of the ten-syllable pentameter. And as soon as we reach the end of a pentameter, the colon pulls us beyond the verse boundary, and so on— consistent concatenation. Two functions are at work here: the forward move and the impeding dam. These are accompanied by other rhythmical factors, for example, FiRst DisoBeDieNce/FRuit/FoRBiDDeN TRee—all capitalized consonants are repeated twice. This is an anti-narrative force.

The whole sentence unfolds over sixteen verse lines. That is a powerful pull forward, subordinating a large number of segments, which dam the flow. But the forward pull encounters another force: the division into cola, which constantly break up and stall the forward drive of our reading. This is the reverse of enjambment. Small devices support this double energy; e.g. the first line starts with "Of"—we don't understand what "of" is of until line 6. By poetic inversion we read: "Sing, Heavenly Muse, of . . ." We move on, but there are further dams on the way. In the end, a whole world opens up for us: the network of a mythological world based on the Bible, to be unfolded and described in detail later (see Chapter 3).

At first glance, Milton's poetics are similar to the Bible's poetics in that they construct a world: a move from *naming* a frame of reference, land or sky, to *unfolding* (through expanding and detailed description). In both texts, names, especially sanctified names (of persons and cities), serve as accumulators of information.

But a major difference lies between them: In the Bible the verse units and the syntactic units overlap; indeed, the syntactic unit determines the rhythmical divisions. In metrical verses a tension is created between the two. The two systematically crisscross each other, creating tensions and non-narrative advancements of the text. This imaginary constructed world has evolved through the dynamization of the syntactic frames. This is hardly an accidental device but a *countersystem,* which accompanies every precise system.

RHYTHM

Meter is the metronome, the regular wave that subordinates all irregular elements in a poetic text (through the rule of correlation). We have: "Ŏf mān's fĭrst dīsobēdiĕnce // ānd thĕ frūit" /ᴗ ‒́ ᴗ́ — ᴗ ‒́ ᴗ/— ᴗ ‒́ /. The physical articulation of language is irregular |x x́|x́|x x x́ x||x x x́|. The five-iamb line is made of irregular units (words) of 2-1-4-3 syllables. The distances between stresses are changing as well. A text is said to have a meter when the metrical matrix can be read in that meter. However, for expressive purposes we may not read it metrically.

Rhythm is the result of all rhythmical inputs that converge in one text or in one local intersection. The total rhythmical impact is a result of a complex performance, which is always different and subordinated to the total reading of a poem. Three forces converge here: (1) the regular meter, absent in free verse; (2) the rhythmical units diverging from regularity in such matters as the size of the words and the place of their stresses; and (3) all non-rhythmical factors that influence the tone and meaning of our reading, for example, the voice of the speaker or narrator, the allusion to a biblical world, the impact of syntax, the suspended syntactic resolutions, and the changed order of words, the total of a rhythmical "image."

Milton makes almost no mistakes in the meter. Clearly, he and most English poets have internalized the iambic pentameter that is used throughout this book—and throughout all English poetry, poetic drama, and narrative.

Even if we rearrange the poem according to its cola, Milton continues thinking in five iambs with a pause in the inexact middle. This is the frame in which he molds language. But he does it irregularly, because language boundaries are not as rule-governed as iambs, with their formal regularity. However, he soon shifts to four and fewer iambs in a line.

If that is the case, why not write a poem, divided according to the syntactic units, the cola?

Because the power of Milton's text lies not in the prosaization but in the counterpoint, in the tension between units of language and units of verse. This tension works on all levels: stressed/unstressed, word/foot, colon/verse.

The Russian Symbolist poet Andrey Bely in his book *Ritm kak dialektika* (Rhythm as Dialectics) suggested measuring rhythm by the number of deviations of one line vis-à-vis its preceding line: deviations not in the meter, but in the counterforces, in the boundaries between words and cola, the placement of stresses, etc. In short lyrics or sonnets the parallels between the two verses mirror each other; in Milton this is vital for the flexibility of a long speech. The internalization of the five-foot meter is such that when the verse is rearranged by the cola rather than the meter, the intersecting cola fall in a five-iamb line:

> Of man's first disobedience,
> and the fruit of that forbidden tree
> whose mortal taste brought death into the world,
> and all our woe, with loss of Eden, till
> one greater Man restore us, and regain
> the blissful seat,
> sing, Heavenly Muse, that, on the sacred top
> of Oreb, or of Sinai,
> didst inspire that shepherd
> who first taught the chosen seed
> in the beginning
> how the Heavens and Earth
> rose out of Chaos:
> or if Sion hill delight thee more,
> and Siloa's brook that flowed fast
> by the oracle of God,
> I thence invoke thy aid to my adventurous song,
> that with no middle flight
> intends to soar above th' Aonian mount,
> while it pursues things unattempted yet
> in prose or rhyme.

The arrangement loses its tension and dynamics, and, frankly, it gets boring. The system is precise in five iambs; the countersystem—the syntactic cola—is relatively free and open to play.

The system of versification is indicated in the meter. But the source of disruption lies in the countersystem. The system is an accentual-syllabic verse; the countersystem lies in the units of language.

Language mostly supplies only four stresses for five accents. There is a statistical reason for this. In English, the average number of syllables per accents is 2.5. The verse must skip a few stresses to be proportionate with the language. But in ternary meters we miss a few unstressed syllables, as in Lord Tennyson's poem "Break, Break, Break." In an abstract scheme it looks like an iambic trimeter with a few additional slacks, and the first line is a radical staccato consisting of three independent stresses with no unstressed syllables between them.

Break, break, break,	/0 0 — 0 0 — 0 0 —/
On thy cold gray stones, O Sea!	/∪ ∪ — 0 ∪ — ∪ —/
And I would that my tongue could utter	/∪ ∪ — ∪ ∪ — 0 ∪ — ∪/
The thoughts that arise in me.	/0∪ — ∪ ∪ —0 ∪ —/
O, well for the fisherman's boy,	/0 ∪ — ∪ ∪ — ∪ ∪ —/
That he shouts with his sister at play!	/∪ ∪ —∪ ∪ — ∪ ∪ —/
O, well for the sailor lad,	/0 ∪ — ∪ ∪ —∪ 0 —/
That he sings in his boat on the bay!	/∪ ∪ — ∪ ∪ — ∪ ∪ —/
And the stately ships go on	/∪ ∪ — ∪ 0 — 0 ∪ —/
To their haven under the hill;	/∪ ∪ — ∪ 0 —∪ ∪ —/
But O for the touch of a vanish'd hand,	/0 ∪ —∪ ∪ —/∪ ∪ —∪ 0 —/
And the sound of a voice that is still!	/∪ ∪ — ∪ ∪ — ∪ ∪ —/
Break, break, break	/0 0 — 0 0 — 0 0 —/
At the foot of thy crags, O Sea!	/∪ ∪ —∪ ∪ — 0 ∪ —/
But the tender grace of a day that is dead	/∪ ∪ — ∪ 0 — /∪ ∪ —∪ ∪ —/
Will never come back to me.	/0 ∪ — ∪ ∪ — 0 ∪ —/

A more cautious reading, especially a second reading, can accommodate a ternary net with "holes" in it. A reading like a metronome will produce three anapests and, in the last strophe, four anapests with deviations in the form of "missing" unstressed syllables.

Assuming that the reader relives the regular distance in time between every two stresses, the more syllables that are missing, the faster the reading goes. The first line produces only a beat, like a drum, setting the tone of the poem. The third line in the third and fourth strophes is a typical enhanced reading in rhythm of 3/2 + 2 in faster tempos. There is no regular meter, but if we consider the expected performance, we sense a background of regularity in the rhythm.

In French poetry the opposite relations obtain: the formal meter is syllabic: it has no predetermined order or number of accents, but it does have a fixed number of syllables. Stress in French verse is hardly heard. In the Alexandrine, there are twelve syllables in a line, divided into two versets, with accents on the sixth and twelfth syllables. After a stress there can be one blank syllable *e muet*. But in order to automatically count six syllables, we break up the line either into three iambs or two anapests. There is no predetermined order, but each hemistich is articulated through their pattern. "Les chats" is a sonnet by Baudelaire:

Les amoureux fervents et les savants austères/∪ — ∪ — ∪ —/∪ — ∪ — ∪ — 0/
Aiment également, dans leur mûre saison,   /0 — ∪ — ∪ —/∪∪ — ∪∪ —/
Les chats puissants et doux, orgueil de la maison,
                    /∪ — ∪ — ∪ —/∪ — ∪ — ∪ — /
Qui comme eux sont frileux et comme eux sédentaires.
                    /∪∪ — ∪∪ —/∪∪ — ∪∪ — 0/

Amis de la science et de la volupté   /∪ — ∪∪ — ∪/∪ — ∪ — ∪ — /
Ils cherchent le silence et l'horreur des ténèbres;
                    /∪ — ∪ — ∪ —/∪∪ — ∪∪ — 0/
L'Erèbe les eût pris pour ses coursiers funèbres,
                    /∪ — ∪ — ∪ —/∪ — ∪ — ∪ — ∪0/
S'ils pouvaient au servage incliner leur fierté./∪∪ — ∪∪ — /∪∪ — ∪∪ —/

Ils prennent en songeant les nobles attitudes /∪ — ∪ — ∪ — /∪ — ∪ — 0/
Des grands sphinx allongés au fond des solitudes,
                    /∪∪ — ∪∪ —/∪ — ∪ — ∪ — 0/
Qui semblent s'endormir dans un rêve sans fin;
                    /∪ — ∪ — ∪ —/∪∪ — ∪∪ — /

Leurs reins féconds sont pleins d'étincelles magiques,
                    /∪ — ∪ — ∪ —/∪∪ — ∪∪ — 0/
Et des parcelles d'or, ainsi qu'un sable fin,   /∪ — ∪ — ∪ —/∪ — ∪ — ∪ — /
Etoilent vaguement leurs prunelles mystiques.
                    /∪ — ∪ — ∪ —/∪∪ — ∪ — 0/

Here the opposite relationship obtains: the meter counts syllables, while the arrangement of stresses represents the countersystem. There is no accentual order in the poem as a whole, but each verset has its arrangement, often different from that of preceding versets.

THE VARIETY OF FORMAL SYSTEMS IN HEBREW VERSE

Because of their interaction with a variety of aesthetic and prosodic norms, most systems of verse known in human culture (except for the Chinese meters, based on musical pitch) have been productive in Hebrew over the past three thousand years at one time or another. Any aspect of the Hebrew word—the number of syllables in a line, the structure and place of stress, the relative length of the syllables, the consonantal root of a Hebrew word, and the word as a whole—could serve as the basis for a different metrical system.

The following prosodic systems have governed the meters of Hebrew poetry at one time or another:

1) **Accentual meter**—a meter based on a fixed number of major stresses in a verse line (in Old English or Old German and in post-Biblical Hebrew poetry)

2) **Free-accentual meter**—a meter relying on several conspicuous stresses (three or four), equivalent rather than equal, which shore up the free syllables around them, as subordinated words, or enclytics (as in the Bible)

3) **Word meter**—a meter based on the number of written words in a verse line (as in the piyut, the major tradition of Hebrew liturgical poetry)

4) **Syllabic meter**—a meter based on a fixed number of syllables per line, irrespective of stresses and their placement (in Hebrew in Italy since the Renaissance and in central and eastern Europe in the nineteenth century)

5) **Quantitative-syllabic meter** (also called simply "quantitative"meter)— a configuration of meter based on both principles, the number of syllables and the distinction between long and short syllables (in classical Arabic poetry and in Hebrew in medieval Spain, Provence, Portugal, and Italy)

6) **Accentual-syllabic (a.-s.) meter in Ashkenazi Hebrew**—a meter based on a configuration of both the number of syllables and the order of stresses (in English, German, Russian, Yiddish, and Ashkenazi Hebrew in the modern age)

7) **Accentual-syllabic (a.-s.) meter in Israeli Hebrew**—a meter based on the same general principles as in Ashkenazi Hebrew, yet the change of dialect to "Sephardi" (Israeli) Hebrew is not a negligible issue: a whole language moved its stresses abruptly from the center of the word to the end, mainly from a penultimate to an ultimate stress, which impacted the whole vocabulary and metrical system—the very character of the language

8) **Deviant accentual-syllabic meter (the "net")**—a meter with a regular number of stresses, with limited freedom in the number of unstressed

syllables; influenced by the verse of Russian Modernism (in Israeli poetry since World War I: Rachel (Raḥel), Bat-Miriam, Alterman, Khalfi)

9) **Balancing phrase groups**—a variety of free verse forms, based on counterbalancing cola and verse boundaries, that emerged in Hebrew in Europe in the early twentieth century during the vogue of Expressionism (the Viennese Ben Yitzhak, Vogel) and in Israel since the 1950s under the impact of Anglo-American Modernism (especially Nathan Zach and Yehuda Amichai)

No other language went through so many prosodic systems as Hebrew.

The earliest known systematic use of rhyme as a compositional device in poetry evolved in Hebrew sometime between the second and sixth centuries CE before the Arabic conquests. It grew out of a biblical cluster of partial parallelisms in semantic, syntactic, morphological, and sound patterns, now formalized and obeying strict numerical rules.

The rhyme patterns, strophic forms, and the principles of composition of a poem have a similar variety. Hebrew verse in the course of its history has run the gamut of rhyme norms: terminal or accentual rhymemes, continuous or discontinuous rhymemes, "grammatical" or sound-autonomous rhyme, rhyme based on suffixes or on the lexical morpheme, rhyme using word repetition or excluding it.

I have formulated a structural model for the understanding of each system. Thus, in the glorious Hebrew poetry in Medieval Spain, one scholar found 57 different meters, another scholar counted 32 meters. Why not 31 or 35? This was a taxonomy in the medieval Arabic tradition. Yet when the structural principles of this system are analyzed, we find 5 basic meters (2 binary and 3 ternary), as in modern poetry. Another example: classical liturgical poetry was known to scholars for its "rich sound-play." However, the sounds are not "rich," because all those consonants are required by the rich norm (maximal sounds in a rhymeme are equal to the minimal). It turns out that rhymes in the piyut follow very strict rules, including the use of discontinuous strings of sounds, modeled on the discontinuous structure of the Hebrew lexeme.

DO SOUNDS HAVE MEANING?

Hebrew poet Nathan Alterman, taking his daughter on a stroll after a rare rain refreshed the streets, shows her the essential elements of the new city: stone, glass, light.[1] In Modern Hebrew, *zgugit* means "glass," and *tsalul* means "lucid, transparent, sober":

> hiney ha-zgugit—shma tsalul mi-shmoteynu,
> umi bekif'on hirhura ya' avor?
> al kav miftana, ke-al-saf nishmateynu,
> ha-ra'ash nifrad min ha-or.[2]

> [here is the Glass, her name (*zgugit*) more lucid than ours, / who can cross through her frozen thought? / on the line of her threshold, at the brink of our soul, / Noise separates from Light.]

1. SOUND AS SIGN

Sound is colorful.
Sound is ubiquitous.
Sound is signifying.
Sound is transparent.

For Husserl, a sign was transparent: we are looking *through* the sign, not *at* the sign. For T. S. Eliot, it is a stained-glass window: we look *at* it, not through it. The mantra of the New Critics in the twentieth century was: "A poem should not mean but be" (Archibald MacLeish).

Sounds can be intentional, emitted by a human source, or symptomatic, indicating an external event in nature or civilization (thunder, an airplane flying by, a voice calling). Sound is sound only if there is a listener and a hearing situation (reception, acoustics, social communication). There are thousands of shades of color distinguishable from one another by human perceivers in laboratory conditions. And there are zillions of shades of sound. Some level of noise (even subliminal noise) is necessary as a context for any communication.

Sounds (or their representations) are ubiquitous in communication. Sounds range from noisy blasts to Silence. They may express an aesthetic preference for noise or a class attitude (vindication, disdain, fear). On the other end of the spectrum, there is Silence. The sound of Silence is not the absence of speech; rather, Silence is part of communication, an intentional, negative reading: suppression of the sound of speech, degree zero. In another poem, Alterman wrote, "Du-mi-ya bā-mer-kha-kim sho-re-ket" (Silence whistles in the white spaces).

From among all the possible sounds and shades of sound that humans produce, languages have codified a small number of interrelated phonemes that constitute a system for the whole language. In a given language a phoneme is the smallest unit of sound; it has no meaning of its own, but can make a difference in meaning. Take the word *raw:* if we change the phoneme *r* to *l*, we get the word *law*—with a totally unrelated set of meanings. But for a Japanese those two phonemes sound the same; both shades of meaning inhabit one English phoneme. Learning to speak is a process of eliminating superfluous sounds that can be produced by a baby but do not make separate phonemes and do not participate in the system. In all human languages together there are only fifty-five phonemes: each language accepts only a selection. Each phoneme is composed of several distinctive features, which coalesce in one phoneme. There are ten–twelve distinctive features.

Phonemes are not precise, measurable sounds. Every person sounds different, and different at different hours and in different moods, like Monet's *Haystacks.* It is often unclear where the boundary lies between the many sounds that belong to one phoneme or another. We often disagree whether we heard a **k** or a **p**, saw green or blue. A cluster of variegated noises and/or printed letters using different fonts can represent the same phoneme. A computer may have a hard time identifying all phonemes correctly if they are scanned from a collection of fonts in a book on typography, yet a human perceiver can adjust the physical data to a hypothetical phoneme, and the phoneme to a word and to a sentence. Phonology reduces sounds to an abstraction, an idea of a distinguishing sound (whether "raw" or "law" is in a legal context or in a meat shop).

2. ДЫР БУЛ ЩЫЛ (DYR BUL SHCHYL)

In extreme situations, there are iconoclastic users of sound. Such was the plea of Italian Futurists for a "music of noises" and the "painting of sounds, noises, and smells." The Dadaists continued with that tradition. In Cabaret Voltaire in Zurich, four Dadaists simultaneously read their different texts on the stage, resulting in a cacophony of nonsense. The radical Russian Futurists spoke of "the word as such" (*samovitoe slovo*) and promoted sound with no meaning attached to it. The Russian poet Kruchonykh wrote a poem devoid of any meaning:

> Dyr bul shchyl
> Ubeshchur
> Rrr
> lll
> Zzz

It means in Russian what it means in English.[3] But it does mean: sound is important. However, the syllables in the first two lines may have allusions to real words, and Mayakovsky wrote, "Est' eshcho khoroshie bukvy" (There are still good [unused] letters [*sic*]: **r, sh, shch**.) The Russian Futurists called it a transrational language (*zaumny yazyk*—literally, "beyond the mind.") In a famous poem by the Swiss Dadaist Hugo Ball, "Karawane," no single word (except the title) has any meaning, but the capricious graphic representations of letters undergo original deformations. Yet the fact is: poetry is threaded with sound networks. A college textbook claimed: "In reading poetry it is important to remember that the major importance of sound must [must?] always be realized in terms of content."[4]

3. SOUNDS IN INTERPRETATION

In Saussurean terms, sound and meaning are equivalent to signifier and signified. In language theory the link between the two is arbitrary and definite, whereas the sound patterns we discuss here are beyond the single word and constructed ad hoc. In the interpretation and teaching of poetry it is common

KARAWANE

jolifanto bambla ô falli bambla
grossiga m'pfa habla horem
égiga goramen
higo bloiko russula huju
hollaka hollala
anlogo bung
blago bung
blago bung
bosso fataka
ü üü ü
schampa wulla wussa ólobo
hej tatta gôrem
eschige zunbada
wulubu ssubudu uluw ssubudu
tumba ba- umf
kusagauma
ba - umf

Hugo Ball, "Karawane," 1917

practice to accept that the interpreter mobilizes the sound effects of the poetic text to reinforce his or her perception of the poem's meaning. The "father" of the New Criticism, I. A. Richards, suggested that poems are written with the "full body" of words, meaning their sound orchestration, connotations, and imagery, not just their lexical meaning.[5] Roman Jakobson intended a similar approach, when he spoke of the "set toward the message."[6] Claims assigning meanings to sound patterns are made not merely by critics interested in the "form" of a poem, but even more so by practical critics preoccupied with the poem's "meaning." Readers of poetry interested in the poet's "message," or "content," sometimes feel uneasy about the dense and complex network of sound patterning in verse and try to incorporate it into their total interpretation. In the other camp, one finds prominent critics and theoreticians who deny altogether that specific meanings are inherent in specific sounds. The two polar positions are well represented, on one side, by M. Grammont, who collected many examples for the classification of "expressive" properties of sounds in French (especially in *Le vers français*), and, on the other side, by P. Delbouille,[7] who provided a resounding criticism of all "expressive" theories of sound in poetry and saw sound as merely a contextual matter.

The problem of the relations between sounds and their meanings, or the reality which language may represent, is as old as Plato's "Cratylos," and the literature in this field has no limits. Besides literary critics and theoreticians, the arguments have been shared by philosophers, psychologists, linguists, and poets of various persuasions.[8]

Sounds can be inherent or relational (in other words: qualitative or quantitative). Inherent sounds will emphasize the sound quality, the "K-ness" of "K," or the "O-ness" of "O," whereas relational sounds depend on their quantitative relation to other sounds. In the word "**di'**gest," pronounced with the stress on the first syllable, "di" is stressed in relation to the unstressed second syllable, and in "di**gest'**," the second syllable has a stronger stress in relation to the first.

All poetic structures of sound use those distinctions: meter is made of relational sounds; rhymes are made of inherent sounds. Strophes are combinations of both: patterns of relational sounds (meters and verse lines) are linked by patterns of inherent sound (rhymes). In both devices there are two major uses: (a) fixed and formal and (b) free and sporadic.

	Formal	Free	
Relational	Meter	Free verse	Rythm
Inherent	Rhyme	Sound patterns	Strophe

Of the four groups of sounds, we shall discuss mainly one: free sound patterns.

> Th' expense of spirit in a waste of shame
> Is lust in action; and till action, lust
> Is perjured, murderous, bloody, full of blame,
> Savage, extreme, rude, cruel, not to trust,
> Enjoyed no sooner but despisèd straight:
> Past reason **h**unted; and no sooner **h**ad,
> Past reason **h**ated, as a swallowed bait,
> On purpose laid to make the taker mad:

Mad in pursuit, and in possession so;
Had, **h**aving, and in quest to **h**ave, extreme;
A bliss in proof, and proved, a very woe;
Before, a joy proposed; behind, a dream.
All this the world well knows; yet none knows well
To shun the **h**eaven that leads men to this **h**ell.

(William Shakespeare, Sonnet 129)

In the formal two classes, meter and rhyme, the function of the sounds is not important and subdued. The last couplet rhymes: *well/hell*—the specific sounds are not functional. But if we read the poem and understand the lovemaking as an action, we discover the heavy breathing, reinforced by the "H" pattern in strategic places. As a result, the "H" accumulates strength in the course of the sonnet and brings the whole sonnet to, and encapsulates it in, the last word, "hell." In addition, the sonnet develops a network of sound patterns, "th' expense–despisèd," as well as "P–R" recurrences (pursuit, possession, proposed); and, finally, the "W" pattern that leads "world well" into the last rhyme, "well" (rhyming with "hell"). The effect here is the accumulation of context, carrying crucial sounds to the final rhyme.

Typically, an introduction to the study of poetry devotes a chapter to sound. The author claimed that "merely to discover alliteration or assonance is but a small part of the total process of dealing with sound; the larger part is discovering precisely what the function of the sound pattern is in terms of the poem as a whole."[9]

With this approach in mind, the author reads an example from Shakespeare's Sonnet 30:

When to the sessions of sweet silent thought
I summon up remembrance of things past,
I sigh the lack of many a thing I sought,
And with old woes new wail my dear time's waste.

The author discusses the "mood" of the poem and argues:

But sound, too, makes its contributions to the mood of the first twelve lines and to the changed mood of the couplet. The sibilants in *sessions, sweet, silent, summon, remembrance, things, past, sigh, sought, woes, times,* and *waste*—all in the first four lines—reinforce with their hushing quality the quiet that is part of *sweet silent thought.*[10]

"Hushing quality": it would be easy to bring counterexamples from English and other languages where repetitions of sibilants—a conspicuous material of sound patterning in poetry—seem to represent quite the opposite. Sibilants may represent not silence but various kinds of sounds—for example:

> the deep sea swell
> . . . .
> A current under sea
> Picked his bones in whispers.
>
> (T. S. Eliot, "The Waste Land," IV)[11]

The sounds represented here are different from those in Sonnet 129 in both their sound qualities and their emotive overtones. Furthermore, there is a fast transition from the powerful noise of a sea swell to the sound of whispers (which, therefore, is overshadowed, bringing forth its metaphoric connotations).

Here is another example:

> There is not even solitude in the mountains
> But red sullen faces sneer and snarl
>
> (Ibid., V)

The conspicuous sound effect of the sibilants in the last line hardly represents any real sounds in the description of the fictional world of the poem: the mood expressed overshadows them. In other cases as well, hardly a trace of either sound or silence appears in the patterning of sibilants:

> And smell renews the salt savour of the sandy earth
>
> (Eliot, "Ash-Wednesday")[12]

or:

> Blessèd sister, holy mother, spirit of the fountain, spirit of the garden,
> Suffer us not to mock ourselves with falsehood.
> . . . .
> Sister, mother
> And spirit of the river, spirit of the sea,
> Suffer me not to be separated
>
> (Ibid.)

As the examples show, patterns of sibilant sounds may represent either noise or silence. Indeed, there are very different kinds of noise that are shaded by different emotive qualities or have no relation to noise at all. It seems that no meaning can be imputed to the sounds themselves. Therefore they cannot be said to have a "hushing quality."

We are not concerned here with the question of whether or not this critic describing Shakespeare's sonnet was right, but with another question: Whenever meanings are imputed to sounds in poetry, how does the transfer occur? What is the process of such a reading *if* and whenever it is activated?

4. CONSTRUCTIVE PROSODY

Let us return to Shakespeare's Sonnet 30. Clearly, not *all* sounds in that quatrain represent *all* co-textual meanings. Sound patterns are not existing facts but either precise or plausible constructs based on such facts. A pattern of silent sibilants is established, based on their proximity to each other and their disproportionately large number, especially in the first line of the sonnet. The primacy effect is so conspicuous, it seems to overshadow other possible meanings and other groupings of sounds, such as the "M" pattern based in line 2 or the "W" in line 4. The S + T pattern, which intersects with the sibilants, starts in "SweeT SilenT ThoughT," covers all four rhyming words: "ThoughT-paST-SoughT-waSTe." Then this pattern intersects with a certain motif or word or other semantic element from the co-textual network of meanings, in our case: "SweeT SilenT ThoughT." The semantic element must be sufficiently important for the global construct of the poem's meaning and must be capable of being expressed or reinforced by the given sounds. In other words, the semantic element must motivate their dense sound patterning. At this point, the reader *transfers* a quality, a tone, a connotation, or an intention from the domain of meaning to the established sound pattern.

From now on, the whole sound pattern is perceived as *expressive* of a certain meaning, tone, or mood. The central theme of the first line, "sweet silent thought," colors the repeated sibilant sounds with a shade of its meaning, and this "coloring" seems to suffuse the lines dominated by the given sound pattern. Even the word "sessions"—part of a metaphor from the court of law—is perceived by our critic as contributing to the expression of "sweet silent thought." Indeed, "sessions," as the first lexical word, is the force that establishes the whole sound pattern; it has nothing to do with the content of the word itself.

A mere alliteration of first consonants in adjacent words (inherited from Old English meters) is so frequent in English—in poetry as well as in prose—that it may almost pass unnoticed, just a lexical item, a word, perceived as automatic, until revived by the opening S-tripling in "sessions."

Thus, we have a bidirectional process: first, a sound pattern is established in part of a text, then certain meanings in the same text are transferred to the sound pattern, and then the tone of this sound pattern, colored by those meanings, is transferred back to the level of meaning, reinforcing it.

5. INTERACTING PATTERNS IN WORKS OF LITERATURE

The interaction of patterns is not a trivial issue concerning sounds alone. The structure of this interaction is similar to that of other interactions of co-textual patterns in literary texts. In Romantic nature poetry, descriptions of nature are often personified; nature carries anthropomorphic features and has human "moods" because its descriptions are imbued with metaphors from the human world in the first place. But then nature will express the mood of the "lyrical I" (usually by metonymy); when the "I" is in the nature scene other persons in the poem are.[13] It is not simply that a person is like (or unlike) nature but, in a circular interaction, that Man is like Nature, which is like Man.

The two stages of transfer appear in this necessary order only in a logical sense: the sounds must be colored by certain meanings before they can return to color the meanings of words. The psychology of perception, however, allows us to see them simultaneously, especially in view of the fact that both sides of the interaction are selected and patterned by the reader for the sake of such an interaction, i.e. when a hypothesis of their mutual dependence becomes plausible.

In sum, we can define a basic trait of literary texts: literary texts unfold parallel bundles of heterogeneous patterns, semantic and non-semantic. Such patterns are co-textual and interact with each other: sound patterns, metaphors, lines of plot, descriptions of nature, characters, threads of ideas, etc. Such interactions bring about mutual reinforcement and mutual motivation of the patterns involved.

I would like to stress an important point: two interacting patterns are not parallel to each other as a whole and do not necessarily interact as a whole. The sound pattern is autonomous in this respect: it stretches over parts of the text irrespective of whether the words carry the related meanings. On the other hand, the meanings belong to larger semantic constructs, parts of which are not related to these sounds at all.

We have an asymmetrical relationship between two autonomous patterns (here, one of sounds, one of meaning), interacting through certain *points of intersection.*

If we represent a sign in a simplified manner as a certain relation between sound and meaning, s/m, poetry dissects this Saussurean tie, separating the sounds and linking them to sounds of other words, and linking the meanings to other meanings. A new relationship between sound and meaning is created, not in one word but in a construct made by readers on the basis of several words—not an arbitrary construct as in Saussure, but a co-textual one, the meaning of which must be deduced from the particular frame of reference.[14]

Our case may be represented in a schematic form, showing two points of intersection:

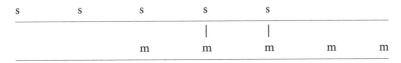

s = sound; m = meaning.

When a point of intersection between two patterns is established, the process of bidirectional transfer occurs:

s	s	s	s	s	s	s
↓2	↓2		↑1		↓2	↓2
m	m	m	m	m	m	m

1 = first stage of transfer; 2 = second stage of transfer.

There may be more than one point of intersection, and sometimes the effect of the sound pattern may be related to the whole mood of a poem ("soft," "harsh," "euphonious," "drastic," etc.).

This interaction is necessary not only between sound and meaning. A similar structure can be observed in the field of metaphor.[15] Take W. H. Auden's poem on the Portuguese colony Macao:

> A weed from Catholic Europe, it took root
> Between the yellow mountains and the sea,
> And bore these gay stone houses like a fruit,
> And grew on China imperceptibly.[16]

In Auden's poem, two *frames of reference* (*fr*) are established: one is the Catholic city of Macao (*fr*$_1$) with its stone houses growing on the side of continental China; the other is a weed (*fr*$_2$), taking root, growing, bearing fruit, etc. The first frame of reference, "Macao" (*fr*$_1$), is presented as *existing* in the fictional world of the poem. The second frame of reference (*fr*$_2$), "the weed," is introduced as *not existing* in the fictional world of the poem, as a metaphor brought in for the sake of comparison.

We could filter out the language of these two frames of reference and separate the language of each frame from the text.

fr$_2$ "the weed"	*fr*$_1$ "Macao"
A weed . . . took root	A [transplant] from Catholic Europe, it took root
Between the yellow mountains and the sea,	Between the yellow mountains and the sea,
And bore . . . a fruit	And bore these gay stone houses . . .
And grew . . . imperceptibly.	And grew on China imperceptibly.

As we see, using the language of the poem alone, a considerable part of the language may be applied, without change, in either direction, one literally, one metaphorized vis-à-vis the other.

There is a textual interpenetration between *fr*$_1$ (Macao) and *fr*$_2$ (plant). Not only is *fr*$_1$ described in terms of *fr*$_2$, but *fr*$_2$ is reinforced in the imagination by the description of *fr*$_1$: Macao is like a weed, but it is a stranded weed, far from its source and also enormous and vital, like Macao clinging to the shore of China. In other words, we observe a two-way process: the image of the weed is magnified by the description (and geography) of Macao, and then, in turn, as a huge, city-size weed, it reinforces the description of the city.

Metaphor:	weed (like Macao)	
	↓2	↑1
Macao (like a "Macao-like" weed)		Macao

The structure of a sound/meaning interaction is similar:

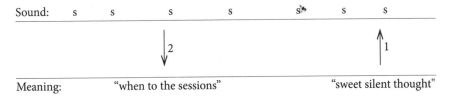

Now, if this is the case, why sibilants? Wouldn't any sound pattern do? Let us try to "rewrite" the Shakespearean lines using words similar in content and sound patterns similar in structure (the asterisk indicates rewriting).

> *When to the CRuX of CRystal QUiet thought
> I CRave and Call RemembRance of things past

We have a very similar structure of sounds, this time based on the repetition of the sound *K,* reinforced by the cluster K + R. Nevertheless, it seems that this sound pattern cannot possibly express silence, although "quiet thought" starts with K as "silent thought" started with S. It is plausible that a reader may impute something strong and harsh to this text, reinforced by the sound pattern and the cluster K + R. The pivotal word may become "CRuX."

In general, in a part of a text where a sound pattern coexists with several semantic patterns, the sound pattern may contribute to shifting the center of gravity from one direction of meaning to another. A specific sound does not have one specific meaning. The sound may join various directions of meaning to the point of creating an impression on the reader that the sound itself carries such meanings.

There seem to be various general qualities accompanying at least some sounds, which lend *potentials* of meaning to these sounds. One sound may have several potentials, representing a variety of shades (such as: whisper, whistle, sound of a sea swell, sneer, and snarl)—or even contradictory potentials depending on contexts (such as: noise, on one hand, and silence, on the other). Some of the meanings of the words in a specific context may activate such potentials in any specific direction, or not at all.

To what extent are such potentials fixed or free? Are all sounds of a language equally endowed, or are there degrees to the ability of sounds to carry meanings? Are such potentials (psychophysiological) human universals, or do they change in specific genres or languages? Are they historically determined or changing? These are complex questions precisely because the sound/meaning relations are not codified, discrete, and "arbitrary" in a Saussurean sense. The main problem is that the co-textual nature of a transfer makes it dependent on the specific combination of sound patterns and meanings.

The effect of sounds in a context is not at all the same as the effect of the same sounds when isolated for experiment or observation. Sounds in a text tend to be subordinated to the meanings of sentences, and their potential effects tend to be subdued, unless they are reactivated through purposeful patterning supported by expectations of a given genre.

Any sound may be activated through a number of parameters in a language: (1) analogues of its articulatory properties; (2) analogues of its acoustic properties; or (3) association with specific words carrying the sound in this language. The use of such sounds in some specific words in the given language may activate one direction of meaning or another.

6. TYPES OF SOUND/MEANING RELATIONS

I shall propose a general model for sound/meaning relations in texts. It seems that many controversies on this issue are pseudo quarrels and cannot be resolved, simply because they lump together several meanings of the word "meaning" or the word "expressive" and regard the whole area as one phenomenon: one meaning relating to one sound.

In fact, there are various types of interaction between sounds and meanings in poetic texts. Though the local configurations may be highly complex, they largely fall into four basic categories.

TYPE 1: ONOMATOPOEIA—MIMETIC SOUND PATTERNS

The seemingly simplest and most direct relation between sound and meaning obtains in the wide area of onomatopoeia. Onomatopoeia occurs when the sounds of a word imitate the sounds of the object that the word denotes. There is a whole range of possible relations. In some cases, the word is directly denoting a sound ("meow," "moo") or naming a kind of sound ("barking," "rustling," "whistle," "whisper"). In other cases, the sounds represent a noise produced by, or connected with, the object denoted by the word. Thus, "cuckoo" is not the name of a sound but the name of a bird producing "coo-coo" or a similar sound. A sea swell denotes the shape of the water, and its sounds may suggest the noise of the sea.

Not all the sounds of onomatopoeic words participate in the imitation. And they do not necessarily cover the whole asymmetry. Therefore, a more correct definition would be: onomatopoeia is a word (or a group of words) in which *parts* of the sounds are equivalent to part (or an aspect, or metonymy) of the denotation. There must be an evocation of a sound in nature for the onomatopoeia to appear.

It is, however, not a real imitation of nature. Though some onomatopoeic words are easily recognizable by their typical phonemics makeup, which deviates from that of regular words in the language, still the sounds of nature are filtered through the rather small selection of sounds that are possible in a human phonemic system of any given language. Furthermore, such sound/meaning words are codified in each language (they are "arbitrary" in Saussure's sense, though not arbitrary in their iconic features). Thus, "whistle" (English), "Pfeifen" (German), "fayf" (Yiddish), "svist" (Russian), "shrika" (Modern Hebrew) all designate the sound produced by the mouth or by a whistle, yet each word foregrounds a different aspect or shading of the sounds as imitating nature.

Similar examples are: "whisper" (English); "shópot" and "shépchet" (Russian); "Láhash" (Hebrew); "flüstern" (German). Each word is perceived to imitate the sound it denotes. Indeed, it actualizes a part or aspect of the sound or its production. The speakers of each language actually tend to hear in nature that direction of the sound which is represented in the word.

There is, thus, a reciprocity between language and perception of reality. In human affairs, language and object may even produce different sounds. A slight but sudden reflex of pain evokes in English an "ouch" or "ow" but in other languages an "ach," "oy," or "ay." In this case the sound itself is an imitation of a psychological response to a physical cause.

As Maurice Grammont pointed out, a cuckoo does not emit the sound "koo-koo" but actually voices a palatal "ou-ou," but for phonetic reasons the two syllables are not left without consonants (Grammont explains why *K* is the "natural" consonant in this place).[17] The examples of differences between languages in onomatopoeic words are well known (e.g. the rooster's call in different languages: "kukeriku," "kikericki," "coquerico," "cock-a-doodle-doo," etc.). The different phonetic developments of the languages influenced this area, too. An onomatopoeic word is as arbitrary as the rest of the language, but it still preserves an indication of iconicity.

Onomatopoeic words may not represent any additional properties of the signified. Indeed, the word is connected to a represented object through the most direct link: between sound properties of the word and sound properties of the object. However, when such a link is established, further properties may be conveyed by the sound combinations of the words in so-called sound symbolism: sound patterns may be "harsh" or "soft," "pleasant" or "disgust-ing," "mellifluous" or "cacophonic," conveying specific qualities of, or emotive responses to, the denoted object.[18]

Other connotations are transferred through the channel of the sound link; the sounds themselves become colored by those connotations, and vice versa. Thus, a "shrill" voice has not merely a high-pitched quality, but often some-thing piercing and unpleasant as well. "Crunch" is defined by a contemporary English dictionary this way: "to chew something with a crushing noise"; "crush" in the same dictionary is defined not as a noise but as a force: "to press with a force that destroys or deforms"; and yet the first definition assigned a noise to it: "crushing noise." In the first word, "crunch," the sound is part of the definition; the meaning of the word is conveyed via an onomatopoeia. This onomatopoeia, however, represents not merely a sound; the sound is colored by the quality of crushing, breaking up (which may be turned in a pleasant direction too, as in munching potato chips). In the second word, "crush," there is no onomatopoeia in the definition; the sound, however, it is a concomitant, a connotation of the meaning.

After a buildup of an S-pattern T. S. Eliot wrote: "red sullen faces sneer and snarl." The triple cluster SNR is repeated in two words that merge into one: "SNeeR-and-SNaRl." Is it an onomatopoeia? Our dictionary has for "snarl": "1. to growl angrily, showing the teeth, as a dog; 2. to speak in a sharp or angry manner." In the first definition the sound is central; in the second it disappears but is still hovering in the faded metaphor ("speaking in a sharp manner"). For "sneer" 1, "to smile scornfully, as by curling the lip," no sound is indicated, except by metonymy (and in 2, "a sneering look or expression," it is further removed metaphorically). It seems that we have here, on one hand, an onomatopoeic expression heavily colored by an emotive connotation and, on the other hand, the reverse. Through the sound structure of the whole pattern, the reader's attention to the sound aspects (and the possibility of onomatopoeia—even the vision of teeth) is sharpened. But then the whole onomatopoeic effect is turned into a metaphor, since sound apparently does not refer in this frame of reference; it is merely a sensuous channel through which the negative effect is conveyed.

As the last example shows, poetry does not merely use onomatopoeic words given in the language (such a use would seem a primitive device, befitting children's stories). As in other aspects of poetic structure (metaphor, stress, parallelism, etc.), poetry employs a principle existing in the language (ono-matopoeia), but makes quite independent use of it, notably by creating new sound patterns based not on one word but on combinations of words, such as "sneer and snarl."

Unlike linguistic onomatopoeia, poetic onomatopoeia is never a feature of a word, but of a whole pattern, abstracting sounds from several words outside syntax for new combinations. Such a newly created sound pattern, spanning parts of more than one word, enters into onomatopoeic relations with some aspect or connotation of the meaning of one of the words. Since such literary onomatopoeias are not codified, the reader has to decide in each case whether or not an onomatopoeic element is at hand and how far it extends.

As in the case of metaphor, poetry may create new onomatopoeic patterns, modeled upon the structure of onomatopoeic words but scattered over several of them. At the same time, it may make use of onomatopoeias existing in lan-guage. As in metaphor, we must distinguish between *conventional* and *novel* onomatopoeias and between *dead* and *vivid* ones. A vivid onomatopoeia is a word or a pattern in which the onomatopoeic aspect is still felt beyond the limits of a grammatical word. That is, in addition to the "arbitrary" relation between signifier and signified, there is also an iconic relation. The relation is still conventional, if codified in the language. A novel onomatopoeia is created ad hoc and supported by a specific context. Poetry may now *deautomatize* and *activate* any conventional onomatopoeia by involving the relevant sounds in a sound pattern spreading over several words.

Here's another example: we can pronounce the word "wind" in English with such an emphasis on the beginning of the word that it will be felt as imitating the sound of a wind. But normally, the "w" in wind is transparent. It is at most a dead onomatopoeia. Etymologically it possibly came from an imitation of blowing wind, but typically this allusion would go unnoticed unless especially emphasized. It may be considered onomatopoeia only in the diachronical perspective of language. The same holds for "east wind," "north wind," "south wind," and "west wind." When Shelley, however, writes "O wild West Wind," in the opening of a poem, he revives the onomatopoeic aspect of the phrase "West Wind" and creates a W-pattern that goes beyond the words as a lexical unit and thus revives the dead onomatopoeia. In much the same way dead metaphors come to life in poetry when their dead vehicle is extended in context.

The borderline between *dead* and *vivid* onomatopoeias in language may be blurred; the activation of either one depends on the nature of the context and the activity of the reader. In a dead, or not sufficiently vivid, onomatopoeia, the sounds of the word are transparent. While making these sounds valuable again, by pointing the reader's attention to them, by involving them in an autonomous sound pattern, the onomatopoeic relation also comes to life.

TYPE II: EXPRESSIVE SOUND PATTERNS

The second type is much more widespread in poetry. Grammont has devoted a detailed discussion to the possible "expressive" qualities of various sounds in French poetry. Others have analyzed expressive sound patterns as "sound symbolism" or "sound metaphors."

In this category the sounds are perceived not as imitating a real sound but as carrying (or reinforcing) a certain content quality, tone, or mood, usually connected not with the meaning of one word but with a whole situation or frame of reference. Ivan Fonagy, for example, brought much statistical evidence to support the claim that in various unconnected languages, "harsh" sounds (such as the plosives: K, P, T) are more prevalent in poems of a drastic or harsh content, and "soft" ones in poems with a "softer" or pleasing content.

The relations established in these two kinds of sound patterns may be graphically represented thus:

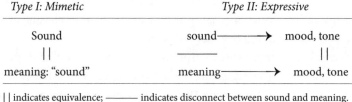

Type I: Mimetic	Type II: Expressive
Sound	sound———→ mood, tone
‖	——— ‖
meaning: "sound"	meaning———→ mood, tone

‖ indicates equivalence; ——— indicates disconnect between sound and meaning.

In the second type not the sounds themselves but rather a certain tone or expressive abstracted quality is perceived as representing a certain mood or tone of content abstracted from the domain of meaning in the given poem.

In semiotic terms we may see the relation as follows: Any sound patterning in poetry breaks up the habitual, automatic link in one word between the signifier and the signified and undermines the transparency of the sound in referential language simply by de-automatizing the sound pattern itself and making it conspicuous. However, the human tendency to read all language elements as signifying, if possible, turns the new sound pattern into a new signifier.

The same device, which broke up the regular signifying relation within a word and pointed out the "split" nature of a sign, has created a new, composite signifier based in part on several words. This signifier, even when falling into conventional combinations, is always perceived as creative, as made up ad hoc, simply because no lexicalization can happen: it is a partial, selective and discontinuous sound pattern, stretching through several words and not related to the full denotation of these words but only to part (or an aspect) of it.

In type I this composite signifier has a unique signified, usually in the denotation of one word or merely in one connotation of it—hence the tendency to read a text as if the meaning has spread (as an overtone) through the whole range covered by the signifier (the sound pattern).

In type II we encounter not merely a composite signifier but a composite signified as well. Here belong Heidegger's *Stimmung* (mood, atmosphere) and the New Critical "tone." Furthermore, its contours and precise meaning remain often vague and open-ended. The reason is obvious: sounds coalescing into a pattern are recognized by their identity, while the "meanings" represented (or "reinforced") are made not of identical elements but of an interacting cluster of word meanings. These words often project an undefined "mood" of a situation or a frame of reference.

The new signifying relations are not lexicalized, not collected as words in any dictionary; the meanings are not discrete. In the first type we have at least a specific sound alluded to. Even so, the same S-pattern must be reinterpreted in each case to make it represent a different specific sound, derived from the individual nature of the object and our extra-linguistic knowledge. In type II, sound groups may be said to represent only very general directions of tone; they gain their specificity from the interaction with the co-textual meanings. And even here we deal with rather vague, composite, and not precisely verbalizable feelings—which is why the use of such sound patterns (especially since Symbolism) is considered suggestive and valuable for poetry.

Since the sound pattern as signifier stretches over several words, it may enter into several kinds of relationships with the co-textual meanings. In E. A. Poe's "Raven," for example, both types interact:

And the silken, sad, uncertain rustling of each purple curtain
Thrilled me—filled me with fantastic terrors never felt before;
So that now, to still the beating of my heart, I stood repeating
"'Tis some visiter entreating entrance at my chamber door—
Some late visiter entreating entrance at my chamber door;—
                                   This it is and nothing more."

The poem was famous and admired in Russia and in France. The sibilants clearly represent here not the silence of sweet thought but the rustling of silken curtains, muted by overtones of uncertainty, sadness, "fantastic terrors," and expectation.

The onomatopoeia in "rustling" is activated in Poe's line "And the silken, sad, uncertain rustling of each **purple curtain**" through a chain of S-sounds strengthened by RP and RT clusters.

Sound? What sound? I can read a poem and not emit or hear any sound. The term "sound" is, in fact, an abbreviation of a chain: seeing signs in print—attributing them to a specific phoneme (abstraction from any possible letters)—translating them into letters, into sounds, into phoneme—into cases of sound. The opening of the first line, "And the Silken, Sad unCertain," creates a strong sound pattern (S, in combination with several other consonants) that is expressive of a certain mood. If we had only "sad, uncertain," the combination of the two meanings would have one direction; when qualified by "silken," it attains a somewhat different tinge, perhaps softened or mysterious. Type II would be preserved if the line continued with a key word change: "And the silken, sad, uncertain swerving of the purple curtain." A sound connotation may be felt (activated from the silken curtain), but it is not directly signified. In the actual poem, however, the sound pattern, already established and imbued with an expressive mood, obtains in "rustling" a link to the first type of sound pattern, onomatopoeia. Schematically, we have two channels:

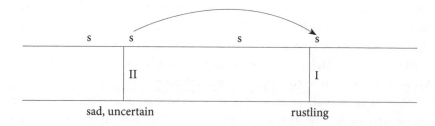

By the rules of semantic integration, all adjectives in one *fr* may qualify each other. Thus "silken" qualifies the "rustling"; it is a rustling as of silk. Then the whole expressive pattern (II) seems to color the onomatopoeia (I) to use it as a channel for conveying the mood. This mood is further colored by the "purple" quality of the curtain and, further again, by the magical-irrational mood of the second line (reinforced, in its turn, by the sound pattern based on an F-thread): "Thrilled me—Filled me with Fantastic terrors never Felt beFore." Since we have not one static unit (a word) but two interacting patterns (of sound and meaning), and each is changing and transforming as the text unfolds, the resultant transfer of meaning changes too and obtains further and richer dimensions as the reading advances. The various changing effects themselves interact, support, or cancel each other.

TYPE III: FOCUSING SOUND PATTERNS

Quite a different kind of sound/meaning relation may be found in the following passage from T. S. Eliot's "Ash-Wednesday":

> If the lost word is lost, if the spent word is spent
> If the unheard, unspoken
> Word is unspoken, unheard;
> Still is the unspoken word, the Word unheard,
> The Word without a word, the Word within
> The world and for the world;
> And the light shone in darkness and
> Against the Word the unstilled world still whirled
> About the centre of the silent Word.

The passage has a wealth of equivalence patterns of all kinds and allusions to the world of Eliot's imagery and beliefs. We shall look here only at two sound patterns. An obvious one is "word-Word-world-whirled." This sound cluster WR + D appears fourteen times in the nine lines (and is further echoed in the repeated "unheard," rhyming with "word"). Neither the specific quality of these sounds nor any tone or mood associated with them plays any semantic role. Nevertheless, the sound pattern focuses our attention to some key words of the passage. What is equivalent here is not sounds and meanings but a *relation* between two or more sound clusters and a *relation* between the meanings of their words. In graphic terms:

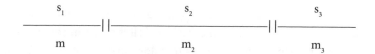

The keys words: "word," "Word" (in the sense of Logos), and "world" are brought together, and the specific relationship between them is left to the reader's interpretation. The focusing pattern, however, does not create any automatic parallelism between sounds and meanings. Thus, the word "whirled" belongs to the sound pattern (reinforced through the almost tautological double chain of sounds unSTILLeD WORLD/STILL WHIRLED) but is not part of the thematic pair "word-world." "Whirled" is rather connected to a central image involving different-sounding words: "unstilled," "centre," "light." Perhaps the sound link calls our attention to the essential link between these two patterns of theme and imagery.

Indeed, a new sound pattern of related consonant clusters emerges toward the end of this passage: "unstilled-still-centre-silent." We have here a cluster of four consonants, at least three of which appear in each word: NSTL–STL–SNT–SLNT. This sound pattern, too, links up central words (perhaps less central thematically, but important for Eliot's imagery). But the sound pattern involves the word "still," which cannot be said to have any thematic importance, although it is as prominent in the sound pattern as any other (even reinforced through the tautological double chain). Furthermore, the same line starts with the word "agaiNST," which leads directly to the opening of the chain in "uNSTilled." "AgaiNST," however, may have been overlooked, being peripheral in a semantic and syntactic respect. Upon rereading, we may further add the words "lost," "spent"—LST, SNT—in the first line. Through an additional consonant P, in the cluster SP, they are developed in an additional thread: LoST-SpeNT → SPeNt–unSPokeN, which, in turn, is taken up by "UNspoken–UNheard," linked to the central sound pattern both by anaphora and by morphological and semantic parallelism and then by rhyme: "unhEARD–wORD."

THEORETICAL SUMMARY

Simple repetitions of sounds or sound clusters may not be felt by a reader unless reinforced by syntactic or rhythmical parallelism or semantic and stylistic prominence. In Eliot's poem there is mutual reinforcement: words central in theme or imagery strengthen the importance of a sound repetition; and the sound pattern, in its turn, focuses attention to the relations between these words (in meaning or in imagery). Eliot, however, does not permit here any complete sound/meaning parallelism. The sound patterning is autonomous because it involves also words thematically not related to the central group; and vice versa—some words related by meaning, or central to the poem, may not participate in a given sound cluster. Again, asymmetry prevails. This is only natural if sound patterning (or any poetic form) is not to become an automatic (and therefore redundant) concomitant of meaning.

A focusing sound pattern is a pattern linking clusters of sounds in several words, some of which are linked thematically. Part of the sound pattern includes *part* of the key words in a context. Focusing patterns do not merely make important words conspicuous or link disparate images; they may also reshuffle the emphasis on the importance of words in a text, thereby imposing upon the poetic text an additional principle of order: that of sound relations.

In focusing patterns, relations between sounds call the reader's attention to relations between meanings (or other properties) of the interrelated frames of references. The specific nature of such relations must be resolved in each case, not resolved at the whim of the reader but supported by a reasoned interpretation of the text and its intertextual adherences. Along with the reinforcement of a link between related words ("word"–"world") or mutually qualifying words ("sad," "uncertain"), totally disparate words may be brought together. For instance, Mandelshtam links wasps (*osy*) with the axes of the earth (*osi*) through a focusing sound link and makes them the pivotal themes of a poem. The surprise here is how T. S. Eliot's revolt against regular rhyme and meter nevertheless promoted free sound networks with the post-Symbolist value of dense text organization.

TYPE IV: NEUTRAL SOUND PATTERNING

The most widespread use of sound patterning has no direct relation to the meanings of the immediate words or to the relations between such meanings. These sound patterns are *neutral* in respect to their co-textual meanings. In this case, sound patterning contributes to the meaning of a poem in a higher sense: it is part of the *Poetic Function* as defined by Jakobson: a "set toward the message." To avoid a conflict with the literary meaning of "message," I have suggested renaming it "set toward the text itself." That is, the text is calling attention to the language and the formation of the text itself. There is both a subversion of the normal sound/meaning relationship and an emphasis on the density of poetic language.

In semiotic terms one might identify the first three kinds of sound patterns as iconic, symbolic, indexical; in the fourth type there is no direct sign relation. I avoided this semiotic terminology because, for lack of discrete signifiers and signifieds, the units are more complex. For example, in the second, expressive type, symbolic relations obtain between the resultant abstractions ("mood"), but each of them is derived metonymically (i.e. "indexically") from the meanings of words.

Diagrammatically, the four categories of sound/meaning relations may be represented thus:

I. Mimetic	II. Expressive	III. Focusing	IV. Neutral
s	s_1——s_2→tone, mood	s_1——s_2——s_3	s_1——s_2——s_3
| |	——— | |	—| |—| |—	———
m: "sound"	m_1—m_2→tone, mood	m_1——m_2——m_3	m_1——m_2——m_3

\| \| indicates equivalence; ——— indicates disconnect between sound and meaning.

In actual poetry we find easy transitions from one type to another. It seems to me that there is a psychological hierarchy by which the reader tries first the most direct transfer, the mimetic, and moves to the next stage only failing that. The signifying nature of language, as well as the tradition of poetry explications and of harnessing every poetic device into interpretation of the individual work of literature encourages such transfers.

The neutral or "poetic" function operates in all four cases but is not felt as such whenever a motivated appearance of sounds may be uncovered. On the other hand, within any pattern of the more abstract kind we may often discern partial relations of the more immediate types. In any text with predominantly neutral sound patterning, an interpretive close-up may detect possibilities for mimetic, expressive, or focusing local transfers, which make at least parts of the poetic sound patterning directly connected to the poem's meanings.

The density of sound patterning in a text may play a role in guiding the reader. Metrical alliteration that appears regularly (as in Old English or German poetry) or regular rhyming automatizes the device and attributes it to the general conventional form; an especially strong schematic or stylistic deviation is needed to revive attention to a possible local meaning transfer. The same alliteration or rhyme, however, when appearing sporadically (as in Russian and Hebrew Modernism), calls for immediate attention to a possible local transfer.

In any case, when encountering a possible sound pattern, the reader has to decide whether a transfer of meaning is feasible, what kind of transfer it may be, and what its specific content is. All this is not codified in any way but must be worked out from the interactions of co-textual patterns. As we have seen, the very decision about bringing a sound pattern to the center of attention may depend on such a possibility of interaction. In this respect, a variety of factors may play a role, including the generic nature of the text (e.g. sound repetitions in casual texts may be overlooked as being teleologically unrelated to the chief functions of the genre, informative or phatic).

7. PROSE

Though most examples here are from poetry, prose fiction and drama, too, abound in sound patterning. In poetry sound patterning may have seemed historically more prominent, for lack of such other "essential" genre features as mimesis or plot and also given the natural link between such patterns, made of sound, and the compositional structures of the poem, which are made of sound material (verse and strophic structure). Sound patterning is, however, as widespread in fiction, the study of which in this respect has hardly begun.

Let us observe one example, from James Joyce's story "Eveline." The first sentence of the story reads: "She sat at the window watching the evening invade the avenue." In this short sentence, the title of the story and its protagonist, "EVEliNe," make a focusing pattern with "EVENiNg," "INVade," "AVENue." The word "invade," however, takes part in the focusing pattern but falls out of this semantic chain and—by relating drastically in meaning to the expected "falls" or "descends"—opens up a pattern of expectation and a symbolic reading of the story as a whole. The question arises: What has invaded Eveline's world? The attention to this word "invade" is concentrated through the focusing pattern. Thus, in simple language, without verse or meter, a poetic density is achieved.

A similar focusing device is used twice toward the end of the story (shown with my added italics):

> [She] felt him *seize* her hand:
> "Come!"
> All the *seas* of the world tumbled about her heart. He was *drawing her* into them: he would *drown her.*

In both patterns there seems to be a transformation of meaning (motivated by the presentation through Eveline's mind, which is associative in general and irrational now): to "seize" her hand is like pulling her into all the "seas"; "drawing" is like "drowning."

In the same story there are other kinds of sound patterns, most of them standing out because the main body of the text is written in a simple prosaic language (reflecting Eveline's point of view) avoiding obvious embellishments—for example, "OF course, her Father had Found out this aFFair and had Forbidden her." Locally, this can only be a neutral sound pattern. In the larger context, however, it may be linked to the fact that both opposing forces, "Father" and "Frank," start with an F. If this connection is made (in a focusing pattern), it may imply that in the very act of forbidding, the father evokes in her mind Frank's name.

At the same time, Joyce is not shy of simple onomatopoeic effects: "she heard his footsteps CLaCKING aLONG the CONCReTe pavement and afterwards CRuNCHiNG on the cinderpath."

8. INTERACTION OF PATTERNS

The structure of sound/meaning relations is similar to other kinds of textual patterns of interaction in the literary text. I shall mention here a few points.

1) A text provides a vast amount of material, only some of which is obviously patterned. Other elements may be constructed by readers under certain conditions.
2) Patterning links up elements into discontinuous chains of heterogeneous nature.
3) Two or more co-textual patterns may enter into relations of hierarchy or interaction. Co-textual patterns may mutually select (or filter) those elements of each other that are relevant for interaction.
4) Interactions enable mutual reinforcement, opposition, or transfer of meaning from one pattern to another (sound to meaning, or meaning to meaning). Such interactions occur in symbol and metaphor; between two characters; between nature descriptions and human emotions; between plot and ideas, etc.
5) Since interactions are not between two static and discrete units but between patterns, each of which is spread out through several language

elements and projected situations, there may be several kinds of transfer, at several points of intersection of these patterns.

6) Since we deal here with semiosis beyond what is codified in language, and with composite signifiers and signifieds, spread through many language elements, there is a necessary process of *construction* by readers. We cannot in advance solve each interpretive case or provide final clues for its solution. But we can describe the parameters influencing such constructions and the structure of such transfers, if and whenever they are made.

3

RHYTHMS OF THE BIBLE REVISITED

In essence, there were two mega-eras in the history of Hebrew poetry and Hebrew prosody: the Biblical Era, beginning with the sources of the Bible in ancient Near Eastern ("Canaanite") poetry and going up to the closure and canonization of the Hebrew Bible in the first century CE; and the Historical Era, which includes the past two millennia of Jewish history as part of the general history of human culture. Poetry and prosody in the Historical Era can be described as a sequence of clearly distinguished, precise, and changing systems of versification interacting with extrinsic trends in time and in the space of recorded history. The first era is the subject of this chapter; the second, the subject of the next chapter.[1]

The impact of the Bible on people in all layers of society in many languages has never subsided. The Bible is one of the most translated books in history. Several essential features of the Bible contributed to this unique position: the sanctity of the text, its "encyclopedic" nature, and the totality of its universe—it placed every modest story in the plain perspective of a historical narrative and ethical values. Typical for the Bible is the use of situational cognition, rather than narrative, combined with challenging indeterminacies and shortcuts.

In spite of considerable differences between the original Hebrew of the Bible and translators' English renditions, those renditions nonetheless open up the compact language, tone, and dominant rhythms of biblical discourse that influenced the literature in many vernacular languages. One difference between the languages of the original and English is the need to use three or four short words in English for one condensed word and one major stress in

Hebrew. To compensate for that discrepancy, I am hyphenating all words in English that substitute for one word in Biblical Hebrew.

The Bible starts with the birth of the universe, then zooms in on the birth of a nation, then on particular kings, on individual persons and individual events—all of them embedded in higher narratives (e.g. the story of David); and all higher narratives are embedded in a dialogic situation between God and his people, in which the expulsion from Paradise ends in Job. The Bible itself describes several narratives along a considerable stretch of real time, yet in later times all those events existed simultaneously in the reader's perception as parallel to each other. These events were not a story but a complex and disrupted panoramic universe presented sparingly. The Bible was read and retold so many times—back and forth—that earlier events were read in the light of later events and the later in the light of earlier: "there is no earlier nor later in the Bible," states the Talmud, anticipating the Christian theory of prefiguration. The sanctity of the Bible brought about the simultaneity of its coexistent stories and images.

Events and discourses in the Bible are co-present. The Biblical Era appears to us as a fixed synchronic panorama of partial fictional worlds embodied in texts, frozen in their movement, recorded in different modes of discourse.

Any discussion of Hebrew poetry after the Bible must take into consideration "the Book of Books," because of its permanent presence—above time—in Hebrew culture and education of all times. The biblical text is a presence, not a story or the presence of a story. And this intention is reinforced by the style of biblical discourse, with the emphasis on parallelism (a counternarrative move) and historical present (*va-yelekh*).

The language of Hebrew poetry in all generations after the Bible was studded with collocations, phrases, and language patterns, either directly quoted or deriving from the Bible. But it did not—and did not intend to—produce any systematic and precise form of versification, a general requirement that will be obligatory for poetry to be poetry in all periods of the Historical Era.

The strength of biblical language did not come to it only because of its holy stature but also because of its prosodic organization. The latter is meaningful but not "pure" in the Bible; it includes a co-textual meeting of various pattern elements and of its syntactic, semantic, and prosodic nature into one combined *rhythmical impact*. It is this *local configuration* and its rhythmical impact that are unique in the biblical texts and allow for variation and individuality of expression. Precisely the lack of fully systematic structures and full predictability sends the reader to work out the local interactions between theme, fiction, and rhythm. The Bible is not a narrative: it is a discourse about a narrative and within a narrative, or a bundle of discourses embedded in a mega-narrative framework, a semi-fictional, semi-sacred total universe.

The Bible includes texts composed over a long period of time, perhaps over the course of a millennium. An additional eight or nine or ten hundred years passed after the canonization of the Bible until its grammatical and methodical vocalization (assigning of vowels to the consonantal core of the written text). In that long double period of two millennia, the language itself was possibly undergoing phonetic and prosodic changes, as languages in use normally do. But since the language was not in use, that may not be the case. In the view of readers of later generations, most of the Bible was one holy text with one language and an almost unified, synchronic system of vowels and musical-accentual markers, which fulfill prosodic and syntactic functions (punctuation and intonation). The text itself was canonized, even the classical corrections were canonized as such, and only pronunciation and interpretations could change.

It is possible that the original biblical texts were read differently than in the reading of the Vocalizers (Nakdanim) or ours. But until unambiguous proof of an original pronunciation is made—that if we correct accordingly, we shall get precise patterns—it makes no sense to amend or "correct" the text. For example, if there is a shift of stress in the whole language one syllable to the left, the metrical relations between stresses remain basically the same and justify analysis in our present pronunciation, which is familiar.

In this chapter, I shall deal with the biblical text as it was given to us, and I shall let freedom remain free.

PARALLELISM

The overall principle conspicuous in the poetry of the Bible is *parallelism*. A verse (as recorded in the tradition with the consecutive numbering of "chapter and verse") is a linear yet syntactically closed segment of text that includes at least two (and sometimes three or four) smaller segments—verse units called *versets,* each carrying two or three (and sometimes four or one) major stresses (or phrase stresses). In a verse, two (or three) versets make a unit enclosed in itself, and we have to reopen it if we want to add more information and more semantic material. A verse is much more limited in size than its equivalent in the vernacular, a sentence, which can be long and open-ended.

The versets are equivalent to each other. For example, the song "Ha'azinu" ("give ear": "Give Ear, O Ye Heavens"), Deuteronomy 32:1–2, opens thus:

> Give-ear, O-ye-heavens, and-I-will-speak;
> and-hear, O-earth, the-words-of-my-mouth.

(Quotations in English are generally from the King James Bible translation—in order to preserve one standard base—but without preserving italics and all capital letters in the translation.)

Where several English words that represent one word in Hebrew are hyphenated, to reconstruct the Hebrew rhythm they should be read as one word with one major stress or phrase stress. The two versets in our example are parallel in the location and number of their phrase stresses (3 + 3), in their syntactic structure, and in their thematic import—and some or all of those features may be overlapping. But the overlap is not always as complete as here. And even here, objectively there is no absolute parallelism. *Give-ear* (imperative) and the earth will *hear* (future tense) are synonyms, but their morphology is different. *O-ye-heavens* and *O-earth* evoke the two original domains of the universe (heaven and earth; see Gen 1), which are two terms of one binary opposition. Then come *and-I-will-speak* and *the-words-of-my-mouth,* which are not synonyms but a metonymy: an action and its object. The Bible itself makes a point of non-equal equivalents, as in "For three transgressions of Damascus,/and for four, I will not turn away the punishment hereof" (Amos 1:3), where three and four are parallel and equivalent.

We must make a distinction between the *versets*—which provide the textual *frameworks* or *vehicles of parallelism*—and the *parallels* (or parallel patterns) that fill them. A *parallel* connects two or more *terms,* related to each other by any principle whatsoever: accentual, syntactic, semantic, morphological, sound patterns, etc. Hence there is *parallelism* between two (or more) versets and several specific *parallels* that fill them.

The terms of the parallelism can be equal or different in size or form; they can be related to each other according to principles like identity, similarity, and binary opposition or a gradual increase or decrease of such principles. The parallels echo between the versets, overlapping them and crossing over from one frame to another, in full or in part, horizontally or vertically.

In the past, the admiration of the biblical rhythm by Western scholars such as Johann Gottfried Herder (1744–1803) was based on this compact language (e.g. Herder's "Vom Geist der ebräischen Poesie" [On the Spirit of Hebrew Poetry]; 1782–1783): the confluence of all major forces of the text in three or more focal points. Typically, while you can have ten words in one poetic line in English ("To be or not to be, that is the question"), we have only three in Hebrew, as in "Ha'azinu": three words carry three major stresses, overlapping with three syntactic centers, three focal points of meaning—and all relate to parallel units in other versets. A verset is a short group of compact clusters focalized by major stresses, rather than a long narrative chain of many words, as is typical of Western prose. The fact of palpable parallelism induces the text to fold back on itself, a strong, symmetrical dam against the narrative forward flow.

HORIZONTAL AND VERTICAL PARALLELISM

The basic principle of this rhythmical organization is an *accentual-syntactic-semantic free rhythm* (in this order). This description implies that elements of the three domains provide parallels, and each parallel is like free verse in modern poetry, with no precise forms. Of these three forces, at least two must appear in every parallelism in poetry, whereas in biblical prose, the first will suffice.

This characteristic explains the power of biblical rhythms with latter-day readers, because almost every prosodic accent is reinforced by means of emphases in rhythm, syntax, and meaning. This phenomenon is unique, for meter and rhyme in most languages rely on sound material only; they constitute a separate layer of language, abstracted from the meanings of the words and are not directly influenced by the content of the specific words. Moreover, the term "free rhythms" entails a sense of both rhythmical text and freedom. Even approximate equality of poetic units cannot be sustained for long, and we do not know in advance when and how the second term of a parallel may come. As a result, most words, sounds, and meanings are locally repeated, at least doubled and reinforced.

In the song "Ha'azinu," the opening three lines (traditionally numbered verses) are relatively regular:

1a: Give-ear, O-ye-heavens, and-I-will-speak; 1b: and-hear, O-earth, the-words-of-my-mouth.

2a: My-doctrine shall-drop as-the-rain, 2b: my-speech shall-distil as-the-dew,

3a: As-the-small-rain upon-the-tender-herb, 3b: and-as-the-showers upon-the-grass.

Here is the opening in Hebrew, to be read first horizontally, then vertically, in the following order: 1a-1b-2a-2b-3a-3b.

וְתִשְׁמַע הָאָרֶץ אִמְרֵי־פִי.	הַאֲזִינוּ הַשָּׁמַיִם אֲדַבֵּרָה
תִּזַּל כַּטַּל אִמְרָתִי,	יַעֲרֹף כַּמָּטָר לִקְחִי
וְכִרְבִיבִים עֲלֵי־עֵשֶׂב.	כִּשְׂעִירִים עֲלֵי־דֶשֶׁא

Every line (verse) here consists of two parallel versets. The boundaries of the versets overlap with the borders of autonomous syntactical units. Unlike modern poetry, here the highest syntactic break in every verset comes before the beginning and after the end of the verset and not in its middle. Thus syntactical and verse units overlap, as if the theme dictated the rhythm. In European modern poetry, on the contrary, built-in tensions are created between the units of syntax and the units of verse which do not overlap (see my reading of Milton in Chapter 1). The nature of the specific syntactic category (subject/predicate, simile, or auxiliary description) is not important, but its size is. A verset is, first of all, a syntactic-rhythmical unit, or *colon* (a term of the Russian Formalists deriving from Latin rhetoric—also: *syntagma*). A "sentence" may stretch over what we would consider several versets, but the rhythmic impulse divides the long sentence into "natural" rhythmical units, equivalent in their number of major or phrasal stresses; and vice versa, such groups of stresses require some syntactic justification. The colon must respond to the requirements of both: the number of major stresses in a line and syntactical coherence.

In the opening of this poem, there are 3:3 stresses in the first two couplets, and the third couplet has 2:2 stresses. In biblical poetics, two and three are equivalent units, yet not necessarily identical. In their syntax, however, the two last couplets are linked together, carrying four parallel similes; indeed, tradition saw both of them as belonging to one verse (Deut. 32:2).

The second and third couplets provide precise parallels: accentual, syntactic, and semantic. Every word has a parallel word in its twin verset, but not necessarily a synonym. Both *rain* and *dew* are water; the first is strong, and the second is soft and delicate—these constitute two polar points in one semantic ladder.

In the first couplet, *heavens* and *earth* are not synonyms but a binary opposition alluding to the creation of the universe and to the first chapter of Genesis. Here, seen from an overall thematic construct, the versets are parallel: *listen* and *they-will-hear* refer to the same phenomenon, the same object that is spoken to and heard. But there is no direct grammatical parallel: *listen* comes in the name of the speaker, and *they-will-hear* in the name of the receiver. The morphological structure is different in both words; *and-I-will-speak* and *the-words-of-my-mouth* are not synonyms, but rather a transitive verb and its object. Though in a higher, thematical construct of this passage, all the versets refer to the same wishful event.

The three verses are linked by concatenation: the object of the first couplet, *the-words-of-my-mouth*, is developed in versets 2a and 2b (in English: *My doctrine . . . my speech*). Furthermore: versets 2a and 2b develop into 3a and 3b. The two key words of verse 2—each opens up in a whole verset (3a). *The-rain* (2a) opens up into 3a: *as-the-small-rain upon-the-tender-herb*. Similarly, *as-the-dew* (2b) unfolds into verset 3b: *and-as-the-showers upon-the-grass*. Every verset of the third couplet—3a and 3b—is as a whole parallel to only one word in the previous couplet (*rain* or *dew*). Hence, there is a vertical parallelism that descends from verset to verset and not just a horizontal one.

UNFOLDING A FICTIONAL WORLD: GENESIS

We started with issues of prosody and are shifting to devices of world building. World building here is a rhythmical event; it involves a higher level of rhythm in the text and in its fictional world. This had to be expected, because the prosody here is based not only on rhythmical but also on semantic material, which entails a fictional world. This device in the unfolding of the biblical text—in poetry and in prose—may be called *opening*. A frame of reference[2] (any object, event, or state of affairs), like "rain," is labeled and projected in the field of consciousness of the reader, and subsequently it gets opened up for its details. A projected frame of reference is essential for biblical syntax, which is formally paratactical and creates short units without syntactic subordination or long-winded intonations; rather, it expands filled-in details of the fictional world in concentric circles, reaching out more and more widely and offering more and more details.

The opening of the book of Genesis is structured in a similar way, with the universe divided between heaven and earth. But the parallelism is not between versets. "Heaven" and "earth" are mentioned in one verset as a closed binary opposition: *"In the beginning God created/the heaven and the earth."* While heaven and earth are packed into one verset, the second verset is a *continuation* of the first, not a parallel. In the song "Ha'azinu," the frame of reference *the-words-of-my-mouth* in the first verset gets opened in the fourth line: *"for I shall call the name of God."* Instead of long and subordinated sentences typical of Western literature, we have here spirals of the *opening* and *unfolding* of the frames of reference that are at first merely mentioned with one word, then increasingly enlarged and expanded.

NATURAL RHYTHMS

If there were no explicit theory of verse, how could poets or prophets know it? They couldn't, unless their sensibility was based on some implicit, psychopoetic "natural rhythm." The rhythmical groupings—regular or free—in most conventional forms in the poetry of various nations are built like a hierarchy of rhythmical waves: in regular stanzas, 2 or 3 syllables make a foot; 2 or 3 feet make a verset or hemistich; 2 or 3 versets join a line; 2 or 3 lines join a semi-strophe; 2 or 3 semi-strophes join a strophe (e.g. *ab ab ab* + *cc* in the Italian ottava rima).

The natural unit on every level of the ladder is a wave of 2 or 3 (with deviations to 4 [3 + 1]).[3] A "natural unit" in rhythm is like a wave that does not divide into regular subunits or like a prime number. Hence, 2 or 3 are the optimal size of natural rhythms, especially in free rhythms, which are not fixed for the whole poem in advance. Four is a borderline case, falling between short and long lines; a unit of 4 subunits can easily divide into 2 + 2.

The Bible reenacts this natural rhythm. Given the lack of a systematic theory at the time, and laxity in precise numbers, the Bible can impress with an unmediated rhythm that is at once natural and strong—emphasized by the overlapping syntactic and semantic forces of the text—and free. A similar use of natural rhythms on a higher level can be observed in the poetry of Walt Whitman, which was obviously influenced by the wide-reaching rhythms of the Bible.[4]

RHYTHM IN PROPHECY

The first chapter of the book of Isaiah evokes both the opening of the book of Genesis and the song "Ha'azinu." Chapter 1 of Isaiah is organized in four moves (I did not impose this systematic structure; it is in the text):

Move I (3 periods) = 7 + 5 + 7 lines
Move II (3 periods) = 7 + 5 + 7 lines
Move III (2 periods) = 6 + 6 lines
Move IV (2 periods) = 6 + 6 lines

We shall examine the first move.

Move I = 3 periods = 3 + 2 + 3 strophes = 7 + 5 + 7 lines.

Each line has 2 or 3 versets, and each verset has 2 or 3 words. The term "period" here means the equivalent to a periodic sentence. The concepts of strophe and line are borrowed from elementary literary prosody. In rising order:

2 or 3 words make a verset
2 or 3 versets make a line
2 or 3 lines make a strophe
2 or 3 strophes make a period
2 or 3 periods make a move
3 + 1 moves make chapter 1 of Isaiah

The four moves of this chapter (4 = 3 + 1) are marked in the text by parallel openings. Three openings call people to listen to God's word: in verse 2, "Hear, O-heavens"; in verse 10, "Hear the word of the LORD"; in verse 18, "Come now, and let us reason together, saith the LORD." And the fourth opening, in verse 24, has a summary character: "Therefore saith the LORD, the LORD of hosts, the mighty One of Israel."

Arrows, here and elsewhere, indicate the direction in which the lines are read.

→

[2] Hear, O-heavens and		
give-ear, O-earth:	for the-LORD hath-spoken,	2 + 2/3
I-have-nourished-and		
brought-up children,	and-they have-rebelled	
	against-me.	3 + 3
[3] The-ox knoweth his-owner	and-the-ass his-master's crib:	3 + 3
but-Israel doth-not know	my-people doth-not consider.	3 + 3
[4] Ah sinful nation,	a-people laden-with iniquity,	3 + 3
a-seed of-evildoers,	children that-are-corrupters:	2 + 2
they-have-forsaken the-LORD,		
they-have-provoked the-		
Holy-One of-Israel		
[unto anger],	they-are-gone-away backward.	2 + 3/2

Period B

[5] Why-should-ye be-		
stricken any-more?	ye-will-revolt more-and-more:	3 + 2
the-whole-head is-sick,	and-the-whole-heart faint.	2 + 2
[6] From-the-sole-of-the-foot		
even-unto-the-head	there-is-no soundness-in-it;	2 + 2
but-wounds, and-bruises,	and-putrefying sores:	2 + 2
they-have-not-been-closed,		
neither bound-up,	neither mollified with-ointment.	3 + 3

Period C

[7] Your-country is-desolate,	your-cities are-burned with-fire:	2 + 3
your-land, strangers devour it	in-your-presence,	2 + 3
and-it-is-desolate,	as-overthrown by-strangers.	3
[8] And-the-daughter-of-Zion		
is-left	as-a-cottage in-a-vineyard,	2 + 2
as-a-lodge in-a-garden-		
of-cucumbers,	as-a-besieged city.	2 + 2
[9] Except the-LORD of-hosts	had-left-unto-us a-very-small remnant,	3 + 3
we-should-have-been		
as-Sodom,	and we-should-have-been like-unto-	
	Gomorrah.	2 + 2

Upon first reading the Hebrew it seems that those are free rhythms; but as soon as we achieve equality in versets, we deviate from rhythms. Still, the deviation itself is so precise that the result may be even more precise than in accentual-syllabic meters.

And there are further rhythmical devices: Period A has predominantly 3 + 3 accents; Period B has predominantly 2 + 2. In this *regularly irregular meter*, local combinations play a key role, with precise local regularities like modern meters. Verse 8 reads like four anapests with a one-syllable omission in each demi-verse. I deliberately register each syllable with modern metrical symbols to illustrate the similarity with or difference from modern meters.

[8]

$\rightarrow$

∪∪ — ∪∪ — ∪∪ — 0∪ — ∪

∪∪ — ∪∪ — 0∪ — ∪∪ —

[9]

$\rightarrow$

∪ — |∪∪ — |∪ — |∪ — ∪∪|∪ — |∪ — | [a predominantly iambic free meter]

|∪ — ∪ — ∪|∪∪ — |∪ — ∪|

But then the segmented meter must change to:

|∪ — ∪| — ∪ — |∪ — ∪ — ∪| [i.e. a precise iambic pentameter]

On the background of threes (3 + 3) the dominance of twos (2 + 2) sounds compact. But two or three has no specific individual meaning. The meaning of such sound patterns has to be derived from interaction with the meanings of the text (see Chapter 2).

		מַחֲזוֹר א' 2.
	וְהַאֲזִינִי אֶרֶץ,	שִׁמְעוּ שָׁמַיִם,
2 + 3/2		כִּי יְהוָה דִּבֵּר׃
		בָּנִים גִּדַּלְתִּי וְרוֹמַמְתִּי
3 + 3		וְהֵם פָּשְׁעוּ בִי. 3.
3 + 3	וַחֲמוֹר אֵבוּס בְּעָלָיו;	יָדַע שׁוֹר קֹנֵהוּ
3 + 3	עַמִּי, לֹא הִתְבּוֹנָן.	יִשְׂרָאֵל לֹא יָדַע 4.
3 + 3	עַם כֶּבֶד עָוֹן,	הוֹי, גּוֹי חֹטֵא
2 + 2	בָּנִים מַשְׁחִיתִים;	זֶרַע מְרֵעִים
	נִאֲצוּ אֶת-קְדוֹשׁ יִשְׂרָאֵל,	עָזְבוּ אֶת-יְהוָה,
2 + 2/3		נָזֹרוּ אָחוֹר.

מחזור ב

3 + 2	תּוֹסִיפוּ סָרָה؟	עַל-מֶה תֻכּוּ עוֹד	5.
2 + 2	וְכָל-לֵבָב דַּוָּי;	כָּל-רֹאשׁ לָחֳלִי	
2 + 2	אֵין-בּוֹ מְתֹם	מִכַּף-רֶגֶל וְעַד-רֹאשׁ	6.
2 + 2	וּמַכָּה טְרִיָּה;	פֶּצַע וְחַבּוּרָה	
3 + 3	וְלֹא רֻכְּכָה בַּשָּׁמֶן;	לֹא-זֹרוּ וְלֹא חֻבָּשׁוּ	

מחזור ג

2 + 3	עָרֵיכֶם שְׂרֻפוֹת אֵשׁ	אַרְצְכֶם שְׁמָמָה	7.
2 + 3	זָרִים אֹכְלִים אֹתָהּ;	אַדְמַתְכֶם לְנֶגְדְּכֶם	
2 + 3/3		וּשְׁמָמָה כְּמַהְפֵּכַת זָרִים;	
2 + 2	כְּסֻכָּה בְכָרֶם	וְנוֹתְרָה בַת-צִיּוֹן	8.
2 + 2	כְּעִיר נְצוּרָה;	כִּמְלוּנָה בְמִקְשָׁה	
3 + 3	הוֹתִיר לָנוּ שָׂרִיד כִּמְעָט;	לוּלֵי יְהֹוָה צְבָאוֹת	9.
2 + 2	לַעֲמֹרָה דָּמִינוּ;	כִּסְדֹם הָיִינוּ,	

This is the prosody of *regular irregularity* using the two possible natural rhythms: two and three. To avoid an artificial sense, the two items have to be intermingled. Move I has three syntactic periods, and each one is both a thematic and syntactical unit, a kind of macro-sentence of the speaker.

Since the strophes are quite long, they divide into "lines."[5] In this hierarchy, there is, on every level, a natural group of subgroups, mostly of two or three subunits. The whole rhythmical hierarchy is reinforced by several kinds of parallelism, which crisscross the units and break the automatic structure of symmetrical parallels using different kinds of asymmetry.

In such a way, the whole move is built like a long chain with parallel versets arranged in a hierarchy of seven levels, which we could describe as an architectonic ladder:

word–verset–line–strophe–period–move–chapter

The chain, the ladder, is not a narrative but a series of unfolding themes, or frames of reference.

Whereas ancient poetry predominantly had lines (traditional "verses") of two versets, the prophet here presents four versets (2 + 2). The traditional verse 4 has seven versets: 2 + 2 and 2 + 1. Verse 4 is unified by a sound pattern of Z or Z + R, culminating in *naZORu ahOR*, a closing chord. This chord has words with less than the Hebrew norm of three consonants in the root. This organization is laid bare if we construct the units not in one linear chain but in a hierarchical structure, as introduced here.

Clearly, there is a planned, though changing, structure. The 7 + 5 + 7 lines indicate an asymmetrical intention and remind us of the Japanese haiku poem (no historical reading), which has 5 + 7 + 5 syllables. In the context of the symmetrical parallelism which is so conspicuous in ancient biblical poetry, highlighting asymmetry underlines the fact that we confront here an advancing speech—the pairs of symmetrical parallelisms are swept up in its advancement. Asymmetry is attained by repeated changing of the numbers of units on every level and by versets that do not participate in the parallelism.

For example, in the first line, there is a parallel between two versets: "*Hear, O-heavens,/and-give-ear, O-earth*" (2 + 2), followed by an "orphan" verset ("for the-LORD hath-spoken") that has no immediate parallel. This structure looks like rhyming: **aam**: the first two versets are "rhyming" (by parallelism) with each other, whereas the third verset has no mate and remains an "orphan" (in printer's language). The symmetry of the first two versets was derived from the traditional poem, and the speaker overcomes the symmetrical structure by the use of a free third term that continues the long move of the argument.

In the poem, the first two versets are parallel. We may observe the reverse order of words in Isaiah in comparison to the ancient song "Ha'azinu":

Ha'Azinu haŠaMayim/vetišMa ha-Arets

[Give-ear, O-ye-heavens/ . . . and-hear, O-earth]

Two sound patterns are crisscrossed in a chiastic figure: $A + \check{S}M/\check{S}M + A$. In Isaiah, however, the patterns are built with regular alliterations; the same four words are used but reshuffled—*ŠiM'u ŠaMayim ve-ha'Azini Arets*—to cover every first consonant of a word. The first pair of words now starts with the consonants Š + M, and the second starts with A (the letter alef): $\check{S}M + \check{S}M/A + A$. There is, however, a third verset: "for the LORD hath spoken," which has no immediate parallel. The symmetry comes from the tradition of biblical poetry, whereas the asymmetry emphasizes the genre of speech or sermon, which uses a wealth of static parallelisms yet subordinates them to the flow of the argument. I observed a similar relationship between a pair of colors in Chagall's twelve windows of the synagogue in the Hadassah Hospital in Jerusalem.[6] The twelve tribes of Israel are represented in the four directions of the world, with three windows each. The windows are multicolored, but each window has a dominant color. For each direction, two windows have shades of the same basic color, and the third is an "orphan"—whose color is picked up by another window.

But in a higher thematic construct, the third or "orphan" verset, which has no direct, immediate parallel, accepts the whole continuous speech as parallel to that orphan sentence: "for the LORD hath spoken." In the next line, the words "I have nourished and brought up" are a parallel, not between versets, but inside one verset; while the last verset, "they have rebelled against me," is not parallel but continues the argument; it is a summary, confronting the details and metaphors. On the level of the general meaning of the text, the fourth verset is directly opposed to the content of the third. The third strophe is an extension of the fourth verset, "and they have rebelled against me." Indeed, thematically, the whole Period A appears as an unfolding of this verset. In the space between opening and unfolding the fictional world, the speaker's argument and the narrative all have enlarged.

In sum: In chapter 1 of Isaiah, the structure is not narrative or directional but hierarchical, and the text is packed with parallels—in both horizontal and vertical order. The parallels are not dominant but subordinated to the dynamic forward-moving speech.

The verset "and they have rebelled against me" starts a theme, which is developed along the move. More concrete language parallels appear as pairs in one line: "The ox knoweth his owner, / and the ass his master's crib." There is no absolute symmetry—for example, the word "know" does not appear in the second verset—but the thematic parallelism runs over from one line to the next. "Israel doth not know" is parallel to "they have forsaken the LORD" and, indeed, parallel to all versets of Period A.

As opposed to biblical poetry, which loves repetition but is reluctant to repeat parallel units of any kind more than twice or thrice, Isaiah has multiple repetitions of the same pattern, in an increasing crescendo. Thus, of the seven versets of biblical verse 4, four versets are parallel to each other. In verse 8, the second verset continues the first verset: "And the daughter of Zion is left / as a cottage in a vineyard." Here the second verset is a continuation of the first, but the text continues with three parallel versets—"as a cottage in a vineyard"—"as a lodge in a garden of cucumbers"—"as a besieged city"—until the fact that we have three versets overcomes the urge of symmetry. It seems appropriate to describe the sequence as a dynamic repetition within the advancement of the speech and not as a static parallel pair.

The same principle stretches above the superstructure of the move as a whole: the three periods are parallel to each other and also unfold the theme as a rhetorical argument: Israel sinned against me → they were punished by physical suffering → their land is a wasteland (metonymy).

RHYTHM IN GENESIS, CHAPTER 1

The book of Genesis is not perceived as poetry. But its use of versets as syntactic-rhythmical units is similar to—and still different from—that accepted in poetry. We may call the rhythm of Genesis *condensed Epic rhythm,* and the genre, *cosmic epic.* Let us observe the first eight traditional verses:

[1] In-the-beginning God created the-heaven and-the-earth.   3 + 2
[2] And-the-earth was-without-form, and-void;
    and-darkness was-upon-the-face of-the-deep.   3 + 3
    And-the-Spirit of-God moved upon-the-face of-the-waters.   2 + 3
[3] And-God said, Let-there-be-light:
    and-there-was light.   3 + 2
[4] And-God saw the-light, that-it-was-good:
    and-God divided the-light from-the-darkness.   4 + 4
[5] And-God called the-light Day,
    and-the-darkness he-called Night.   4 + 3
    And-the-evening-[was] and-the-morning
    were-the-first day.   4 + 2
[6] And-God said, Let-there-be-a-firmament in-the-midst-of-the-waters,
    and-let-it divide the-waters from-the-waters.   4 + 4
[7] And-God made the-firmament,
    and-divided the-waters which-were-under the-firmament   3 + 4
    from-the-waters which-were-above the-firmament:
    and-it-was-so.   3 + 1
[8] And-God called the-firmament Heaven.
    And-the-evening-[was] and-the-morning-were the-second-day.   4 + 3

2 + 3	אֵת הַשָּׁמַיִם וְאֵת הָאָרֶץ ;	1. בְּרֵאשִׁית בָּרָא אֱלֹהִים
3 + 4	וְחֹשֶׁךְ עַל-פְּנֵי תְהוֹם ;	2. וְהָאָרֶץ הָיְתָה תֹהוּ וָבֹהוּ
3 + 2	מְרַחֶפֶת עַל-פְּנֵי המים ;	3. וְרוּחַ אֱלֹהִים
2 + 4	וַיְהִי אוֹר ;	4. וַיֹּאמֶר אֱלֹהִים יְהִי אוֹר
	5. וַיַּרְא אֱלֹהִים אֶת-הָאוֹר כִּי-טוֹב ;	
4 + 4	וַיַּבְדֵּל אֱלֹהִים בֵּין הָאוֹר וּבֵין הַחֹשֶׁךְ ;	

3 + 4	6. וַיִּקְרָא אֱלֹהִים לָאוֹר יוֹם וְלַחֹשֶׁךְ קָרָא לָיְלָה ;
2 + 4	וַיְהִי-עֶרֶב וַיְהִי-בֹקֶר יוֹם אֶחָד ;
	7. וַיֹּאמֶר אֱלֹהִים יְהִי רָקִיעַ בְּתוֹךְ הַמָּיִם ;
4 + 4	וִיהִי מַבְדִּיל בֵּין מַיִם לָמָיִם ;
	8. וַיַּעַשׂ אֱלֹהִים אֶת-הָרָקִיעַ
4 + 3	וַיַּבְדֵּל בֵּין הַמַּיִם אֲשֶׁר מִתַּחַת לָרָקִיעַ
	וּבֵין הַמַּיִם אֲשֶׁר מֵעַל לָרָקִיעַ
1 + 3	וַיְהִי-כֵן ;
	9. וַיִּקְרָא אֱלֹהִים לָרָקִיעַ שָׁמָיִם ;
3 + 4	וַיְהִי-עֶרֶב וַיְהִי-בֹקֶר יוֹם שֵׁנִי ;

GENRES AND DISCOURSE

The boundaries of genres in the Bible are often blurred. They are not genres of fictionality (tragedy) or genres of form (sonnet) but genres of discourse (e.g. cosmic narrative or human narrative). At first, we are struck by the fact that half of the versets have four stresses each (a number absent from poetry). Is it poetry? Or is it prose of some sort? Most of the traditional verses here come in two versets each, and some are doubled (2 + 2) (like the biblical verses 2, 4, 5, and 8). Verse 7 has three versets. In contrast to poetry, which favors twos and threes, half of all the versets here have four stresses, and several have one stress. The range can be described as one–four stresses per verset, or phrase, whereas poetry has mostly two–three.

A special device is the short chord that often comes to close a pair of versets. The chord never uses full Hebrew words with three-consonant roots and presents a rhythmical bow with two stresses with only one unstressed syllable between them: $| - \cup - |$. A regular biblical word has the opposite, a majority of unstressed syllables: $| \cup \cup - \cup |$.

In addition to the numeric differences, the prose lacks semantic parallels between the early pairs of versets, but it does have *continuation* and *complementation*—e.g. *And-the-Spirit of-God moved upon-the-face of-the-waters.*

There are many repetitions in the text, especially in pairs of words: *heaven* and *earth, tohu* and *bohu, light* and *darkness*—yet such pairs appear each in its own verset and do not create parallelism between versets. In Isaiah, *heavens* and *earth* appear in parallel versets, while in Genesis, *heaven* and *earth* together fill in one verset, and the second verset is not parallel to it but its continuation.

The theme is cosmic: the creation of the world. The word ברא (created) seems to have arisen from the opening word of the Bible, בראשית (in the

beginning) and is phonetically included in it: BRA/BRAshit (ברא/בְּרֵאשִית).[7]
And right away, the theme ("the universe") splits into a binary opposition:
above/below → heaven/earth. And then, in a chiastic move, the text opens
the framework "earth" and, after it, the framework "heaven."

There are no long sentences here, as in Western literature, with subordina-
tion of secondary clauses, but every concept, or frame of reference, is first
evoked by an opening word, then unfolds into a new pair, and then, perhaps,
provides more details or becomes a stage for such to come.

After the earth was described as darkness, there comes the binary opposi-
tion to darkness—light. And both open up to a new parallel pair: day and
night. Only after the darkness is presented in this perspective do we return to
heaven in more detail. In this detailing, the firmament appears that separates
waters from waters, and from here, on the third day, comes an additional
binary opposition: water—dry land. The land and the earth, later in the text,
give birth to a new pair—grass and fruit tree—which prepares the stage for the
expulsion from paradise. All those pairs of oppositions appear in one verset
each and not in parallel versets. And new thematic units are introduced by
derivation rather than as new themes.

In several instances, there are more than two versets in a verse. The biblical
poets or editors inserted unusual short versets into the same verse (verses 2,
5, 7), like chords. The chords are short and dense, mostly three-syllable, with
short words and two-stressed syllables (the opposite of what is normal):

y-hí ór,   vá-ihí ór; yóm-eḥád; yóm shení; vayhí-kén:

→

|∪ − −||∪ − −||−∪−|| −∪−|| ∪ − −|
[let-there-be-light] [one day] [second day] [and-it-was-so]

There are no three-consonant roots here as in most Hebrew words. And the
function of the chord is to show conclusion, acceptance.

The beginning of Genesis plays between many penultimate words (*hamayim*,
haʾarets, *tohu*, *bohu*, etc.) and the short, pragmatic closures of two short stresses.

←

|− − ∪ || − − ∪ || − − ∪ ||− ∪ ||− − ∪|| − ∪ − || − − ∪ |
ויהי כן. ,יום אחד ,לאור יום ,כי טוב ,ויהי אור ,יהי אור על-פני תהום

In this selection, there are thirteen stressed syllables and eight unstressed
syllables—a rarity in any language. The previous example (Gen 2:2) has the

exact opposite: four stressed syllables over against twelve unstressed ones. This is rhythmical-solemn prose, featuring short and equivalent units.

In addition, the whole text is organized vertically, with an often-repeated anaphora: *And the Spirit of God—and God said—and God saw—and God made—and God called.* This is like a continuous rhyme (like the Spanish "string" rhyme [*haruz mavri'ah*]), except that in this case the place of the rhyme is not at the end of the lines but at the beginning, nor is this rhyme made of sounds but of repetitions of the same word, "God."

The text represents a staircase structure (Shklovsky's term), in which every rung projects a frame of reference, which gets filled in, in the continuation of the text and builds an ever-enlarging world (though still very short and compact). All that is opposed to directional, linear unfolding, either narrative or descriptive, which is prevalent in Western literature.

In terms of genre, this poetry is the closest in form to pairs of ideal symmetrical parallels but deliberately stops short of that. The prose is similar in its rhythm, but the versets are more fluctuating and poor in parallels. On the other hand, the prophecy is richer than the poetry in its use of parallels and promotes both horizontal and vertical forward-moving patterns.

In sum: the prose is poorer in parallels than the poetry, while the prophecy is richer than the poetry, especially in raising the vertical as against the horizontal structures. There are various kinds of rhythmical prose in the Bible that go as far as five or six stresses in a verset. In prose, the second verset in a pair is usually not parallel but complementary to the first verset, as in the first verse of Genesis: "In the beginning God created / the heaven and the earth."

In the Bible, as in European poetry, it stands to reason that we could guess a solution that does not employ the principle of equivalence between versets of various lengths. Let us assume that an abstract and fixed metrical pattern of three accents in a verset is superimposed on the text using clear rules of coordination between meter and language, as in modern poetry. A word may have two or more metrical accents, provided the *rule of coordination* of meter and language is observed: *in an abstract grid, if any accents fall on a word, at least one accent must fall on the stressed syllable.* This holds as true for Milton as for Leah Goldberg (see Chapter 4). The fact is that at least one word in a verset of only two words is a long word—a word which has three or more syllables and enables two or more rhythmical accents with at least one unstressed syllable between them. That is, it is easy to imagine that a meter of three accents was superimposed on this text. In a modern manner, we can represent this as follows:

כִּשְׂעִירִם עֲלֵי-דֶשֶׁא וְכִרְבִיבִים עֲלֵי-עֵשֶׂב.

→

Kīsĕirīm ălĕy-dēshĕ /   vĕ   khīrĕvĭvīm   ăley ēsĕv.
| — ∪ ∪ — | ∪ ∪ — ∪ || ∪ || — ∪ ∪ — | ∪ ∪ — ∪ |

In modern poetry, except for the conjunction, this is a regular ternary meter (a dactylic hexameter). In other words, the meter is separate from the language and does not use all language stresses. The question is whether we can adjust the text to achieve a given metrical order, as in modern accentual-syllabic poetry.

In the continuation of the song "Ha'azinu," there are more versets of two words, but always at least one word is long: *Bĕtŏĕvōt yăkh'īsūhŭ* בְּתוֹעֵבֹת יַכְהִיסֻהוּ יַכְעִיסֻהוּ← — ∪ ∪ — | ∪ ∪ — ∪ | (Deut 32:17). Knowing this enables us to see the possibility of a unified reading of the poem with three accents (not stresses) per verset. On the other hand, the opposite is not true; not all long words get secondary stresses: *yĭsŏvĕvĕnhŭ yĭvōnĕnēhŭ* יְסֹבְבֶנְהוּ יְבוֹנְנֵהוּ (32:10) → | ∪ — ∪ ∸ ∪ | ∪ — ∪ ∸ ∪ |. This phrase could have carried four accents, but the meter does not require it and is satisfied with three accents; it is reasonable to read the phrase this way: יְסֹבְבֶנְהוּ יְבוֹנְנֵהוּ → | ∪ ∪ ∪ — ∪ | ∪ — ∪ — ∪ |. This is not the only possible reading; we can read the phrase in several different ways on condition that there is correlation between language and meter.

Thus, we have two hypotheses about reading. One allows some freedom in the length of the verset (between two and four stresses per verset), based on three accents as a dominant number that one can deviate from or challenge. The alternative assumption is that a permanent meter of three accents imposes its regularity on the language of the verse, provided there is no clash between meter and language. This rule is precisely as in modern poetry and emphasizes those syllables that fit the metrical scheme, that is, by overlooking some short words and adding secondary stresses in selected long words when the meter requires it.

OVERALL RHYTHM

The syntactic or semantic equivalences between parallel versets calls the reader's attention to the phenomenon of parallelism itself. But the phenomenon of parallelism is revealed, first of all, in the *rhythmical* structure of the text, even if there is no semantic or syntactic support. The rhythmical structure of biblical texts is organized mainly around stress. The principle of organization is accentual, but the number of accents in each verset does not have to be fixed and defined. We can have precise repetition (3:3 accents) or a free relationship (e.g. 4:3) or numbers of accents that change with the unfolding of the text.

The numbers are often equal or similar. Moreover, even if the number is changing and not fixed, it is not just "free." Every verset is at least a rhythmic-syntactical colon, the basic unit of overlapping syntax and rhythm. The small size of a verset and the semantic density of Biblical Hebrew also contribute to the conspicuous status of every major word in the line, especially when its status is reinforced in a parallel verset. Two unequal versets—if they come in similar numbers (4:3)—convey the sense of equivalence between two syntactical clauses.

THE LEVEL OF SYLLABLES

We can assume that rhythm in the Bible is based on limited free variations of the three forces at work: rhythmic, syntactic, semantic. The focal organizing factor is stress. Biblical poetry is based on versets with a nearly equal number of stresses. The meter is a free-accentual meter. Indeed, the number of unstressed syllables between two stressed ones is not regular, as in modern accentual-syllabic meters. And yet, clear constraints are at work here. There is practically a taboo in the Bible on placing two adjacent stressed syllables inside one syntactic unit; if two stresses collide with each other, we use the rule of "retreat" (*nasog aḥor*), and the first of the two stressed syllables must move backward. For example, the genitive collocation *anshé ḥésed* (generous people), has such a clash, and as a response, the stress on the first word moves one syllable back: *ánshe ḥésed*. On the other hand, long words (three or more syllables) usually receive secondary stresses, apart from the syllables with major stresses. As a result, there is at least one syllable between two stressed syllables and usually not more than two. The stresses are not allowed to be too far from each other. In rhythmical terms, every stress carries on its shoulders two or three syllables (and sometimes four). This is similar to the rhythm of deviant meters (the "ternary net") in modern poetry, which mostly hovers between one and two (and sometimes three) unstressed syllables, i.e. between modern iambs and amphibrachs—the natural rhythmical units.

Yet on the level of syllables and stresses, there are several local configurations, and it is hard to imagine that their appearance is accidental. Ostensibly, there is freedom in the number of unstressed syllables, yet this is true only if we work with statistical averages. If we observe some conspicuous local configurations, we can discover the wide range of rhythmical effects in the Bible.

As the poetry creates local parallels between two versets or between local pairs within one verset, the same rhythmic effects work on the lower level of syllables and stresses. The Bible is full of pairs of words that have an equal or similar syllabic structure. A parallel syntactic structure invites a similar syllabic structure, and vice versa.

Let us turn again to the song "Ha'azinu" and mark all the syllables for stress, as in modern poetry. Sound orchestration is not a mere slogan when the text as a whole is saturated with sound patterns. In fact, the numeric relations keep changing constantly, but in the local rhythm they may all play a role.

Here, read each column vertically:

→		→	
ha-azinu	∪ ∪ — ∪	vetishma	∪ ∪ —
↓ ha-shamayim	∪ ∪ — ∪	haarets	∪ — ∪
va-adabera	∪ ∪ — ∪	imrey-fi	∪ ∪ —

The same configurations are in the original:

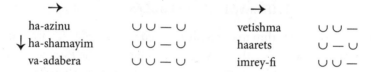

In the first column, all the words are long and penultimately stressed—a typical effect of a hymnic, musical tone, which is felt especially because of the paucity of penultimate stresses in the language. In the second column, the words are shorter and there is a shift to ultimate stresses. Thus, a clear opposition is formed between a verset of long, penultimately stressed words and the closure in ultimately stressed words:

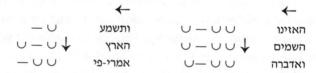

This rhythm is as precise as in classical meters, but the regularity appears only in short segments that are juxtaposed to each other and change constantly for local rhythmical effects. The rhythm is local and interacts well with the local elements of meaning and voice. On the other hand, the meter of a text institutionalizes the text, subsumes it under one mandatory, leveling institution.

Contrary to the three penultimates in the opening, we move here from anapests to *chords* in short and strong iambs. And there is also internal rhyming that reinforces the impact: *tizal / katal; kematar / katal; likhi / amarti.* The syllabic structure is mirrored in both versets. A secondary stress in the long words is possible in order to realize three accents:

$$\longleftarrow$$

$$\cup - \cup \cup \mid - \cup \cup - \qquad \text{כשעירים עלי-דשא}$$
$$\cup - \cup \cup \mid - \cup \cup - \cup \qquad \text{וכרביבים עלי-עשב}$$

Here we see clear amphibrachic flow. The second verset starts with an extra unstressed syllable that is justified by the conjunction *v-* (and), which brings together the two identical versets.

This is not a fixed metrical system but, on the contrary, constantly changing local rhythmical configurations, their meter reinforced by the strong stresses and the heavy independence of the single word in the Bible. When we are looking for the unity of the meter, such differences are suppressed, but in the analysis of the rhythmical effects, it is important to emphasize the local differences and juxtapositions between metrical segments of syllables. The space of freedom is used here to produce internal equivalents and oppositions, which are organized on the lower level, the level of syllables. And this is rhythm rather than meter; this is the tightest link between sound and meaning, because it gets reassessed with every new word. The same "irregular" syllables, which on the level of the text exhibit, in principle, that the rhythm is "free," serve, on the local level, as meaningful configurations. One of the principles of this book is precisely this reversal: the syllables that are not organized are put under scrutiny so we can unravel the inner rhythms of the local text.

SOUND ORCHESTRATION

At first, it seems strange: in the poetry of the Historical Era, the function of poetic language relies on the density of the text in every respect. But there is a difference: the semantic patterns—metaphors and images—are scattered in the text with no consistency, whereas the sound patterns—meter and rhyme—are employed to support the formal structure of the poem. On the other hand, the Bible treats meter and rhyme as free form. Like metaphors, sound patterns are scattered in the text to serve as "ornaments" or to call attention to the co-textual poetic language, not to serve as compositional devices. From here, it is an easy transition to an organized poem, as in the post-biblical piyut—the liturgical poetry in Christian Palestine.

All possibilities of patterns with the sounds of words are tried out in the Bible, and those are used later in the piyut in formalized, regular forms (see the next chapter). In the Bible, however, their structure remains free and open. Their functions are local and coextensive with other aspects of the local text's meaning, imagery, metaphor, etc.

Within the framework of rhythmical parallelism comes a whole gamut of sound repetition and sound patterns, freely distributed, but profusely and clearly embellishing the text. Whatever the origins of Hebrew rhyme and puns or sound patterns in later poetry, the later poets were able to draw on a variety of such devices in the Bible. There are:

1) simple alliteration הֹוד וְהָדָר, חֵן וָחֶסֶד—the same letter at the head of two or more words

2) a chain of one repeated sound צַדִּיק מִצָּרָה נֶחֱלָץ (Prov. 11:8)

3) repetition of the same root, which is syntactically justified: אָחוּדָה נָּא חוּדָה לָכֶם חִידָה ("I will now put forth a riddle unto you," Judg. 14:12), חִידָתְךָ וְנִשְׁמָעֶנָּה ("Put forth thy riddle, that we may hear it," 14:13)

4) puns on similar sounding roots: אַל תַּחֲרֹשׁ עַל רֵעֲךָ רָעָה (Prov. 3:29); פַּחַד- פַּחַת פָּח ; אִישׁ אֵשׁ-אֵשֶׁת

5) root rhyming בָּבֶל - בָּלַל (cf. Gen. 11:9), צְדָקָה - צְעָקָה (cf. Isa. 5:7)

6) occasional end rhymes in the modern sense יַיִן – שְׁלָחָה (cf. Prov. 9:4), צֶמַח קֶמַח (Hos. 8:9)

Rhyme is sometimes obviously linked to the structure of parallelism, as here:

וּשְׁנוֹתֶיךָ לְאַכְזָרִי	פֶּן-תִּתֵּן לַאֲחֵרִים הֹודֶךָ
וַעֲצָבֶיךָ בְּבֵית-נָכְרִי	פֶּן-יִשְׂבְּעוּ זָרִים כֹּחֶךָ
u-šnotekha le-akhzari	**pen**-titen la'aḥerim **hodekha**
va-atsavekha be-veyt nokhri	**pen**-yisbeu **zarim kohekha**
And-thy-years unto-the-cruel;	Lest-thou-give thy-vigor unto-others,
And-thy-labors be-in-the-house-of-an-alien.	Lest-strangers-be-filled with-thy-strength,

The two sentences are similar in rhythm (3:2 stresses) and are linked by an anaphora, as well as by parallel syntax, meaning, morphology, and end rhyme. Though the symmetry is pervasive and multiple, it is, however, neither regular nor permanent. The first versets of each line are parallel in meaning as a whole but not in each word; אֲחֵרִים ("others") and זָרִים ("strangers") are parallel in morphology and rhyme; וּשְׁנוֹתֶיךָ ("thy years") and וַעֲצָבֶיךָ ("thy labors") are not parallel in the same sense; אַכְזָרִי ("the cruel") and בֵּית נָכְרִי ("the house of an alien") are not synonymous in the language but become so when enforced by this context and rhyme. In the same way, all parallel words rhyme with each other, except for the first word.

This is perhaps an extreme example of all-pervasive order; the biblical patterns are often less symmetrical, and the verset that follows may not have any of the above devices. Rhyme, as it is known at present, as a regular organizing device of a poem, is not a mere internal ornament; rather, it was created as concomitant to an unequivocal strophic structure and a formalization of poetic patterns. This development occurred centuries after the Bible was written, in the Palestinian piyut of Yannai and Eleazar Kallir.

4

THE SYSTEMS OF HEBREW VERSIFICATION

HEBREW VERSIFICATION IN CULTURAL HISTORY

The general theory and morphology of versification systems could not offer a historical and linguistic example richer and more variegated than the Hebrew language and culture.[1] These are like a nomadic laboratory for the metamorphosis of poetic forms in the context of Jewish history, a history of "wandering centers," as the historian Simon Dubnov perceived it.

After the closure of the Bible and its Jewish canonization, verse and rhyme of one kind or another became omnipresent features of Hebrew culture in all periods and in all centers of the Jewish dispersion. Thousands of Hebrew poems have been written in Palestine / Eretz Israel and throughout the Diaspora, most of them following strict normative rules which were often quite complex and elaborate. Marked by strong tendencies toward formalism and conservatism, the forms of Hebrew verse nevertheless changed radically as Hebrew culture selectively encountered, in time and space, Near Eastern mythopoetic narratives and networks of parallelism (*The Goddess Anat*), Hellenistic secular culture, Arabic classical poetry, Italian Renaissance versification, German eighteenth-century genres, Russian Romanticism and Futurism, Yiddish folklore, and English Modernism.

Almost all possible systems of rhythm and rhyme had been active in Hebrew poetry (except Chinese tonic meters). In the course of the centuries, Hebrew poetry unfolded twelve different prosodic systems. This is understandable yet most unusual: English poetry has had only four systems in history: (1) the Old English "native" accentual meters; (2) the French-inspired syllabic system; (3) the accentual-syllabic system of English poetry in its richest period, from the sixteenth to the twentieth century; and (4) the modern diversity of free verse.

The term "form," used here in a limited sense, refers to all poetic patterns that *employ elements of sound for the composition of poetic texts.* The term "poem" here indicates any text organized in such a manner—whether it is a lyric or an epic and whether it fulfills any individual experience or aesthetic function in a modern sense or not.

As we saw in Chapter 3, the Bible exhibits a thick network of free, sporadic sound patterns, repetitions, parallelisms, quasi-strophic structures, and other devices which serve both the orchestration of the text as a verbal, "musical" accompaniment and focus the reader's attention on the text itself. Like metaphors in poetry, which may appear rarely or often unexpectedly and irregularly in a poem, so do sound patterns embellish and intensify many poetic texts without building any formal structure of composition and expectations.

Unlike other languages, Hebrew, though continuously used in writing, was seen as a "dead" language until the twentieth century; it was nobody's "mother tongue," and it did not serve as the spoken language or the Base Language of a social group.[2] It has never changed the core of its vocabulary, the written forms of its words, its basic morphology, certain patterns of lower syntax (e.g. *smikhut*—genitive), certain idiomatic collocations, or the fundamental framework of its historical, semantic, and "mythological" allusions. The major changes in the language occurred in its pronunciation, since the language could not be dead during prayer and education—you have to pronounce it somehow. The language was bound to be influenced by how it was spoken. In eastern Europe, the higher yeshiva studies for Jewish boys were conducted in a dialogue between two students or between a teacher and a student, with each profusely quoting the classical texts of the Holy Tongues, Hebrew and Aramaic.

As recorded in the beginning of the twentieth century, about five thousand Hebrew words and collocations were found in the spoken language, Yiddish, and were pronounced according to local Yiddish dialects. Thus, the Grand Rebbe of the Lubavich Hassidic sect made his long, learned speeches in Lithuanian Yiddish, pronouncing "š" like "s," etc. But even these facts did not alter the basic forms of the written, sanctified Hebrew word and its biblical spelling—which are most relevant for written poetry.

THE EXTRAORDINARY NATURE OF
HEBREW LITERARY HISTORY

A study of the changes in the forms of Hebrew verse should take into account the peculiar nature of its history. A Hebrew poet, regardless of his time, lived at the crossroads of three cultural horizons: (1) the historical perspective, common to all literatures: the interaction between synchrony and diachrony, i.e. between trends of the poet's own generation and those of both the near and the classical past; (2) the influence of contemporary poetry written in Hebrew in other countries; (3) the impact of non-Hebrew poetry in a non-Hebrew language the poet spoke, read, and studied.

The tensions between the three systems were of primary importance to the history of Hebrew poetic forms. Quite often cardinal differences existed between the three. Thus some Hebrew poets living in Rome around 1300 CE still wrote in the Hebrew strophic forms of the piyut, the Hebrew liturgical poetry developed in Eretz Israel under Byzantine Christian rule, then brought to Italy and canonized long before any Italian language even existed. The system of the piyut relied on the number of words per line rather than the number of syllables. Rhyme was mandatory, and each rhyme had multiple members but did not alternate with other rhymes. The poets rhymed *aaaa, bbbb, cccc*, etc., rather than alternating: *abab* or *aba bcb cdc*, etc. At the same time, they were confronted with two other poetic systems. Contemporary Italian poets wrote strophes in syllabic meters and alternating rhymes, creating sonnets and other strophic forms in the Provençal manner in Hebrew. At the same time, Hebrew poets in Spain employed precise syllabic and quantitative meters. It took several generations until Hebrew poets in Italy changed their poetic system and adopted quantitative meters of Arabic origin, developed in Spain, to write secular strophic poetry in Hebrew in the Italian sonnet form and in Italian numbers of syllables (mostly eleven—the number of choice in most European languages). Emanuel of Rome, a major sonnet writer in Hebrew at that time, wrote his Oriental-type adventure fiction, *Maḥbaroth Emanuel*, in freewheeling rhymed prose, studded with anecdotes and poems, using the Oriental, rather than the Italian or Spanish-Hebrew, rhyming rules.

Similar dilemmas faced Jewish poets in other generations and countries. Saul Chernikhovsky in the late nineteenth century grew up in Tavriya on newly settled Russian lands near the Black Sea, speaking a Ukrainian dialect of Yiddish at home. He studied Hebrew texts with a Litvak *melamed* and learned the language of culture and power, Russian, with a private teacher. From the Yiddish base, Chernikhovsky learned German and went to Germany to study medicine in the prominent University of Heidelberg, There he acquired ancient Greek and translated Homer into Ashkenazi Hebrew. In Hebrew he revived a German eighteenth-century narrative-descriptive poetic genre, the idyll, at a time when descriptive poetry was already seen as inferior in German literature. Chernikhovsky used the idyll in its German interpretation, as an epic genre without rhyme, which was otherwise no longer acceptable in German poetry. "Descriptive poetry" became a derogatory epithet in Goethe's Germany. Owing to the German misunderstanding of the Greek hexameter, Chernikhovsky interspersed trochees between the predominant dactyls, which sounded like limited free rhythms to Russian ears. In Greek hexameters, the poet could substitute one long syllable for two shorts, a dactyl could be read / — ∪ ∪ / → / — — /; but in the Russian reading of Hebrew there were no short syllables, and the result was just a trochee: / — ∪ ∪ / became / — — /, two syllables, read as a trochee, which resulted in free rhythms.

According to a Turkish proverb, "Arabic conquest meant imposing Islam and 'arud meters." The 'arud was imposed even on languages very different from Arabic, such as Persian, Turkish, and Hebrew. In this context, the Arabic meters were not copied in Hebrew but were confronted with a different language; Hebrew poets tried to build Hebrew equivalents to the Arabic meter. For example, the basic foot in Arabic meters consists of one long and one or more short syllables, whereas in Hebrew it is the opposite: one short and one or more long syllables.

As we shall see, the network of Hebrew creativity covered the globe. Versification is a precise discipline and can map the territory precisely. Since that is so, how did new systems of verse suddenly appear in new places? How did Spanish Hebrew meters, adopted from Arabic versification, spread way beyond Spain and suddenly pop up in the poems of the Ashkenazi Rabbi Barukh from Magenza, on the Rhine River? And Bialik's melodious neo-Romantic poetry, written in Russia, showed up in Henderson, North Carolina, alongside Negro spirituals, themselves inspired by the Hebrew Bible (El Lissitsky).[3]

How can we talk about one global network of Hebrew versification? Why didn't the poets each live on his own island, separate from other Jewish groups in Diaspora? Why didn't their poetry develop separately as Romance or Slavic languages did? The main reason was that wherever Jews appeared, they carried with them the Torah and the one biblical language—to be interpreted and discussed globally. The Bible and the language of the Bible supplied the linguistic infrastructure that supported the distant islands of verse and versification. Arguments about the meaning of the holy texts unified all Diasporas.

A Jewish poet was closer to each of the three intersecting traditions than poets usually are when experiencing the influences of a foreign literature. The impact of Hebrew poetry written in other countries was enhanced by the closeness of the language in all Diasporas, the community of culture and interpretations, the dispersal of written and, later, printed books, and the mobility of men of letters (e.g. Abraham ibn Ezra, 1089–1164, a Spanish Jew who traveled in the towns of Italy and argued about Hebrew rhymes).

In spite of traditional Hebrew conservatism, the influence of aesthetic norms dominant in other languages was particularly strong because most Hebrew poets did not primarily speak Hebrew but were intimately acquainted with other languages in which they read, studied, translated, and used in everyday life. In many cases they knew at least one more language spoken by Jews and one or two foreign languages—for example, Russian, German, and old Greek (in eastern Europe), Arabic and Spanish (in Christian Spain), Yiddish and Italian (in sixteenth-century Venice), Yiddish and Russian (in nineteenth-century eastern Europe), or Yiddish, Russian, and English (in America in the late nineteenth and the early twentieth centuries). Hebrew poetry usually made a sudden leap from one of the three traditions to another, a leap brought about by a realization of potential influence.

Foreign "influences" on Hebrew poetry were not necessarily contemporaneous. While accentual-syllabic versification was introduced into Hebrew poetry under Russian influence, it occurred not in the sixteenth century, as in German, English, and Yiddish, or in the mid-eighteenth century, as in Russian, but only toward the end of the nineteenth century, when Modernism emerged in Russian poetry itself and undermined the nineteenth-century cycle of Russian poetry. Belated though such an impact may have been, it was not necessarily accepted in all its aspects. Thus, YaLaG (Yehuda-Leib Gordon) was influenced by his Russian contemporary Nekrasov in some of his themes and genres and in the tone of the poet's voice, although they lived together in the same city, Saint Petersburg, but did not accept the Russian verse system. When asked on a doctoral exam where YaLaG was born, and helped by the examiner's "It starts with a 'P,'" the student was relieved and said "Petersburg," but the examiner laughed: "Ponevezh!" Of course, this was Jewish inverted geography.

The poetry of Abraham Shlonsky of the 1920s and 1930s in Eretz Israel was influenced by the imagery and slogans of Russian Futurism, but in meters it was as classical as the verse of Pushkin, which he translated profusely into Hebrew. Yet those translations into the Russian "classical" verse came after Shlonsky's Futurist period, in a "reverse" historical order.

On the other hand, many Hebrew poets were very much aware of the relativity of prosodic systems. They knew how to use diverse and sometimes opposing systems for the different genres or for the different languages they wrote in—especially in the case of bilingual or multilingual poets, such as Elia Levita, who wrote poems in Sephardi as well as Ashkenazi Hebrew and epics in Yiddish in Italian strophic forms (about him, see Chapter 5), and YaLaG, who spoke against Yiddish and accentual meters but wrote in both.

Despite these complex circumstances and the considerable body of rhymed and versified Hebrew texts, the varying norms of Hebrew poetry can be described exactly, since in most ages and places these norms were conventional rather than individual, appearing in clear-cut areas rather than diffused. A further problem was what Hebrew language to use. In most generations there was a clear awareness that poetry has to be written in the "pure" language of the Bible; however, the Hebrew the poets actively used in writing about their life situations was Rabbinical Hebrew, often commingled with Yiddish and Aramaic. Therefore, each area developed its own version of Hebrew for poetry. Professor Dr. Yosef Klausner, the promoter of the revival of Hebrew and the first professor of Hebrew literature at the Hebrew University in Jerusalem, claimed that there were four separate Hebrew languages, the speakers of which would not understand each other's language: Biblical Hebrew, Mishnaic, Tibbonite (the scientific language of the Middle Ages named after the Tibbon family of translators), and Modern. We could probably add the languages of Sephardic Hebrew poetry and Ashkenazi Rabbinical Hebrew.

THE TWELVE TRIBES OF HEBREW VERSE

The precise number twelve is not material. We can compress the number of styles of Hebrew verse to ten, or nine, or add all styles we find in the Bible. I include here Ashkenazi and Sephardic accentual-syllabic meters as two different systems with radically different poetics, and, on the other hand, the Bible as one system of verse. I suggest the symbolism of the twelve tribes as identity dispersed in history and geography.

The peculiar nature of Jewish history does not permit the development of Hebrew poetic forms to be divided into pure historical periods or geographical spaces but rather into "areas," determined by a combination of historical, geographical, and generic factors. For example, the Hebrew poetry created in Spain and called Spanish Hebrew poetry spread piecemeal to other countries or continued for generations; and the forms of secular verse spilled over to religious poetry. Moshe ibn Ezra's collected poetry, for example, appeared in two big volumes: *Secular Poetry* and *Sacred Poetry*.

The following major areas of Hebrew poetic forms can be discerned:

1) *biblical poetry* (discussed in Chapter 3).

2) *post-biblical poetry*, representing several trends or quasi-genres: Wisdom Poetry (Ben-Sirah), short poems of religious experience, and the beginnings of liturgy.

3) *the rhymed piyut*—a complex and formal form of liturgical poetry written under Byzantine Christian rule in Eretz Israel. Unrhymed prayers and blessings were interlaced with formal poems. A vigorous strain in this tradition, which created the rich yet difficult "Kallirian" rhyme, flourished in the tenth–eleventh centuries in Italy and in the Rhine area. A small group of Hebrew scholars and poets, especially of the Kalonymos family, moved from northern Italy to a German-speaking area on the Rhine during the period of the Carolingian Empire. For them, the formal criteria, especially the Kallirian rhyme, determined what to include in the Italian and Ashkenazi *maḥzor* (prayer book).[4]

4) *Hebrew quantitative versification in Spain,* which represented a breakthrough into a rich and variegated system of versification. Theories of Hebrew linguistics and poetics written in Arabic accompanied the system, which was the first precise syllabic system of versification in Hebrew: every syllable counted, according to the changing laws of quantitative meters. Under such constraints, a plethora of neologisms flourished, mainly deriving from biblical language. The very taste of the words was changed and refreshed. The Hebrew of Spanish Hebrew poetry is a different language from the Hebrew used by Bialik, for example. This poetic system was developed in Spain under the impact of classical Arabic poetry and created an internal Hebrew tradition. Written in Hebrew since the tenth century, this poetry flourished in Muslim and Christian Spain and Provence until the fifteenth century and dominated the meters

of Hebrew poetry in Italy and throughout the Islamic East almost until the twentieth century.

5) *Hebrew poetry in Italy,* written in the geographical center of the Jewish world, where cultural trends of Eretz Israel, Ashkenaz, Spain, and Babylonia were mediated. Hebrew poems were written in Italy from the ninth to the beginning of the twentieth century. Symbolically, the last poem in J. Schirmann's canonical anthology of Hebrew poetry in Italy was an Italian-type Hebrew sonnet dedicated to the death of Theodor Herzl.

6) *Ashkenazic poetry.* Hebrew poetry was written throughout the Middle Ages by Ashkenazi Jews, at first in the Carolingian Empire, then in Slavic countries—Czech, Polish, Russian, Ukranian ("Goyish"). The Palestinian-Italian tradition formed its early stages in the tenth to twelfth centuries as part of the formation of "Yiddish"-speaking Ashkenazi religious culture. A "weaker" line of rhymed poetry descending from the Palestinian piyut followed, continuing until modern times, especially in several religious shorter genres, notably the *seliḥah* (supplication) and the *kinah* (lamentation) and bilingual (Hebrew-Yiddish) historical chronicles in rhyme.

7) *Eastern poetry,* from Babylonia, North Africa, Iraq, and other countries under Islamic rule, which passed easily from the old piyut forms to the Spanish-Hebrew tradition of versification. In principle it had meters similar to the classical Arabic meters that Jews in Muslim countries knew.

8) *Haskalah poetry,* of the belated Jewish version of the European Enlightenment, which emerged in the eighteenth and nineteenth centuries in German, Austrian, and Russian territories in central and eastern Europe. Here purely syllabic versification, derived from Hebrew poetry in Italy, which itself derived from Italian poetry, was the norm, defying the more complex norms of the German and Russian host cultures. This form continued to be the medium of Hebrew verse in the Austrian and Russian Empires until the end of the nineteenth century.

9) *Hebrew "Revival" or "Renaissance" poetry.* Since the late 1880s, Hebrew poetry written in Russia and by exiles from Russia in other countries using the standard Ashkenazi pronunciation of Hebrew accepted the Russian accentual-syllabic meters. A new class of young Jewish intellectuals, in particular, the "Externs," who were not allowed to attend Russian gymnasiums, learned huge quantities of poetry by rote (my

own mother knew by heart the whole of Pushkin's *Eugene Onegin*), thus entering Russian culture through a rhythmical channel. The system spread immediately from its Russian epicenter to all countries of Hebrew creativity: Germany, Eretz Israel, the United States, elsewhere. We can see such inscriptions on Hebrew poems as "Henderson, North Carolina" (El Lissitsky) and "Swinnemünde," a reference to a German town near the North Sea (Saul Chernikhovsky). The meter of this poetry was called "classical," which referred to the precise use of accentual-syllabic meters.

10) *"Classical" verse in Israeli Hebrew.* Accentual-syllabic meters, transmorphed to fit Israeli (not quite Sephardic) pronunciation, appeared at the beginning of the twentieth century and started to dominate Hebrew poetry around 1928, when both prominent Hebrew poets, the Russian "Imagist" Shlonsky and the Yiddish Expressionist Uri-Zvi Grinberg shifted from Ashkenazi to the new Hebrew language spoken by the starving worker-pioneers in Palestine.

There were two strains of "free verse":

11) *accentual-syllabic (a.-s.) deviant meters, or the "net,"* which are Russian-influenced strophic and rhymed free rhythms. They are close to regular a.-s. meters yet deliberately deviate from them.

12) *free irregular verse,* based on *interacting phrase groups* written in Hebrew in Europe early in the twentieth century and in Israel and the United States especially since the 1950s. These forms vaguely followed foreign examples (English, German, Italian "existentialist" lyrics) and were based on the cadences of the new, spoken Hebrew.

We shall examine the rules of Hebrew verse in the Historical Era (poetic forms 2–12) as they developed.

THE POST-BIBLICAL PERIOD

Chapter 3 discussed some of the "free" rhythms in different genres of the Bible. Hebrew writing in the Bible and in post-biblical literature shifted from an emphasis on personal narrative, historical narrative, poetry, and prophecy toward an emphasis on Wisdom Literature and Talmudic dialogical discourse. Whenever an anaphoric, formulaic phrase or a short poetic text was needed, basic forms were used ad hoc. The tendency, however, was to regularize the biblical accentual tradition, primarily by changing the aesthetics of "natural" rhythms (built by twos and threes) into a symmetrical four-accent pattern.

This was a radical shift of Hebrew rhythms. There were, however, three distinctly different interpretations of this basic four-accent rhythm:

(a) One version had a fixed number of words per verset (mostly four words), as in some of the *Hekhalot* hymns and in several short Talmudic epigrams or idiomatic passages.

Those who erase bad decrees	מְבַטְּלֵי גְזֵרָה

Those who erase bad decrees,	מְבַטְּלֵי גְזֵרָה,
transgress their own vows,	מְפֵרֵי שְׁבוּעָה,
Annihilate wrath, send back jealousy,	מַעֲבִירֵי חֵמָה, מְשִׁיבֵי קִנְאָה,
Recall love, restore friendship,	מַזְכִּירֵי אַהֲבָה, מְסַדְּרֵי רֵעוּת
Before the-Splendor of-the-Glory of-the-Awesome Palace.	לִפְנֵי־ הֲדַר גְּאוֹן הֵיכַל נוֹרָא:

(Carmi 195)[5]

And here the syntax is similar to the pattern poems of Yanay's piyut:

Funeral Oration	גֶּזַע-יְשִׁישִׁים

The-Scion of-an-Ancient-Stock has immigrated from-Babylon	גֶּזַע-יְשִׁישִׁים עָלָה מִבָּבֶל
And-brought the-Book-of-the-Wars of-the-Lord.	וְעִמּוֹ סֵפֶר מִלְחֲמוֹת אֲדֹנָי,
Both-vulture and-raven multiply to-see	קָאַת וְקִפּוֹד הִכְפְּלוּ לִרְאוֹת
The-ravage and-ruin which-has-come from-Shinear.	בְּשֹׁד וָשֶׁבֶר הַבָּא מִשִּׁנְעָר.

(Carmi 192)

Sometimes the verset has not four but three words, as in the *akeda* "איתן למד דעת."

Akeda: The Sacrifice of Isaac			אֵיתָן לִמֵּד דַּעַת

Abraham made You known,	A	א	אֵיתָן לִמֵּד דַּעַת
Before You were known by the world,	B	ב	בְּטֶרֶם יְדָעֲךָ כֹּל,
He revealed to all creatures	G	ג	גִּלָּה לְכָל יָצוּר
The road which they should take.	D	ד	דֶּרֶךְ לְהִתְהַלֶּךְ-בָּהּ.

(Carmi 201)

This poem has a strong alphabetical acrostic and keeps three words in a line.

(b) The second version has a fixed number of major or phrase stresses (not words), whereby one stress can subordinate two or more short words in an enclitic (preceding the major stress: *im-ein*) or attached after the root (proclitic: *ani-li*) structure. This *avodah* by Yose ben Yose (Carmi 209) lends itself to a reading in a regular pattern, as most scholars take for granted: 4 + 4 (or 2 + 2 / 2 + 2) major stresses (phrase stresses):

אזכיר גבורות [אלוה]. נאדרי בכח // יחיד ואין-עוד, / אפס ואין-שני

The meter was meant to be 4 × 2 words, yet out of four hemistichs, only one has two words, while the others have three words each. The rules for imposing one accent on two words are rhythmical rather than syntactic. *Eyn-od* (no more) and *eyn-sheni* (no other) are each treated like one-word units. The only hemistich with three major stresses is the first, which means that we have to subordinate two short words to one accent. A particular issue is the word *eloha* (God), which can be seen as a necessary interpolation in an earlier text because the following two words can serve as an epithet for God: the epithet makes the name superfluous. There are other cases in the piyut where elimination of the word "God" leaves a better metrical number.[6] The word "God" itself is not necessary if an epithet stands for him. The length of the poem and the very possibility of reading it in this precise and regular manner support such a reading.

(c) In the third version a four-accent matrix is imposed on the semi-regular verse line, as in modern poetry. Some accents are provided by the stresses of the language, and the others are constructed. If there are fewer than four graphic words in a verset, the long words (of three or more syllables) can accept two accents each as required. This system is diametrically opposed to the one mentioned in type b. The options are several words to one major stress in type b or several metrical accents on one word in type c.

We have a major historical transition from the biblical "natural" rhythms of twos and threes to a symmetrical, sometimes rigid and monotonous aesthetics of four. And instead of parallelism, we have the internal symmetry of rhythmical units (hemistichs).

We do not know how readers of Hebrew treated a *shewa* or *ḥataf* (half-syllable), but probably with the same hesitation with which we proceed today.

Lament   בָּאֲרָזִים נָפְלָה שַׁלְהֶבֶת

If a flame fell upon the cedars,	בָּאֲרָזִים נָפְלָה שַׁלְהֶבֶת—
What will do the moss on the wall?	מַה יַּעֲשׂוּ אֲזוֹבֵי-הַקִּיר?
If a Leviathan has been hauled in by a fishhook,	לִוְיָתָן בְּחַכָּה הוֹעֲלָה—
What hope is there for the minnows?	מַה יַּעֲשׂוּ דְּגֵי-הָרְקָק?
If the streaming river has been struck by drought,	בְּנַחַל שׁוֹטֵף נָפְלָה חָרָבָה—
What hope is there for the water holes?	מַה יַּעֲשׂוּ מֵי-גֵבִים?

(Carmi 192)

The basic meter here is an 8-syllable iambic tetrameter with freedom at the end of the verse. The last line has seven syllables, but the tetrameter is still preserved if we interrupt at the caesura. The first line has nine syllables, with an added syllable at the end. The poem is sung to this day.

The Cows' Hymn to the Ark of the Lord   רַנִּי, רַנִּי הַשִּׁטָּה!

Sing, o-sing, acacia!	רַנִּי, רַנִּי הַשִּׁטָּה!
Flutter in your great splendor—	הִתְנוֹפְפִי בְּרֹב הֲדָרֵךְ—
The desired in golden embroidery,	הַמְחֻשָּׁקֶת בְּרִקְמֵי-זָהָב,
The praised in the palace sanctuary,	הַמְהֻלָּלָה בִּדְבִיר-אַרְמוֹן,
The resplendent in the jewelry of jewelries.	הַמְפֹאָרָה בַּעֲדִי-עֲדָיִים.

(Carmi 194)

In this poem, each line has three graphic words, but one of the words is long and can accommodate two accents. By imposing two accents on words of three or more syllables (with some deviations in the caesura), we get a rhythm similar to a modern trochaic or iambic tetrameter. In this poem, the long word is in the first hemistich of the line (except in line 1). Applying the same principles, we find that this meter is predominant throughout the writings of Ben Sirah. It creates a regularity in the number of syllables: mostly one unstressed syllable between stresses, but sometimes two.

Jos'ua Ben Sirah begins his "Praise to the Fathers of the Universe" thus:[7]

שֶׁבַח אֲבוֹת עוֹלָם

אֲבוֹתֵינוּ בְּדוֹרוֹתָם:	א אֲהַלְלָה נָא אַנְשֵׁי חָסֶד
וְגָדְלוּ מִימוֹת עוֹלָם:	ב ר'ב כָּבוֹד חָלַק עֶלְיוֹן
וְאַנְשֵׁי שֵׁם בִּגְבוּרוֹתָם:	ג דּוֹרֵי אֶרֶץ בְּמַלְכוּתָם
וְחוֹזֵי כֹּל בִּנְבוּאָתָם:	ד הַיּוֹעֲצִים בִּתְבוּנָתָם
וְרוֹזְנִים בְּמֶחְקָרוֹתָם:	ה שָׂרֵי גוֹיִם בִּמְזִמָּתָם

ו חַכְמֵי שִׂיחַ בְּסִפְרָתָם   וּמוֹשְׁלִים בְּמִשְׁמְרוֹתָם׃

ז חוֹקְרֵי מִזְמוֹר עַל חוֹק   נוֹשְׂאֵי מָשָׁל בִּכְתָב׃

ח אַנְשֵׁי חַיִל וְסוֹמְכֵי כֹּחַ   וְשׁוֹקְטִים עַל מְכוֹנֹתָם׃

ט כָּל אֵלֶה בְּדוֹרָם   וּמִימֵיהֶם תִּפְאַרְתָּם׃

י יֵשׁ מֵהֶם הִנִּיחוּ שֵׁם   לְהִשְׁתַּעֲנוֹת בְּנַחֲלָתָם׃

יא וְיֵשׁ מֵהֶם אֲשֶׁר אֵין לוֹ זֵכֶר   וַיִּשְׁבְּתוּ כַּאֲשֶׁר שָׁבָתוּ׃

יב כַּאֲשֶׁר לֹא הָיוּ הָיוּ   וּבְנֵיהֶם מֵאַחֲרֵיהֶם׃

Clearly, two long words take the space of four accents: *avotheynu bedorotam* (optionally: one extra syllable in the caesura). On the other hand, four short words take the same space: *rov kavod ḥalak elyon*. The hemistich divide is very strong: long words appear either in the first two iambs (1 + 2) or in the last two (3 + 4) but never cover slots 2 + 3 in the middle. To have this meter, the poet uses the law of *nasog aḥor;* for example, in *ánshey ḥésed,* instead of the regular *anshéy,* ultimately stressed, the stress recedes to the preceding syllable: *ánshey ḥésed, ḥákhmey síaḥ,* and *ánshey ḥáyil* are all stressed on the first syllable. Initial consonant clusters cancel the stress altogether. The poet deals freely with "short" syllables (with the *shewa* or *ḥataf*). In the caesura, after the first hemistich, there can be one unstressed syllable or two. For example, *avotheynu /— ∪ — ∪/ bedorotam / ∪ — ∪ — /* has two unstressed syllables in the caesura. Auxiliary one-syllable morphemes—prepositions—are dealt with as full syllables as in Modern Hebrew (N. Alterman!). We have a perfect iambic tetrameter.

The trajectory of the basic unit of Hebrew verse went through the following stages:

1) A verse is a segment of a text composed of two (or more) versets;
2) "natural" rhythms have two or three stresses in each verset.
3) Within this norm, sometimes a fixed number of accents is observed, such as the three accents in the old song "Ha'azinu,"
4) transforming into four accents per verset—in late biblical books and post-biblical texts—with a strong tendency to create
5) a symmetrical division of the long verset into 2 + 2, which often grows into
6) *the longest verset,* 4 + 3 or 2 + 2 / 3.

Thus the rhythm hovered between the biblical long and short lines: 4 + 3, equivalent and descending; and the split of four into two symmetrical subunits, 2 + 2 to 2 + 2 / 3.

EXUBERANT RHYMES: THE *POIETAN* AND THE PIYUT

The Hebrew word *piyut* (poem or poetry) is derived from *paytan* (poet, maker of piyut) from the Greek *poietan* (maker, poet). The consonantal spelling *PYTN* (פיטן) can be vocalized in Hebrew as *poyetan*. *Piyut* (plural: *piyutim*) is the common term applied to a variety of genres of Hebrew liturgical poetry which originated in Eretz Israel under Christian Byzantine rule up to the sixth century CE. The use of Greek words—*poietan, kiklar* (cycle), *Kallir* (Cyril)—is evidence of the Hellenistic culture that influenced Hebrew discourse at the time.

From a formal point of view, the history of the piyut can be divided into three periods: (1) its beginnings, primarily in Eretz Israel and in Babylonia, from the canonization of the Bible until the creation of the formal, fully rhymed "classical" piyut; (2) the classical period, with strophic and rhymed poems, formalized and patterned in complex yet fixed cycles; (3) simplification, mainly in Ashkenaz. To place all cases in perspective, we shall first dwell on the full-fledged classical period.

HIGH PIYUT: THE CLASSICAL PERIOD

A broad gamut of rhythmical expressions and sound patterns was widespread in biblical and post-biblical literature during the first centuries after the canonization of the Bible. The attention to the text itself (Jakobson's "set toward the message") sanctions the importance of the text, either as "poetry" or as "sacred" text. There is no contradiction between the sacred and the formal; on the contrary, making the text "palpable" ("A poem should not mean but be") lends weight to the extraordinary text. Yet only by an act of formalization were the new complex structures established. Rhyme, meter, refrain, strophe—whatever had been sporadic in the Bible was now formalized and organized in complex cycles of poems governed by strict rules and precise numbers. The idea of form may have been influenced by a Hellenistic aesthetic taste, but the specific forms did not emerge in Greek poetry but in Hebrew.

Since the complex structures of the piyut are determined by the genre, it is preferable to describe the formal structure together with the thematic aspects of each genre, its liturgical function, and the particular method of its inclusion in the basic text of the prayer book. The difficulty of such a detailed description is highlighted by our present limited knowledge of the history of the piyut. Objective circumstances contributed to this state of scholarship: thousands of poems and fragments, found in the Cairo Genizah, are in the process of being deciphered. These poems are, by and large, undated, often fragmentary or written in a cryptic language that requires an archaeology of spelling and allusions, and either anonymous or associated only with the first name of the poet, who in most cases is unknown from other historical sources. A considerable number of piyutim were known for centuries because they were included in the Ashkenazi prayer book. They were printed like prose, and nobody was interested in uncovering their forms.

THE STRUCTURE OF ONE CYCLE

As an example of the complexity and formal constraints working in the piyut, I shall describe the structure of one cycle following the detailed liturgical description by a major scholar of the piyut, M. Zulay.[8] The complexes of poems called *kerovah* and *yotser* are cycles of an intricate nature. A *kerovah* by Yanay has a superstructure of nine parts with a permanent separate set of rules for each part, repeated in dozens of *kerovot*. Yanay may have written hundreds of *kerovot*—a different cycle for each week in the triennial cycle of reading the Torah. The structure of each of these poems is governed to the smallest detail by one set of rules. Other poets wrote cycles of poems for the Sabbath and the festivals and sometimes several different sets of poems for the same purpose, apparently written for services in different years or different synagogues.

Yanay's *kerovot* are mostly of the *kedushta* type. The *kedushta* is a poetic cycle incorporated in the prayer, the *Amidah*, in which the *Kedushah* is recited. The *kedushta* ("holiness") has a fixed theme for every week based on the weekly biblical portion. The theme and its language are integrated in the poems of the cycle. There are a number of main elements.

1) The poem for the first benediction of the *Amidah* prayer, including three strophes of four versets each. Every strophe has a separate fourfold end rhyme linking all its versets. Every verset begins with a separate letter, following the order of the Hebrew alphabet, and each is linked by an unfinished acrostic employing the first twelve letters of the alphabet, א to ל (A to L). The concluding verset alludes to the first sentence of the weekly portion of reading the Torah, which follows and introduces a series of biblical sentences in their original form, which has neither rhyme nor meter. The biblical passages give authoritative support to the content of the poem. This chain of biblical sentences is linked to a closing strophe of three or four versets, with the last word of the chain repeated at the beginning of

the closing strophe. The last verset of this strophe is again linked to what follows, alluding to the *Magen Avot* benediction recited after this poem.

2) A poem for the second benediction, similar in its strophic structure to the first poem. It continues the interrupted acrostic (from the letters מ to ת, M to Th) and uses the last two letters twice in order to fit the twenty-two-letter Hebrew alphabet into the framework of a series of four-verset strophes (altogether twenty-four versets). A chain of explanatory sentences also leads toward a closing strophe in which the final verset anticipates the following benediction, *Meḥayeh ha-Metim.*

3) A short poem of four strophes, each starting with a letter that is part of an acrostic of the poet's name, Yanay (יניי). Every strophe consists of four short cola of two or three words each. The poem ends with an allusion to the first word of the *haftarah* (the portion of the Torah reading) that follows, together with an explanatory passage.

4) A poem of a rather free structure, usually consisting of three fourfold strophes. Concluding the first part of the piyut, the poem is marked by the obligatory use of the final word—*Kadosh* (Holy).

5) A poem traditionally called *asiriyyah* ("the tensome") because it is composed of ten strophes that are rhymed couplets having quite often a large variety of internal rhymes.

6) A poem consisting of eleven strophes, each using a separate fourfold rhyme. The poem introduces a group of poems and is preceded by the biblical statement which it discusses. Frequently, the biblical statement or parts of it are interwoven into the poem as beginnings of the first lines of the poem or of its strophes. Thus, the non-rhyming and non-metrical but sacred biblical phrases are supported on every side by completely formal poems.

7) One to three *pattern poems* that make up part 7 of Yanay's poem (more in later poets). Each pattern form has an individual structure, a complex form, that fills the text precisely and in every detail. Only in this slot is the poet allowed to use rigorously organized poems without rhyme.

8) The *silluk* (finale), a kind of open-ended free rhythm poem that introduces the *Kedushah*. It has a free structure which varies from *kerovah* to *kerovah* and is richly rhymed in an unrestricted manner. In the poetry of Yanay's follower (or disciple) Eleazar Kallir, the *silluk* developed into a very long, exuberant, richly orchestrated yet unconstrained, often asymmetrical poem.

9) The *kedushta*. In principle, it has neither rhyme nor strophic structure. In Yanay's time there was no fixed version as yet, and the poet was free to formulate his *Kedushah* in every cycle anew. It was based on an exegesis and elaboration of the formula *Kadosh, Kadosh, Kadosh* (Holy, Holy, Holy).

Every cycle was determined by a combination of certain pragmatic, thematic, verbal, and formal elements. Though the intricate rules for each cycle changed from genre to genre, there was no free combination in each new creation: the *basic forms* used in these compositions were quite restricted and independent of the specific themes and textual context. Some of these basic forms are discussed below.

FORMS OF COMPOSITION

Within a given cycle the form and length of each poem was restricted, depending on its place in the cycle, its use of acrostics, and its strophic form. The major strophic forms used in the piyut were the following:

(1) *One continuous poem with one rhyme.* One single end-rhyme runs through the poem, like the *ḥaruz mavri'aḥ* (literally: "string of beads") in Spain. At the beginnings of the lines there is a mandatory acrostic that covers the whole Hebrew alphabet. Each letter is repeated one or several times: hence the number of versets is either 22, 44, or 88. The acrostic fulfills the function of an initial rhyme.

(2) *Regular strophic compositions.* Each poem is composed of a number of strophes of a determined form and length. Every strophe has its own independent rhyme both differing from and not interfering with members of other rhymes; the rhyming pattern is: *aaaa bbbb cccc,* etc. The length of strophes may vary from two to ten versets. A strophe of four versets became the major form of the *seliḥah,* especially in the variant created in Ashkenazi Europe. The multiple (fourfold or eightfold) repetition of each rhymeme and the lack of rhyme alternation in the rhyming piyut create an effect quite distinct from that of standard European strophic poetry, which uses its rhymes in alternation.

The poetic text is like a cube surrounded by sound patterns on all sides: beginning rhyme (acrostic), end rhyme (sound), pattern of initial consonants of the words within a line (alliteration), and strophic end line (refrain). In Eleazar Kallir's masterpiece *kerovah* to the *Musaf* prayer of the Day of Atonement (in the Ashkenazi prayer book), the cycle *Essa De'I le-Merahok* is based on a stanza of nine versets. The following is one stanza of the poem:

יַשְׁלְגוּ אָדְמֵי שָׁנִים	שֶׁל כָּל-יְמוֹת הַשָּׁנִים	חֲדָשִׁים וְגַם יְשָׁנִים
יַלְבִּינוּ כְּתֻמֵּי שׁוֹשַׁנִּים	וְיוֹשְׁבוּ לְתַעֲרֶם שְׁנוּנִים	בְּפִלּוּל אֲשֶׁר מְשֻׁנִּים
רֻחֲצוּ וְהֻזַּכּוּ מֵעֲשׁוּנִים	לְאַוֶּלֶת מִהְיוֹת שׁוֹנִים	וְעַל מִבְטָחֵימוֹ שְׁעוּנִים

On the rich rhyming and sound patterns of this piyut, see the section below on Kallir's masterpiece.

This poem belongs to the *kiklar* (from the Greek κύκλος, cycle) genre, in which there is a refrain-like shorter stanza of three (rather than nine) versets after each regular stanza. There are three different refrains, alternating between the seven regular stanzas. In the general scheme of the poem, each verset of the regular stanzas is represented by the letters *A* to *G,* the refrains by the letters *p* to *r;* capital letters represent versets linked by an acrostic:

Aaa		Ddd		Ggg	
Aaa		Ddd		Ggg	
Aaa		Ddd		Ggg	
	ppp		ppp		ppp
Bbb		Eee			
Bbb		Eee			
Bbb		Eee			
	qqq		qqq		
Ccc		Fff			
Ccc		Fff			
Ccc		Fff			
	rrr		`rrr		

Can anybody assume that these sound patterns are accidental or just rich? Doesn't this constitute a manifesto of a vertical horizontal structure, hence a written text? The elaboration of the trinity—is it symbolic? Was three a symbolic number? Or the signature of Eleazar Kallir? The vertical structure is as follows. The term "line" is a metaphor from written texts.

3 words = 1 verset
3 versets (a + a + a) = 1 line
3 lines ⌈aaa⌉ = 1 strophe
         |aaa|
         ⌊aaa⌋
3 strophes = 1 refrain cycle
3 different refrains change in every cycle

The poem is organized both horizontally and vertically. We may call it a *grid* (as in Isaiah). The triadic principle is dominant throughout: three words make a verset (one letter in the diagram), three versets make a line, three lines make a strophe, three strophes complete a refrain cycle, all three different refrain rhymes are repeated (three times each). This is a great tradition, going back Isaiah (see Chapter 3 in this book). However, in Isaiah, the similar grid is formalized, and the number of units is free, though limited. The third refrain cycle is not completed, however, since there are seven strophes only (seven is as sacred as three). This grid was followed by such Spanish Hebrew poets as Yitzhak Ibn Ghiyat (Isaac ibn Ghayat) and Yehuda Halevi. Such an intricate formal structure was probably unknown in world literature at the time.

(3) *Pattern poems.* An unusual kind of formal poem—the *pattern poem*—was developed in the piyut especially by Yanay. A pattern of a line elaborated in all its details—syntactic, semantic, morphological, and with sound devices—was established in the poem and was then repeated throughout its twenty-two lines (the number being determined by an acrostic of the Hebrew alphabet). A great variety of such patterns appear in Yanay's poetry, all in the seventh part of any *kerovah* cycle. The following is an example of a very simple kind.

If you loved, who would hate?	A	א	אִם אֲהַבְתָּה מִי יַשְׂנִיא
If you blessed, who would curse?	B	ב	אִם בֵּירַכְתָּה מִי יָאַרֹר
If you fenced, who would break out?	G	ג	אִם גְּדַרְתָּה מִי יִפְרֹוץ
If you joined, who would separate?	D	ד	אִם דְּבַקְתָּה מִי יַפְרִיד

Every line embodies a rhetorical pattern with two fixed and two free words. The initial letter of the first free word ("you loved") starts with a letter of the alphabet: (ד ג ב א) arranged in an order. This word is a verb in the second person past tense, and its meaning has a positive connotation. The second free word is opposite in meaning, it has a strongly negative connotation, and it is a verb in the third person future tense. All verses are semantically parallel, almost a tautology of each other.

There are more complex patterns, such as this one:

A	אָהוּב (ל . . .) חס וְשָׂנאוּי לְמַאַס	A	תּוֹלְדוֹת אָהוּב וְשָׂנאוּי
B	בָּחוּר לְסֶגֶל וּבָזוּי לְסֶגֶר	B	תּוֹלְדוֹת בָּחוּר וּבָזוּי
G	גְּדִי לְרָצוּי וְנָמֵר לְנִיצוּי	G	תּוֹלְדוֹת גְּדִי וְנָמֵר

[The story of a loved one and a hated one / loved for respect and hated for neglect
The story of a chosen one and a despised one /
                              chosen for virtue and despised for rejection
The story of a lamb and a tiger / a lamb for pleasing and a tiger for strife.]

Every line consists of two versets, of three and four words respectively. The first verset refers to a story of two personae: one positive, the other negative. The second part of the line elaborates on the first, repeating the two personae and modifying the description of each. The first word is permanent, creating an anaphoric chain ("The story of . . ."); the second word is positive in meaning and is strung on an acrostic of the Hebrew alphabet; the third word is either a direct or indirect opposite of the second. The second hemistich repeats words 2 and 3 and qualifies them, explaining the reason for this binary opposition: in what perspective are the personae to be cast. The modifiers do not provide a full explanation; rather, they allude to a biblical text. Both modifiers—words 5 and 7—are introduced by a preposition of purpose (ל) and are linked to each other by some kind of rhyme. Since the morphology of most words of the pattern is fixed, the rhyme is inevitable in all cases where suffixes are used. Here are examples of alliterations.

4 × A	וירא אהובים ויאמל ואבה לארם
4 × B	וירא **ב**אים ויבעת ו**ב**יקש לבלעם
4 × G	וירא גרים ויגר וגמרם לגרשם

The meaning of the pattern is: "He saw (positive personae) and he was hostile to them (or frightened, or shocked, or worried, etc.) and he wished (or planned, or hurried, etc.) to curse them (or swallow them, or uproot them, etc.)." All four changing words are linked by one letter to the acrostic; the second and the fifth words, using plural suffixes, each create a chain of rhymes concomitant with the morphological rhyme. In the rhyming chain of the second words, however, there are two exceptions: המון, רבבה—a mass of people, "ten thousand" (the highest number in Hebrew words)—words that designate plurality but do not have the grammatical plural form. Indeed, rhyme here is not yet independent but is still tied to grammatical parallelism.

The form of the pattern poem is basically derived from biblical parallelism, but two new principles were applied: (a) two symmetrical versets, parallel in the Bible, were turned into a chain of twenty-two synonymous sentences; and (b) there was a rigorous formalization of the spontaneous pattern, and all deviations were excluded. Repeating the same structure twenty-two times makes the semantics synonymous and redundant.

(4) *Free strophic forms.* These are of two kinds: (a) the unrhymed piyut, an exceptional form, fulfilling strict liturgical functions and employing phrases of a formulaic nature; and (b) the rhymed yet free poem, especially the *silluk* (finale), developed by Kallir into a long chain of rhymed versets, with changing rhymes and shifting rhyme principles and without any strophic structure or fixed measure of verse length. Each rhyme usually has many members: 25 LAKH + 20 MU + 18 SEV + 13 MEM, etc.—rhyme for rhyme's sake in Kallir's *silluk* to *Chapter Zakhor*. Besides such sound rhymes there may be in the rhyming-position semantic rhymes (names of rivers or time periods), word repetition, words of one root—in short, any aspect of the Hebrew word can serve as a compositional frame.

ON THE ORIGINS OF RHYME

Hebrew rhyme preceded systematic rhyme in all European languages, although I cannot prove it. And there is always the possibility that Hebrew rhyme came several hundred years earlier without influencing other languages directly. The concrete historical events have not been discovered, or cannot be for lack of evidence, but circumstantial evidence may support this view.

Rhymes are so widespread in most cultures that any spark can ignite an encompassing fire. To this day, rhymes are made by children around the globe for fun and in play, and by adults for embellishments in poetry and in narratives. The great invention that Hebrew rhyme made was double: separating a cluster of sounds, detached from any meaning or syntax, and using them as frames for the composition of strophic poetry.

In a different historical moment, in the 1880s, suddenly all Hebrew and Yiddish poetry around the world accepted accentual-syllabic meters. Kallir's rich rhyme sprang all of a sudden from nowhere. The same happened in Provençal poetry with its complex strophic forms, as Paul Zumthor showed, and other such events occurred. Poets are masters of the language, and an invention of laissez-faire language use triggers a flood of innovations. As soon as the principle is presented, it is easy for poets to switch over. In the case of Hebrew we can observe the crystallization of the complex final forms. If Hebrew had just been borrowing a readymade device, we would have received ready rhymes. But we see here a widespread net, encompassing a great variety of sound-patterns, and then the process of eliminating discarded items. This is the process of structuration, as we saw in phonology in Chapter 1: the zillions of possible sounds are reduced to a few dozen in order to have not a list but a system. In the piyut of Yanay and others we can see the groping toward, the experimenting, until the final product was crystallized. The product is not just a structure linked by a rhyme but a reduced structure of reduced sounds. At first, all aspects of the word are equally important—semantic, grammatical, or sound patterns can serve compositional purposes—but soon enough the pure sound patterns are privileged. Sound is convenient in a rhyme because it is pure form, independent of the theme or any individuality of the poem.

Compositional rhyme serving both as a sound pattern and as the compositional frame of strophic poems—the second great innovation of the piyut—was a landmark in the history of world poetry. Since not many of the piyutim were known before the studies of the Cairo Genizah, and since the external circumstances of the piyut were obscure and its language puzzling, it was not until recently that scholars have become aware of this original contribution of Hebrew poetry as it went through the stages between stammering and profuse experimentation.

It is clear by now that Hebrew rhyme grew out of the internal development of Hebrew poetry and became in Hebrew a permanent, indeed obligatory, feature of poetry earlier than in any other language in the Mediterranean world. It is possible that the principle of rhyme was then transferred to the poetry of the Syriac church, which was written in Aramaic. Aramaic is a language closely related to Hebrew, spoken inter alia by Jews converted to Christianity, and written in Greater Syria. Through this mediation it was introduced into Latin Christian poetry and from there into all other languages of Europe. However, most of the rhymes in Christian languages (consider St. Augustine) are very simple, without the rigorous complexity of the Hebrew rhyme, which became simplified later. In the major European languages regular rhyme did not appear before the eleventh century and always came from a Latin source. Hebrew poetry was far ahead of other languages in that respect. The question remains: Did Hebrew have a direct influence on other languages? There is no direct proof that it did. Historical research is needed if at all possible.

KALLIR'S MASTERPIECE: THE DISCONTINUOUS RHYMEME

A rhyme is a pattern linking two or more appearances of sounds in strategic spots in a text. The cluster of equal or equivalent sounds is called a *member* of a rhyme; the group of equivalent sounds is a rhymeme. Not one, but several kinds of rhymeme were used in the piyut, and each was associated with different strophic forms or genres. The *rhymeme* (like *phoneme* and *morpheme*) is a cluster of sounds repeated in all members of a rhyme. The most important was the rhyme of the strophic poems. The basic norm of this rhyme is unknown in the poetry of other languages. Each rhymeme of a strophic piyut had to meet two requirements: (1) parallelism of all the sounds of the last syllable of a line, where the last syllable includes the consonant preceding the last vowel (the French *consonne d'appui*); and (2) parallelism of two out of three consonants belonging to the root of each rhyming word, even if there are gaps in the middle of a word—hence we call this kind of parallelism *discontinuous rhyme.*[9]

Kallir's *kerovah Essa De'i le-Merahok* (discussed above for its strophic structure) is based on a strophe of nine versets. The following is one stanza of the poem. It should be read first horizontally, then vertically. The " + " in the list that follows represents the possibility of inserting other sounds (2Š + NIM).

←

חֲדָשִׁים וְגַם יְשָׁנִים	שֶׁל כָּל-יְמוֹת הַשָּׁנִים	יֵשְׁלְגוּ אָדְמֵי שָׁנִים
בִּפְלוּל אֲשֶׁר מְשֻׁנִּים	וְיוּשְׁבוּ לְתַעֲרָם שְׁנוּנִים	יֵלְבְּנוּ כִּתְמֵי שׁוֹשַׁנִּים
וְעַל מִבְטַחֵימוֹ שְׁעוּנִים	לְאֶלֶת מְהִיּוֹת שׁוֹנִים	רֻחֲצוּ וְהֻזַּכּוּ מֵעֲשׁוּנִים

Rhyming Words	Rhymeme
Š + ŠaNIM—Š + haŠaNIM—Š + ye-ŠaNIM	Š + Š + NIM
ŠoŠaNIM—Š + ŠeNuNiM—Š + meŠaNeNIM—	Š + Š + N + NIM
'iŠuNIM—ŠoNIM—Š'uNIM	Š + NIM

Here, the requirement of two root consonants is fulfilled. In the first line, the Š is redoubled (2Š + 2N + IM), in the middle line both Š and N appear twice, and in the last line the required consonants appear once (Š + NIM): the sound repetition is minimal (and almost the whole word is employed). (Here are literal translations of the rhyming words: *red silk, the years, ancient, roses, smart ones, they are learning by rote, from smoke, different ones, they are leaning.*)

The rhyming words bring together distant semantic fields. As required, each rhyming word contributes two of its three root consonants to the rhymeme (in this case, Š + N), as well as the last syllable of the word, including the supporting consonant: NIM. The strophe is unified by means of a particular rhyme, which is thus repeated nine times—in our case: Š + N + NIM. In addition, each line begins with a letter from the acrostic: first the full alphabet, followed by the poet's first name. In this case, the alphabet had twenty-two lines, and then came the poet's name: *Kalir* (Kallir). In our strophe, we have the ending IR: *kalIR*, with **I** repeated twice, followed by **R**. This particular poem belongs to the genre of *kiklar*, in which there is a refrain-like shorter strophe of only three versets after each regular strophe.

The rhymeme in this system is both terminal and discontinuous. The principle of terminality means that the rhymeme covers the final syllable of each rhyming member, whereas in European or in Modern Hebrew poetry its basis is not the last syllable but the last *stressed* syllable. In many cases in Hebrew, the two overlap, but in instances of discrepancy, stress in the rhyme of the piyut is disregarded. And so it was later, in Hebrew poetry in Spain.

The principle of discontinuity of the rhymeme is unique in rhyming systems; it mirrors the nature of the Hebrew lexical morpheme (root), which is discontinuous and consists mainly of consonants. The changes of vowels inside such Hebrew words as ŠaVar–ŠeVeR–ŠoVeR cause morphological but not semantic differences. Š + V + R is a root meaning "break"; the vowels in this example add grammatical categories: past tense, noun, present tense, whereas in English the similar differences between LeVeR–LiVeR–LoVeR are lexical: every word has a different meaning. On the other hand, the suffix in Hebrew words is continuous and mirrors the last syllable in this rhymeme.

Rhyme in the piyut became an autonomous language, independent of grammar, meaning, or word repetition. The discontinuous rhymeme is merely similar in structure to the Hebrew root, but it does not necessarily come in words of one root. In the above case, the rhymeme is Š + NIM, no matter what was between those letters. Š and N are the root consonants; NIM, the last syllable. Between the discontinuous sounds of the rhymeme there appeared changing vowels and even changing consonants, though usually consonants of the kind found in the rhymeme (as in our case: Š twice and N twice).

Since a traditional Hebrew root usually has no more than three consonants, only one consonant is free for variation. If, however, there are only two *sounding* consonants in a word (which excludes such muted root consonants as א, ה, ח, ע), the poet will use only one root consonant for the rhymeme. In other words, the rhymeme includes *all sounding consonants minus one*. The one consonant must *sound* in order to signal the difference: in all rhyme systems a rhyme is the maximal unity of similarity and difference. In strophes with many rhyme members, it is extremely difficult to find enough words to meet such requirements, especially when the rhyming words are at short distances from one another (in our case, only two words apart). Such rhyming was possible in the piyut due to the difficult "Kallirian" style, which, on the one hand, allowed for an almost unlimited number of neologisms and, on the other hand, was abundant in ellipses and allusions to the common Hebrew library, which permitted words from distant semantic fields, situations, and original texts to be brought together. Of course, this required an author with a Hebrew library in his head. An allusion brings up a whole text and/or a situation between one word and the next. Michel Riffaterre, in our time, claimed that the proper reader has all of French poetry in his head (as he did).

In this Hebrew piyut system, there are five major forms of rhyme, dependent upon the morphological structure of the rhyming words:

1) If the final syllable is open (e.g. LA), an additional preceding root consonant is necessary—e.g. in Kallir's rhyme: GoLA–GeuLA–beGiLA–niGLA–GiLA–veeGLA–aGuLA–meGiLA–veGoLA (the rhymeme is G + LA).

2) If the final syllable is closed (e.g. NIM) and only one consonant belongs to the root, a root consonant has to be added, as in the above case, with a plural suffix: ŠaNIM–haŠaNIM–ŠeNuNIM, etc. The rhymeme is Š + NIM.

3) If the final syllable (NU) has no root consonants, two discontinuous root consonants are added—e.g. צוּרֵינוּ – נֶעֱצָרֶנּוּ – יוֹצְרֵינוּ - מִצָּרָתֵינוּ (our Rock [God], we shall stop him, our creator, from our calamity): TsuReNU–naaTsReNU–yoTsReNU–TsaRateNU. The rhymeme is Ts + R + NU.

4) The same holds for a morphological suffix in a closed syllable—e.g. MoReHEM: M + R + HEM.

5) If the final syllable is closed and includes no grammatical suffix (ḥaRAD–yaRAD), then in itself it meets both requirements. There is no discontinuity, but the difficulty in finding or inventing rhyming words remains.

Illustrating point (5) is the famous strophe that for "enlightened" readers in the nineteenth century served as a symbol of Kallir's unintelligible and cacophonous style:

← / אָץ קוֹצֵץ בֶּן־קוֹצֵץ / קְצוּצֵי לְקַצֵץ / בְּדִבּוּר מְפוֹצֵץ / רְצוּצֵי לְרַצֵץ / לָץ בְּבוֹא לְלוֹצֵץ /

פְּלָץ וְנִתְלוֹצֵץ / כְּעֵץ מְחֻצָּצִים לַחְצֵץ / כְּנָץ עַל צִפּוֹר לְנַצֵץ.

→ (aTS koTSeTS ben KoTSeTS / KeTSuTSay lekaTSeTS . . . etc.)

Here, the final syllable *TSeTS* fulfills both requirements: it is both the last syllable in a line and has two root consonants. The inherited text is not vocalized. The reader is sent out to chase allusions using those sounds. In this case, the doubling of the same sound 30 × *TS* includes all the repeated *ts* sounds in non-rhyming positions. Altogether there are 30 *TS sounds in eight versets*—quite a mouthful. And clearly, it is a challenge for the poet to find that many allusions using these sounds. Owing to the neologisms, the allusions, and the elliptical syntax, this passage succeeded, but it is almost unintelligible without a commentary. But without the passage, there is no rhyme.

Using several symbols—N, the norm; R, a root consonant; C, a morphological consonant; V, a vowel; +, a permitted discontinuity in the sound string—the five forms of the Kallirian rhymeme listed above may be summarized as follows:

$$N_1 = R + RV$$
$$N_2 = R + RVC$$
$$N_3 = R + R + CV$$
$$N_4 = R + R + CVC$$
$$N_5 = RVR$$

If you look from the left, you consistently see two R's; if you look from the right, you see a complete syllable at the end of each line.

A typical case of a discontinuous rhymeme can be found in the *Hoshanot*, read on the first and second days of the Sukkot holiday, where the poet rhymes שׁ + עִי twenty-two times (in the poem אֱעֱרוֹךְ שַׁוְעִי) and שׁ + עוֹת twenty-two times (in the poem מוֹשָׁעוֹת – שְׁבוּעוֹת – בְּשַׁוְעוֹת – שׁוּעוֹת – שַׁעֲשׁוּעוֹת :אֵל לְמוֹשָׁעוֹת), etc. The two required root consonants are שׁ (š) and ע (ʻ) followed by a grammatical suffix: **i** (my) and **ot** (feminine plural).

This game of sounds in the rhyme has no superfluous sound, it would seem, just the required minimum (which occupies most of the rhyming word).

In Yanay's poetry, repetitions of four equivalent or similar words are often found in rhyme (such as לְפָנִים-לִיפָנִים-פָּנִים-פָּנִים). Any repeated full word automatically meets both requirements of the rhyme norm. But Yanay's pupil Kallir excluded plain repetition of a word as a substitute for a strophic rhyme, thus enforcing his difficult norm. A few hundred years later, in Spain, a one-rhyme poem (*qassida*) accepted the Arabic norm and allowed a repetition of the same word in rhyme only after seven lines.

LANGUAGE AND RHYME

The rhyme norm described above was primarily based on sound. Sound was not identical with the letter representing it or with the later-canonized vocalization. For the sake of rhyme, the *qamats* (ָ) and the *pattah* (ַ) were equivalent. As a result, in Israeli Hebrew, half of all vowels sound as **a**. *Tsere* (ֵ) and *segol* (ֶ) are both **e**. The letters א, ה, ח, ע lost their consonantal qualities, and in the rhymeme of the piyut they are interchangeable with each other and may be either disregarded or counted as vowels. Kallir rhymes לִשְׁלוֹחַ – אֱלוֹהַּ, קֵמְעָה – טְמֵאָה (like Shlonsky and Alterman). The sounds ב and ו seem to be equivalent: מַחֲשָׁבָה – שָׁוֶה , אֵבָה – גַּאֲוָה, etc. On the other hand, consonants with or without a hard sign (*dageš*) rhyme freely with each other: נֶפֶשׁ – טִפֵּשׁ :פ/פ *tippeš-nefeš* and קוֹבֵץ :ב/ב מַשְׂבֵּץ – רוֹבֵץ – מַרְבֵּץ. The equivalence of ב/ב (B/V), according to the graphic principle, and that of (V) ב/ו, according to the sound principle, established a new equivalence for the language of rhyme: ב, ב, ו (B, V, V). Kallir rhymes רְבִיד – מַעֲבִיד – לְהַאֲבִיד – הִרְבִּיד – דָּוִד or דְּבָרִים – שְׁוָרִים – גְּבוּרִים.

This tradition of equivalents for the sake of rhyme was carried with the piyut into Italy and Ashkenaz (Franco-Germany). Meshullam Ben Kalonymus of the tenth century (born in Italy, lived in Mainz) rhymed freely: הֶרְבָּה – רָוָה-מְרִיבָה, etc.[10] Rabbi Meir Ben Baruch of Rothenberg in the thirteenth century rhymed טְבוּעִים – מַצְבִּיעִים – מְשַׁוְּעִים (teVi'im matsbi'im m'săv'im).

THE HISTORY OF KALLIRIAN RHYME

The forms of Kallirian piyut spread throughout the Diaspora. In the West (Spain) they were superseded in the tenth and eleventh centuries by the Hebrew forms of Arabic versification. Syllable counters had no use for word counting. In Italy and Ashkenazi Franco-Germany they dominated the unrhymed core of the *mahzor* (prayer book) and do so to the present day. With time, the difficult rhyme norm was simplified: poets dropped the requirement to include two root consonants; now rhyme was based on a repetition of the final syllables alone and became terminal, as is the standard Hebrew rhyme scheme everywhere in the Middle Ages. Indeed, in a time of Crusader pogroms, how could poets play with sounds? The word "play" may be too strong, but sound patterns were required.

The process of simplification apparently originated in Eretz Israel. In the ninth century the Palestinian-influenced rhyme in the piyut of southern Italy was based on the final syllable only. But the "strong" norm prevailed again in the tenth century in Babylonia, Italy, and Franco-Germany, to be dropped finally toward the end of the eleventh century. Yet perhaps the chain of events was different. A historical study considering the forms as well as other historical evidence is still not available and perhaps (for lack of evidence) cannot be done.

OTHER KINDS OF RHYME

In Yanay's and Kallir's poetry the rich, discontinuous rhymeme of the strophic poem is not the only rhyme form. Indeed, rhyme emerged from a culture of parallelism on all levels. All aspects of the Hebrew word were separated and employed, in one form or another, for the sake of rhyme: the sound, the root, the suffix, the meaning, and, finally, the word as a whole. In pattern poems this is obvious: not only the final sounds of the parallel words are repeated, but also their meanings and morphological structure. In this genre of pattern poems, however, rhymes, like other kinds of repetition, are tied: they serve the composition of the poem not independently but as a whole cluster. The function of rhyme was not to create a euphony but to provide the text with a compositional frame. What its building material was did not matter. Still, it was obvious that the terminal sound rhyme would prevail, because sound was emancipated from any semantic unfolding of the text.

The question is: Why was this interesting, complex, and precise system of strophic cycles and discontinuous rhymes not discovered earlier? My friend, the great scholar of piyut, the late professor Ezra Fleischer, saw the plethora of sounds in the piyutim of Shlomo ha-Bavli (the "Babylonian"), collected in his edition of Bavli's poetry, several pages' worth, and finally sent his readers to me.[11] One formula is enough to subsume all cases and solve the quandary. There is no especially rich sound layer; all the sounds are predictable and accounted for by the complex *norm*. The maximum and the minimum of sounds meet in the same place. Rarely, a single sound is superfluous.

The reasons for this neglect are several: (1) scholars of religious topics are not used to studying structural forms and are even flabbergasted by all this formalism; (2) many key poems in the *maḥzor* are printed as continuous prose rather than as strophic structures, as I reconstructed above; and (3) although virtuoso works in the language are screaming for attention, the study of religious texts is influenced by Romantic notions of "religiosity" and "spirituality." Once, lecturing on these discoveries, I was accused of making the rabbis into "Russian Formalists," to which I responded: "Not Russian but Jewish" (and how about the *Halachah?*). The love of sound play, repetition, and structural complexity is overwhelming. There is not much new in the content of the piyut—it is attached to the theme of the weekly reading—but what is wrong with innovation in form?

On the way to the final form, the following kinds of rhyme may be discerned.

1) *Sound rhyme,* a rhyme based on the parallelism of sounds, including initial rhyme, which led to rhyme as we know it: discontinuous and terminal rhyme.

2) *Morphological rhyme,* based on a repeated suffix. It appears sporadically in the Bible and was used several times at considerable length in the Dead Sea Scrolls and by Ben Sirah. It was widely used in *kinot* (lamentations) with the suffix *ekha* (‎ךָ‎), "yours" (used when talking to God in the plural), and picked up by Uri-Zvi Grinberg in *Reḥovot Ha-Nahar,* his book of Holocaust poems. It became a legitimate variety of rhyme in non-strophic piyutim, especially in pattern poems.

3) *Semantic rhyme,* where the relations of the rhyming terms are in parallelism of meaning rather than in sound: ‎אכילה – שתיה , זמר–רנן‎ (eating–drinking, song–melody). "Rhyme" represents any device that frames the composition of the poem. Such a device may rely on any aspect of the word. It may be any of the following:

a terminal sound rhyme	[riTSUY–niTSUY]	‎רצוי – ניצוי‎
an initial rhyme	[SEGEl–SEGEr]	‎סגל – סגר‎
a rhyme of letters	['ZuZ–le ' ZaZel]	‎עזוז – לעזאזל‎
a semantic rhyme	[right–duty, life–death]	‎זכות – חובה , חיים – מוות‎

Even in a strophic poem, in a chain of sound rhymes, Yanay writes suddenly: ‎סוס – סוס – חמור – חמור‎ (horse–horse–donkey–donkey), rhyming "horse" with "horse" and "donkey" with "donkey."

4) *Root rhyme,* found in the rhyming of words of one root. The words do not necessarily have similar sound endings—e.g. ‎תוצדַּק – יצדק – צדיק – צדק‎ (will be justified—he is right—a saintly man—justice) or ‎גּאה – גּאה – גּאוה – גּאים‎ (proud [she]–overflow–pride–proud [plural]).

5) *Word rhyme,* based on the repetition of a whole word, usually a key word (life, death, night, war, etc.), throughout a poem. This type is older than systematic rhyme and is often employed in piyutim.

Semantic rhyme and root rhyme are used only occasionally, especially in free strophic forms, such as the *silluk,* or as an additional device within the line. They are of particular interest for the understanding of the origins of sound rhyme, which grew in an environment of repetition and patterning of any possible aspect of the language (including pattern poems as repetition of syntactic patterns).

A distinct kind of piyut uses a word rhyme together with sound rhymes in one single rhyme-chain of a long poem. Such is Kallir's rhyme of the word *tal* טל (dew), in his "Prayer for Dew" "תפילת טל", where it is repeated endlessly and interwoven with words ending with the same sounds only as TAL: נטל, טלטל (*natal, taltal*) (he grabbed, a curl), etc. Piyutim were functional genres working for specific functions in the liturgy. After the Bible, there was little secular poetry in Hebrew. It arrived with full dignity during the creative revival in Spain.

REFINED QUANTITATIVE METERS IN SPAIN

Hebrew poetry entered a new era with its emergence in Islamic Spain in the tenth century. The principles of Arabic versification were adopted by Hebrew poetry. Quantitative meters—regularly alternating "short" and "long" syllables—became the dominant system of versification in Hebrew poetry in Spain from its beginnings, through the "Golden Age" and the Christian advances, until the destruction of Jewish life in Spain at the end of the fifteenth century. Owing to the authority and the achievements of Hebrew culture and poetry in Muslim and later in Christian Spain and the role of the poet as an individual, the language and metrical system of Hebrew poetry in Spain spread to other countries. It dominated Hebrew poetry in Provence, and was prevalent in Italy until the eighteenth century. Even though Jews in Italy could not hear the difference between short and long, they nevertheless kept a precise distinction in writing. This was the mode of Hebrew poetry throughout the Islamic world as well—in Egypt, Babylonia, Yemen, North Africa, the Ottoman Empire—until recent times, and even some rabbis cum poets (*paytanim*) in medieval Ashkenaz wrote their piyutim in the "Spanish" meter.

Hebrew poetry in the East, especially in Babylon/Baghdad during Arabic rule, though situated in the very heart of Islamic culture and influenced by Arabic science and literature—and perhaps because of that—shows no sign of having come under the sway of the forms of Arabic poetry. Local Jews were so steeped in Arabic culture that they saw no Hebrew alternative. Saadiah Gaon of Babylon (tenth century), a religious leader, distinguished philosopher, and Arabic linguist was the author of a large *Sidur* (prayer book), composed of his Hebrew piyutim, and a Hebrew rhyming dictionary. His piyutim followed the norms of the pre-Islamic piyut. Saadiah used the strophic structure of the ancient piyut with a separate and multiple rhyme in each strophe. There was no trace in his poetry of any syllable-counting meter.

However, Saadiah's pupil, Dunash Ben Labrat (920–990), a native of Fez, Morocco, who was educated in Baghdad and went to Córdoba, Spain—traveling from the far east to the far west of the caliphate—introduced the Arabic quantitative metrical system into Hebrew poetry in the middle of the tenth century. Ben Labrat's radical innovation was seen by his critics as violating the nature and grammar of the Hebrew language. Still, Hebrew discourse in quantitative meters was the engine which had generated the high-level production of Hebrew poetry in Spain, Provence, and Italy and provided the disciplined form of its expressions.

Unfortunately, the same symbols, $|-|$ and $|\cup|$, are conventionally used both for stressed and unstressed syllables in modern poetry and for longs and shorts as in Greek and Hebrew quantitative meters written in Spain. To distinguish the two in the following discussion, I shall use a variant for the Spanish short, V, and, in a foot, $|V---|$. For the modern unstressed syllable, I shall use $|\cup|$, and, for a foot, $|\cup\cup-|$.

In Spain, the new meters were "quantitative," based on the opposition long versus short, as in Arabic poetry. In Hebrew, the mobile *shewa*, the *ḥataf,* and the conjunction ו (when pronounced "u") were considered short vowels; all other vowels in the Hebrew vocabulary were considered long. A well-known poem by Solomon Ibn Gabirol opens thus. Here the poetic line is transcribed from left to right, and I use an apostrophe to indicate a short vowel.

→

m'litsati b'dagati h'dufa / u'simhati b'anhati d'ḥufa
/ V — — — / V — — — / V — — // V — — — / V — — — / V — —

or

P   CC   P   CC   P C//P   CC   P   CC P   C

The two rhyming words are neologisms in Hebrew and need interpretation.

←

/ —V / —V / —V // —V / —V / —V /

מְלִיצָתִי בְּדַאֲגָתִי הֲדוּפָה, וְשִׂמְחָתִי בַּאֲנְחָתִי דְחוּפָה

In modern meters, on the contrary, the majority of syllables are unstressed.

→

/ ∪ ∪ — / ∪ ∪ — / ∪ ∪ — / ∪ — ∪ /

There is no clear agreement as to how the *shewa* was pronounced: as part of a cluster of two consonants or as a "half"-syllable of sorts. The Spanish reading is

→ *m'litsati* | V — — — |

considered as four syllables, while in Ashkenaz and later in Yiddish, the word was pronounced *mli-tsa-ti,* without a vowel between the first two consonants.

In Modern Hebrew there is a clear difference between a consonantal cluster at the head of a word, MLI, and the vowel inserted between the consonants: MLi/Meli.

The number of "short" syllables in Hebrew is conspicuously smaller. The *movable shewa* appears only in a few places in the language: (1) it indicates the break between a lexical word and its prefixes: *be-vo* (in-coming), *ve-lo* (and no), *ke-sus* (like a horse), etc., for the prefixes *b* (in), *l* (to), *v* (and), *k* (like); (2) it separates a word from its prepositions: *be-Polin* (in Poland); (3) when a word (or its derivative) has three syllables, the third from the end is contracted (indicated with a *shewa*), as in *ma-kom* (place)–*me-ko-mot* (places), *me-ko-mi* (my place), where the first syllable is shortened to a *shewa*; (4) for short words (two root consonants), the *shewa* comes at the beginning: <אשר ;בְּנֵי ;אֲנִי>; (5) if a word has more than two consonants, the first may be a *shewa* (<ד->).

Furthermore, in Greek verse, a long syllable is the distinguishing unit of a foot: a foot is a regular pattern, repeated several times in a verse line and consisting of one strong (either long or stressed) vowel and several short (or unstressed) vowels. The length (or stress) is the pivotal point of the foot. Thus, a Greek dactylic foot consists of one long and two short syllables | — ∪ ∪ |, which may be shortened to two syllables |— —|. In medieval Hebrew, however, with many more long than short syllables, the pivotal point is a "short" unit: a foot with one short and one or several long syllables ("vowels"): → |V— — —| or |— —V—|. It is hard to conceive how such a weak element (weak in length and in stress) could provide a rhythmic basis for a foot. There is probably no versification in the world that is organized around its weaker marker. And as we shall see, it is not here, either.

HEBREW QUANTITATIVE METERS

A quantitative meter is based on a regular pattern of alternating "short" and "long" syllables—rather than stressed and unstressed syllables, as in modern poetry. Hebrew quantitative meters, though derived from Arabic versification, were quite different from their prototypes. This was basically due to the different properties of the Hebrew language and the shortage of truly "short" syllables in it. After the initial Arabic impulse, Hebrew verse developed its own forms and preferences, autonomous of its source. But the principles remained the same.

Descriptions of Hebrew versification in Spain did not distinguish between problems of diachrony and synchrony. The derivation of a particular meter from this or that Arabic prototype seemed to satisfy modern-age scholars as well, more than understanding its place in the synchronic system of Hebrew verse. The accepted classification of medieval Hebrew meters, basically unchanged for the past millennium, relies on medieval Arabic taxonomies. One finds usually long taxonomic lists of individual patterns rather than structural rules to explain the nature of these quantitative meters.

Including the many derivations, the number of particular metrical lines runs into several dozens (David Yellin's list has 67; Schirmann's, 32), whereas the irregular patterns of the whimsical "girdle" poems (many of them in the collected poetry of Yehuda [Judah] Halevi) may account for dozens of individual schemes. The patterns may be irregular inside the flow of one line, using several kinds of changing feet, but precisely the same "irregularity" of the model verse line is repeated throughout the whole poem: there is a regular irregularity.

The traditionally identified meters will not be enumerated here—no need for that. I shall instead explain the deep structures, or "rules of the game," of all possible meters. One reason for the large number of metrical types recorded is that each meter is used as a label for an individual pattern of a whole line which has not been analyzed into its distinctive features. Three such features should be considered: (a) the basic metrical unit, or the recurring group of syllables (the so-called foot); (b) the number and order of such feet, which determine the length of the line; (c) the form of the last foot—whether complete, short, or changed, rhymed ultimately or penultimately. Compare, in accentual-syllabic poetry an analytical term such as "iambic pentameter," where the first word indicates the basic repeated foot, the second the length of the line, and the third the end of the line in terms of its so-called rhyme gender: "feminine" (penultimate), "masculine" (ultimate), or "dactylic." (Rhyme gender has nothing to do with gender, just its French heritage.)

The difference between the two widespread and traditionally distinct Spanish Hebrew meters,

> *ha-merubbeh* / V — — — / V — — — / V — — / and
> *ha-marnin* / V — — — / V — — — /

is one of length of line only: three feet or two feet. For a similar difference between

> / — V — — / — V — — / — V — — and
> / —V—— / —V—— /

only one term has been used: *ha-kalu'a* (a) and *ha-kalu'a* (b). While a difference in the length of a line may be an important rhythmical factor, it should not justify the use of unanalyzed terms.

Basically, there are three groups of words: (1) prepositions, *b-, v-, k-* (in, end, to, like), to separate the semantic from the grammatical morpheme; (2) marked forms of long words (feminine, plural), which cause contraction: *makom* (place) → *m'kom, mikomot* (places); (3) short words, based on fewer than three consonants. The majority of words in use have no *shewa*.

THE BASIS OF HEBREW QUANTITATIVE METERS

Hebrew poets in Spain did not resort to the distinction between the short and long vowels of the traditional biblical vocalization (ˌ /ˍ or ˌˌ /ˌˌ). Only the *mobile shewa*, the *ḥataf*, and the conjunction ו (when pronounced "u") were considered short vowels. (In what follows, I call them all *shewa*.)

Moreover, whereas in Greek verse a long syllable (as the strongest point in a foot) constitutes the distinguishing unit of a foot, in Hebrew the short (weaker) unit is considered to fill that function; that is, in Spain, a foot has one short and several long syllables (e.g. the most used meter, *ha-merubbeh*, V — — —). The whole foot hinges on one short syllable! It is hard to conceive how a single weak unit could provide a rhythmic basis for a foot.

In Spain we can find yet another way of describing this kind of meter (notably summarized by Saadia ibn Denan, who was expelled from Spain in 1492 and felt obliged to teach the Italian Jews the principles of this versification).[12] The description is based on the use of another kind of contrast, namely that between a *cord* (C = / — /; in Hebrew: *tenu'ah*, "vowel") and a *peg* (P = / ∪ — /; *yated*, or heavy syllable), using Arab desert imagery of a tent. A peg is one and a half syllables long. A quantitative "short" followed by a "vowel" was called a peg: it was a cluster of two consonants and the following vowel. You hang the cords on a peg; several syllables are subordinated to one peg in each foot. Indeed, in some medieval Hebrew grammars (Radak-David Kimchi) a peg / ∪ — / as a cluster of two consonants is considered one syllable—the strong syllable, the focus of a foot: break, crown, small. All other syllables are not "long" but regular cords = vowels. "Short" and "long" together correspond to the contemporary initial consonantal clusters: here, *mli* is one syllable: *mli-tsa-ti*. In Italy, in contrast, *mli-tsa-ti* has four syllables: *me'-li-tsa-ti*. The question is whether certain consonant clusters are permissible in Hebrew. For the line from Ibn Gabirol (written from left to right) the traditional meter is: →/V — — — / V — — — / V — — /. The new notation is: → PCC PCC PC//PCC PCC PC.

In the traditional notation a foot may have one short initial consonant cluster and two or three vowels, but now the same foot is described as PCC, consisting of one peg and two cords. This system of description is justified because in the Hebrew language every "short" syllable must be followed by a "long" one. The so-called short syllable cannot exist by itself, as an independent language unit, and never appears without a "vowel" following it. Thus a quantitative meter may be described as a regular alternation of pegs and cords: usually, one peg and one or several cords.

Now we can understand the logic of the system. The basic group of syllables recurring several times in a line in a fixed order is called a *foot*. A foot must have one peg and one or several cords, so a foot may consist of either two or three "new" syllables; in the old system of notation, the feet could be four syllables long, and many more combinations would have been possible. The basic feet are listed here:

Number of Syllables	Place of the Peg	Equivalence to the Modern Foot
Binary:	PC (initial)	trochee / — V /
	CP (final)	iamb / V — /
	CC (neutral)	/ — — /
Ternary:	PCC (initial)	dactyl / — V V /
	CPC (medial)	amphibrach / V — V /
	CCP (final)	anapest / V V — /

This is precisely the map of options that we have in European accentual-syllabic meters, two binary and three ternary, but instead of length we distinguish stress versus no stress. In medieval Hebrew, however, there was also a meter without pegs, the so-called *mishkal ha-tenu'ot* meter of vowels (syllables), made of eight "long" syllables, but it retained the consciousness of the quantitative opposition long/short and excluded the *shewa* from the text. In the table it appears as "binary neutral." The five basic meters have the same structure as in modern poetry, except for the binary neutral meter, because there can be no language text without any stress, but there can be a text without a consonant cluster (*shewa*).

The verse form of Classical Hebrew poetry in Spain is a distich (called *bayit* [house]) consisting of two versets either identical or differing slightly in the meter of the last foot: the first verset is called *délet* (door, opening), the second *sogér* (closure). In each line, at the end of the *sogér* there is a rhyme term linking the line to the whole poem; the ends of the distichs are strung on one rhyme like a string of pearls. Indeed, *ḥaruz*—rhyme in Hebrew—means "pearls (on a string)." A poem often consists of several dozen distichs repeating again and again the same rhymeme, with the typical double effect of enchantment and monotony. Only in the first distich are both versets rhymed. In the rest, only the end of the closing verset carries the rhyme. Ostensibly, the double verset looks like a biblical verse, but it comes from Arabic prosody, and there is no parallelism between the two versets, except for the repeated metrical grid.

Hebrew meters in Spain exhibit the aesthetic principle of "maximum unity compatible with maximum diversity."[13] To have a meter as a verse unit, we need at least two identical feet; but repetition of an identical third foot would be redundant and should be abbreviated. If the first two feet are not identical, both of them together constitute the basic unit, so the cluster of both feet together has to be repeated twice, thus making four feet in a verse line. This metrical pattern, however, is in all its details permanent throughout the poem. In each verset the basic foot is repeated several times, but the last foot may be incomplete, usually by being shorter. All the feet of a line may be either of one kind only or of two alternating kinds, a pattern unknown elsewhere in European verse. Thus, the beginning of a metrical line determines its continuation. The length of a line is not as free as in Hebrew or in European poetry of modern times. Indeed, to my great surprise, it turned out that the length of the line is totally determined by the nature of the feet. There is a precise interdependence between the structure of the feet and their number.

There are two rules governing the length of a line, as predicted from the first two feet:

a) If at least one of the first two feet is binary, there must be four feet in that line:

→ /PCC/PC //PCC/PC/ or /CC/CC/CC/CC/.

b) If both first feet are ternary, there can be only three feet in a line,

→ /PCC/PCC/PC/,

and the third foot may be either complete (which is rare), shortened, changed, or avoided.

Hence, in a verset, the optimal size of a line is eight syllables: if the beginning two feet are ternary, we have 2 × 3 basic feet + 2 for the unfinished third foot = 8; if the two feet are binary, we have 4 × 2 = 8 two-syllable feet.

The last foot of a line can be described separately: if it is a third foot, it is either complete or shortened.[14] (The symbol P/C shows two alternative endings for the two versets in a distich. Binary meters have practically no variations: because of rule (a), there are four feet with no shorts. The reason for rule (a) is that if one foot is binary and the other ternary, the whole group must be repeated twice, thus having four feet; and if both first feet are binary, there can be no abbreviated third foot. There is no regular ternary meter of cords alone, as there is no language without stresses. And there is practically no binary final meter. No other regular meters are possible. In the ternary meters, the third foot may be completed only if the peg is at the very end.

A *shewa* ("short") at the end of the line is impossible in Hebrew. And a *shewa* before the last vowel is very rare in the Hebrew language. Certainly, there are no "short" vowels in Hebrew; no word ends in a *shewa*. But ending in a peg is not easy either. If, in a word, the *shewa* comes before one vowel, there is no *shewa*. For example, *makom* (place) in its plural becomes *m'komot* | ∪ — — |. But this shortening of the first syllable comes only if two vowels follow the *shewa*. The same occurs in *m'komi, m'komo,* etc. If only one syllable follows the *shewa*, as in *m'kom*, it happens, e.g. in the genitive, when a second word is attached: *m'kom ha-kraw* (the battlefield). To break up the line after *m'kom* is possible in the break between the two versets, but not at the end of the whole line: there is no enjambment in this poetry. This weak position of the last peg calls for a variety of substitutes.

VARIEGATED METERS

Here, unlike in European meters, the feet in a verse line do not have to be identical. The structure of the variegated meters also follows from the rules of length. There are two kinds of variegated meters:

A) *Alternating meters.* According to rule (a), if one of the first two feet is binary there must be four feet in a line: PC PCC are two different feet, and the whole group must be repeated twice. The result is PC PCC/PC PCC in the meter *ha-arokh*.

B) *Changing meters.* According to rule (b), if both first feet are ternary— and different—there cannot be four feet; that is, there can be no repetition of the whole group within each line. In this case, if there is a third foot, it either repeats the first or is changed (as the last foot of a line).

Alternating Meters. In alternating meters the following rules hold for the basic patterns: (1) there are four feet in a line ; (2) the meter is based on a regular alternation between ternary and binary feet ; (3) both kinds of feet go in the same direction: they are either initial or final ; (4) in each hemistich, if there are two pegs, they are removed from each other by only one cord. From rules (3) and (4) it follows that there may be only two basic alternating meters, as follows, which means that the pegs in both feet are either at the beginning or at the end of each foot:

alternating initial	PC PCC PC PCC	הארוך	*ha-arokh*
alternating final	CCP CP CCP CP	המתפשט	*ha-mitpashet*

There can be no medial feet since there must be a common rhythmical denominator; if it is not the foot, it is its direction. Since each line has two

symmetrical hemistichs, variations of the scheme may be accepted at the end
of the line as well as in the second foot—e.g. the alternating falling meter has
a variant PC CCC PC CCC with only two pegs in the whole line. That was the
meter of Dunash Ben Labrat, who could avoid a lot of the trouble of finding
shewas. The variants will not be listed here.[15]

Changing Meters. Change means moving a P in the second foot one slot
forward. Only two ternary feet can combine: the medial and the final (the
name derives from the place of the first peg). Hence the two basic schemes
of changing meters are:

medial and changing	CPC CCP CPC	הקל א׳	*ha-kal* (a)
final and changing	CCP CPC	הקל ב׳	*ha-kalu'a*

Here, the designation final or medial refers to the first place where a peg
appears. That means that if the first foot has a medial peg, the change can only
be to the final foot; if the first foot has a final peg, the change can only be to
the medial foot. Variations occur in the third foot (at the end of the line) and
in the second (at the end of the basic foot). These meters, however, are rare
and shall not be enumerated here.[16]

THE METERS USED IN MEDIEVAL HEBREW POETRY

In actual poetry the situation is even simpler. To be sure, some poets liked
experimenting. As David Yellin has shown, Samuel ha-Nagid used fifty-seven
different metrical schemes. The bulk of Hebrew poetry in Spain, however,
employed only a small number of basic meters, with some variations, of which
the most widespread are (in this order): initial and final ternary meters and
the meter of cords. More precisely:

(1) ternary initial, especially,	PCC PCC PC	המרבה	*ha-merrubeh*
but also	PCC PCC	המרנין	*ha-marnin*
(2) ternary final, especially,	CCP CCP CC	השלם ב׳	*ha-shalem* (b)
but also	P/C	המהיר ב׳	*ha-mahir* (b)
	CCP CCP CC		
(3) cords (binary neutral)	CC CC CC CC	התנועות	*ha-tenu'ot*

These three groups, with a few variations, account for 94 percent of Moses ibn
Ezra's meters in his secular poetry. The major meter, *ha-merubbeh,* (1), found

in about half of the Hebrew poems in Spain, later gave way to *ha-shalem* (b), (2), which requires a penultimate stress and a penultimate ("feminine") rhyme, hence fits the environment of Romance languages like Italian and Spanish that promote the penultimate accent and penultimate rhymes.

Following these three groups, though far behind, are the alternating meters: initial (PC PCC PC PCC—*ha-arokh*) and final (CCP CP CCP CP—*ha-mitpashet*). An unusual thing happened here: since the third foot has to be shortened and the peg is at the end, we have to cut the last peg: CCP CCP CC. In compensation for that, a criterion from a different prosodic system is used, and a language stress is placed on the penultimate syllable: CCP/CCP/ ĆC. In spite of the quantitative meters which made stress irrelevant, this is the surprising general rule: whenever the ending line is shortened and a peg must be cut, this cut is compensated for by a feminine stress. A penultimate accented rhyme is mandatory for all these meters. Hence, it pleased the ears of Romance-language speakers. Only such feminine meters are used in Italy, and *ha-shalem* (b) became the dominant meter in Italy as well as in Christian Spain and Portugal. The preference of initial over final meters is due to the structure of the Hebrew word; the majority of *moving shewa'im* ("shorts") are at the beginnings of words, and a *shewa* may easily be added before a word with a preposition or conjunction (כ, ב, ל, ו) to keep the meter.

The bulk of the poetry uses ternary meters, with three feet in a line (the last one usually incomplete). Since the length of the line is regulated, it varies only within narrow limits. There are only lines of six to ten syllables. If the "short" syllables are also counted (as they will be later, in Hebrew poetry in Italy), the limits are eight–fourteen. Since in contemporary Israeli poetry about half of the *shewa'im* are considered syllables, those limits are comparable to seven–twelve syllables today.

If the special effect of the *ha-marnin*, which has the typical rhythm of a short line, is excluded, all other meters compare well with the variations given in a.-s. poetry in the space between four iambics and four anapests. The shape of the syntactical units, covering a whole verset, is about the same, irrespective of the specific meter. Indeed, besides the rhythmic-syntactical form, the length of a line in Spanish Hebrew poetry is similar to the length of typical Hebrew lines in modern poetry. The optimal line has eigth to nine "long" syllables; in Italy, where the short syllables are counted as full syllables, this means eleven to twelve. Eleven is the ideal Italian meter (*endecasylabo*), which is similar in length to a line of four or five iambs today. The Hebrew language in poetry is comfortable with such units of syntax and fits the typical syntactical units.

There are many variations of verse endings in the last foot of the basic metrical matrix. Any such variant creates a permanent pattern, repeated in all the lines of a poem. Hebrew poets allowed very rarely—if at all—for changes from line to line (foot-"substitutes") or deviations from a given metrical scheme. In Hebrew, in the changing meter CPC CCP CPC, the second foot may be replaced by PP (CCP = PP). This is yet another argument for selecting the peg as the stronger unit, because P = CC.

In sum, the two basic shapes of verse lines are (a) four binary feet or (b) three feet, including ternary feet with an abbreviated third foot. The variations in Hebrew in the third foot are felt not against the pattern of the poem but against the rhythmic impulse of the first two feet of the same verse.

The quantitative binary opposition short/long provides the Hebrew poet with a matrix framework in a written text rather than with a pervasive rhythmic movement in the experience of reading. In Hebrew, the "long" syllable is called a "vowel" but not "long." The two major meters in Arabic, *tawil* and *basīt* (equivalent to the Hebrew alternating final and initial meters), are far from being major meters in Hebrew. Moreover, every possible substitution of longs for shorts is resorted to in Hebrew. Thus, the scheme of the Arabic *basīt* is (from left to right), in its Hebrew derivation:

$$/\cup - \cup - / \cup \cup - / - \cup - \cup - / - \cup \cup - /$$
$$/ - - \cup - / - \cup - / - - \cup - / - \cup - /$$
$$\quad \text{CCP} \qquad \text{CP} \qquad \text{CCP} \qquad \text{CP}$$

Instead of eight shorts to six longs, in Hebrew the proportion became four shorts to ten longs (vowels). A common variation of this meter has even fewer shorts:

$$/ - C \cup P - / - C$$
$$- C /$$
$$- C - C \cup P - / - C - C/$$

No two consecutive short syllables are possible in Hebrew (*shewa* after *shewa* cannot exist); therefore some Arabic meters could not be adopted in Hebrew.

On the other hand, in many Hebrew poems, in addition to the short/long distinction, a strong tendency to regulate stress order and word boundaries—both outside the theory of Hebrew poetry and within the intuition of the poets—can be distinguished. The meter is quantitative, but the rhyme carries strong stress orders. Ostensibly stress is not part of Hebrew Spanish versification or its theory, but accentual tendencies are clearly felt. Thus, in the poem by Ibn Gabirol in quantitative symbols, the first line reads, as its *formal quantitative meter* requires:

נֵחַר בְּקָרְאִי גְרוֹנִי דָּבַק לְחִכִּי לְשׁוֹנִי

הָיָה לְבָבִי סְחַרְחַר מֵרֹב כְּאֵבִי וְאוֹנִי

←

$$|--\text{v}-|-\text{v}---||---\text{v}-|-\text{v}--$$

The formal division of the quantitative meter in this poem is perfect, yet when read aloud, it seems artificial. The order of shorts is perfectly executed, but the quantitative feet often cut into the boundaries of words. Reading according to the feet, we get such absurd sound groups as *ni-har-be-kor i-ge-ro-ni*. There are no such words in Hebrew. The language of the poem follows a different pattern quite clearly, even if subconsciously: an accentual-syllabic pattern, though not in all the lines. That means that overlapping of word/foot boundaries and the use of metrical accents rather than "short" ones are distinguishing markers. If we transcribe the same text in accentual terms, we get a perfect amphibrach, and the boundaries of words coincide with the boundaries of feet. This is the *implied accentual reading*:

נֵחַר בְּקָרְאִי גְרוֹנִי דָּבַק לְחִכִּי לְשׁוֹנִי

הָיָה לְבָבִי סְחַרְחַר מֵרֹב כְּאֵבִי וְאוֹנִי

←

$$||-\cup\cup|-\cup\cup|-\cup||-\cup\cup|-\cup\cup|-\cup$$

The accents are clearly regular, and so are the word boundaries. Though it is not an absolute rule in this poem, in 85 percent of the cases there are word boundaries where feet boundaries should be (but are not), whereas only 36 percent of the cases follow the formal foot boundaries of the quantitative meter. This kind of regularity in stress order and word boundaries is partly due to the correlation between the following factors: (1) "short" syllables cannot be stressed in Hebrew; and (2) short syllables are most common at the beginnings of words, so a boundary usually precedes them. It seems, however, that the major force behind this tendency is the subliminal rhythmical sense of stress and stress order in Hebrew, felt especially in the works of the great poets, Ibn Gabirol and Yehuda Halevi.

Relative regularity in stress order may be felt as a rhythmic substitute in accentual meters without the peg/cord alternation. Thus, in the meter of mere cords (eight cords) there are lines which are clearly "iambic" in the modern accentual sense. Using *accentual symbols* gives a precise iambic tetrameter:

$$\leftarrow$$

$$\cup - \cup - \cup - \cup \,||\, - \cup - \cup - \cup - \cup \qquad \text{accentual meter}$$

כָּתְנוֹת פַּסִּים לָבַשׁ הַגַּן וּכְסוֹת רִקְמָה מֵדֵּי דִשׁוֹ

$$|-V|-V|-V|-V||-V|-V|-V|-V| \qquad \text{quantitative meter}$$

GIRDLE POEMS

The main body of Hebrew poetry in Spain used regular meters and one rhyme running throughout the ends of all lines. The rhyme, called a *running rhyme (haruz mavriah)*, with as many members as there were lines in the poem, in some cases many dozens, provided the combined effect of magical enchantment and monotony typical of Arabic aesthetics and reflected as well in the ornaments of the classical mosques and synagogues.

The *muwaššah*, or "girdle" poem (שִׁיר אֶזוֹר *shir ezor*), an original development of Arabic and Hebrew Andalusian poetry, was represented in Hebrew poetry almost from its beginnings (eleventh century). This was the form of some of the best Hebrew lyrical poems and love poems of the twelfth century. The girdle poem combines in its composition two extremes: the strophic principle of changing rhymes with every strophe and the rhyme principle of a running rhyme which runs through all the lines of the poem in a refrain-like manner and unifies the whole poem with one girdle. The first aspect supported in its rhymes the autonomy of each image (one or several lines), and the girdle provided the narrative of long poems.

In every poem, there are two kinds of strophes: (1) the changing strophes with changing rhymes, where every such strophe has one or several distinct rhymes different from the rhymes of other strophes and repeating their structure; and (2) the "girdle," a strophic pattern like a refrain recurring after every changing strophe, with the same rhyme or rhymes repeated in all girdle strophes throughout the poem. As the "guiding" strophe, a girdle strophe often appears at the beginning of the poem before any changing strophe. In many poems the final girdle, the so-called *ḥarğa*, is written not in Hebrew but in popular Arabic or the old Romance language of Spain. Usually it is a love poem and a quotation from a love conversation. The *ḥarğa* thus determines the meter and rhyme of the girdle, as well as the melody. Most girdle poems were apparently created as songs to known melodies, indicated in the motto of the poem.

The meter of the changing strophes and the meter of the girdle may be identical, but they often are not. Each line may consist of one, two, or three parts, rhymed in their own internal columns or unrhymed. The metrical pattern may be either regular in its own framework (verset) or irregular. If irregular, within the line there is a free combination of all kinds of feet, which seems often to constitute a kind of free verse. But the same irregular free verse of one line is frozen and repeated throughout the poem, in the strophes of each kind separately. The two metrical schemes are often related to each other, in a variety of ways; e.g. one may include a partial repetition of the other. A simple example is Yehuda Halevi's song ‏"בִּי הַצְּבִי בִּי אֲדוֹנִי"‏ ("Bi ha-tse-vi, bi adoni"). In this case, the meter of the changing strophe is

→   CCP CPC

and that of the girdle is

→   CC CPC /CCP CPC

The strophe has a simple but irregular scheme. The metrical pattern of the girdle repeats the meter of the strophe in its second part, but the first part of the girdle is different (in this case, there is a slight variation: a missing peg in the first foot).

An example of a complex rhyme scheme can be found in a poem by Joseph ibn Jacob ibn Zaddik (1075–1149), which begins with a guiding girdle:

←

מֵאֲהָלִי!	בָּרַח, אֲהָהּ, גּוֹזֵל	נוּמִי, אֲהָהּ, נִגְזָל–
מִי גוֹאֲלִי?	עָפְרִי אֲהָהּ, אָזַל–	דִּמְעִי, אֲהָהּ, יִזַּל –
טוֹב מַעֲנֶה,	לָעוּת חֲלִילֵךְ	נוֹגֵן ! שְׁלַח אֶצְבַּע
כֵּן יַעֲנֶה.	צְחוֹת, כְּקוֹלֵךְ	אִלֵּם – אֲבָל יַבַּע
בִּשְׂמֹאל מְנֶה.	עַל פִּי נְבָלֵךְ	שָׁלֹשׁ וְגַם אַרְבַּע

מִפִּי כְלִי-   שָׂפָה, וְאַל יֶחְדַּל   שִׁירִים נְצֹר עַל דַּל

לֹא מֵחֲלִי!   עִתִּים, וְעֵת יְדַּל -   שִׁיר – קוֹל, אֲשֶׁר יִגְדַּל -

The rhymeme is from left to right:

			ZAL	ZAL	LI
girdle			ZAL	ZAL	LI

BƏ	LEXA	ƏNE
BƏ	LEXA	ƏNE
BƏ	LEXA	ƏNE

			DAL	DAL	LI
girdle			DAL	DAL	LI

Variations are obvious.

The rhyme pattern in the whole poem is as follows (capital letters represent the girdle rhymes, from left to right):

→

PPR	↓ abc	def	ghi	jkl	mno
PPR	abc	def	ghi	jkl	mno
	↓ abc	def	ghi	jkl	mno
	PPR	PPR	PPR	PPR	PPR
	PPR	PPR	PPR	PPR	PPR

The principles of the girdle poem were also used in religious poetry, especially by the great poets Yehuda Halevi and Abraham ibn Ezra.

RHYMED PROSE

The *maqāma* is a genre of rhymed prose, usually written as a chain of dialogues and stories in the Oriental manner and interwoven with anecdotes, fables, and metrical poems, including Italian sonnets in Hebrew. Several books in this genre were written during the Middle Ages or translated and adapted from the Arabic (notably by Judah Ben Solomon al-Harizi and Emanuel of Rome). Usually the prose text of the *maqāma* rhymes throughout, though it has no meter and no limit to the number of syllables between rhymes. The number of members of each rhyme is not fixed, the distance between the rhyming members changes at will, and the sound patterns of such rhymemes also vary, from minimal matches to near homonyms. On the other hand, the quantitative poems, which are frequently introduced into this rhymed prose, are clearly marked by their strict adherence to classical meters and rhyming.

A typical case of a different kind of rhymed prose is the religious-philosophical poem "Keter Malkhut" (Royal Crown) by Ibn Gabirol. Though rhyme and rhythm play an important role in this work, their use is neither permanent nor regular; the poem may be considered a kind of richly adorned free verse, changing its rhythmical tone from densely rhymed sound orchestration to mere prose and from time to time employing parallelism.

RHYME IN MEDIEVAL HEBREW POETRY

TERMINAL RHYME

Rhyme in Hebrew poetry in Spain, and throughout the Diaspora in the Middle Ages, was terminal: rhyming the last syllable, disregarding stress or morphology. The rhymeme included all sounds from the consonant preceding the last vowel to the end of the line. Hence, there were three basic forms of the rhymeme:

DO	נוֹדוּ	הוֹדוּ -	לְהַגִּידוֹ -
DOT	חֲרָדוֹת	חֲמוּדוֹת -	חִידוֹת -
DOD	וְנָדוֹד	מָדוֹד -	כְּיָדוֹד -

The norm is N = CV(C). The number of sounds included in the rhymeme (two or three) depends on the language: whether the final syllable is open or closed.

In order to make rhyming easier, the poets made wide use of rhymemes with open syllables (DO) or with suffixes (DOT), as in the first two of the above examples, thus having to change only one root consonant. This tendency was motivated by other principles of medieval poetics. Since there was no requirement for individuality in imagery or theme, the poets could use the Hebrew plural suffixes throughout their long poems. The same holds for possessive particles, such as ךְ, ("yours," when addressed to God), ךְ ("to Zion"—feminine), etc.

The obligatory requirement that a consonant precede the final vowel, similar to the French *consonne d'appui*, was peculiar to medieval Hebrew poetry and not necessary in other languages. It was a compensation for the missing stress that is required in Modern Hebrew poetry. Here is a typical example:

	Medieval Hebrew		*Modern Hebrew*	
	סוֹרֵג		מְדַלֵּג	סוֹרֵג – מְדַלֵּג ÉG
REG		LEG		
	דֶּרֶג		שֶׁלֶג	שֶׁלֶג – פֶּלֶג ÉLEG

In Modern Hebrew, as in European languages, ÉG is a perfectly sufficient rhymeme if the stress is equivalent. In medieval poetry an additional preceding consonant had to be included in the rhymeme (LEG). On the other hand, in penultimately stressed rhymemes (feminine) in modern poetry the inclusion of one syllable is not enough. The principles changed, but the overall proportion between the vocabulary of the language and the rhyming patterns remained similar.

This relationship between modern and medieval Hebrew rhyme may be compared to the difference between English and French rhyme. Whereas in French, *rime riche* (rich rhyme, using *consonne d'appui*) was welcomed as a way to avoid grammatical rhymes, in English that "intrusive consonant" was often excluded from the rhyme. The situation is similar: French rhymemes are based, for practical reasons, on the last syllable, the words are longer, and an addition to the minimal rhymeme is welcome in order to avoid hackneyed rhyming. Only in Hebrew, however, was the use of the *consonne d'appui* obligatory; hence it may be called the *Hebrew terminal rhyme*. Its peculiar impact was felt especially against the background of Italian, German, Yiddish, and Russian rhyme, where such "enrichments" were discouraged.

THE RULE OF THE MAXIMUM

If the final syllable was based on a suffix, poets often strove to enrich the rhymeme, adding to it at least some part of the root. Though this was not a necessary rule (there appeared rhymemes of pure suffixes too), there was a strong tendency to include two root consonants in the rhymeme if possible.

But rich rhyming in Hebrew was limited by unwritten rules:

1) If the required final syllable (N = Norm) included two root consonants, no sound could be added to N. Rhymemes such as מִיד, דּוֹד, בָּל are both minimal and maximal.

2) If the final syllable (N) included one root consonant, a preceding vowel could be added; thus there are rhymemes such as לִי, כִּי, לִים, רִים but also לִי, רֶם, etc.

3) If the final syllable (N) included no root consonant, one root consonant could also be added; thus, besides rhymemes such as –הֶם, -נוּ, -יְךָ there are יְהֶם, יָנוּ, and נֵינוּ, לֵיהֶם, רָיְךָ.

PENULTIMATE (FEMININE) RHYME

Stress as a criterion for rhyme was disregarded in medieval Hebrew poetry. Counting meter meant counting the syllables (or words), yet a secondary, "subterranean" accentual tradition developed a "penultimate" rhyme based on penultimately stressed endings. These are in a small minority of words and are represented by several suffixes and in word endings with ה, ע, like a *stealthy a* (עַ, וֹעַחַ, וֹחַ).

Penultimate accentual rhyme became obligatory in one kind of meter, a meter composed of unequal hemistichs in which the final foot has a cord instead of a peg, e.g. the *ha-shalem* (b): CCP CCP CCP/CCP CCP CCC. The ending presents a change in the regularity of the meter—where a P was expected, a C appeared instead. As a compensation for this frustrated expectation, the poet used in this case a stress-bound penultimate (feminine) rhyme, unheard of in the theory and criticism of this poetry.

Penultimate rhyme always appeared in all meters with no exception where the end of the line was shortened and an expected P was cut. With the meter *ha-shalem* (b) it became prominent in countries where a Romance language was spoken, especially in Italy, where penultimate rhymes were the dominant rhyming form. This meter, *ha-shalem* (b), provides eleven-syllable lines and a feminine (accentual) penultimate rhyme as well—meeting two principles of Italian aesthetics, for which responses were found in the internal tradition. This became the majority meter, instead of the old *ha-merubbeh*: PCC. This is a total phenomenon; all poems with a suppressed ending are written in accentual feminine rhymes.

Elsewhere, in the majority of Hebrew medieval poems, stress was disregarded. Words ultimately and penultimately stressed—Sephardic and Ashkenazi—rhymed freely with one another in their last syllable.

THE DISPERSION OF THE HEBREW TERMINAL RHYME

The Hebrew terminal rhyme originated in the Palestinian Hebrew liturgy as an alleviated form of its "difficult" rhyme. It may be found both in Eretz Israel after Kallir and in ninth-century Byzantine southern Italy. It developed again, as a simplification of the "Kallirian" rhyme, in tenth-century Babylonia (Saadiah Gaon) and in eleventh-century Germany. It was strengthened by the comparison with the Arabic rhyming norm (which required one consonant and the vowel following it) and later with European terminal rhyme, which knew no discontinuous rhymeme.

This norm, of rhyme in the last syllable, stressed or not, persisted in Hebrew throughout the world until the end of the eighteenth century, except in Italy, where a feminine stress requirement had been accepted in rhyme since the seventeenth century (but in Italy, too, no violation of the Hebrew norm could be found). The norm also remained obligatory throughout the Ashkenazi domain (today's Germany, Poland, etc.), though Ashkenazi Hebrew had become a penultimately stressed language.

The Ashkenazi penultimate stress in Hebrew caused a neutralization of all final vowels. Nevertheless, the rhymeme remained exclusively in the final syllable, contrary to reason but in accordance with conservative tradition. Thus Meir ben Samuel of Sczebrzeszyn, in his historical chronicle, rhymed in eight-line strophes words such as פָּקִיד־נִפְקָד־עוֹיקֶד, obviously pronounced *pokəd–nifkəd–oykəd,* in the last, unstressed, syllable. The paradox is that though the original *i, o, ey* (or *i, a, e*) were blurred into one ə-sound in an unstressed position, rhyme remained terminal: a repetition of the sounds in the final syllable only. This Hebrew conservatism is even more astounding in bilingual poems, such as the *Megiles Vints* (about 1616), with its regularly alternating Hebrew (H) and Yiddish (Y) strophes: H–Y–H–Y–HY. In the Yiddish strophes all rhymes are stress-bound (ultimate–monosyllabic and penultimate, making a two-syllable rhymeme). Even Hebrew words in Yiddish follow this rule. But in the parallel Hebrew strophes the same Hebrew words disregard stress: terminal rhyme is preserved. For example, *tfÍLE* rhymes in Yiddish with *megILE* (in two syllables) and in Hebrew in one syllable: *LA-megiLA.*

In only some cases, under the influence of foreign poetry, did Hebrew rhyme relinquish the requirement of the *consonne d'appui,* but in closed syllables only, where rhyming N = VC. Such was the case in some of the girdle poems (patterned on rhymes in a foreign language); e.g. Yehuda Halevi rhymes צָח-פֶּ-נֶאֱמָנָה

(AH—without a preceding consonant), which he would not dream of in his original Hebrew poetry. The same holds for the bilingual Hebrew-Arabic strophic poems of the Yemenite poet Shalom Shabazi and for the strophic songs of the sixteenth-century kabbalist poet of Safed, Israel Ben Moses Najara, who was apparently influenced by Turkish strophic songs.

HEBREW POETRY IN ITALY

The Jewish community in Italy was among the oldest in Europe; though small in number, it was an important cultural center throughout the Middle Ages. Located in a central position, between Eretz Israel, Yemen, and Babylonia in the east and Spain and Provence in the west, between North Africa in the south and Germany and France in the north, Italy was at the crossroads of the major cultural trends in Jewish history. Furthermore, it was situated in the most advanced culture of the European Renaissance. Hebrew poetry in Italy—the earliest examples of which are from the ninth century (*megilat ahima'ats*)—continued to be produced uninterruptedly until the twentieth century.[17] The changes of the poetic systems in Italy may be representative of the shifts in global Hebrew prosody throughout the centuries. But Italy was not one country; it was divided into many fiefdoms that often fought with one another. There are five major formal periods of Hebrew prosody in Italy.

(1) The poetry of southern Italy under Byzantine rule in the ninth century consisted of strophic piyutim, from two to ten lines in a strophe, each strophe having one separate rhyme. The rhymes were simple (terminal norm). Usually an acrostic was required in the beginning and sometimes a permanent refrain was used to close all strophes of a poem. Contrary to the "Kallirian" piyut, the early Italian piyut required a mandatory meter, based on a constant number of words in a line.

Though strophic poems were known in Latin and in Greek-Byzantine poetry of the period, in these languages rhyme was not yet a required, regular, or permanent device. Only in Hebrew did rhyme serve as a criterion for strophic structure, and it was obligatory in most genres (except for traditional blessings, written before rhyme was invented).

(2) In the tenth century and at the beginning of the eleventh, Italy accepted again the "difficult" Kallirian rhyme. It was, as it were, a "reversed evolution."[18] Shlomo (Solomon) Ben Judah ha-Bavli and other poets of that period composed in this vein. Their followers who moved to the Rhine area introduced

this norm into the Hebrew piyut of Ashkenaz (Franco-Germany). These circles edited the Italian and Ashkenazi *maḥzor* (prayer book) and included in it only such rhymed poems as were written by Kallir or followed his rhyming norm. (There are no Jewish Formalists?) In the following centuries, a number of *yotserot* cycles and a large number of *seliḥot* were created in this style.

(3) In the eleventh and twelfth centuries the norms of the ninth century were again revived: the piyutim were strophic poems with changing but separate rhymes, written in exact meters based on the number of words. The simplification of rhyme was apparently due to a variety of factors, one of the foremost being the influence of the Hebrew rhyme of Spain and Provence (though neither the concatenation of one running rhyme nor the syllabic meter was now required). The Spanish scholar and poet Abraham ibn Ezra propagated the simpler rhyme in Rome in the eleventh century. A second main factor was the decline of the difficult enigmatic style of Bavli, based on neologisms, ellipses, and allusions, which occurred in Franco-Germany too. Without this style, "Kallirian" rhyming was almost impossible.

In the thirteenth century Italian poetry in the vernacular emerged and flourished. Hebrew poets living in Rome could not have been unaware of the differences in the respective prosodic systems: (a) Hebrew strophic poems used changing but separate rhymes (*aaaa bbbb cccc,* etc.), whereas Italian rhymes were usually alternating (*abba; aba bcb,* etc.); (b) Hebrew meter was based on the number of words, Italian on the number of syllables; (c) Hebrew rhyme required a consonant preceding the last vowel, N = CV(C); Italian rhyme was stressed, usually penultimate: N = VCV. The Hebrew rhymeme spread over one syllable, the Italian over two rhymemes; Hebrew was based primarily on consonants, Italian on vowels. Hebrew poetry in Italy eventually adopted the Italian norms, but over a period of centuries, primarily through the transformation of forms existent in some other Hebrew tradition.

(4) Alternating rhyme was introduced into Hebrew poetry in the thirteenth century. The major poet who initiated this change was Benjamin Ben Abraham Anav. But Benjamin Anav did not directly imitate Italian forms; he switched to alternating rhymes by adopting the patterns of the girdle poem which had been developed in Hebrew poetry in Spain and Provence and meeting thus an Italian aesthetic norm. However, the poets of this generation did not transfer the system of quantitative meters from Spain; only a semi-regular syllabic meter, as in many a strophic piyut of Yehuda Halevi and Yitzhak Ibn Ghiyat,

was employed. Many such poems, of both Italian and Spanish origin, had by that time been absorbed into the Italian Jewish prayer book (*mahzor*).

(5) Emanuel of Rome (end of the thirteenth century–beginning of fourteenth century) was the major Hebrew poet who shifted to the use of both quantitative-syllabic meters and Italian strophic forms, primarily the sonnet. In both techniques he had predecessors, but the major achievement was his. With him, Hebrew poetry in Italy switched from liturgy to secular poetry. It seems that in order to find an equivalent for Italian poetic forms, Emanuel had to seek a language for secular poetry in Hebrew; this he found in the Spanish Hebrew tradition, which he accepted, with its rhymed prose (*maqāma*), quantitative meters, and imagery. Suddenly Hebrew poets discovered exact syllabic meters, as required by the Italian aesthetic taste, in their own language and tradition. In poetry every "short" was now counted as a full syllable. Nevertheless, the poets rigorously observed the places in the verse line where a "short" should have been.

Though the distinction between long and short syllables, a vestige of Arabic influence, was disregarded in the Italian Hebrew pronunciation of poetry, and every "short" syllable was seen as a full-fledged "long" one, such artificial quantitative meters persisted until the twentieth century: Isaac Hayim (Vittorio) Castiglioni wrote his sonnet on the death of Theodor Herzl in 1904 in a quantitative meter. Hebrew poetry in Italy moved from God to Herzl.

Moreover, Hebrew poets in Italy found meters in the Spanish Hebrew tradition which fitted the lengths of line favored in Italian poetry. The major meter, especially in the sonnets, was the endecasyllabic line (eleven syllables), for which a Hebrew poet could use either the most popular meter *ha-merubbeh* or the new cynosure, *ha-shalem* (b), counting both "longs" and "shorts" as whole syllables. *Ha-shalem* (b) became the major meter of Hebrew poetry, (P = V —) → CCP|CCP|CCC / — — V — / — — V — / — — — /, in the countries where Romance languages were spoken, owing to its mandatory penultimate rhyme, which fitted both Spanish-Hebrew and Italian taste. Emanuel of Rome accepted it for his sonnets, breaking each distich into two sonnet lines, with a rhyme for each distich. Lines with an even number of syllables had an ultimate rhyme, and those with uneven numbers, a penultimate rhyme. As in English poetry, the tenth syllable had to be stressed.

Here, simplified, is a *short story of a penultimate rhyme* through almost a millennium, told by stages:

1) *Ha-merubeh,* → /V — — — /V — — — /V — — /, was the most wide-spread quantitative Hebrew meter in Spain, with the last foot abbreviated: PCC/PCC/PC.

2) By rule, after two identical ternary feet, a third foot, abbreviated, closes the verset.

3) In Italy, the short syllables were counted as full-length syllables. Hence the line was read as an Italian eleven-syllable meter: → /V — — — / V — — — /V — — /. The "short" did not matter at all, yet it was precisely observed as a conventional gesture to Hebrew tradition in language and poetry.

4) The same could have applied to a meter, where the "short" was not at the beginning of the foot. The difference between short and long is only in writing. *Ha-shalem* (b) cannot be at the beginning of a foot: → / — — V — / — — V — / — — V/. This is impossible in Hebrew, because no Hebrew word can end in a *shewa* ("short").

5) If such a shorter line eliminated one "short" syllable, the last foot must be shortened, making the meter: / — — V — / — — V — /— — — /.

6) In such a case, the loss is compensated for. The rule for that comes from a different prosodic system: switch from quantitative to accentual meters—which were unknown until this moment in Hebrew or elsewhere.

7) The compensation for the lost "short" syllable comes in the form of a penultimate stress in accentual-syllabic terms. This is an absolute rule, with no exceptions. All the lines in this meter end in a penultimate (feminine) rhyme. Hence, for example, all the poems ending with a stealthy vowel in words ending in *ḥet* and *'ayin* have a penultimate rhyme (*eyah, oaḥ*).

8) The same is true for all other meters (with no exceptions), which end with a curtailed "short." An example is Yehuda Halevi's "Zionide," written in a verse meter: / — — V — / — V — — /, CCP/CP//CCP/CC. The rhyme is *asiráikh–ÁYIKH*. The last syllable has to be shortened, but at the end of the line there is no *shewa* in Hebrew, and the loss is compensated for by a feminine ending from another system (accentual).

9) The accentual penultimate ending pleased the ears of Italian and Spanish readers. But such endings were used long before there was a Christian environment.

10) The advantages of *ha-shalem* (b) are that the number of syllables is eleven, and the rhyme is accentual-penultimate. This became the leading meter in Italian Hebrew poetry for centuries.

11) In the central and east European Haskalah, the short/long distinction is dropped overnight, in a direct derivation from the Italian model. All lines have to end and/or rhyme with a penultimate ending.

12) A further paradox lies in the requirement to use only such penultimately stressed syllables (*mil'eyl*) that are accepted in the Sephardi/ Italian reading (*mil'ra*).

13) The Hebrew poets in eastern Europe pronounced words according to their Ashkenazi pronunciation, where most of the words were given a penultimate stress. Yet they were forced to use only Sephardi-sounding rhymes, which constituted only about 8 percent of their language.

14) Emanuel of Rome introduced stressed rhyme and alternating rhyming only for his Italian strophic forms. In other parts of his book *Maḥbaroth Emanuel,* he completely accepted Spanish Hebrew traditions, employed the running rhyme widely, rhymed his prose, disregarded stress, etc. His was the combination of two systems with a common denominator: the quantitative meter.

15) After Emanuel of Rome, Hebrew poetry adopted a variety of other Italian strophic forms (in addition to the sonnet, which became the most popular): ottava rima, Dante's terza rima, sestina, canzonetta. Nevertheless, strophic forms of the piyut on the one hand and the Spanish running rhyme on the other lived on for centuries.

16) Despite the domination of quantitative meters, a new syllabic meter (counting syllables and disregarding stress) evolved. Its first major exponent was Moses Ben Isaac Rieti (beginning of the fifteenth century), nicknamed Il Dante Ebreo for his book *Mikdash Me'at,* written in the form of Dante's terza rima. Rieti understood that Hebrew had to rhyme primarily in ultimately stressed words (ultimate rhymes) and accordingly reduced his line from eleven to ten syllables, with a stressed rhyme on the final syllable. Whereas previous Italian attempts at Hebrew syllabic meters (thirteenth century) disregarded "short" syllables altogether, according to their Spanish prototypes, Rieti counted short syllables as completely equivalent to long ones. He abolished the limitation of shorts to particular spots in the metrical scheme. But Rieti's innovation, i.e.

syllabic meters without the quantitative distinctions, did not become prominent in Italian Hebrew verse until the eighteenth century.

17) For several centuries, Hebrew poets retained the distinction between Italian strophic patterns and the liturgical tradition in the structure of their rhymes. On the whole, rhyme was terminal, accentual rhyme being reserved for the sonnet and other Italian patterns. Thus Joseph ha-Zarefati (twelfth century) writes his octaves in ultimate rhymes but still follows the Hebrew rule of a required *consonne d'appui* (thus פֶּר PAR and בֶּר BAR are for him two different rhymemes). Only in the seventeenth century was the change completed; accentual rhyme according to the European norm became mandatory. Despite the nature of the Hebrew language, which favored ultimate rhymes, under Italian influence penultimate rhymes became dominant. Since the eighteenth century penultimate rhyme has been almost exclusively used. It was employed primarily in the *ha-shalem* (b) meter, or in derivations of it: either one or both "short" syllables were dropped or the line was shortened, as in Moses Hayim Luzzato's *la-yesharim tehillah,* where there are two kinds of verse line, (a) eleven-syllable, → / — — V — / — — — — / — — — /, CCP/CCCC /CCC, and (b) seven-syllable, / — — V — / — — — /, CCP/CCC, with each retaining merely one historical "short" syllable. Some of Luzatto's followers in Italy and in Amsterdam dropped this last vestige of quantitative metrics, thus paving the way for the forms of the new era, the Haskalah.

18) Another Italian development should be noted: the earliest invention of accentual iambs in Europe, which was accomplished in Yiddish rhymed romances by the Venetian multilingual Ashkenazi poet Elia Levita about 1508/1509.[19] Northern Italy was at that time a center of Yiddish literature and its early printed books. Elia Levita, a grammarian, a versatile scholar, and a poet, was fluent in several languages. He wrote Hebrew verse both with the Sephardi pronunciation, using quantitative meters, and in the Ashkenazi vein, using free-accentual verse. When adapting long Italian strophic romances, such as *Buovo d'Antona* (in Yiddish, the *Bovo-bukh*) and *Pariz un Viene,* and creating strophes in pure ottava rima in a quite modern Yiddish, he merged the Italian syllabic principle with the Germanic accentual principle (which ruled Yiddish poetry until his time) and developed his iambic tetrameter. The process of this invention should be of major interest to comparative prosody, but with the decay of the Yiddish center in Italy, his iambic tetrameter did not last in Yiddish

poetry. Accentual-syllabic meters reappeared in Yiddish and in Hebrew under Russian influence as late as around 1890.

The overlapping of principles from three metric systems—the Hebrew quantitative, the Italian syllabic, and the biblical accentual—in one verse line did not hamper but rather encouraged the creation of a fourth system in the same verse: the accentual-syllabic meter in its iambic form. How did that come about? The major quantitative meter used in Hebrew in Italy was *ha-shalem* (b): → / — — V — / — — V — / — — — /. Since short syllables cannot be stressed in Biblical Hebrew, the third and seventh syllables were unstressed. Italian poetry opposed a stress on the fifth syllable before the caesura. On the other hand, the tenth syllable was stressed by the rule of rhyme. The biblical rule precluded two adjacent syllables from being stressed (if that happened, the first stress would move backwards by the rule of *nasog aḥor*, which was the law in Hebrew poetry until Fichman practiced it in the 1930s–1950s). The ninth and eleventh syllables were also excluded from stress, being adjacent to the tenth, stressed syllable. The syllables on both sides of a definite stress must be unstressed: / 0—0 /. The following pattern emerged:

Syllable Number:	1	2	3	4	5	6	7	8	9	10	11
Spanish		0					0		0	–	0
Italian				0					0	–	0
Rhyme & caesura					0	–	0		0	–	0
Summary		–	–	0	–	0	–	0	–	0	–	0

In Italy, all Hebrew short syllables (*shewa* and *ḥatafim*) are considered full syllables. Why use *ha-shalem* (b) for Italian Hebrew poetry? The Italian eleven-syllable line could be served by the most widespread Spanish meter, *ha-merubbeh*, as well: /V — — — / V — — — /V — — /. After two ternary feet, the third foot must be shorter, a rule which this meter fulfills. But if the first two feet are ternary, → / — — V — — / — — V — / — — V/, the third foot cuts the line after a "short," i.e. in the middle of a peg, or after a *shewa*—which is impossible in the Hebrew language. Hence the "short" has to be converted to a long: CCP/CCP/CCC/, or →/ — — V — / — — V — / — — — /.

This lack of a quantitative solution led, surprisingly, to an accentual-syllabic device: instead of the missing short syllable, there came as compensation an accentual penultimate rhyme, involving two syllables in the rhyme with the first one stressed. In hundreds of poems using this meter all rhymes are *mil'eyl* (penultimate). And so are all other meters that have a shortened "short" syllable—for example, Yehuda Halevi's "Zionide" (Carmi 347):

$$\rightarrow / -- \mathrm{V} - / - \mathrm{V} - / -- \mathrm{V} - / \stackrel{\smile}{-} - /\text{CCP CP CCP CC.}$$

As compensation for a problem in one system (quantitative), there was a shift to another system (accentual), a meter never heard before! Any cursory look at a Modern Hebrew Spanish anthology will show mandatory penultimate rhymes. Clearly, in spite of the Arabic theories, stress in Hebrew still occupied a place in poetic consciousness. This meter answers two questions about the Italian norm of eleven syllables and a penultimate (feminine) rhyme.

Only even syllables were allowed to receive a stress—and perfect iambic pentameter evolved. (Only the first foot was free to vary, but this is also the case with English or German iambics.) These iambs did not materialize until the Italian norm of not stressing the fifth syllable was disregarded.

Stress was apparently strong in Hebrew, and this tendency was felt and spread to other meters too. Despite the obvious iambic tendency, however, it was never formulated as such, being rather an automatic, unintentional result of the overlapping rules of several different prosodies. The nineteenth-century Haskalah poets in Germany and Russia were strongly influenced by late Italian Hebrew poetry (eighteenth century), but having a different pronunciation—Ashkenazi as opposed to the Italian "Sephardi"—they could not feel this underlying iambic meter. Though they entirely dropped all distinctions of a quantitative nature, they interpreted this verse as purely syllabic. Only poets in Eretz Israel of the 1930s–1940s, such as J. Fichman (Y. Fikhman), writing iambs again in a "Sephardi" (= Israeli) dialect, rediscovered the iambs of their Italian predecessors, especially iambic pentameter.

HASKALAH POETRY

The modern age of Hebrew literature began with the revival of Hebrew poetry in Germany in the eighteenth century. It is regarded as a "secular" period (though many of the poets were religious), since there was a conscious creation of poetry and prose written in the genres of contemporary European literature, which were conspicuously different from the genres of liturgy. Haskalah poetry was a direct descendant of Hebrew poetry in Italy and

Holland, especially in poetic narrative and drama. However, since this poetry emerged in a new social and politicized trend, the Enlightenment movement, and flourished more closely to the centers of the Jewish population in eastern Europe, it expressed a reorientation of Hebrew literature and may rightly be considered the poetry of a new period.

Haskalah literature was written and published by small groups of writers and their followers in Germany, Austria, Hungary, and Russia (including Lithuania and Crown Poland) throughout the nineteenth century. Though their ideas were, to some extent, typical of the European Enlightenment of the eighteenth century, Haskalah poetry cannot be considered to have a monolithic nature but rather to be an eclectic body of verse. This new poetry was indeed, from its beginnings, influenced primarily by eighteenth-century European literature, especially in the typical genres of epic or narrative long poetry (the Russian *poema*) and fable. It also embraced, however, genres developed previously in Hebrew in Italy, such as allegorical drama, and absorbed themes and motifs from nineteenth-century European lyrical and social poetry. An important genre that emerged here was translation, including *The Mysteries of Paris* by Eugene Sue (translated and abbreviated) and *The Negro Ithiel* (Shakespeare's *Othello*).

It seems that Hebrew literature lagged considerably in its development, compared with the evolution of European poetry, going through the stages of neighboring literatures only after those had been established as "classical." Thus one of the major Hebrew writers of the Haskalah in Russia, Yehuda-Leib Gordon (YaLaG), who lived for many years in the capital of Russia, wrote poetry in the vein of the Haskalah in the 1860s and 1870s, in the time of the unique giants Tolstoy and Dostoevsky and long after the poetry of Pushkin, Lermontov, and Tyutchev. But though Haskalah verse seemed to be a fossilized remnant of the eighteenth century, couched in a limited, biblical language and untouched by the poetics of Russian classical poetry, YaLaG also absorbed some influences from the social and "civic" poetry of his Russian contemporary Nekrasov. On the other hand, he continued to use metrical forms in Hebrew which antedated the Haskalah.

The meter of Hebrew poetry throughout the Haskalah was syllabic. Thus the poets continued to use the basic form of Hebrew versification in Italy (derived from Arabic Spain) despite the fact that their prototypes in German and in Russian were written in accentual-syllabic meters. Even translations from German poetry were transposed in Hebrew into syllabic meters, regardless of the German prototype; e.g. Schiller's "Die Glocke" ("The Bell," originally written in accentual-syllabic meters) was translated into Hebrew in syllabic meters, without stress regularity, and into Yiddish—the opposite—in accentual meters, without syllable counting. Stress, strangely enough, played no role in the Hebrew meters of this period, in spite of the fact that it was prominent in the daily speech of these writers and was even dominant in the meter of folksong in their spoken language, Yiddish, as well as in the small amount of Yiddish poetry that they wrote themselves, and, further, in spite of the fact that it ruled the versification of the German and Russian poetry which they strove to imitate. There was no traditional Hebrew poetic authority to back up this choice of syllabic versification—the venerated poetry of the Bible was accentual and relatively free in its verse forms. The only explanation could be a sense of continuity and the typical conservatism of Hebrew verse.

A fact that may have contributed to this situation was the move of eastern European Jewry from Poland to Russia, especially since Polish poetry was syllabic. In particular, the Vilna poets who read Polish acquired Russian a generation or two later. A few attempts were made in the second half of the nineteenth century to introduce accentual-syllabic meters—notably by A.-B. Gotlober and in a small poetry book by Luboshitski, published in Warsaw in 1900, with the meters of all poems marked in Sephardic Hebrew. But only Shimon Frug—one of the first Jews writing Russian poetry and accepted in circles of Russian poetry lovers—automatically accepted the Russian system of versification when he wrote poetry in Russian and inadvertently continued writing in the same meter when he moved back to Yiddish. H. N. Bialik in the 1890s, who read Frug under the table as a yeshiva student and absorbed Frug's major motifs, was among the first to use predominantly accentual-syllabic versification in his Hebrew poetry, in the yeshiva dialect of Ashkenazi Hebrew.

The new meters, influenced by the Russian and recent Yiddish prototypes, swept Hebrew and Yiddish poetry in the 1890s, paradoxically enough at the same time that the Symbolist movement, which eventually tried to break away from precise meters altogether, emerged in Russian.

THE SYLLABIC SYSTEM OF VERSIFICATION IN HEBREW

Haskalah poetry used the pure syllabic system that had developed in Hebrew poetry in Italy after the last vestiges of quantitative versification had been dropped. Every poem had its own meter, a permanent number of syllables in each line, with a stress on the penultimate syllable. Otherwise stress was not regulated. A permanent caesura was rarely implemented. The rhetorical and didactic tone supported this prosaic poetry.

Apart from marginal uses of quantitative meters—in writing, yet not in reading—inherited from medieval Spanish Hebrew, the poetry of the Haskalah did not apply the distinction between short and long syllables. The traditionally short syllables, *shewa* and *hataf,* confused the poets and were considered sometimes as syllables and sometimes as non-syllables. Naphtali Herts Wessely (Weisel), who introduced this system, used the *hataf* as a syllable at the beginning of words and as a non-syllable in the middle of words, and the mobile *shewa* as a syllable in the middle of the words and as a non-syllable at their beginning. It seems that Wessely tried to avoid the mobile *shewa* at the beginning of words in order to obviate the problem. With time, however, it became impossible to refrain from using a whole class of words (beginning with the mobile *shewa*) in Hebrew poetry.

SHIREI TIFERET (SUBLIME POEMS)

Wessely's epic poem was the classical prototype of all the poetry of the Haskalah. The prologues to each of the eighteen parts of his epic were written in eleven-syllable rhymed strophes, but the body of the epic itself was composed in thirteen-syllable unrhymed poetry. Wessely (Vayzel, in Hebrew) used penultimate endings exclusively, in both his rhymed and his unrhymed poetry. Unrhymed penultimate endings in his poem conformed with the Hebrew tradition inherited from Italy (where the penultimate syllable was stressed) and with his poem's German prototype, Friedrich Gottlieb Klopstock's *Messiah.* Wessely, however, in accordance with his Italian prototypes, resorted only to words which were penultimately stressed in both the Sephardi and the Ashkenazi pronunciation; these constituted a small and very specific part of the Hebrew vocabulary and caused an artificial tone in the style of their poems.

The firm grip of tradition meant the exclusive use of penultimately stressed (*mil'eyl*) endings in the Sephardi pronunciation in much of Haskalah poetry; their use was an absolute rule in the higher genres of poetry, especially in poetic drama and epic verse, and in the "higher" circles of the Haskalah, such as the centers in Germany and Vilna as opposed to those in Galicia and Hungary. The paradox of this use of *mil'eyl* in the Sephardi pronunciation is underscored by the fact that in other respects Hebrew was pronounced according to the Ashkenazi dialect, even in specific Ashkenazi subdialects. Thus in the Hebrew poetry of Lithuania (a major center of Haskalah literature in the second half

of the nineteenth century) the rhymes often betray the poet's domestic pro-
nunciation: נֶפֶשׁ - חֹפֶשׁ *kh'ofesh–n'efesh* became *kh'eyfes–n'eyfes* (both *holam* and
segol were pronounced as *ey, kheyfes–neyfes*, and *sh* and *s* sounded alike, as
in the pair רַעַשׁ - כַּעַס *ras–kas*, with שׁ and ס being equal to *s*). Though Lithu-
anian Ashkenazi pronunciation is evident in the poetry, two vowels merged
into one and penultimate stress were the general rule of the Hebrew words
in all varieties of the Ashkenazi dialect, and the Haskalah poets did not dare
use Hebrew in their own pronunciation as a natural resource for the manda-
tory use of penultimate rhymes. Such rhymes in the Sephardi dialect were a
minority in the Hebrew language. Consequently most of the vocabulary was
excluded from rhyming and final verse positions.

The poet Mikhal (Micah Joseph Lebensohn), when he was young, was
negligent in this respect and rhymed words which were perfectly equivalent
in his own Lithuanian Ashkenazi dialect but which appeared as a mixture of
milera and *mil'eyl* (ultimate and penultimate) rhymes to a distant Sephardi
ear. He was scolded by the Italian Hebrew scholar Š. D. Luzzatto (SHaDaL).
Both Mikhal and Yehuda-Leib Gordon, in his later period, broke the rule
and, on and off, used words which are penultimate only according to the
Ashkenazi pronunciation. But even then the majority of rhymes were still
based on words which are considered *mil'eyl* (penultimate) in the Sephardi
pronunciation. What used to be a mandatory rule became a habit or even a
matter of merit in poetic style.

This phenomenon had a strong effect on the style of Haskalah poetry. In the
Sephardi dialect, words of the *mil'eyl* form exist only in several specific groups:
(1) a small group of nouns penultimately stressed (אֶרֶץ - קֶרֶץ – פֶּרֶץ) which
recurred endlessly in the rhymes of the Haskalah and became clichéd emblems
of this poetry; (2) a variety of archaic forms (אֲחֵלוֹמָה, בָּמוֹ, לָמוֹ, מֶנְהוּ) ; (3)
several forms of the verb (הפריעה, אמרתי), notably in the biblical end-stop
pronunciation (יִנְהָרוּ, יְבָעָרוּ); (4) a group of penultimate endings (אוֹמֶרֶת
תֵּבִינִי). Since other sources were limited, the penultimately stressed forms of
the verb became prominent in the rhymes of Haskalah poetry. As a further
and radical result, the rules of rhyme caused sentence inversion, since the
verb was closing a verse line, and enjambment was excluded; all comple-
ments of the verb—similes, etc.—preceded the verb rather than followed it
(as the usual word-order would require). The following is a typical strophe
of this kind:

וּבֵין כֹּה וָכֹה הַדְּמָמָה הִפְרִיעוּ

תּוֹפְשֵׂי הַמָּשׁוֹט בַּמַּיִם יַחְתֹּרוּ;

גַּם קוֹל עַל הַמַּיִם עַם רָב הִשְׁמִיעוּ,

גַּם דָּוִד גַּם רֵעוֹ מִשְּׁנָת נֵעוֹרוּ.

> Meantime the silence they interrupted,
> The crew in the water rowed;
> A voice on the water a multitude emitted,
> And David and his friend from their sleep awoke.

In spite of the accepted Ashkenazi pronunciation in the later poetry of Yehuda-Leib Gordon, most of the words in his poetry were excluded from the rhyme position: a relatively small group of words (Sephardi penultimate), constituting only 8 percent of the normal language continuum, were used in 90 percent of his rhymes. With the collapse of the restriction to the Sephardi stress, no revolutionary change occurred in the rhymes of the Haskalah, since the typical rhymes became part of the poetic style as such. Only a fundamental change in poetic style and in the very conception of poetic language, introduced by the neo-Romantic poet H. N. Bialik and his generation, was to alter radically the resources of Hebrew rhyme, making available for rhyme practically the whole range of the Hebrew language. During the Haskalah, this freedom was enjoyed only sometimes in minor genres and by poets on the geographical periphery (poets from Galicia and Hungary).

Though the tradition of epic poetry in the Haskalah began with Wessely's blank verse, rhyme became, in time, dominant in this domain too, especially in the Lithuanian center and other places under the influence of Russian poetry. Very often the poets of the Haskalah used a variety of strophic forms of more than four lines, notably the strophe developed by Wessely consisting of six lines and rhyming *aabccb,* the ottava rima inherited from Italy, *ab ab ab cc,* and other strophic patterns, especially of six or eight lines. The four-line strophe was also widespread, primarily in the form of *abab,* but it was not as predominant as in the Russian-oriented poetry of later generations.

The strophic forms in all their variety usually used alternating rhymes, the members of one rhyme alternating with the members of another rhyme. Rarely did a Haskalah poet systematically use one rhyme more than twice without alternating. In this respect, Hebrew poetry conformed to the prevalent European sense of rhyme variation. On the other hand, there was no alternation whatsoever of rhymes insofar as their rhythmical properties were concerned. Though Russian poetry alternated, as a rule, not only the rhymes but also their rhythmic patterns, combining ultimate and penultimate rhymes, or ultimate and dactylic rhymes, throughout a poem, Hebrew poetry of this period did not accept this norm. Penultimate feminine rhymes in the Ashkenazi dialect were the absolute rule, except for sporadic, non-systematic uses of ultimate rhyming words.

In Italy such a restriction of the language could be understood as influenced by a taste formed through the reading of Italian poetry, in which predominantly penultimate rhymes are used; this is a concomitant of the structure of the Italian language. In Russia, however, the restriction made no sense at all and can only be explained through the compulsion exerted by the internal Hebrew tradition. Paradoxically enough, this requirement continued to obtain even at a time when penultimate rhymes were drawn merely from the words regarded as penultimate according to the Sephardi pronunciation, i.e. when the bulk of the language could have been used for the purpose of ultimate rhymes. It was only Bialik's generation that, again paradoxically, attempted to alternate between penultimate (feminine) and ultimate (masculine) rhymes, in spite of the scarcity of the latter in the Ashkenazi dialect, which became in this generation the accepted language of Hebrew verse.

Nevertheless, though poets disregarded stress in the syllabic system, it may have subconsciously played a role in forming the rhythmic nature of Hebrew verse in the Haskalah period. The most widespread meters involved thirteen and eleven syllables. Such line lengths conformed very well to the structure of four major accents, or four words, grouped together mostly in two pairs. This correlation may have played a role in the acceptance of Haskalah poetry, for there was, to the ear, an underlying quasi-biblical meter, felt even more because of the primarily biblical language used in this poetry. A line of eleven or thirteen syllables, using four major stresses, in a language in which the average number of syllables to each stress is about three, can easily be brought to approximate an amphibrachic tetrameter. For example, the first strophe of A. D. Lebensohn's poem לַבֹּקֶר רִנָּה in the Ashkenazi pronunciation can be read:

←

|∪ — ∪∪ — ∪|∪— ∪∪ — |	קוֹל תִּשְׁמַע נַפְשִׁי הֲמוֹן צִבְאוֹת חַיִל
|∪ — ∪∪ — ∪|∪— ∪∪ — |	רְנַת כּוֹכָבִים וּבְרֹאשָׁם יָרֵחַ;
|∪ — ∪∪ — 0|∪ — 0∪ — ∪∪|	עַל מִשְׁמֶרֶת אֶרֶץ עָמְדוּ בַּלָּיְל,
|∪ — ∪∪ — 0|∪ — ∪∪∪ — |	עַתָּה כִּי בָא שַׁחַר לְבָם שָׂמֵחַ;
|∪ — ∪∪∪ — ∪0| — ∪ — ∪	גַּם נָגַע זֶה עַל עֵינִי וַיְעוֹרוּ,
|∪ — ∪∪ — |∪ — ∪∪— ∪|	וּמְלֹא כָל הָאָרֶץ אֶרְאֶה כִּי אוֹרוּ.

This is a typical Haskalah strophe (*ababcc*), with its syllables and rhyming counted only as Sephardi *mil'eyl*. But an Ashkenazi reading reveals the underlying ternary dactylic-amphibrachic meter in the poet's consciousness, sidestepped here only in the first hemistichs of lines 3 and 4, and in the second hemistich of line 5.

Toward the end of this period the unregulated stresses within the line became more and more often ordered, with many lines approximating four amphibrachs (perhaps with an extra syllable or a missing syllable in the caesura). Such were, for example, the poems of Š. L. Gordon (SheLeG) in the early 1890s.

Thus, for the second time in the history of Hebrew syllabic verse, the development was again toward an accentual-syllabic meter, dominated, however, by the amphibrach rather than by the iamb, which was prevalent in Italy, and it followed the Ashkenazi rather than Sephardi pronunciation.

Such is the story of the transformations of a major Hebrew metrical form. The quantitative meter of Spanish Hebrew poetry, originating in Arabic versification, was reinterpreted in Italy as syllabic meter under the influence of Italian versification. Hebrew syllabic poetry as written over a period of centuries (from the twelfth to the nineteenth) adopted Italian strophic forms without relinquishing the quantitative patterns of the Arabic heritage but shifted time and again into accentual-syllabic iambs. The poets of the Haskalah took up the same syllabic verse forms, continued to use them in spite of a literary environment which exclusively accepted accentual-syllabic meters, and imbued them with an underlying accentual, semi-biblical rhythm. They finally brought Hebrew poetry again to the verge of accentual-syllabic meters.

The development of Hebrew poetry should be considered as series of linked transformations rather than as a series of totally opposed and separate changes. There was no fundamental change in sentence structure and syntactical rhythm. Similar groups of words could constitute a verse line, since a line of eleven syllables was the most frequent length in all these periods, regardless of meter and dialect.

THE MODERN AGE: THE HEBREW RENAISSANCE

THE HISTORICAL SETTING

Though echoes of European literature and European poetics of the modern age had been heard in Hebrew poetry since the days of Dante and the Hebrew sonnet in Italy, Hebrew poets did not accept fully, until the very end of the nineteenth century, the consequences of the lyrical revolution accomplished by Goethe, Pushkin, and the English Romantics.

In this context we can observe the striking fact that Hebrew meter was based, until the end of the nineteenth century, on syllable counting rather than on the subtle and complex instrument developed in other languages with accentual-syllabic versification. English poetry since the sixteenth century, German poetry since Opitz (seventeenth century), Russian poetry since the middle of the eighteenth century—the whole modern period of these poetries—cannot be imagined without this metrical system. It is a system whose exact structures made possible the clear-cut distinction of a large variety of forms and also provided the background for clearly pronounced effects of particular rhythmical configurations, as observed by "close readers." These two assets were of primary importance for a poetry characterized by the individuality of the writer, the individuality of the poem, the reliance on a living language, and the immediate appeal to the imagination of the reader in concrete, sensuous images. Even free verse was rich and effective against this background. Such a poetics was accepted and absorbed by the Hebrew poets who, through an "externist's" secondary education, came to know the classical Russian heritage of Pushkin, Lermontov, and their followers. ("Externists" were Jewish students not allowed into a Russian gymnasium who took their matriculation exams outside the school.) A major method for studying Russian poetry was to memorize vast bodies of it (e.g. all of Pushkin's *Evgeny Onegin*).

The first poet to write most of his Hebrew poems consistently in accentual-syllabic meters was H. N. Bialik, whose first poem "El ha-Tsippor" (To the Bird) was published in 1894, about the same time when Russian Symbolism emerged; that movement strove to break away from the regularities of this very same metrical system. Bialik became the Hebrew national poet, but not because of his Zionism. Zionism simply continued the earlier poetry of the

"Love of Zion" movement. Rather, he became the national poet because he was the first poet in Hebrew who wrote poems as they should be written: in precise accentual-syllabic meters. "El ha-Tsippor" was both the first national poem and Bialik's last Zionist poem.

In Odessa before World War I, Hebrew poets wrote some of the best Hebrew poetry in the poetic mode of Russian literature of the 1830s, while young Jewish poets, writing in Russian, launched modernistic journals such as *The Flying Omnibus*. The beginning and the end of the major cycle of modern Russian poetry in Hebrew and in Russian seemed to meet at that one time and that one place. Obviously, Hebrew poetry could not for long be excluded from general developments, especially because it was being written by the same poets in Yiddish, a language closer to reality than Hebrew, which absorbed the waves of Modernism more rapidly. Thus, in one generation Hebrew poetry not only caught up with the European classical heritage as it had been conceived by the early nineteenth century but landed, in one grand leap, in the European twentieth century. The struggle and interaction between a variety of poetic trends—evolution turning rapidly into contemporaneity—make this one of the most fascinating periods of Hebrew poetry. But in a survey it is difficult to keep apart the "generations" and trends of poetry in which unequivocal norms persisted. Free verse was developed almost contemporaneously with the emergence of exact meters. Modernistic rhymes were intermingled with exact "classical" rhyming, on the one hand, and with blank verse, on the other. Such developments make it advisable to discuss forms and formal systems— "regular" or "modernistic"—rather than periods of poetry.

Another objective difficulty in discussing the rhythms of Hebrew poetry in the twentieth century is due to the revolution in the pronunciation of the Hebrew language itself, which undermined its whole prosodic foundation. The rhythm and sound orchestration, so essential to the classical poetry of the preceding generation—H. N. Bialik, S. Chernikhovsky, J. Fichman, J. Steinberg, Z. Shneour—is lost to Israeli readers. The poetry of the Hebrew revival in Russia at the end of the nineteenth century (in the so-called *Teḥiya* [Renaissance]) was concrete and sensuous and subtle in rhythm and sound, the subtlety the result of employing Russian sensibilities; it unfolded the sound values of the language in the Ashkenazi dialect. But almost at the same time there was in Israel a revival of Hebrew as a spoken language, which used the Sephardi or, more precisely, an "Israeli" pronunciation. The Israeli dialect of Hebrew is marked by open, productive creation. It adapted logical European shifts in syntax for purposes of argument and dialogue and adopted the least common denominator in the range of phonemes. Specifically, Israeli Hebrew adapted all—and only—the vowels of the Sephardic dialect and only the consonants of the Ashkenazi.

The most prominent change is in the placement of stress: on the ultimate or penultimate syllable. The clash between the two dialects was sometimes fierce. One example may suffice. The two words עֹז־רֶתֶת (courage–trembling) were a perfect rhyme in the Lithuanian Ashkenazi poetry of the poet U. N. Gnessin. In the new, Israeli dialect, they are pronounced *oz-rétet* rather than EYS–rsEYS (with both *ḥolam* and *tsere* being pronounced *ey,* and ת sounding like *s; z = s* in a rhyme according to the Russian convention of neutralizing voiced consonants in end positions). The Sephardi pronunciation was also employed in Hebrew meters in this period—indeed, as early as 1900 (not counting some experiments during the Haskalah period or the unintentional iambs of Hebrew poetry in Italy). The Ashkenazi pronunciation was still dominant in the Hebrew poetry of the 1920s and was alive with some poets until the 1940s. This coexistence again complicates any precise discussion of historical trends.

The shift of dialects brought a revolution in the sound system of the language; nothing like it occurred elsewhere in such an abrupt manner. In the process most of the poetry of the period of revival was lost in terms of its musicality and rhythm, but the poets who moved from one Hebrew tongue to quite a different one, despite the pangs of readjustment, remained the same people, and so did their poetic ideals and norms. If they took a ship from Odessa to Jaffa or from Trieste to Haifa, they landed in a different linguistic universe and had to readjust to the new sound system or—the opposite—regain a way to work with the spoken language. Therefore it is possible, despite the crucial shift, to discuss prosodic norms, at first using illustrations from Hebrew poems with the contemporary Israeli pronunciation and later retreating.

THE TWO SUPER-DIALECTS OF MODERN HEBREW

When Hebrew became a spoken language, the seventeen teachers in all of Eretz Israel (Palestine) decided to adopt the principles of the "Sephardi" pronunciation, as spoken in Haleb, Syria, in which the location of the stress is based on the accent marks of the Bible. The majority of words in this Israeli pronunciation have a stress on their final syllable, and half of the vowels are lost. Only a small group of words are penultimately stressed; these are of two varieties: the so-called *segoliyim* with two *e* vowels, patterned as in *degel* (banner) and *regel* (leg), and words with the "furtive *pattah,*" ending in an originally guttural consonant, like תַּפּוּחַ (*tappúah*), רֵיחַ (*reíah*), and לָנוּעַ (*lanúa*). A larger group of penultimately stressed words is provided by several suffixes, such as the penultimate forms אוֹמֶרֶת (*oméret*—versus the ultimate form *omér*); verbs in some perfect forms, אָמַרְתִּי, אָמַרְתָּ, אָמַרְנוּ (*amarti, amarta, amarnu*), but those produce the dull and disparaged "grammatical rhyme"; and nouns in the plural with some possessive pronouns (דְּבָרֶיךָ, דְּבָרַיִךְ—*dvarekha, dvarayikh*). A new large group of penultimately stressed words consists of "international" borrowings: *akadémya, gimnázya,* etc.

Several distinctions in the quality of the sounds marked in the biblical vocalization system are blurred in the Sephardi dialect. Thus both *pattah* and *qamats* are pronounced **a** in Sephardi Hebrew; *tsere* and *segol* are pronounced **e**; and תּ and ת are both pronounced **t**.

The Ashkenazi pronunciation of Hebrew, developed in central and eastern Europe at least since the fourteenth century, is based primarily on the penultimate stress. With a few exceptions, a penultimate stress is absent only when it is impossible to implement it: (a) in monosyllabic words (a small group in Hebrew); (b) in bisyllabic words if the first syllable is a short one (*hataf* or *shewa*), e.g. בְּנִי, אֲנִי—again, a minority in the language; (c) in longer words where the penultimate syllable is a short one, in which case the stress moves to the third-to-last syllable to make a dactylic rhyme, e.g. הַמְּחוֹנְנִים (*ha-mehónenim*) and נַעֲרָה (*náarah*). In (b) and (c) there are exceptions, based on the fact that historically short syllables became normal and may be stressed, as were Hebrew words in Yiddish (e.g. חֲלוֹם should be *khalóym* but is often pronounced as in Yiddish: *khólem*). Compared to Sephardi Hebrew, Ashkenazi Hebrew has a wider range of vowel qualities: *qamats* is distinguished from *pattah; holam* and *tsere* are diphthongs. The weak ת (**th**) is pronounced **s** (rather than like the Israeli **t**). In general, the sounds of the Ashkenazi subdialect are a combination of the least common sounds of both: the vowels in Sephardic and the consonants in Ashkenazi.

Within the Ashkenazi domain there were several dialects, on the whole resembling the co-territorial dialects of Yiddish. In poetry these subdialects are felt not so much in the meter as in the rhyme.

Ashkenazi Hebrew with its diphthongs and penultimate stress was felt by poets to be "softer," less flat, and more "musical" than the tough, "masculine," and "harsh" Israeli Hebrew, which was ultimately stressed and in which the rather "pedestrian" sound **a** makes up 50 percent of all vowels in a text. Until the late 1940s several scholars and teachers tried to keep poetry in the traditional Ashkenazi dialect, but finally they had to give in and use the spoken language of Israel. Several poets attempted "translating" their poetry into the new dialect. By and large they succeeded in producing a mechanical meter, but in most cases the poem was severely harmed in the process. A variety of interesting transitional forms developed. One example is provided by Uri-Zvi Grinberg, a poet still writing in Ashkenazi Hebrew and accepting the institution of Ashkenazi poetry, who, in Israel in 1928, let the Israeli workers in his Ashkenazi poems speak in their authentic Israeli pronunciation while the poet's voice remained in Ashkenazi; he thereby created a reverse relation between frame and quoted speech.

ACCENTUAL-SYLLABIC METERS IN MODERN HEBREW

The dominant system of Hebrew prosody since the 1890s was accentual-syllabic. This versification system came to Hebrew poetry under the influence and in the forms of the Russian tradition of the nineteenth century, though some rhythmical characteristics of these meters are due to the structural properties of the Hebrew language.

Accentual-syllabic meters are based on ordering both the number of syllables and the location of stresses in a verse line. But it is rare, especially in Hebrew poetry, for the actual stresses in the language of a line to constitute a neatly ordered pattern, copying the metrical scheme exactly. Indeed, there is a discrepancy between the units of language and the units of meter: language stress and word boundaries, on the one hand, and metrical accents and feet, on the other. A meter "exists" in a poem if its actual stresses and word boundaries meet certain rules of correlation with the underlying metrical scheme.

TYPES OF METERS

A meter establishes a regular order of accented and unaccented syllables that underlies all lines of a poem (or a defined part of a poem). The sign (—) represents a metrically accented syllable, the sign (∪) an unaccented one, the sign (x́) a stress. The elementary recurrent group of syllables is called a foot. Thus in a line of the type →/ ∪ ∪ — ∪ ∪ — ∪ ∪ —/ there are three feet in the form: /∪ ∪ —/ (anapest). A foot is not a rhythmical unit; its boundaries do not mark any stop in reading; it is a mere abstraction of the basic principle underlying the pattern of a verse line.

Logically, there are two binary feet:

iamb /∪ —/
trochee /— ∪/

and three ternary feet:

anapest / ∪∪ —/
amphibrach / ∪ — ∪/
dactyl /— ∪∪/

Sometimes I use a four-syllable unit—paeon, but a paeon easily falls apart into two binary feet, a paeon III /∪∪ — ∪/ into two trochees, for example. The decision on this matter is impacted by the rhythms in other lines, the tempo of the text, and other non-metrical devices. Each foot has one accented and one or two unaccented syllables. A meter of a line is determined by the kind of feet and their number; an iambic pentameter is a line of five iambs. The number of feet is determined by the number of accents; the last foot may be incomplete and may vary throughout a poem. Thus, in an iambic pentameter there may be either ten or eleven syllables, ∪ — ∪ — ∪ — ∪ — ∪ — (∪), depending on the line ending or the gender of the rhyme. Usually in Modern Hebrew poetry there is only one kind of foot in a poem, i.e. one form of alternating accented and unaccented syllables (binary or ternary).

DEFINITION OF METER

There are two distinct ways to read a poem: (1) scanning (pronouncing the meter precisely while disregarding syntactic or intonational variations); and (2) stopping after every word boundary and at any intonation in between. A poem has a certain meter, not when it embodies a certain pattern, but when it *can* be read according to such a metrical pattern without going against its language. The general rule of correlation is: if a word receives any metrical accents, at least one of them must fall on the stressed syllable. According to this rule, (1) a word may be used for the accent on its stressed syllable; (2) a word may carry no accent in the given text; or (3) a word may have several accents, one of them falling on the stressed syllable. The following is an example of a Hebrew meter of four anapests: נוֹשֵׁב עֶרֶב אָפֹר וְעוֹרְבִים עַל תְּרָנָיו ← nŏshĕv ērĕv ăfŏr vĕ-ŏrvīm ăl trănāv / ∪ ∪́ – ∪ ∪ – ∪ ∪ – ∪ ∪ – / (Alterman, *Ha-ruaḥ im kol aḥyoteha*). The stress of the first word is disregarded by the meter: both syllables are unstressed, while the stresses of other words are employed by the meter as regular accents:

אָז חִוָּרוֹן גָּדוֹל הֵאִיר
אֶת הָרְחוֹבוֹת וְהַשְׁוָקִים.
עָמַד נָטוּי עַל פְּנֵי הָעִיר
נַחְשׁוֹל שָׁמַיִם יְרוּקִים.

→

Az hivaron gadol heyir	/ Ú — ∪ ∠ ∪ ∠ ∪ ∠ /
Et ha-rkhovot ve-hašvakim	/ ∪ — ∪ ∠ ∪ — ∪ ∠ /
Amad natuy al pney ha-ir	/ ∪ ∠ ∪ ∠ ∪ ∠ ∪ ∠ /
Nakhshol shamayim yerukim	/ ∪ ∠ ∪ ∠ ∪ ∠ ∪ ∠ /

The metrical scheme is a precise iambic tetrameter, but the language response is variegated: all second and fourth iambs in a line are stressed in the language, but only half of the first and third accents are materialized as stresses.

The first word of the first line (*az*) is stressed in language but unaccented in the meter, and the second word has two accents (*hĭvărón*, one of them on the stressed syllable). The second line provides only two stresses in its language: hence, the third line has full four iambs.

RHYTHMIC VARIATION

An expressive reading of a poem will consider language stress and word boundaries rather than the mechanical pattern of the metrical accents. Thus rhythmical variation is created primarily by the fact that not all accents of the meter are realized in the language. The division of actual stresses and word boundaries may vary from line to line, creating, for example, a trochaic strophe. Here, every "x" denotes a syllable, and an "x́" denotes an accented syllable. (The quotation is from Alterman's *Shirim she-mikvar.*)

דוּמִיָּה בַּמֶּרְחָבִים שׁוֹרֶקֶת.
בֹּהַק הַסַּכִּין בְּעֵין הַחֲתוּלִים.
לַיְלָה, כַּמָּה לַיְלָה! בַּשָּׁמַיִם שֶׁקֶט.
כּוֹכָבִים בְּחִתּוּלִים.

→

Dumiyá ba-merhavím shoréket.	|xxx́|xxxx́|xx́x|
Bóhak ha-sakín be-éyn ha-hatulím.	|x́x|xxx́|xx́|xxxx́|
Láyla, káma láyla! Ba-shamáyim shéket.	|x́x|x́x|x́x|
Kokhavím be-hitulím.	|xxx́|xxxx́|

[Silence whistles in the wide spaces.
Shining of a knife in the eye of cats.
Night. How much night! Silence in the sky.
Stars in diapers.]

In this case, the length is not equal in all verse lines: there are five, six, six, and four trochees in consecutive lines. The number of stressed syllables changes too, from three, four, five, to two, irregularly dispersed.

When read according to its language, every line seems to be rhythmically different. (The vertical lines mark off words.)

x x x́	x x x x́	x x́ x	
x́ x	x x x́	x́ x́	x x x x́
x́ x	x́ x	x́ x	x x x́ x	x́ x
x x́ x́	x x x x́		

The metrical pattern is an abstract grid. We have to fill it with language units.

In the Israeli Hebrew language there is, on average, one stress to each three syllables. In binary meters, which constitute the bulk of Modern Hebrew metrical verse (as of English verse), rhythmical variation is based primarily on omitting stresses in accented positions. This tendency usually follows the Russian symmetrical pattern of variation. Thus, in a tetrameter, a meter of four iambs or trochees, the fourth and the second accents are almost always stressed (unless changed for a special rhythmical effect). This is obviously different from the pattern in English binary meters, where the variation is largely based on the opposite possibility: stressing unaccented syllables.

DEVIANT METERS (TERNARY "NET")

In binary meters any variation is built into the system: there is a 3:2 relationship between the number of accents and the number of stresses. However, in ternary meters almost all accents coincide with stresses. In Israeli poetry, where, in most words, stress coincides with word boundary, the effect becomes tedious, especially in the anapest, where almost every foot is a word and almost every accent provides a stress. Poets did their best to create variation here, too, but the solution came in the form of a kind of free verse, *dol'nik*, adapted from Russian Modernist poetry (Akhmatova, Esenin, Mayakovsky, Tsvetaeva). In this system, the number of accents per line remains regular, but the number of syllables is to a certain degree free.

Usually, an impulse toward a ternary meter is created, to be disturbed on and off: instead of two unaccented syllables between two stresses, there is occasionally one or none (and with some poets, three). In a diagram, the abstract pattern looks like a "net," a ternary scheme with "holes" in it, which appear without any regularity but rarely enough so as not to destroy the underlying ternary pattern. Beginnings of lines are usually free, too, thus abolishing any distinction between the ternary meters, anapest, amphibrach, or dactyl. Two strophes by the poet Rachel are illustrative:

$\rightarrow$

Hen damá be-dami zorém	∪∪ — ∪∪ — 0 ∪ —
Hen kolá bi rán—	∪∪ — 0 ∪ —
Rachél, ha-ro'á tsón laván	0 ∪ — ∪∪ — ∪∪ —
Rachél—em ha-ém.	0 ∪ — ∪∪ —
Ve-al kén ha-bayit li zar	∪∪ — 0 ∪ — ∪∪ —
Ve-ha-ir zara	∪∪ — 0 ∪ —
Ki haya mitnoféf sudará	∪∪ — ∪∪ — ∪∪ —
Le-rukhot ha-mid-bár.	∪∪ — ∪∪ —

[Her blood turns in my blood
Her voice turns inside me
Rachel—the shepherd of Labon's sheep,
Rachel—the mother of mothers.
And therefore, the house is alien to me
And the city is alien,
For her shawl was fluttering
To the desert winds.]

The conversational tone is achieved here by breaking the anapestic flow. The same principle may be used for a variety of rhythmic tendencies and poetic themes and tones. It has become a major form of Hebrew poetry since the 1920s, developed by Rachel, Elisheva, Alterman, Khalfi, Zusman, Leah Goldberg, Bat-Miriam, and other poets who followed the Russian tradition. Except for the learned Leah Goldberg, almost all women poets wrote in deviant meters, influenced mainly by Anna Akhmatova.

FREE RHYTHMS

Since the beginnings of Hebrew accentual-syllabic meters, varieties of freedom from their strictures have been sought. Chernikhovsky used the dactylic hexameter widely in his idyls, varying one or two unaccented syllables. The effect was similar to that of the ternary net, but the excuse (or motivation) was that meter was an interpretation of the Greek quantitative meter followed by German poets, who varied the dactyls by using trochees (instead of the Greek spondee). Bialik tried his so-called biblical rhythms; but unlike in the Bible, the number of accents was fixed and the number of unaccented syllables varied in a limited way: one or two (and occasionally three) syllables in each interstress interval.

Just ten years after the initiation of the accentual-syllabic meters in Hebrew, a Hebrew poet appeared who wrote purely free verse: Avraham Ben Yitzhak (Dr. Sonne). The trend, based on the balancing of small word groups and phrases, was enhanced by the influence of German and Austrian Expressionism. That influence was exerted on such poets as Dr. Sonne and David Vogel, who both lived in Vienna. The trend was renewed by some of the young poets of the Palmach generation (1948) and was refreshed in the 1950s under the influence of English Modernism. The forms of free verse are too varied to be enumerated here.[20] Basically they lean on syntactic patterns, strengthened by parallelism and sound orchestration. At present, the whole range of Hebrew poetry from strict metrical verse to prose-like free verse is productive.

RHYME IN MODERNIST POETRY

Though rhyme in Hebrew is older than in any of the surrounding languages, and though its forms changed over the centuries, it was not before the 1890s that Hebrew rhyme accepted fully the European rhyming system. The principle of stress-bound rhyme had already been adopted in Hebrew poetry in Italy in the seventeenth century, but it actually applied to feminine (penultimate) rhymes only and did not involve the whole language until the end of the nineteenth century.

Viktor Žirmunskij, in his classical book, *Rhyme: Its Theory and History* (Russian), distinguishes "exact" from "inexact" rhymes. In Modern Hebrew poetry it is convenient to do the same. In "exact" rhymes, the rhymeme always extends to the very end of the rhyming members: *šMA–eyMA, novÉYAX–KerÉYAX*. In "inexact" rhymes some of the final sounds are not identical; i.e. the rhymeme does not always reach the end of the verse line, and the last consonant in each rhyming word is deliberately different: *mesoRÉGEt–baRÉGEv; lehaDŠÍ–kiDuŠIn; HA–xÓFEn–HA–ÓFEk*.

The inexact rhyme, a demonstrative dissonance and a symptom of Modernism, will be discussed after the basic exact norm, from which it deviated.

THE BASIC NORM OF THE EXACT RHYME

I distinguish four degrees of normativity in the structuring of texts, based on earlier definitions in Hebrew:

a) A *norm* is a law governing all instances of a phenomenon in texts.

b) A *tendency* is the appearance of a certain device that is not obligatory to be used in all instances.

c) A *symptom* is an instance typical of a body of text but appearing infrequently. For example, the first image of T. S. Eliot's "Love Song of J. Alfred Prufrock" is symptomatic of Modernism, but neither the rest of the text nor all the metaphors in it need to follow suit.

d) Free or localized expressions appear without establishing any requirement for the text as a whole.

Naturally, prosody is more rigorous in these requirements than other aspects of a text.

The basic norm of the rhymeme in Modern Hebrew poetry, as it is in most European languages, includes **all sounds from the last stressed vowel to the end of the line**: $N = \acute{V}(\ )$. The parentheses represent all sounds that may come after the last stressed vowel.

This accentual-terminal rhyme norm is opposed to the terminal Hebrew rhyme of the Middle Ages. An example is *šovÁX–heÁX; šenavÓXA–kamÓXA; dÁY LA–LÁYLA; lirkOŠ ET–KharOŠET.* The rhymeme in these cases includes at least two sounds (V́C, V́CV, V́CCV, V́CVC). All of these are minimal rhymemes: they may be enlarged ad hoc, but deleting one sound may destroy the rhyme.

Thus, the basic norm is not determined by the number of sounds involved in the rhymeme but by their position. The number of sounds following the last stressed vowel depends on the structure of the words; it is a matter of language rather than a matter of rhyming norm. In this system, a *rime riche* is based not on the number of sounds in the rhymeme but on the employment of sounds additional to the required norm, as in *tits–NAX–aNAX* (תִּצְנַח - אֲנָךְ). Though the rhymeme *NAKh* has only three sounds, it is a rich rhyme, since *AKh* would be good enough, whereas *ÉSET* in *IÉSET–nogÉSET* (לֶסֶת - נוֹגֶסֶת) is not rich, though it has four sounds, since it is the minimal sound group of the penultimate rhymes.

SECONDARY NORMS

In addition to the basic norm, several secondary norms are at work. Some are more general, while others are less obligatory or more restricted to certain poets or trends.

The Numeric Norm

Hebrew poetry with the Israeli pronunciation requires a minimum of two sounds in the rhymeme. In English, German, and Yiddish poetry, one stressed vowel at the end of a word is sufficient; *free–tranquility–sea, be–we,* and *go–snow* are perfect rhymes, well used in English poetry. But in Israeli Hebrew, as in Russian, a consonant has to precede the final vowel in such cases: *bitfiLÁ–leoLÁ* is a minimal rhyme (N_2 = CV́). Two sounds are enough, even when there is no consonant: *ligvÓA–elÓhA.*[21]

Hebrew poetry in the Ashkenazi pronunciation did not require this numeric norm. Bialik rhymed just **I** in lÍ–bnÍ (לִי - בְּנִי) and just **e** in *hazE–hapE* (הַזֶּה - הַפֶּה), using just the rhymeme **e** or **i** alone. The reason for this difference is obvious: there are in the Ashkenazi pronunciation very few ultimately stressed words (they are primarily monosyllables, a rather small group in the Hebrew dictionary) and even fewer monosyllabic words with open syllables. With the additional rule it would be almost impossible to rhyme these words. On the other hand, in the Israeli pronunciation most of the words are ultimately stressed, the number of vowels in the language is reduced to five, and an enormous number of words terminate in **a** (a relic of the historical *pattah, qamats,* and *hataf*). The use of this **a** for a rhyme would be too easy and trite to be effective.

The Historical Factor

A historical factor was at work in this development. Bialik and many of his contemporary "Ashkenazi" poets at the end of the nineteenth and the beginning of the twentieth century (Z. Shneour, I. Katzenelson, Jacob Steinberg, J. Fichman) wrote Yiddish as well as Hebrew poetry. Yiddish, like other Germanic languages, does not require the numeric norm, but the Hebrew poets of the next generation (Rachel, A. Shlonsky, Leah Goldberg) were overwhelmingly influenced by Russian poetry, where this norm is required.

The historical factor is felt again in the "young" Israeli poetry of the 1950s. Hebrew poetry now moved from the Russian to the English sphere of influence and away from rich and "colorful" imagery and rhyming to a rather prosaic poetics. Here again rhymes appeared, based on a single stressed vowel: *kÍ–tsivonÍ; lezokhrÓ–be–motÓ,* etc.

The Morphological Norm

In the Israeli pronunciation *šIR–kabIR* and *nIM–alIM* (אַלִים - נִים) are perfect rhymes, but *mexusIM–alIM* (עָלִים - מְכוּסִים) is not, since *IM* in this case is a morphological ending: the plural suffix of a noun, a verb, or an adjective. This secondary norm invites the participation of at least one root consonant in a rhyme. Minimal rhymes in this case are *mekhuSIM–maʾaSIM* or *aLIM–keLIM*.

Three Criteria of the Rhyming Norm

The basic norm may now be combined with the secondary norm: an exact rhyme in Modern Hebrew poetry in the Israeli pronunciation requires in its rhymeme all the sounds from the last stressed syllable to the end of the verse line, provided there are at least two sounds in the rhymeme and at least one is part of the root of the rhyming word. This complex rule makes three kinds of demands, regarding (a) the place of the rhymeme; (b) its minimal size; (c) its morphological structure.

Relativity of the Morphological Norm

The three heterogeneous norms have different degrees of validity in the writings of different poets or generations. The morphological subnorm seems to be the most flexible. Some suffixes are less susceptible to this norm, and some more. Thus Rachel, a poet of the 1920s who preceded the Hebrew "young" generation of the 1950s in the use of "prosaic" language in her lyrical poetry, was influenced not by English Imagism but by Russian Acmeism, especially in the poetry of Akhmatova. Rachel strictly applies the morphological norm to the non-feminine plural suffix IM (e.g. *raVIM–asaVIM*) but disregards this requirement for the feminine plural OT (*kalOT–netivOT*). Some "young" poets of the 1950s use even obvious grammatical rhymes, with the plural suffix IM as a sufficient rhymeme.

On the whole, the more widespread and comprehensive the use of a suffix in the language, the stronger the tendency not to rely upon that suffix alone. The opposition to "grammatical" rhyme, inherited from Russian poetry, was the strongest with the plural IM. On the other hand, the requirement to add a root consonant is weak in two-syllable suffixes, which are penultimately stressed, such as the dual *áyim*.

The "mistrust" of grammatical rhyme is often expressed in poetry written with far more adherence to poetic standards than is required by the norm. Thus Shlonsky uses rich rhymes especially when a suffix appears, as if to compensate for the very use of a suffix in a rhyme: *DIRIM–aDIRIM* (D + IRIM where IM would be sufficient), *MeDuROT–MiDoROT* (M + D + ROT), where *RIM* or *ROT* would be sufficient.

Minimum and Maximum

The norm defined above concerns the minimal group of sounds required in a rhymeme. In Hebrew poetry in the Israeli pronunciation there is a wide discrepancy between the minimum sounds required and the maximum actually used. Some poets, such as A. Shlonsky or N. Alterman, influenced by the poetics of Russian Modernism, employ rhymes as rich as possible: *tiKTE-FÉNU-KTEFÉNU, AKuMÓT-hAKoMÓT,* etc. The words in Modern Hebrew, having no secondary stress, are usually long (three syllables or more). Most of the sounds in the rhyming words of the poets under discussion are employed in the rhymeme. This tendency is doubly connected with the poetics of Hebrew "imagistic" poetry: (a) This poetry, which abounds in striking imagery, rich sound patterns, "strong" themes, etc., is associated with the general "colorful" aesthetics. There is a strongly expressed "set toward the message" (Jakobson), a high "density" of poetic language. (b) Since many sounds are involved in each rhymeme, it is quite difficult to find words to rhyme with one another. Only a poetic language with a high degree of flexibility in imagery and an elliptic combination of words could enable such freedom in connecting rhyming words drawn from distant spheres of meaning. The poetics of Eleazar Kallir can be considered the product of similar conditions.

The maximal limit for a rhymeme consists in leaving a minimal difference between the rhyming members. In such rhymes as Yehudah Karni's *K'I LU MAT-KIL'UMAT* (כְּאִלּוּ-מַת - כִּלְעוּמַת) and *YIF' AM-YIF AM* (יִפְעָם – יִיף עָם), the difference may only be in the place of a junction between two words. In Alterman's rhyme repeating twice, *LEXAYAYIX* (בְּגוּמַת לְחָיַיִךְ – לְחַיַּיִךְ), the difference lies merely in the different morphological structure of the two uses: in the first case ("your cheeks"), the *l* is part of the root לחי (cheek); in the second case ("for your life"), the *l* is a separate morpheme ("for") connected only graphically with the word חיים.

A COMPARATIVE PERSPECTIVE

Rich rhyme in Israeli Hebrew can be explained by more than the influence of one kind of Modernist poetics (coming from Russian Futurism). The properties of the language also encourage this tendency. Most of the words in the Israeli pronunciation are stressed ultimately, and most of the words are multisyllabic. Rhyming merely one syllable time and again would be tedious. Moreover, since most of the words are stressed ultimately, there are a multitude of words available for each rhyme ending. Israeli Hebrew may be compared to other languages. In Russian, where many words are also multisyllabic, accents may occur on any syllable of a word, so the number of words rhyming ultimately is relatively smaller, and multisyllabic rhyme is usual. In Yiddish, too, the number of penultimate and dactylic rhymes is much higher than in English.

In English the number of monosyllables is so high that ultimate rhymes are usual, as in Modern Hebrew. But the neutral sounds of each member are not strongly felt, since they are few. In a usual Hebrew word one of three syllables does not participate in a minimal rhymeme. Compare the English *pARTS–mARTS*: though the rhymeme is monosyllabic, most sounds of each rhyme member are covered by it. Compare that with the Hebrew *mešuXzÁR–veaXzÁR*, where the non-participating, "neutral" sounds of each member are conspicuous. Moreover, English has some different rhyming vowels (as compared to the mere five of Israeli Hebrew) and many consonant clusters, preceding and following the vowel, which makes the number of possible rhyme endings incomparably higher and the number of words available for each rhyme relatively much smaller. Since there are not many possible rhyme endings in Israeli Hebrew, it is much easier to meet the minimal rhyme requirements and also easier, and more necessary, to add sounds and "enrich" the rhymeme. French with its ultimate stress, though the language is more abundant in rhyme endings than Hebrew is, also tends toward *rime riche,* offering at least one sound more than the basic norm.

RHYME IN THE ASHKENAZI PRONUNCIATION

The basic norm of the accentual-terminal rhyme is identical in the poetry of "Sephardi" ("Spanish," including Italian) Hebrew since the Renaissance and in the poetry in the Israeli pronunciation, on the one hand, and in Ashkenazi Hebrew, on the other. It was accepted in European Ashkenaz at least from the fourteenth century on, but entered rhyme only in the nineteenth century. But the realization of the norm differed strongly owing to the difference in the rhythmic structure of the Hebrew word in both super-dialects.

Since the Ashkenazi stress falls on the second or third syllable from the end, most rhymes are automatically polysyllabic and most sounds of a word are included in the rhymeme. Thus, *mÍDBOR–nÍDBOR* (desert— had agreed) is a minimal and very usual penultimate (feminine) rhyme in Bialik's poetry, but the same pair makes a very rich rhyme in the Israeli pronunciation: *mIDBÁR–nIDBÁR* (five sounds, whereas two *AR*s would be enough). Therefore, rich rhymes are scarce in Ashkenazi Hebrew but could abound in Israeli Hebrew (at least in the practice of some poets). Moreover, the necessity in most cases to include at least two syllables in the rhymeme leads poets to search for alleviating devices. Thus Bialik in his early poetry tends to use grammatic rhymes which already have one syllable as part of the morphological suffix, so the poet has to find words which differ in one syllable only. This necessity also leads to the use of archaic endings, feminine forms, etc. In short, any marked form of a word will enrich the rhyme. The Israeli rhymeme EL נוֹזֵל - צוֹהֵל is thus pronounced *tsóyel-nóyzel* in Ashkenazi: this is not a rhyme. But the feminine form, with an added syllable, is: צוֹהֶלֶת נוֹזֶלֶת - (*tsoyhéles-noyzéles*). Therefore Bialik uses not the usual נוֹזֵל, or *nozel* ("running light") but a more archaic form, which is feminine: אוֹרָה נוֹזֶלֶת ("she-the morning light"). Feminine verbs or adjectives in rhyming position bring feminine nouns in the middle of the line. The same holds for other archaic, feminine forms and plurals.

"MODERNISTIC" RHYME: THE INEXACT RHYME

Modernistic Hebrew poetry uses a large number of inexact rhymes, such as Alterman's *ŠKuFÁ hI–miŠKaFAyIM; KoS HaM ÁyIM–KsuMÁ hI*, etc. In such rhymes at least one member ends with a neutral sound that does not participated in the rhymeme. But the effect is strong, since such rhymes usually have many sounds. There are a great variety of concrete forms, but in all cases the stressed vowel is constant—i.e. it is an accentual rhyme. In most cases the rhymeme is discontinued, and, using Kallir's model, the system may be called accentual-discontinuous. In addition to the fixed stressed vowel, the rhymeme is based primarily on consonants. This phenomenon of the discontinuous rhymeme, which is peculiar to Hebrew poetry, is based on the nature of the Hebrew lexical morpheme, which is discontinuous and basically consonantal with at least one obligatory stressed vowel.

This system, representing a strong break from the standard European norm, where the rhyme is accentual-terminal and is usually continuous, had its forerunner in the earliest system of rhyme, in old Hebrew liturgy (the piyut). But the concrete immediate influence that created this norm in Hebrew Modernism came not from the piyut but from the poetry of Mayakovsky, beloved by those who were excited by the Russian Revolution, and Pasternak, "our" Pasternak, where rhymemes were also inexact in their endings and moved back deeper into the middle of the line. While discontinuity in Russian rhyme was an occasional form of deviation (Voznesensky) rather than the rule, for Alterman and his contemporaries it became the norm, based on the characteristics of the Hebrew language.

Alterman uses both exact and inexact rhymes in the same poems. The minimal requirement for a rhymeme now is two sounds, at least one of which is the last stressed vowel. But only rarely was the minimal rhymeme employed. (An exact rhyme is, e.g. *zahÁV–yadÁV,* and an inexact rhyme is, e.g. *koXÓ–harXÓv.*) Most of the rhymes include many sounds. The sound contrast between the rhyming members was strongly emphasized by introducing neutral sounds in between the sounds of the discontinuous rhymeme, e.g. *SiPuNÉXA–kaSE PaNÉXA, LEORÉR–LEOR nER,* or by changing the order of the parallel sounds: *miTPARÉTSet–TRAPÉTSioT (TPAR*–TRAPTs). This discontinuous rhyme is, in principle, similar to the discontinuous rhyme in Kallirian piyut: both respond to the structure of the Hebrew word.

In sum, Modernist rhyme cannot be described merely in negative terms, as a dissonance or a deviation from a classical norm. The norm of the accentual-discontinuous rhyme creates a system as consistent and as effective as the accentual-terminal one, though the range of variation given to particular poets may be considerably wider now.

A BIRD'S-EYE VIEW OF THE HISTORY
OF HEBREW VERSIFICATION

A PAN-HISTORIC SYNOPSIS OF HEBREW PROSODIC SYSTEMS

The preceding historical survey presented a long chain of changes. When pan-historical comparisons are made, one finds inherent logical relationships, as well as mirroring and contrasts between systems which are distant in time and context but molded in the structures of one and the same language and culture. Table 4.1 presents the basis for such a comparison. In it the major systems of Hebrew verse are arranged clockwise, in the order of their emergence in the history of Hebrew poetry. Except for a meter based on musical pitch, all known verse systems were productive in Hebrew at one time or another. As can be seen in the table, there was a logical pattern, a kind of cyclic movement in this history. The foundations of the meter moved from phrase to word to syllable and back. In the end, rhyme was finished, unless the words were accompanied by song. Will there be a new cycle?

Table 4.1: The Major Systems of Hebrew Verse (in Their Logical and Chronological Order)

Time Period	Free Line Length	Fixed Line Length	
	Basis of Meter: Phrase	*Basis of Meter: Word*	*Basis of Meter: Syllable*
Antiquity and Middle Ages (From phrase to syllable)	I. *Bible*: free accentual meter • varying semantic-syntactic-rhythmic parallelism in phrase groups • sporadic rhyme	II. *Rhymed Piyut*: word meter • number of words • rich discontinuous rhyme based on whole word	III. *Spain*: quantitative meter • number of syllables + order of long/short syllables • rhyme based on last syllable
			IV. *Late Italy & Haskalah*: syllabic meter • number of syllables • stress-bound rhyme
Modern Age (From syllable to phrase)	VII. *Modernist*: free rhythm • changing balance of phrase groups • rhyme not obligatory	VI. *Modernist*: accentual "net" (in the Russian tradition) • number of major stresses + deviation from syllabic order • rich discontinuous rhyme based on whole word	V. *Modern*: accentual-syllabic meter • number of syllables + order of stressed/unstressed syllables • stress-bound rhyme

As the table shows, the earliest (I) and the latest (VII) verse systems, unconnected culturally to each other, were based on the free rhythm of phrase groups. In the Bible there was a strong rule of free symmetricity or parallelism, whereas in Modernist free verse there is an asymmetrical flow and line-to-line continuity, and the length of lines may be highly varied. In Modernist free rhythms in the post-classical period (VI), poets often employed different segments of accentual-syllabic meters as well as the effects of irregular rhyme. They were not exercising the freedom of "primitive" poetry, poetry that preceded any system, but the freedom of a "late" post-classical period, which included the freedom to employ any device developed in the "classical" rules of previous periods.

From biblical rhythm, based on the semantic-syntactic-rhythmical free parallelism of phrases (I), the development of Hebrew verse moved toward basing its meters on more and more exact measures, i.e. ordering smaller elements of the language—from phrases to the number of major stresses, through the exact number of words, to the number of syllables according to their prosodic features: length of syllables (III), then stress (IV).

Meters based on syllable counting ruled Hebrew poetry from about 950 until almost 1950. These were the most exact and varied systems of versification. Within this tradition, the change in the internal organization of the verse line from organization by a quantitative principle to organization by an accentual principle represented the general development of European poetry, but marked also the shift from the artificial "high" style of reading poetry to the intrusion of the cadences of the spoken language.

In Hebrew religious poetry of Franco-Germany (Ashkenaz) throughout the Middle Ages, a system based on the number of words persisted (II), i.e. a meter which, though numerically rigorous, was closer to representing some phrase patterns and resembled the rhythm of medieval Yiddish and German poetry.

In modern poetry the movement of the early centuries CE was reversed from strict syllable counting (III–IV), to a semi-regular meter, relying almost exactly on the number of major word stresses (VI), to a free verse system, based primarily on a rhythm of phrase groups (VI) and relying on the tension between the verse line and the syntactic units. But in this period, even within the domain of free verse (VII), the previous regular norms, accentual-syllabic (V) and accentual, deviant net (VI), were still widely employed. On the other hand, the essential difference between the major systems of Hebrew verse should not lead us to overlook some basic consistent trends which cut across several systems. Within each system not all possibilities were equally employed. In any system, a rather small number of possible forms were prevalent.

Observing the syntactic possibilities of Hebrew verse in different periods, one finds a predilection for a certain optimal length of line, persistent through the ages: three or four major stresses (nine–twelve syllables) in the Bible, four or five graphic words, eleven or thirteen syllables (including "short" ones), and three or four amphibrachs (nine–twelve) or iambs (ten), which are very similar in length of line and conveniently accommodate similar groups of words and phrases.

THE MAJOR SYSTEMS OF HEBREW RHYME

A similar pattern can be discerned in the history of Hebrew rhyme norms. Here, again, Hebrew poetry completed a whole cycle in its development. But rhyme was not as obligatory as meter. The earliest and the latest periods have no regular rhyme, that is, no rhyme in the strict sense of a sound device used regularly for the strophic composition of a whole poem. Table 4.2 presents typical rhymemes using the following symbols: V, vowel; C, consonant; R, root consonant (only where relevant); V́, stressed vowel; and +, discontinuity in the rhymeme. When read clockwise, the table represents the history of Hebrew rhyme as related to the major periods of versification shown in Table 4.1.

Table 4.2. The History of Hebrew Rhyme

No Regular Rhyme	*Decisive Vowel*	*Form of Rhymeme*			
		Discontinuous		*Continuous*	
I. Bible: free sound orchestration	Final	II. Kallirian Piyut: terminal-discontinuous		III. Medieval: terminal	
		RVR	ריק	CVC	ריק
		R + RV	מ+רי	CV	רי
		R + RVC	מ+ריס	CVC	רים
		R + R + CV(C)	מ+ר+הם (תִּי)	CV(C)	הם (תִּי)
VI. Modernist ("Free"): scattered rhymes	Stressed	V. Modernist ("Russian"): accentual-discontinuous		IV. Modern (Italy, Haskalah): accentual-syllabic	
			מבריק	V́C	יק
		CV́+	רי+מֹורי		
			דְּבָרִים	CV́	רי
		VC (V)+	וֹר+(אֹרַת עֹורֶק)		
		CV́C(V)	דְר+(דֶּרֶךְ-קֹודֶר-אַןְ)	RV́C	רים
		C + C + CV́ + (V)+	ק+ס+מָ+?י	V́CVC	וֹרֶק
		(KoS HAMAYIM–KSuMA HI)			

Disregarding some secondary developments, we find four major rhyme systems in Hebrew. The similarities and the differences between these systems are related to the form and location of the rhymeme. The upper part of the diagram is opposed to the lower part of the diagram with respect to the decisive vowel: in the Middle Ages the rhymeme relied on the final vowel in a line, in the modern age on the last stressed vowel. On the left are shown the extremes of rhyme, when the rhymeme could be discontinuous. On the right are shown the "classical" periods, when the rhymeme had to be a continuous and terminal chain of sounds.

There is also a correlation (though not an overlap) between the corresponding major systems of meter and rhyme, as may be seen from a comparison of both tables. At the extreme ends of this cycle, when rhythm was based primarily on phrases, i.e. was dominated by a balancing of syntactic and semantic patterns, no regular rhyme was necessary. In the "classical" periods (II–V), when meter was based on the number of syllables, rhyme, too, was syllabic: the medieval rhymeme was based on one (terminal) syllable; modern rhyme based its major distinction of rhyme gender (ultimate-penultimate) on the number of syllables. Typically enough, in verse systems in which the prominence of one word was basic, discontinuous rhyme developed—that is, rhyme mirroring the nature of the Hebrew word. However, this parallelism, essential as it was, was by no means automatic; word meter continued a long time after the suppression of the early discontinuous rhyme.

5

THE DISCOVERY OF ACCENTUAL IAMBS
IN EUROPEAN POETRY

METER AND RHYTHM: A MULTICULTURAL SYNOPSIS

Rhythm in poetry—whether conventional or original, whether schematic and trite, or sophisticated and individual—has always rested upon, or deviated from, or otherwise related to a central metrical system. Without the foundations of such a system no rhythmical effect is possible.[1] And without an analysis of the relations between the metrical framework and the pertinent properties of a given language, there can be no understanding of the basic rhythmical trends of any national poetry, either in its historical development or in its most idiosyncratic expressions.[2]

All this should be well known by now; however, in the large body of studies in this field we do not always find a clear understanding of the independence and interdependence of meter and rhythm, the dialectical tensions between norm and variation, between the historically predominant and the individually expressive, between general tendencies and on-the-spot configurations.

Assuming an awareness of such tensions and their historical contribution to the development of national literatures, I shall outline the problem of transition from one basic metrical system to another. I shall then discuss the concrete structural and cultural conditions of such transitions in several European literatures—in particular, the emergence of **accentual-syllabic (a.-s.)** metrical systems,[3] which prevailed in several languages between the Renaissance and the avant-garde (in the order of their acquisition or discovery: Yiddish, English, German, Russian, Hebrew) but not in Romance languages, such as

French and Italian, which developed different metrical systems, based on the number of syllables, while accent became secondary.

THE TWO METRICAL SYSTEMS OF ACCENTUAL POETRY

Languages with phonological and free stresses—for this study they were English, German, Russian, Hebrew, and Yiddish—have developed at least two accentual systems. By languages with a "phonological" stress I mean languages where a change in the place of the stress in a word can cause a change in meaning, as the change of a phoneme does. By "free" stress I mean that, at least on the face of it, stresses may occur in different syllables of a word. Thus in English we can find such pairs as dígest/digést, rébound/rebóund, rébel/rebél, présent/presént, próduce/prodúce. At least in some cases, the shift of the stress may cause a difference in meaning.

The two accentual systems have been (1) the "native," "tonic," or "*accentual*" meter, based on a regular number of accents per line (3+3 or 3+4) and a free number of syllables—as in parts of the Bible, in Old German, and in Old English; and (2) the accentual-syllabic (a.-s.) system that regulates both stressed and unstressed syllables, as practiced by Shakespeare, Wordsworth, Milton, Goethe, Pushkin, and most poets in their generations. Here, the number of syllables in a line is fixed but the order of stresses is fluctuating and is only *correlated* with an abstract metrical scheme. Using the expression "accentual iambs," I refer to all meters, not just iambs, but iambs were the first and most widespread a.-s. meter in every poetry, especially in English.

The same languages have also had for a period of time purely syllabic poetry; the number of syllables per line was fixed, but eventually the syllabic system was seen as "foreign" and, with its disappearance, lost all relevance for the living rhythms of poetry, which continued variously to oscillate between the two poles. The syllabic system remained central in languages that have a fixed, automatic place for stress, such as Polish (on the penultimate syllable) and French (on the ultimate syllable), which makes stress automatic, concomitant, and less conspicuous than in languages with varying stress.

The tension between the two accentual systems comes to light in the so-called "free verse" of modern poetry, where they play in various ways in the no-man's land between the two major accentual systems. Some poems have (1) a fixed number of stresses with a free number of syllables, and others have (2) the opposite, a relatively free number of stresses and fixed number of syllables.

By referring to two basic systems I do not mean two entirely different groups of stress patterns or the separate language material of a verse line. Accentual poetry was never unlimited in the number of syllables; nor did a.-s. poetry ever have its language stresses fall exclusively into the abstract metrical scheme. There have been various tendencies of syllabic order within the free accentual frameworks, and—vice versa—various degrees of deviation or violation within the strict a.-s. meters. Thus one specific individual line of "strict" a.-s. meter may be less regular in its actual language pattern, in the actual number of stresses and in the syllabic distances between two adjacent stresses, than a specific line of an ostensibly "free" accentual poem. To emphasize this point, the Russian Formalist V. M. Žirmunskij cites a poem by Shelley that is supposed to be iambic yet deviates further from the iambic scheme than a sonnet by Dante, although Dante's Italian syllabic meter did not require regularity of stress.[4]

The first task of scholarship in this domain would be to define the inherent rules by which the dominant metrical system remains dominant, thus making possible the *rhythmical* effects of local, on-the-spot regularities (where they are not metrically required) or local irregularities (those deviating from a metrical norm). Despite the ease with which a meter is usually identified, the definition raises overwhelming difficulties. The pitfalls which it creates have led to general agreement that rhythm is "eine der heikelsten und umstrittensten Fragen . . . nicht nur der Literaturwissenschaft" (one of the most delicate and argued-about questions . . . not just of the science of literature).[5] The reason is precisely in this oscillating between systems and principles, a wavering which makes poetry so varied and rhythmically alive. K. Vossler,[6] as a true Crocean, has argued that the difficulties of definition are not so much in the theorist as in the ever-changing "protean" nature of the verse itself. The second step is to assess the changing relations between stresses and the number and location of unstressed syllables between them.

In recent times—especially under the impact of free verse and its role in modern lyrical poetry, as well as the changes in the tone and manner of reading poetry—voices have been raised in praise of the "native," "tonic" system, in deprecation of the monotony of a.-s. meters, or in appreciation of overlooking these meters where the poetry is valued positively. L. Benoist-Hanappier (1905) observed that his contemporaries were already turning verse into free verse by the manner in which it was read.[7] The "theatrical" reading can be seen (heard) at the Comédie- Française, while English poetry and Shakespeare have always striven toward the "spoken language." An anecdote related by W. Kayser tells of a theatergoer who was worried that a Shakespeare play he wanted to attend might be written in poetry, to which his interlocutor responded: "Indeed it is, but you don't feel it." "You don't feel it" because of the manner of speaking the dramatic text and the many enjambments that break the five-iamb unit of the verse line (iambic pentameter).

One should not underestimate the importance of such a reorientation in reading poetry, and this for two reasons at least. First, it has helped to abolish "grammar school" requirements of strict numbers for poetry and monotonous, metronome-like scanning and has served in the rehabilitation of irregular (non-a.-s.) verses previously assumed to be inferior or primitive. We may cite the new prestige of free rhythms in modern poetry or in works by such poets as Goethe, Hölderlin, Whitman, Coleridge, and Arno Holz or in old accentual systems in epic poetry and in folksong. In Yiddish prosody, the rule of a.-s. meters was first opposed by the linguist Max Weinreich. His argument, based on Yiddish literary history, received support from an unexpected quarter: the revolt in practice by the young Modernist Yiddish poets of the 1920s.[8] Second, the reorientation of reading poetry has enabled attention to be drawn to previously overlooked non-metrical yet rhythmical devices, which are conspicuous in free rhythms when there is no regular meter but which play a significant part in creating the whole rhythmical impact of a metrical poem as well. These may be either rhythmical factors in the narrower sense, which, despite their prosodic nature, do not take on a constitutive role in the given meter (stress, number of syllables, word limits, intonation); or syntactical factors that influence a rhythmical reading, such as phrase-groupings and their relation to the order of lines, word-order tensions, etc.; or even "higher" factors influencing both rhythm and the rhythmical reading of a poem, such as the personal tone of the poet, the dynamics of meaning, or the genre of the poem.[9]

Literary theory cannot completely accommodate some of the "anti-meter" theories (actually anti-a.-s. meter), at least on the following points.

(1) Claims for "freedom" in the name of a return to original, "natural" forms—in expressions such as Germanic "organicity" as opposed to French "formality"—are historically unsound, as are references to "the freedom inherited from the Old English" and "der germanische Drang zur freien Füllung

der Takte" (the Germanic drive toward free filling of the musical measures).[10] Foreign influences are more complex than was assumed by those scholars. Andreas Heusler, in his synoptic paper "Deutsche Verskunst" (German Art of Versification) (1943) was preoccupied with this problem: "Druckt auch der Versbau deutsche Volksart aus?" (Does the structure of verse also express German "Volk" ways?)[11] Heusler, who wrote three volumes of a history of German versification, published a short summary in 1943 [*sic!* where were we then?], then reprinted it in *Kleine Schriften* in 1951. In the mechanical use of meters he sees poetry as dead for 150 years. Even in the three volumes of his massive *Deutsche Versgeschichte* (1925–1929), written before Hitler, which are full of exact technical knowledge, Heusler vents his feelings about rhythmical monotony in the following manner: "Der buchfähigen Versen von 1600 bis 1750 fehlt jeder Hauch von deutschen Erdgeruch, von urwuchsiger und treuherziger Deutschheit" (The bookish verses of 1600–1750 lack any breath of the smell of German soil, of the homegrown and heartily faithful Germany; III, p. 131). Proclaiming that "deutsch ist, was der Silbenzählung fernliegt in dem gleichformigen Stark— Schwach" (German is that which is far from counting syllables in the uniform Strong–Weak), he is led to describe as "stammfremd" (racially alien) the iambs and trochees that A. W. Schlegel felt to be the "natürlichsten und gleichsam freiwilligen Silbenmasse" (the most natural and voluntary syllabic measures) of the German language (according to Heusler's own quotation).[12]

Wolfgang Kayser has emphasized that in the complexities of cultural interrelations there are virtually no historically independent national forms.[13] It should be added that Klopstock's metrical "freedom" was based on Greek examples, as was Hölderlin's. In the seventeenth century, it has been observed, "rhythmisch wurde das deutsche Lied gerade durch das italienische Tanzlied vom italienischen Metrum befreit" (in its rhythm, the German song [*Lied*] was liberated of the Italian meter by the Italian dance song itself).[14] Even the so-called "kurze Reimpaare" (short rhyming couplets), which for Heusler constitute the true "volksmässige deutsche Versart" (folkish German verse art), came from the Latin language and ultimately from the Semitic Orient. In a similar case in Russian, Dostoevsky advised the poet Maykov to use rhyme instead of the Old Russian meters, since "now rhyme is in the folk spirit, and the old Russian meter is academic."[15]

These claims are meaningless in their nationalistic overtones: the ostensibly German or Old English freedom, and the similar Germanic role of stress, may be found in Russian folklore and in Russian Modernism, in the Hebrew Bible and in Hebrew Modernism. It is thus a matter of linguistic structure rather than a national or "racial" trait.

These claims, finally, are misleading in that they overlook the radical differences between the rhythms of old, *pre-a.-s.* poetry and the Modernist, *post-a.-s.* verse. The differences between the "old" and the "new" are enormous. In the latter, both poet and reader have an ingrained metrical memory and a subtext of regular meter in their field of consciousness that they can deviate from.

(2) Extreme reliance on variation as the measure of rhythm (e.g. according to the theories of the Russian Symbolist poet Andrey Bely; see Andrey Bely, *Ritm kak dialektika* [Rhythm as Dialectics]) or as the expression of a "life-principle" of the *Seele* (soul or mind)—as opposed to the mechanical principle of *Geist* represented in meter (Ludwig Klages)—overlooks not only the rhythmical values of parallelism, repetition, recurrence, symmetry, but also the fact that variations and deviations are felt only when there is deviation from some order, whether in the poem itself or in the poetic system. We have T. S. Eliot's testimony to "the constant suggestion and skillful evasion of iambic pentameter." Without reference to an underlying regular system—in the poem itself or in the poetic context being opposed—all the subtleties of rhythmic variations are lost.

(3) The claims that accentual poetry implies "natural" reading are not substantiated. The ambiguity of stress (of a word, a group of words; secondary stress, etc.) causes even accentual meters not to be automatically given. In some cases, as Heusler admits in connection with German Stabreim poetry, one needs training to be able to read the text rhythmically at all: "Man muss tief Atem schöpfen" (One must take a deep breath), and so on. After that, it is not clear how Heusler can make a claim about "Widerstreit zwischen Versmass und Sprache, worunter wir später so viel gelitten haben, gibt es in der Stabreimdichtung nicht" (the clash between the measure of the verse and the language, for which we later suffered so much).[16]

(4) Metrical poetry remains metrical poetry. The perception of irregularities of the language material, or of principles of organization other than the meter (actual stresses, phrase grouping), is important for the description of rhythm, but it is no substitute for the meter. The meter in such poems exists and serves as a basis for every other organization or expression; moreover, the meter may be distorted if only one syllable is changed in a place where the given system does not permit it.[17]

But above all: (5) Whatever judgment we may pronounce on a particular issue of rhythmical impact, we may agree that the major periods and the highest artistic achievements of poetry in languages with free stress in modern times have been in a.-s. meters.

These achievements owed a great deal to the subtle and complex metrical instrument, created anew at the beginning of the Modernist poetic ascent. It is an instrument whose exact structures provided the background for clearly pronounced effects of local rhythmical variations and also made possible the clear-cut distinction of a large variety of forms. These two assets—rhythmical variation and variety of forms—were of primary importance for a poetry characterized by the individuality of the writer, the individuality of the poem, the reliance on spoken language, the immediate appeal to the senses of its readers, the plurality of genres, and the independence of poetry from music.

History-minded literary scholarship has been able properly to appreciate the role of a.-s. meters in the modern era, and hence also the importance of the reform which has established the new a-.s. system. Thus D. Čizevskij dedicates a special chapter of his *History of Russian Literature* (The Hague, 1960) to the verse reform; B. Tomaševskij (*Stilistika i stixosloženie* [Leningrad, 1959]) devotes some forty pages to it. Cf. also W. Kayser's *Geschichte des deutschen Verses* (Bern, 1960). Recent English criticism, generally less formal-oriented and more "meaning"-minded, has on the whole shown less appreciation of innovation as such (in form, language, and theme), but has preferred to judge the quality of the new features as they were subsequently employed in great poetry.

THE TRANSITION TO ACCENTUAL-SYLLABIC METERS IN EUROPEAN POETRIES

Accentual-syllabic (a.-s.) meters, though similar in their diagrammatic patterns to Greek meters (by substituting the opposition stressed/unstressed for the Greek long/short), did not grow out of any direct Greek influence.[18] The mechanism of their appearance was never smooth and was everywhere a result of acts of individual creation. These creative acts were preceded by earlier tendencies in the same direction. A syllabic (Romance) system in poetry clashed with native accentual traditions or prosodic features inherent in the spoken language. Thus we had either a syllabic or an accentual principle; one principle is easy to internalize, and it is easy to count the syllables. But an a.-s. meter was organized as a double helix, with constant interaction between the two patterns along with the text. This enabled a rich texture, combining similarities and contradictions.

A.-s. meters "governed English verse from Spenser to the Edwardians."[19] They continued to appear in several forms or served as a background in Modernist poetry (see the young T. S. Eliot in *Poems Written in Early Youth*, collected by John Hayward [New York: Farrar, Straus and Giroux, 1967]). The innovator was probably Wyatt (1503–1542), although there are still arguments as to how fully he meant what he did, and as to whether the clashes between metrical *accent* and language *stress* in his decasyllabic lines are due to rhythmical subtleties or to the early stages of his "apprenticeship." Wyatt's work parallels the pre-Opitzian state of affairs in Germany. In Germany the reform was consciously and completely made by M. Opitz at the beginning of the seventeenth century. In both cases there was both the impact of the Italian Renaissance and reliance on the native spoken language.

In Russia, the syllabic system based on a fixed number of syllables in each line of a poem was reformed in several stages and turned into a.-s. system by Trediakovsky and Lomonosov toward the middle of the eighteenth century. Their work was influenced in part by German poetry and appealed to the accentual element in Russian folklore.

Thus it seems quite natural that the hero of our story—a poet and a bachelor (of arts), born in Germany, who went to live in Italy and used Italian plots, themes, and poetic forms while writing in a language with a tradition of Germanic stress patterns (Yiddish)—should come upon the discovery of accentual iambs more than one hundred years before Opitz canonized them in Germany.[20] This versatile, highly talented, and learned individual was Eliahu Baḥur (in Hebrew), or Elye Bokher (Elye the Bachelor, in Yiddish), known in Christian Europe as Elia Levita. He was a Hebrew grammarian, a teacher of Christian Renaissance scholars, and a Yiddish and Hebrew poet. Levita's discovery was not made all at once and has not been noticed until now. It is the more interesting for the available evidence of the author's laboratory and the structural developments which led him to his discovery.

THE MAIN ASPECTS OF THE TRANSITION
OF A NATIONAL POETRY TO A.-S. METERS

Although the time, the characters, and the national circumstances have differed from one language to the next, the transitions to a.-s. meters seem in their general traits to have been similar; i.e. they are the proper study of comparative literature. "Comparative" here refers, specifically, to the basic structural similarities of literature in several languages and not just to influences between nations, although in the present case these, too, played a role. The following points seem to be particularly pertinent.

(§1) *Syllabic background.* The innovation of accentual-syllabic (a.-s.) meters grew out of a cultural background where "higher" or learned poetry was syllabic. This was the sequence in English, German, Russian, Polish,[21] and twice in Hebrew. The first reform in Hebrew that led to iambic meters took place within the syllabic framework of post-Renaissance Hebrew poetry in Italy, where the accentuation of Hebrew was primarily ultimate (so-called "Sephardic"): the stress was on the last syllable of most words. The meter emerged again in Hebrew poetry in Russia around 1890[22] without there being any knowledge of the previous achievement and against a background of primarily penultimate, "Ashkenazic" accentuation.

(§2) *Accentual strain in "lower" poetry.* In most of these literatures there was an accentual strain in "lower" poetry, especially in the melic element of folksong. Even in predominantly syllabic poetries, such as French and Polish, an accentual element seems to have been prominent in folksong.[23] Learning connoted syllabism; the lower (or more popular) the poetry, the greater its reliance on the spoken language and its stress.[24] Even in Greek poetry stress came to the fore.[25] In some languages, there had been an accentual versification in the past (in Old English, German epics, the Hebrew Bible, and perhaps also Russian epics).

(§3) *Periods of approaching (a.-s.) regularity.* The two independent prosodic systems—the syllabic and the accentual—approached a.-s. regularity during certain periods. These always involved verses of varying length, some clearly regular, some probably accidentally so (as a result of the structure of the language or of the author's personal sensibility). But in these preliminary periods a.-s. meter never became the governing rule of a whole poetry in the same sense that it did after the final transition, when it was in accord with the specific language.

Thus in syllabic poetry, though its descriptions by prosodists differ widely (it was called everything from "syllabic," a term applied without consideration of any regularities of stress, to "iambs" and "pentameter"), the scanning of a complete text invariably entailed the violation of some language stresses. The well-known *Dictionary of World Literature*, for example, states: "Chaucer's verse is itself predominantly iambic" and proceeds to speak of "iambic meters" or of "the so-called heroic line of five iambs."[26] But a broader description would have to admit that "the number of instances in which the speech stresses coincide with the metrical accents is less than half." The judgment of the rhythmical merits of such a pattern is an entirely different question; thus H. S. Bennett praises "this power of counterpointing the speech rhythm against the metrical pattern," though admittedly it is "not probably as a result of any very conscious design on Chaucer's part."[27]

We must emphasize that it is not the number of deviations of the language material from a metrical scheme which is decisive, as A. Bely assumed, but their specific nature. In fact, in the verse of many later, truly a.-s. poets the number of deviations increased, but they always fell within the limits of some law and could be explained as inoffensive to the contemporary ear. In accentual poetry, on the other hand, even in periods of clear iambic tendencies, when numerous lines had quite regular numbers of syllables and stress order, there remained a free anacrusis (a missing preliminary syllable or two before the first stress of the line), and extra syllables continued to appear unexpectedly.

In German poetry, which is particularly relevant for our case (the distinction between Yiddish and German was not yet clear-cut), several approaches to iambic regularity had been made, but the transition was not final before Opitz. Such is also Kayser's point of view. As he summarizes it: "Der deutsche Vers steht im 16.Jh. vor der Entschiedung: wird er die metrische Schematisierung gegen die Sprache durchführen oder nicht?" (German verse in the sixteenth century stands before a decision: will it promote the metrical schematization against the language, or not?)[28] Kayser sees the turning point in the conscious decision of Opitz. Heusler has described several approaches of this kind from both sides—the syllabic and the accentual.

The closest approximations to iambs in German occurred around 850 (Otfrid) and again around 1300 (especially Konrad von Würzberg, d. 1287). There was no continuous development, however: "Von der ritterlichen Glatte um 1300 zu Opitzens Jamben und Trochäen ware kein so grosser Schritt gewesen. Aber es ging nicht geradlinig; der frühneudeutsche Vers biegt seitab" (From the smooth knightly meters around 1300 to Opitz's iams and trochees there was not such a step. But the development did not proceed in a stream-lined way. The early New German verse bent sideways).[29]

In view of the careless formulations about the "iambicity" of previous periods, it may be appropriate to emphasize the point: "Danach können wir *das Neue* [italics in original] an der Opitzischen Forderung in die Worte fassen: ein richtiger 'Vers' muss ein Jambus oder Trochäus sein, und zwar ein *sprachgemässer* [italics supplied]. Diesen Doppelgrundsatz hatte keine der früheren Gruppen so folgerecht erstrebt" (Hence we can formulate *the New* in Opitz's requirement as follows: a correct "verse" has to be an iamb or trochee, provided it fits the language. This double law was not followed so persistently by any of the previous trends).[30] In the German *Reimvers* of the ninth century there arose, under Latin influence, what we would call iambic tetrameters, but these lines remained in the minority; instead of the Latin eight syllables, we have lines containing four to twelve syllables.[31] In Konrad's semi-iambic four-beat verse, there is a free anacrusis and several other forms of freedom that enabled Heusler to quote six lines of the "same" meter that would in Opitz's time have counted as six different meters.[32]

(§4) *Transitional stage.* Before the final reform there was a transitional stage in which the strict number of syllables per line was enforced and some kind of alternating (i.e. "iambic" or "trochaic") scanning was probably effected. To this stage belongs in England—Wyatt; and in Germany—the strict variety of *Knittelvers* in the *Meistersang* of the sixteenth century (notably Hans Sachs). In Russia, too, a transitory stage developed, though not quite identical in nature with the English and German ones. I refer to the experimental floundering of Russian verse from Trediakovsky's first stress-regulations within the syllabic framework to Lomonosov's later poems; Lomonosov actually overruled the strictures of his predecessor and of his own more advanced a.-s. reform.

With respect to both English and German, the interpretation of this stage remains a subject of continuing argument. When one reads according to a strict scheme, one violates the language stresses: "Ach, wie manchén, seufftzén ich séngk" (Hans Sachs); or, "The lóng love thát in mý thought dóth harbór"; or again, "With hís hardíness táketh díspleasúre" (Wyatt). Whatever the modern reading may be, what did this accentuation mean at the time of writing? These variations cannot, apparently, be construed as intentional rhythmical subtleties. We must rather conclude that the principle of accord of metric accent with language stress was not yet decisive (as can also be seen from §5, below: in rhyme we *have* to violate stress). Scholars like Heusler, Kayser, and Lewis agree—in spite of criticism or the scruples of their own modern ears—that at least in writing the poet did not consider language stress, but scanned mechanically.

For example, Gerald Bullett in his introduction to *Silver Poets of the Sixteenth Century* suggests a reading which introduces five irregular accents per line without contradicting language stress: but he does not explain why there are ten syllables per line, or why he reads "wherewitháll" with a single accent and "révérénce" with two, or how "harbár" can rhyme with "banér" and with "súffre."[33] (The spellings in *The Golden Hind* are "harbor–banner–suffer.") The modern ear, accustomed to a.-s. meters, may be pleased by such irregularities, but there is no doubt that when Wyatt does scan, he "ticks out regular meter with the ruthless accuracy of a metronome."[34]

On the other hand, it is hard to accept Heusler's assumption that in writing, the poets counted syllables, while in reading they stressed them: and that the number of stresses in a line, though not regularly arranged, is constant.[35] Even if this had been the case, the merger into a.-s. meters would not yet have occurred. It seems rather that this was a stage in which the meter as such was being learned, and was improved upon by the subsequent generation as far as the handling of language stress is concerned.

(§5) *Rhyme.* It, too, testifies that a reading existed that clashed with stress. We call a sound pattern somewhere in the end of a line an *end rhyme.* An end rhyme covering the final syllable in a line will be called a *terminal rhyme.* In all these poetries, there were rhymes based on final syllables without stress correlation: "bacheler-ryver" (Chaucer), where the rhymeme is ER; "harbor–banner–suffer–displeasure" (Wyatt); and a Russian/Polish rhyme, "komú–inómu" (Simeon Polockiy). In German, there were words rhyming terminally: "ungléich," "Weishéit," "Wirtsháus," "Elénd," etc. Perhaps the reading of poetry singled out the last syllable for special emphasis.

In Russian such rhymes were rare because of the convention that favored penultimate (feminine) rhymes in syllabic poetry, which contributed two rhyming syllables at the end of each line. Terminal rhymes are opposed to *stress-bound* rhymes. A stress-bound rhyme matches the positions of stress in the rhyming words. If the stress falls on the last syllable in a line, and does so in all rhyme members, the rhyme is ultimate (masculine, m); if the stress is on the penultimate syllable, the rhyme is penultimate (feminine, f).

In Hebrew poetry, terminal rhymes in conflict with stress were widespread not only in Spain (tenth–fifteenth centuries), where the Hebrew meter was a matter of precise syllable counts and ignored stress, but also later, until the nineteenth century, in all countries from Yemen to Lithuania (of course, except Italy). In Hebrew poetry, this phenomenon was incomparably more profuse than elsewhere, probably because the language was not spoken. In Ashkenazic Europe the words were pronounced differently and did not match from the ostensibly "Sephardic" (actually "terminal") rhymes of the prayer book.[36]

In all these poetries rhymes conflicting with stress disappeared with the final establishment of a.-s. meters, which are based on a principle of strict stress regulation. The abolition of terminal rhyme implied also the final establishment of rhyme gender and the use of rhyme gender in alteration, starting from the last syllable back, the ultimate (masculine), from the next-to-last syllable (feminine), and later also from the third-to-last syllable (dactylic). This comparative finding shows that all explanations of such rhymes adduced from the history of pronunciation are insufficient (e.g. the argument about French influences on English rhyme or ultra-Sephardic pronunciation in Ashkenazic Hebrew). The truth is that the very concept of rhyme was different in the earlier period, when it was connected with sound repetition and special emphasis of the *last,* rather than the *last stressed,* syllable.

There is a special category which consists of words that have their major stress on the third syllable from the end. These may be used either in dactylic rhymes ("sublímity"/∪ — ∪ ∪/) or in ultimate rhymes, i.e. stressing their final syllable ("sublimitý–whý"). Since rhyme is in a metrically prominent position, it prefers complete accord with stress. In German poetry before the metric reform, when metrical rhymes still predominated, this category was widespread. Opitz avoided it, as did Goethe, but Schiller still uses "begrábenèn–Hóffnungèn" and the like.[37]

In Russian poetry, where dactylic rhymes are not uncommon, this category was strongly disliked. In English poetry its use is not banned, but it sometimes functions as a device of archaism. Thus Byron, whose work abounds in dactylic rhymes, uses the same words in both ways. On the one hand, he has dactyls, such as "sŭblīmĭtŷ–mǎgnănīmitŷ" (Byron, *Don Juan,* Canto I, Stanzas XII, XXIX) and "ĭntĕllēctŭāl–hĕn-pēcked yŏu ǎll" (Canto I, Stanza XXII), but in the same context, he also has ultimate rhymes: "why–try–curiosity" (Canto I, Stanza XXIII) and "war–Trafalgar–pópular" (Canto I, Stanza IV). On the other hand, the rhyming of the last syllable when the stress is on the penultimate syllable (e.g. "will ein gast betreuben"),[38] common in folksong, was abolished in a.-s. meters, which require the alternation of stressed and unstressed syllables. Vestiges of such rhyming are found in folksong[39] and in songlike genres (Thomas Hardy, for example, rhymes "sing–giving" in "To Lizbie Browne").

(§6) *Stages.* The first step everywhere was the counting of syllables in each line, under the influence of some Romance poetry (in Russian, this influence came via Polish). The second step consisted of correcting the relation of the verse to language (stress) without changing the syllabic framework. This is the corrective implied in Opitz's strictures against the *Knittelvers* and, practically, also in the differences in Sidney's and Spenser's verse compared with Wyatt's. The transition involved an appeal for support both in the prosodic structure of the native language (Opitz, Lomonosov) and in folksong; Wyatt, too—the first to introduce French and Italian strophic forms (sonnet, terza rima, ottava rima, rondeau)—wrote "native" songs.

K. Vossler, in his *Dichtungsformen der Romanen,* emphasizes that "lower" poetry and folksong were based on stress. An interesting parallel to our case is provided by his description of Latin poetry: "Und andererseits ist sicher, dass das Auseinandergehen von Vers-ictus und Wort-akzent sehr stark sein kann und besonders stark ist bei den gelehrten, feierlichen, gräzisierenden Dichtungsarten, und dass es andererseits sehr schwach ist bei den Komikern, in der familiären Dichtung, in den Episteln—, kurz in denjenigen Stilarten, die sich der Sprechsprache, der Umgangssprache nähern" (On the other hand, it is certain that the split between verse accent and word stress can be very strong, especially in learned, solemn, gracious kinds of poetry, and on the other hand is very weak in familiar poems, epistles, in short, with those kinds of poetry which approximate spoken, even casual language; p. 33).

(§7) *The impact of Italy.* It is, apparently, not a matter of coincidence that the transitions came about when the Romance influence was not French but Italian (as it was in the case of Chaucer or medieval German poetry). The impact of Italy was felt in poetries where a.-s. meter was created as a crossbreed of the syllabic and the accentual principles. The chronological order of this merger was probably as follows: Yiddish, English, Dutch, German, Italian, Hebrew.

Somewhat different is the case of the secondary introduction of a.-s. meters. But there, too, most of the characteristics listed in this chapter hold, including the appearance of a transitional stage. There is no automatic transfer of forms; a foreign poetry may exert its influence for a long time without its prosody being adopted. But when the change does occur, the model is available, and the transition is shorter and easier, floundering being confined to the "taming" of the native language. Thus in Russian around 1735 there was a German background: Lomonosov wrote his famous letter to the Academy while he was studying in Germany, and it was from German that he took over the iambic tetrameter.[40] Lomonosov's occasional precursors, too, were Germans writing in Russian. The influence was, of course, not in form alone, but in the whole poetic or even cultural atmosphere. Several non-Italian scholars, alert to the prominence of stress, observed accentual tendencies in Italian syllabic poetry.[41]

The flexible position of word stress, as compared to its position in French, provides convenient ground for such tendencies without causing monotony. That this is so, at least for the foreign ear, can be inferred from the fact that Italian strophic forms have always been naturalized in a.-s. poetries as iambic, and that Hebrew poetry in Italy grew into iambic regularity without experiencing any other foreign influence.

(§8) *Not by meter alone.* The innovation was never a matter of meter alone. It was connected with explorations of strophic forms, changes in genre and poetic diction, and apparently also changes in the manner and tone of reading poetry. On the one hand, it involved the independence of poetry from music, and on the other hand, it dispensed with artificial or high-toned manners of reading.[42] The whole atmosphere in which the new meters were introduced was one of literary renaissance.

(§9) *The first a.-s. meters: binary.* The first a.-s. meters—in England as well as in Germany, in Russian as well as in Hebrew—were binary: iambs (prevailing) or trochees, i.e. a simple alternation of stressed and unstressed syllables. Ternary meters have historically come about as a much later development.[43]

(§10) *The first verses: short.* In most cases short lines preceded long lines. Opitz's dominant length is a four-stress line. Lomonosov wrote his odes in four-iamb lines. Wyatt was more regular in his short lines.

(§11) *Accord of accent and stress.* The establishment of a.-s. meters constituted a complete accord (not identity) of metrical accent and language stress. The form of this accord in the first stages was quite strict and strikes the modern ear as mechanical because of the maximum overlapping of stress and accent, of verse and syntactical unit. C. S. Lewis says of Wyatt: "Both phases are what we should expect in a man who was escaping from the late medieval swamp; first his floundering, and then, after conversion, a painful regularity."[44] And Kayser, quoting Opitz, asks: "Sind es eigentlich gute Verse?" (Actually, are those good verses?) Indeed, when we apply our experience of the rich rhythmical patterns of later poetry, every line here seems isolated: "Sie spüren, dass die Zeile als Einheit genau, ja zu stark funktioniert. Hier fehlt eben jene Spannung, die von einer Zeile in die nächste hinüberführt. Hier sind die Akzente regelmässig gesetzt, aber es fehlt jener unterirdische Strom, der nun alles trägt" (You sense that the verse line functions precisely, even too strong. Here the tension is lacking that leads us from one line into the next. The accents are set out regularly, but that underground torrent that carries it all is missing).[45]

(§12) *Syllable/stress ratio.* In the beginning of the a.-s. meter, the tendency was to hear the alternating meter as exactly as possible; every placement of accent required by the meter needed a stressed syllable. Therefore some of the early theoreticians excluded from poetry words "unfit" for the meter, i.e. words whose stress could not overlap with the accentual scheme of mechanically scanned iambs. Thus Lomonosov excluded the pyrrhic (a substitute for the iamb, or an iambic accent not realized in a language stress), and Opitz similarly excluded words like "óbsiegen."[46] But this rule could not be kept permanently, especially in languages with many long words, and the restrictions were subsequently abandoned.

In Russian, Lomonosov already had to break his rules in his own poetry. At first Lomonosov calls verses with such long words "incorrect," but he is unable to exclude a large part of the Russian vocabulary from poetry. In the text of his "Ode" of 1741 he has an average of 2.2 syllables per stress (whereas the Russian language has an average closer to 3.0, compared to 2.5 in English). But in the "Ode" of 1762 the ratio is already 2:8: long words and pyrrhics have been admitted, and they have remained acceptable to the Russian tradition ever since.[47]

(§13) *Discrepancy.* In later developments, when the discrepancy between the metrical scheme and language that filled it increased, the correlations between them were always limited by different immanent laws. What is disturbing in the poetry of the transitory stage is not the existence of the discrepancy but its kind.

We can define a general rule for poetry: regular metrical structure may or may not utilize a distinction made by the language, but it must not run counter to such a distinction. Such is the opposition stressed/unstressed, or the distinction between grammatical genders, or between a primary and a metaphoric meaning of a word. Alternatively: poetic structure may apply a similar rule to neutral material but should not contradict a distinction in the language. A meter is not given automatically in the text of a line: no reading of all the language stresses, defined by any strict rule, guarantees a metrical scheme. In iambic verse there are always small words which are not accented by the meter, or long words which receive more than one accent (in Russian there may be as many as four iambic accents in one 8- or 9-syllable word). Even syllabic verse cannot be defined simply by the constancy of the number of syllables per line. Thus Vossler quotes a line from Lamartine which can be read as twelve-syllable, but can also be read as eleven- or ten-syllable, and still remain an Alexandrine verse.[48] H. S. Bennett, writing on Chaucer, says that his ten syllables may "melt to nine, or swell to eleven or twelve."[49] Iambic lines, too, lack not only an "objective" number of stresses but an "objective" number of syllables as well. For example, "favorite" may be read as disyllabic ("**fave**-rit," *Don Juan*, I, 12) or as trisyllabic ("**fa**-vo-rite"), according to the needs of the meter. To be sure, an expressive reading might render it trisyllabic when only two syllables are required, so that deviation is felt.

A metrical poem is a poem which does not *dictate*, but *allows*, scanning without violation of the language; in other words, it is a poem, a schematic reading of which is not *given*, but *possible*. The schema is therefore felt as a background in a more natural, content-oriented, or expressive reading. For all the languages discussed here, the general rule for a.-s. meters, most simply formulated, seems to be this: *if a word (or a group of words) is accented, at least one of the metrical accents must fall upon the major (stressed) syllable.* Thus Byron may once use "pŏstĕrĭty" with a dactylic ending[50] and then, immediately, "pŏstērĭtȳ" as two iambs, /∪ —∪ —/ (*Don Juan*, Dedication, 7, 9), but he never uses the word without an accent on the "stér." Similarly, a word like "banner" may be either not accented at all, "banner," or accented, "bānnĕr," but never "bănnēr" (in a French way, as it is still used by Wyatt).

The same rule holds in most periods, though not quite as rigidly for phrasal stress or colon stress, i.e. for any group of two words or more (important especially in languages with many monosyllables, such as English). That is to say, any syllable of a weaker word will be stressed, where this rule holds, only if the stress of the stronger word is also accented. Under many conditions this additional rule does not apply, but in particular cases it may supersede the rule for a single word.

For some periods in some languages (notably English) one should add a reservation: deviations from the rule may occur with onsets of rhythmical groups (at the beginning of the line, or the place after a caesura, and sometimes also as the place after a syntactical pause).

For the sake of this study, the detailed form of our rule matters less than a general agreement that an iambic poem is recognizable as such. The rules of "substitution" can hardly explain rhythmical dynamics; i.e. they fail to explain the reasons why, and the places in which, substitutions can be made without dissolving the meter. The construction of such rules also runs counter to the general discontent with mechanical "feet" theories, which are, to some, "a fantastic fabric of fancy, without any foundation in fact" (W. Scripture).

(§14) *Rhythmical variation.* This law permits a great deal of rhythmical variation on the very level of stress-accent relations: the use of small words (especially words of contextual importance) in unstressed positions (notably in English); the use of long words, i.e. without linguistic realization of all accents (in Russian or Hebrew); variation in the degrees of stress to realize the accentual pattern of a line (notably in German); or all of these combined, in symmetrical or asymmetrical, repeated or changing patterns, to achieve all kinds of poetic tones and rhythmical effects.[51]

But everywhere the full use of these possibilities has come only with time and after the instrument had become more refined and the reader's ear so attuned to the dominant meters that a poet could indulge in the most subtle departures without their being felt to be violations of some permanent pattern.

ELIA LEVITA AND THE BACKGROUND OF HIS DISCOVERY

Eliahu ben Asher Halevi Ashkenazi,[52] hereinafter referred to as Elia Levita, was born in southern Germany, near Nuremberg, in 1469. He lived in Venice (at least in 1496) and in nearby Padua (1504); returned to Venice with his manuscript in 1509, stayed in Rome until 1527, later worked in publishing houses in Venice and in Germany, and returned to Venice, where he died in 1549.[53] In his romance, *Bovo-bukh,* he mentions "unzer bruder fun Veneydig" (our brother from Venice), apparently referring to himself.

He was a linguist, a biblical scholar, and the author of many books on Hebrew grammar and lexicography. He taught Hebrew to several Christian humanists, notably Sebastian Münster and Paulus Fagius (both of whom later translated his books into Latin), George de Selve (who was later French ambassador to Venice and who invited Levita to teach at the University of Paris), and Cardinal Egidio di Viterbo, to whom Levita taught Kabbalah and in whose house in Rome he lived between 1514 and 1527.

A multilingual writer, Levita compiled a Latin-German-Hebrew-Yiddish dictionary. In Hebrew, besides his scholarly work, he wrote verses in complex forms, notably to rhyme some of his grammatical rules. Of his Yiddish works extant today there are only a translation of the Psalms; two rhymed epics, *Bovo-bukh* and *Pariz un Viene;* and two long poems on local current events, with scurrilous overtones.

What was his poetic background? Jewish communities in Italy and southern Germany were small, were often confined to ghettos, and had small intellectual classes. Whatever creativity they showed was performed on the margins of traditional religious learning. Nevertheless, Hebrew and Yiddish writing were separate, with entirely different genres, forms, versification, rhyming, and language. Rarely did a Hebrew writer contribute to Yiddish literature. We know of no sonnets written in Yiddish, though hundreds were written by Hebrew poets in Hebrew and in Italian.

Until Levita's time, Yiddish poetry had been closely linked to German literature in its genres, forms, and turns of language. Yiddish poetry contained entire texts that had been rewritten in Yiddish letters from German sources. On the other hand, as emphasized by Ch. Shmeruk, there was a persistent trend, Jewish in theme and independent of German, that continued with topics, genres, and forms developed earlier in Hebrew poetry.[54] Johann Christhof Wagenseil, a famous Christian Bible scholar, noticed that there were in Yiddish "eigene Metra und Gedichte-Arten welche sonst in der teutschen Poësi nit üblich zu Nachahmung ihrer Hebreischen" (its own meters and types of poems, which are not usual in German poetry, to imitate the Hebrew). He then quotes "Merubah" (Quatrain), rhyming: *aaabcccbddddb* . . . , in the Hebrew tradition. Thus, two long poems, for Hanukkah and Purim, written in Venice about 1555, have a German rhyming pattern. The author admits that it was a mistake to use a German "tune" but explains that he did so for lack of time.[55] This trend is conspicuous also in the tradition of bilingual poems: a Hebrew strophe alternating with a Yiddish one, sometimes with an acrostic running in one chain through both, which is destroyed when the poem is taken apart according to a unilingual principle. Now Yiddish language and poetry moved for the first time in their history into a non-Germanic country, namely into northern Italy, and there it flourished for a short time in the beginning of the sixteenth century.

As we review Levita's background three strains of Hebrew poetry may be relevant: the Bible, Hebrew poetry of medieval Ashkenaz (i.e. Germany, northern France, and subsequently eastern Europe), and Hebrew poetry written in Italy. The rhythm of the Bible is based on pairs of versets each containing an equivalent number of stressed syllables, formed in groups of four or fewer words per verset, but not constant numerically; instead, syntactic and semantic parallelism played a central role. But these biblical forms had almost no direct continuation in the Middle Ages. In Hebrew liturgy a cluster of stresses became a matter of word counting; the rhythm was based on complex strophic chains and repetition rather than semantic parallelism, as in the Bible.[56]

In Italy, Hebrew poetry was written from at least the ninth century (before there was any Italian language) to the nineteenth century. At first the old liturgical forms prevailed, but by Levita's time the strict syllabic patterns of rhymed quantitative meters were dominant. These meters had been developed in Arabic Spain, based on a regular order of short and long syllables, and had served Hebrew poetry in its "Golden Age" in Spain and Provence from the tenth to the fifteenth centuries. In Italy they were contaminated with Italian syllabic measures (primarily the endecasyllabic line). In the Italian Hebrew poetry of Levita's time, rhyme was not yet connected with stress (see the discussion of Hebrew poetry in Italy in the previous chapter); this connection did not become established in Hebrew until the seventeenth and eighteenth centuries.

The forms of Hebrew poetry in Ashkenaz have not yet been studied properly. It seems that both its liturgical and its secular genres (of which few examples have survived) were either "free" or based on stress. The latter system can be considered a contamination of the forms of Jewish folksong with the old Hebrew liturgical tradition of word counting. Some poems were linked to tunes and therefore used rhyme order according to either German or Hebrew strophic forms. But there was no syllable counting of any sort in Ashkenaz. The rhythm of the internal part of the line was similar to that of Yiddish or German: a more or less regular number of stresses (four or three) with a syllabic filling that was, in principle, free.

On the other hand, the sound patterns of Hebrew rhyme—both in Ashkenaz and in Italy—were governed by the rules created in the old liturgy and established in Spain: a rhyme in Hebrew in all countries throughout the Middle Ages required equality of the ends of a line, counting *from the last vowel*, along with the consonant preceding it (*consonne d'appui*), but disregarding stress. Thus in *Megiles Vints* (about 1616),[57] with alternating Yiddish and Hebrew rhymed stanzas, the Yiddish stanzas, insofar as they are masculine, rhyme "kAM–nAM" (vowel and consonant with no preceding consonant), while the Hebrew ones rhyme "beyaDAM–lehoriDAM" (with the obligatory supporting consonant). The same difference was maintained in other bilingual poems (cf. Ch. Shmeruk, "Which Holiday Is the Best? A Versified Dispute between Hanukkah and Other Holidays")[58]: the famous "Shabes-lid"[59] and bridal songs such as the one printed in *Mitsves Noshim*, Venice, 1588.[60] In medieval Yiddish poetry the minimum and maximum rhyming norms coincided; as far as I can determine, the preceding consonant was never utilized for the sake of "richer" rhymes, as is done in Modern Hebrew poetry. Paradoxically, before Levita's reform, Yiddish poetry rhymed Yiddish words of Hebrew origin according to the Hebrew terminal rhyme—on *the last vowel in a verse line and the consonant preceding it*—but not according to the stress-bound principle, which starts with the last *stressed* vowel. But it had to give up even the consonant, which was compulsory in all contemporary Hebrew texts. Thus, in the *Shmuel-bukh* (stanza 587), "Eyn-Gédi" rhymes with "zi," although the stress in "eyn-gédi" is penultimate in all forms of Hebrew pronunciation. We observe the same in a pair of words of Hebrew origin: "irakhmieli–keni" (stanza 794).[61] There is just one vowel! In Yiddish, as in English, one vowel alone is sufficient for a rhymeme: see / sublimity.

This supporting consonant provided compensation, as it were, for the missed possibility of multisyllabic rhymes that terminal rhyming does now allow. Its use parallelled French tendencies toward "rich" rhyming as contrasted with German or English minimal rhymes. In Yiddish, as in English, the supporting consonant did not take part in the rhyme.[62] In bilingual poems, too, this difference in rhyming principles was consistently observed, as it was observed by Levita in his own unilingual writing in each language.

Thus Levita's sense of the relativity of prosodic systems was due not only to the difference between Yiddish poetry or its German background, with which he may have been acquainted, and the Italian poetry on which his work leaned, but also to the differences between Hebrew and Yiddish and those within Hebrew itself (Ashkenazi/Sephardi). In his own writing he employed at least two systems: accentual meters with stress-bound rhymes in Yiddish and quantitative-syllabic meters with terminal rhymes in Hebrew regardless of stress.

How did Levita meet the general conditions of transition to a.-s. (accentual-syllabic) meters? Yiddish is the only language of the group discussed above which had had no tradition of syllabic meters in the past (contrary to §1), perhaps because it was not the prestige language of learned circles, as Hebrew was (even Levita wrote his Yiddish ottava rima stanzas ostensibly "for women"). Yiddish poetry never renounced the direct appeal to the reader's senses through the reliance on stress. The rhythm had always been accentual (§2) with tendencies toward regularity similar to those of the German folksong (§3). Hence there was no problem of a transitional stage or of "*Tonbeugung*"— bending the accent (§4), some of the traits of which had to be tackled by Levita himself. Related to this is the fact that rhymes in conflict with stress (§5) were very rare in Yiddish outside of words of Hebrew origin.[63] Levita is almost pure on this score: stress is prominent in his rhyme, and gender is the rule. He was probably the first Yiddish poet to rhyme words of Hebrew origin according to their Yiddish accent. That is to say, he rhymes them in their penultimately, "Ashkenazically" stressed form, although in his own Hebrew poetry the stress in the same words is ultimately, "Sephardically" stressed because of the terminal norm of the Hebrew rhyme.

Quite possibly the clash between the daily (Ashkenazic) pronunciation of Hebrew words and the rhyme norm of medieval Hebrew poetry was the major reason for the avoidance, or peculiar utilization, of Hebrew-origin words in Yiddish rhyme. In the Cambridge Manuscript[64] only Hebrew names appear in rhyme—probably because Hebrew names terminally stressed had the backing of Christian pronunciation as well (*Davíd* rather than *Dávid* or *Dóvid.*). The same applies, with one exception, to the *Shmuel-bukh* and the *Doniel-bukh*, although words of Hebrew origin abound in both, in the text as well as in the caesura position (which in the *Doniel-bukh* is penultimate). In the Oldendorf collection there appears (in number 22) the rhyme "umgehn–kheyn–gewinnen." This is clearly a terminal rhyme, using a monosyllable of Hebrew origin (*kheyn* rhymes with *ehn*), which is identically stressed in all conditions.

Levita's breakthrough in giving penultimate stress to Yiddish words of Hebrew origin in penultimate feminine rhymes was freely repeated in *Megiles Vints* and in later folksongs. In Hebrew such rhymes apparently were not introduced until the nineteenth century. But this achievement in Yiddish was not immediately accepted in full. Thus Gumprecht of Szczebrszyn, in Venice in 1555, still uses a few words of Hebrew origin in rhyming positions (13 out of 1,591); some of these are terminal, and only three or four are feminine, penultimate. In the latter case, both words are of Hebrew origin, so that a reading "loymer–shoymer" accords with Ashkenazi pronunciation.

Levita's a.-s. meter is iambic (§9); the lines are short for the most part, and the longer ones are less regular than the short ones (§10): the meter is far more regular than in modern times (§11), but (toward the end of *Pariz un Viene*) Levita does employ longer words with double stresses (§12), according to the general law (§13). He uses an occasional enjambment and shows flexibility—for example, by means of varying stress length (§14); on the whole, however, one feels the simple meter and the rhetorical uses of the work's symmetrical structures. It seems to me that his art made a change in the tone and language of Yiddish poetry (§8). His language strikes the modern ear as more familiar than that of the earlier epics, whose formulaic style is colored by literariness and Germanness. The Italian influence on his poetic forms (§7) is obvious.

Thus Levita's metric transition displays a complex of traits similar to those found in parallel phenomena in other European poetries, though it is independent of them. But Levita's was the only a.-s. reform effected not from the syllabic (§6), but from the accentual side, or from popular rather than aristocratic language. Consequently it was a much more unequivocal transition. It was determined above all by the fact that Levita had first adopted an Italian strophic form without giving up the rhythm of the line of his own poetry. Instead of adopting the syllabic meter, as was often done in Germany, he combined the Italian strophic form with the four-beat line of folksong, leaving aside the syllable count. Then, after a careful rhythmical development, he made a leap, adopting Italian syllable counting without giving up the four-beat line, and thus, fusing them, he discovered the iambic tetrameter (later reinvented by Opitz in Germany).

RHYME AND THE EVIDENCE OF THE POET'S WORK IN PROGRESS

Two long poetic narratives by Levita are known to us: the *Bovo-bukh* (*BB*) and *Pariz un Viene* (*PV*),[65] both original adaptations of European medieval romances, based on Italian versions, skillfully written in ottava rima rhymes, in a fluent, often witty language, interspersed with Jewish elements and ironic digressions.

BB, written in 1507 in Padua and printed by the author in Isny in 1541,[66] was based on the Toscana version of the romance *Buovo d'Antona* (in English, *Bevis of Hampton*). The plot subsequently gained great popularity both in rhymed and prose versions. The name of the hero is Buovo d'Antona; in Hebrew letters, *Bovo* →; בּבֿא and in casual Ashkenazic reading, *Bobe*, which also means "grandmother." From here we get to *bobe-mayses*, "grandma's stories"—stories about medieval knights and their exploits cannot be real! Thus, a shift in pronunciation and a shift in material culture brought about a transformation of the meaning of *bobe-mayses*. The rhyme pattern is that of ottava rima, *abababcc*. But it is only the sequence of the rhymes, not their gender or their meter, which corresponds to the Italian ottava rima.

Levita was the first to use the rhyme pattern of ottava rima in any Germanic language; in German itself—with a much stronger literature than Yiddish—it was not introduced until 1626, in a translation of Tasso's "Jerusalem Delivered." But this fact, though it emphasizes Levita's independence of his background, is in principle of minor consequence, since Yiddish poets were already familiar with complex strophic forms, of both German and Hebrew origin. Levita's achievement lies rather in the masterly execution of this scheme of triple rhymes in texts of considerable length (650 stanzas in *BB* and about 800 in *PV*) and in a language perhaps more difficult to rhyme than the Italian of the prototype;[67] his achievement also lies in his progressive work in rhythmical variation and regulation, which led him to his important discovery.

The rhyme gender of the Italian ottava rima, which was the major form of epic poetry at the time, was naturally penultimate (feminine) throughout; that is to say, the penultimate syllable of every line was stressed, and all sounds from the penultimate vowel onward were rhymed. It is in this form that this strophe was adopted in Germany in the seventeenth century.[68] Only late in the eighteenth century did Heinse and Goethe, as W. Kayser has stressed, "introduce the felicitous innovation of alternating feminine and masculine line endings."[69] Levita had already struck upon the idea of alternating the rhyme-stress relation in *BB*, although the execution was not yet consistent.

In a book on *BB*, a modern Yiddish critic wrote: "It is conspicuous that when [Levita] is telling a story, when he simply relates bits of content, or when he is describing things and events, the feminine rhyme plays a role. [But] when he arrives at parts in which he wants to convey movement, haste, or strong emphasis, the masculine rhyme dominates."[70] No content analysis is needed to disprove this claim. All that is necessary is to follow Levita closely in the progress of his work.

Levita starts out in *BB* with stanzas of purely penultimate (feminine) rhymes, as in Italian poetry. Stanza 23 is the first one to alternate ultimate (masculine) and penultimate (feminine) rhymes in its sextet (*ababab*). In the first 60 stanzas we find only 6 cases of such alternation: in the following 70 stanzas (nos. 60–129), 21 cases; in the next 70 (nos. 130–199), 42; from stanza 200 onward, this form dominates: out of 62 stanzas, only 6 still have purely feminine penultimate rhymes. But from number 262 to the end of the book (number 650), there is not one single alternation! In other words, the poet started, as in his Italian prototype, writing in feminine penultimate rhymes, then slipped accidentally into an ultimate rhyme (masculine—quite natural in Yiddish speech and in

Yiddish poetry before him); next, he used the alternation occasionally, moving into it as his dominant form; and finally, from stanza 200 onward, it becomes a rule with few exceptions, which disappeared entirely after about one-third of the book. This transition was apparently noticed by a modern translator of *BB* into Yiddish, M. Knapheys.[71] At first his rhymes are purely penultimate, as in the Italian, but suddenly, without any gradual transition, he switches into Levita's alternating stanza. The switch in Knapheys's modern Yiddish version is slightly later than in the original (p. 262): it occurs after the equivalent of stanza 279 (p. 107). That means that when Knapheys understood Levita's form, he took it over, while in *BB* we see groping, change, and development.

There is no sharp change in this development. A check of the content shows that there is no possible pause at either of the above-mentioned "turning points" (after nos. 23, 130, 200, 262), i.e. that Levita's awareness of the form grew gradually as he went along and was not the result of any break in the process of writing. This process took a year's time, from Iyar to Nissan in 1507 (if one may believe the testimony of an ironic writer in an otherwise factual stanza, number 649). Moreover, this as well as other evidence of gradual change within the book seems to show that *BB* was written in the same order, in the same flow in which it is presented to the reader.

PV, printed posthumously in Verona in 1594, has survived in a single copy,[72] of which the first twenty-four numbered leaves (about 250 stanzas) are missing. The text has not yet (1964) been reprinted, though it is quoted at length in literary histories. Dr. Max Weinreich, who was the first to describe *Pariz un Viene* and was also the modern discoverer of the first edition of the *Bovo-bukh*, wrote: "I do not mean to decide which of these books was written first. If the question can be answered at all, it will be only through a detailed analysis."[73]

The analysis of the rhyme pattern yields sufficient evidence for placing *PV* after *BB*: as a rule, *PV* has the same pattern as prevailed in *BB* (of ottava rimas with alternating ultimately stressed and penultimate rhymes in the sextets).[74] If we had one work with regular and one with irregular rhyming, we could perhaps suppose the reverse order. But:

(1) since *BB* is not simply irregular, but shows a clear development toward a particular form of rhyme alternation which finally prevails with consistency; and

(2) since, moreover, *BB* begins with the rhyme pattern of its Italian prototype and moves away from it, there can be no doubt that *PV* was written later.

The date of *PV* can be established. Since internal evidence shows it to postdate *BB*, it cannot have been written before 1508. Now, in *PV*, Levita still refers to himself as a bachelor, but in the so-called "Sreyfe-lid," which Ch. Shmeruk has proved to have been composed in Venice between 1510 and 1513, he mentions his wife. Apparently he did not marry until the age of forty (hence his surname Bokher, i.e. "bachelor"). But Levita fled from Padua probably when Padua was conquered, in May 1509. Although Max Erik believed that *PV* could have been written in Venice,[75] this does not seem likely. In the opening of chapter VII of *BB*, the author mocks the Venetians for their inhospitality, which is opposed to the customs of Mantua, Ferrara, Padua, and other cities (such as Genoa, where the hero Pariz's arrival provides a transition for the story). The insulting tone used toward Venice and the casual inclusion of Padua among other cities does not support the view that the poem could have been created after the war and the author's exile in 1509. Thus the time of composition can be set with considerable certainty in 1508–1509.

As to the authenticity of *PV*'s authorship, no name remains in the extant version, although in the nineteenth century an author's name was seen.[76] We agree with M. Weinreich's argument about Levita's authorship.[77] To this is added the evidence of continuity with *BB* in numerous complex, subtle, and detailed points. The uniqueness of these patterns in Yiddish poetry and their unconscious nature makes any hypothesis other than that of the identical authorship of *BB* and *PV* inconceivable. (See below, especially the discussion of chapter V.) On the other hand, we must disagree with L. Landau's hypothesis that Levita was also the author of the third known Yiddish epic in ottava rima, the "Artushof."[78] As M. Weinreich said of the stanza version of this poem, "the language, the style, the descriptions are in the 'Artus' so different that it must belong to another author."[79] Judah A. Joffe has questioned Weinreich's contention, pointing to the remark in the "Artushof" that the "tune" of *Bovo-bukh* fits it.[80] Indeed, the "Artushof," like *BB*, alternates the rhyme gender in the majority of its stanzas and has a large minority of stanzas with purely penultimate rhymes. But this, though it corresponds to the overall statistics of *BB*, does not reflect the decision made by the author after the first third of *BB* had been composed. If "Artushof" had been written before *BB*, it should have had purely penultimate rhymes, like the beginning of *BB* (this is not plausible in any case, since "Artushof" mentions *BB*). On the other hand, would the author, after finishing *BB*, have regressed from his rule of gender alternation, which dominated both of his epics? Moreover, it is hard to conceive of Levita's using dull and repetitious rhymes such as "Der kineg shprokh: riter oyz der korn / ikh bin farflukht gevorn / ikh bin der kineg hokh geborn / der oyz zayn shlos iz far lorn / nun bin ikh eyn hersh gevorn / land un layt far lorn gevorn / un ikh veys ir zayt drum gekumen / daz ir aykh mayner hot on genumen." Elsewhere, Levita never uses the same rhyme six times; nor does he ever repeat the same word in one rhyme, whereas here "gevorn"—an auxiliary verb—is repeated three times.

The following observations may be added:

(3) In a few stanzas of *BB* the author tried out rhyme alternation in the reverse order: penultimate-ultimate (feminine-masculine). In *PV* the reverse order does not appear (this fact is important for the metrical pattern):

$$\cup - \cup - \cup - \cup \mid \cup - \cup - \cup - \cup - \qquad \text{bad}$$
$$\cup - \cup - \cup - \cup - \mid \cup - \cup - \cup - \cup - \qquad \text{good}$$

If the order is feminine-masculine, two lines cannot be read in one breath, for two slacks are crowded in the caesura.

(4) Though the overwhelming majority of *BB* stanzas end in a pair of penultimate rhymes, there are thirty-one scattered cases of ultimate rhymes (masculine) in the couplet (cc): this does not occur in *PV* at all.

(5) In addition to such internal evidence as may still be found, the external structure of the books is different: whereas *BB* is written in one sequence, *PV* is divided into ten chapters, and the author makes skillful use of the beginning and ending of each chapter of poetic deviations.

(6) Characteristically, too, in *PV* Levita seems to have dropped the use of Italian words for which, in *BB*, he felt obliged to provide a glossary.

(7) Another innovation, though not regularly formalized, is Levita's highly effective employment of dactylic rhymes (rhymemes which start on the third-to-last syllable). This type of rhyme later played a prominent role in modern Yiddish poetry, especially under Russian influence. In Russian, such rhymes were later used conspicuously in the ottava rima of Byron's "Don Juan" (where the rhyme gender is also alternating, but not regularized). In Germany this type of rhyme (*Gleitreim*) appeared only rarely in the seventeenth century and probably never in the Volkslied[81] (the patterns of which underlie Levita's poetry): as late as 1647 Harsdörfer calls them "fast ungebräuchlich" (almost unusable).[82] Levita's use of the dactylic rhyme reflects his independent feeling for language, perhaps even for the specific traits of spoken Yiddish (which must by that time have abolished secondary stress). The pioneering nature of his *Sprachgefühl* (language sensibility) is also evident from the fact that he was probably the first to use Yiddish words of Hebrew origin with their

Ashkenazi penultimate stress, i.e. exactly as they are pronounced in modern Yiddish, despite the fact that in his Hebrew poetry he rhymes them with terminal rhymes, i.e. with the accent on the final syllables, in accordance with the Hebrew medieval tradition.

Levita still made occasional use of the secondary accent of compound words, e.g. "glaýkh–kónigraýkh" → / — / — ∪ — / (*PV* 62v.iv). These rhymes later became rare in Yiddish, although they did survive in English poetry. All this evidence seems to support the notion that in Levita's time Yiddish was already characterized by one major word-stress, without *Nebenton* (secondary stress).[83] Yiddish therefore did not have the same problem as German with words that are either banned from iambic meter or are squeezed in on the penalty of stress violation ("ein Grossváter" or "der Gróssvater").[84] According to our rule §13, such words are easily dealt with in any meter: if the stressed syllable of a "compound" word is accented, any other syllable may be accented too.

The dactylic rhymes appear only in place of penultimate rhymes, and primarily in the couplet (cc). *BB* had only three dactylic rhymes altogether: *vándern–Flándern–ándern*[85] (couplet 188 and repeated thrice: in couplets 200, 292, 380); *póyern–tróyern–móyern* (397); and *geshvíndern–híndern–kíndern* (221). The first two triplets had already appeared in the *Shmuel-bukh* (684, 1650) as its only dactyls. As for *PV*, the first 75 stanzas of the surviving section have no dactylic rhymes; the first to appear is, again, *ándern–Flándern*. The dactyls then show up in considerable variety, almost on every leaf (though they are rare again in chapter 8). In *PV* their dactylic nature is pronounced because of the exact iambic meter and the exact observance of rhyme/stress relations: the two final syllables are really additional, and this prevents a secondary stress on the last syllable. Clearly, dactylic rhymes remain in the minority; that is, they serve merely as a stylistic effect. It is another instance of internal development, but in this case the development was not toward regularity. Levita's dactyls come mostly from the Germanic component of the language: *kémerlikh–yémerlikh* (47v.i), *léydign–shéydign–préydign* (41v.iii); but also from the Italian component: *Alisándria–Mándriah* (54r.iv); and from the Hebrew component: *tátern–pátern* (67v.ii), *Ir hĕrcĕ vēynĕt blāt, Iř āgĕn trēhĕrn/un irgĕshtālt ăz zōlt măn zi glăykh tēhĕrn* (53r.iii).[86] The dactyls, "irrational" for an iambic pattern, lend life to the rhythm of the stanza. In later Yiddish poetry they have been used in binary meters only by such form-minded Modernists as A. Leyeles, e.g. in his masterful "Woodfern Farm."[87]

METER AND RHYTHMICAL DEVELOPMENTS
IN THE *BOVO-BUKH*

The author of *BB* compounded the rhyme scheme of ottava rima with an accentual meter much closer to the ear of his Yiddish audience than the syllabic prosody of his Italian source or the quantitative meters (coming from Arabic Spain) which he used in his own Hebrew poems. The accentual system with a limit of four stresses per line had until that time been the exclusive pattern of Yiddish poetry (in conformity with the dominant medieval German form) and in every probability also the dominant strain of Ashkenazi Hebrew poetry.

Thus, the internal rhythmical movement of the poem was determined neither by the strophic pattern, nor by the thematic material, but by the inherited language continuum. This is not as natural as it may seem. English poetry in the Middle Ages, under French influence, and Russian poetry in the seventeenth century, under Polish influence, both used syllabic meters, quite unnatural to their native traditions and unfitted to the prominence of accent in the respective languages. Conventions are stubborn.

The same applies to the Italian influence on German poetry at the end of the sixteenth century. The *Villanelles* written by Jakob Regnart (1574), for example, make use of lines of either ten syllables (and a feminine variant of eleven) or six syllables (and a variant of seven)—a pattern quite unusual in the German *Volkslied*. It was only gradually that he allowed the Italian influence on the form of his songs to slacken. A second wave of Italian influence, around 1590, was caused by the introduction of another strophic form, the *canzonette*.[88] Only after a.-s. meters were firmly established in Germany, in the seventeenth century, did accent come to be considered in adapting Italian strophes, as in the case of the ottava rima (although even here the number of syllables was preserved). By preserving the stress as a constitutive factor, Levita both maintained the familiar flow of the phrase-patterns in Yiddish and provided a basic asset for the slip into a.-s. meters, which he was still to make.

A similar feeling for form led Levita to choose the length of his line. The form was in complete accord with the tone of his writing, the audience envisaged, and the language used to write the epic poem in his German four-beat line. For that he disregarded both his Italian prototype and the Yiddish (German) epic tradition. As far as we know, Yiddish epics in the Middle Ages—both those which were versions of German prototypes and those which came from Jewish sources (like the book of Samuel and the biblical epics in its wake)—used German epic forms, which amounted basically to a rhymed pair (or double pair) of "long lines." In the *Shmuel-bukh,* for example, these had six stresses each, with a caesura in the middle.

Basically—other factors being equal—lines with fewer than four stresses are "short" and "light"—as opposed to their "heavier" effect in longer lines. This is a universal of prosody.[89] No folk poetry makes regular use of lines longer than four-stress ones; that is to say, folk poetry gives preference to a line which constitutes a "simple (or: natural) unit," one which does not tend regularly to fall apart into two or more rhythmical units. W. Kayser generalizes: "Aber grundsätzlich dürfen wir sagen, dass bei den Zeilen bis zu vier Hebungen die einzelne Zeile eine viel deutlichere, wirksamere Einheit bildet als bei den umfangreicheren Zeilen, für die in wachsendem Masse kleinere Einheiten wichtig werden" (But essentially we must say that with lines with up to four stresses the individual line makes a much more conspicuous, impactful unit than do comprehensive lines for which smaller units become increasingly important).[90]

To this argument, based on the number of stresses, may be added the ideas of Žirmunskij and Tomaševskij.[91] Žirmunskij has shown that all languages have a "normal," basic, firm group of syllables, both in the texts of songs and in popular poetry, as well as in prose (insofar as artistic prose can be divided into segments playing a semi-rhythmical role). The normal length is eight to nine (or seven or ten) syllables. Such, indeed, is the average (and also the usual) number of syllables per line in *BB*: eight in the sextet, ten in the closing couplet.

Such an unbroken unit, it may be added, easily combines with similar units into complex stanzas, in which adjacent lines, opposed to each other by rhyme, clearly bring out rhythmical regularity (or regular variety) and symmetry, without hampering the forward movement of the long poem. Longer lines in epic poetry occur for the most part either in blank verse or in rhymed couplets, i.e. either where pronounced strophic organization was given up or where the finality of the couplet is overstressed. Such symmetry does not provide a convenient ground for individual lyrical poetry, for the individualizing epithet, for attention being given to individual words, nuances, or ambiguities in particular places. Nor is it the intention of *BB* to do that. Its effects are primarily rhetorical and based on the syntactic-rhythmical level.

Genetically, the four-beat line combined with alternating rhyming (oppositions of adjacent lines in length and in gender) came to Levita from folksong, light verse, and short poems both in Yiddish (of which few have survived) and in their German prototypes (reflected, for example, in a collection of German *Volkslied* which was still in use one generation later, about 1530).[92] But the author avoided the playfulness of light verse when he used the maximal line of these lyrics, while the lyrics proper mostly combined or superseded the limiting four-beat line with a three-beat line.

The meter of *BB* does not imply that there are four stresses or words in the language of each line discoverable by any a priori linguistic description, but that every line *can* be read with four major accents. Even without a "tune" (about the existence of which the author hints, though admitting that not every reader will know it), a lay reader will fall naturally into the metrical pattern—due to the inertia of reading and the rhythmical qualities of this simple, symmetrical, and internally semi-regularized form, supported by the symmetry and parallelism of the rhyme scheme and the dominant sentence structure. But this reading is no more a "natural" or "prose" reading than in the case of a.-s. meters: in neither case is there an automatic relation between "objective" word stress (or phrasal stress) and prosodic accent. In general, the metric accents in *BB*, when realized, coincide with central words, but not exclusively. There are usually more than four words per line; secondary stresses fall either on auxiliary or on shorter words; they may be realized or subdued—according to the numeric relations in each line. And in many cases it is difficult to decide exactly which one of the shorter words has to be accented in reading.[93]

In principle this meter is purely accentual, the number of syllables being inconstant and irrelevant. Thus, within the same framework of four stresses there appear lines of from five to fifteen syllables (counted up to the last stressed syllable, but omitting the syllables after it, since these are determined not by meter but by rhyme; there are actually six to sixteen syllables)—e.g.: *Vilstu es yo hobn* (stanza 641: 6 syllables) and *un do zi eyn gute vayl bay anander vorn gezesn/do ruft men zi ale beyd zi zoltn kumen cu dem esn* (stanza 201: 13+15 syllables).[94]

Such is the general principle. But the actual rhythmical impact—here as elsewhere—does depend upon the relation between stress and number of syllables, though not in the refined manner of on-the-spot configurations, which is typical of modern free verse. We may say, as has been said of German historical poems more than a hundred years after they were written: "Von einer gegenseitigen Durchdringung von Stoff und Form kann jedoch in unsern Liedern kaum die Rede sein" (In our songs [*Lieder*] we can hardly speak of interpenetration of theme and form).[95] In other words, the primary task of the on-the-spot rhythmical variations is not so much to support local subtleties of meaning as to convey the general characteristic of the rhythmical movement. And in this there are significant changes as the book develops.

In general, in a typical line of *BB*, the number of unstressed syllables moves between one and two, occasionally also between zero and three, especially in the middle of the line, where the major syntactical pause of the given line usually falls. For example:

$$- X X - / X X X - X - || X - X - / - X - X ||$$
Bove der vor in zaynem hercn fro || Do er di reyd hot fornumen ||

$$| X X - \cup \cup - \cup - \cup - || X - X X - X X - X - X$$
Er gidokt keynes zoymen iz nit do||Tsu brukhim hayoyshvim vil ikh glaykh kumen.

(300)

A statistical study of the continuous stress-syllable relations could be of great interest, but even a mere examination of the length of lines indicates significant tendencies, as can be seen in Table 5.1. In Table 5.1 the number of syllables refers to the number up to the last stressed syllable (including it), since we consider any addition a matter of rhyme.[96] What can be learned from the table?

(1) Wherever a marked change in the statistics occurs, the break takes place in the same part of the book, the part where the dominant rhyme pattern has changed: around stanza 200. There is also a critical region of experimentation between stanzas 151 and 250, after which all tendencies are either dropped or finally established. Thus the final decision as to the rhyme pattern of the book was taken in stanza 262, although the new form became dominant earlier, in the critical region.

(2) Levita developed a clear rhythmical difference between the lines of the sextet and the couplet, not distinguished earlier by anyone. The lines of the couplet, though somewhat longer from the beginning, become considerably longer after the critical region (columns 2, 3).

(3) The average length of line is already close to what became the regular pattern in *PV*, where the sextet lines have eight syllables (= four iambs) each, and the couplet lines ten syllables (five iambs) each. Here the average is still somewhat longer: 8.8 and 10.2, respectively. Indeed, though the formal meter is a four-beat line, a natural reading of the couplet often gives five stresses. W. Kayser speaks of the "*Wandel im Rhythmus* mit dem bei Goethe wie in allen

Table 5.1. Length of Line: Its Patterns and Developments in the Bovo-bukh

Stanza Numbers	Average Number of Syllables per Line		Gap between Shortest and Longest Lines		Number of Lines (for Every 20 Checked) Having Fewer or More Than 10 Syllables				Percentage of All Stanzas Having Rhyme Gender	
	Lines 1-2 of each stanza (rhyming ab)	Lines 7-8 of each stanza (rhyming cc)	Lines 1-2	Lines 7-8	Lines 1-2		Lines 7-8		Alternating in sextet (ab)	Masculine in final couplet (cc)
					Fewer	More	Fewer	More		
/1/	/2/	/3/	/4/	/5/	/6/	/7/	/8/	/9/	/10/	/11/
1–50	8.3	9.1	7–12	7–11	18	1	12	3	10%	6%
51–100	9.1	9.2	6–11	7–12	13	4	12	5	28%	8%
101–150	8.9	9.1	7–12	8–11	14	1	13	2	42%	2%
151–200	8.9	9.6	7–11	7–11	14	3	8	4	58%	10%
201–250	9.0	10.0	7–11	7–15	14	1	11	4	92%	6%
251–300	9.0	10.2	7–11	8–13	13	3	8	9	96%	8%
301–400	8.9	10.3	6–13	-8–14	15	1	6	7	100%	4%
401–500	8.6	10.1	7–12	7–13	15	3	8	9	100%	6%
501–600	9.0	10.6	6–11	8–14	13	4	6	10	100%	2%
601–650	8.5	10.1	5–11	8–13	14	1	8	10	100%	0%

Note: In column /2/, rows 1–50 through 151–200 are bracketed with an average of 8.8, and rows 201–250 through 401–500 are bracketed with an average of 8.8. In column /3/, rows 1–50 through 151–200 are bracketed with an average of 9.3, and rows 201–250 through 401–500 are bracketed with an average of 10.2.

guten Stanzen die Zweiteiligkeit ohrenfällig wird" (the shift of rhythm which makes the duality in Goethe and in all good stanzas conspicuous), which is in his opinion "das wirksamste Mittel . . . das dem schliessenden Reimpaar seine Eigenheit gegenüber den vorangehenden Zeilen gibt" (the most effective means that accords the closing rhymed couplet its unique quality vis-à-vis the preceding verses). (He does not refer to changes in quality. The modern Yiddish translator of *BB* caught the general tendency that led to the norm of *PV:* he translated the *BB* meter in the sextet into four iambs. But he did not feel the statistically different rhythm of the couplet, and did not translate it into the pentameter which characterizes the original *PV.*)[97]

(4) The same differentiation is supported by an account of the longest and shortest lines used. In the beginning there is no difference; later the couplet clearly has longer lines than the sextet and avoids the very short lines (columns 4, 5). The statistics show us clear tendencies, though no fixed numbers can be detected.

(5) In the sextet about three-quarters of all lines have fewer than ten syllables, and only a few have more than ten. In the couplet this relation changes in the critical region: lines longer than ten outweigh the shorter ones (columns 6, 7, 8, 9).

(6) For comparison, the rhyme-patterns are shown again (columns 10, 11— here all rhymes are counted, being now divided mechanically into groups of fifty stanzas). In the critical region there occurs a rise in the rhyme variation of the couplets, too (the use of masculine rhymes), but it drops again (column 11). *PV,* as usual, draws on the consequences: masculine rhymes are banned from the couplet.

(7) Table 5.2 shows the actual distribution of lines of different length in the couplet. The picture is clear: whereas the number of short lines drops sharply, the long lines dominate in the critical region, then drop again (around stanza 250), but this time in favor of the very long lines.

(8) In Table 5.3 we see that around stanza 400 Levita developed a new difference between the first and the second line of a pair: the second became shorter, as it so often is in Yiddish and in German folksong. Moreover, the shortest lines (of five or six syllables) now always appear to belong to the second line. It seems that in these shorter lines natural reading would use only three stresses; for example, *Der nóx záx er Bóvo un di fróy / un hórt zi réydn un láxn* (stanza 386) has four stresses in the first line, three in the second.

Table 5.2. Distribution of Lines of Different Length in the Couplets of the *Bovo-bukh* Stanza

Stanza Numbers	Number of Lines (for Every 20 Checked) Having a Length of:			
	7-8 Syllables	9-10 Syllables	11-12 Syllables	13 or More Syllables
1–50	6	11	3	0
51–100	6	9	5	0
101–150	6	12	2	0
151–200	2	14	4	0
201–250	2	14	2	2
251–300	2	9	8	1
301–400	1	12	5	2
401–500	2	9	8	1
501–600	2	8	8	2
601–650	4	6	9	1

Grouped percentages: 7-8 Syllables — 1–50 to 101–150: 30%; 151–200 to 601–650: 11%. 9-10 Syllables — 1–50 to 101–150: 53%; 151–200 to 201–250: 70%; 251–300 to 601–650: 44%. 11-12 Syllables — 1–50 to 201–250: 16%; 251–300 to 601–650: 38%. 13 or More Syllables — 1–50 to 151–200: 0%; 201–250 to 601–650: 8%.

Table 5.3. Relations of Length within Each Pair of Lines in the Stanzas of the *Bovo-bukh*

Stanza Numbers	Average Number of Syllables per Line			
	Line 1	Line 2	Line 3	Line 4
1–50	8.2	8.3	8.8	9.3
51–100	8.5	9.6	9.1	9.3
101–150	8.9	8.8	9.0	9.3
151–200	9.4	8.4	9.8	9.4
201–250	9.1	8.9	10.1	9.9
251–300	8.8	9.2	9.8	10.4
301–400	8.8	9.0	10.0	10.6
401–500	9.3	7.9	9.9	10.2
501–600	9.7	8.2	10.1	11.0
601–650	9.0	8.0	9.9	10.2

Grouped averages: Line 1 — 1–50 to 151–200: 8.8; 401–500 to 601–650: 9.3. Line 2 — 1–50 to 151–200: 8.9; 401–500 to 601–650: 8.0. Line 3 — 1–50 to 151–200: 9.2; 201–250 to 601–650: 10.0. Line 4 — 1–50 to 151–200: 9.3; 201–250 to 601–650: 10.4.

This tendency, which is occasionally in evidence at the beginning of the book, may be linked to the unusual order of rhyme gender: ultimate/penultimate, masculine/feminine (type b; see below). In folksong, where the first line cannot as a rule be shorter than the second line, the order ultimate/penultimate (masculine/feminine) occurs only if the second line has fewer stresses (the usual numbers are four and three, respectively, for lines 1 and 2), with eight syllables in line 1 and seven in line 2. But in *PV* the order ultimate/penultimate, though causing the first line to be shorter than the second, is employed in support of the metrical structure.

type a   ∪ — ∪ — ∪ — ∪ — ∪   (4:3)
           ∪ — ∪ — ∪ — ∪ —
type b   ∪ — ∪ — ∪ — ∪ —
           ∪ — ∪ — ∪ — ∪

This variation of four and three accents appears later in Levita's "Sreyfe-lid," but it was not used in *PV*, probably to prevent the kind of excessive lowering of the seriousness and compactness of a strophe which is possible in shorter lyrics, or to keep the conformity of the stanza (cf. point 11 below).

(9) A less pronounced, though quite consistent, tendency is to make the final, eighth line somewhat longer (on the average) than the seventh, as a kind of closure of the strophe.

(10) In both above-mentioned aspects there occurs some change in the critical region: the first attempt to differentiate between the first and second lines (then dropped, to be regained toward the end), and a similar differentiation of lines 7 and 8 (later reversed in direction).

(11) A further study of the final third of the book (not detailed here) shows that in the third couplet, too (but not in the second), the first line is longer on average. Thus the alternation is twofold: the first and third pairs of lines are alternatively longer and shorter; the second and fourth pairs are even in length, with a slight tendency to be shorter and longer; and the fourth pair (the closing couplet) is considerably longer than the preceding ones. In *PV*, only the most marked and consistent difference—the length of the couplet lines—was adopted and canonized.

One should not forget that those are only statistical tendencies, expressed in actual occurrences; they are not obligatory rules (and there are enough contradictory cases—e.g. the occurrence of a line of thirteen syllables in the sextet). It is not clear to what extent such subtle rhythmical tendencies were conscious. Their use seems to reflect Levita's subliminal sense of rhythm and musicality (which he called "tune"). It is clear that *PV*, taking over a whole network of such merely statistical tendencies, must be a direct immediate continuation of *BB*:

a	long	
b	short	
a		
b		
a	long	
b	short	
	c	longer
	c	

THE IAMBIC PATTERN OF *PARIZ UN VIENE*

In *PV*, Levita took a further step: he adopted the Italian principle of a constant number of syllables per line. But instead of taking over the Italian line of ottava rima, he projected the syllabic principle upon the pattern developed in his own *BB*: it was as if a model stanza of *BB* was frozen, regularized, and canonized. We lack the first quarter of *PV*; in the surviving portion of *PV*, the fusion of the two principles, the accentual and the syllabic, is complete: we find not just eight-syllable lines with four scattered accents, as in the German *Knittelvers*, but regular iambs. To be sure, there are still deviations, inconsistencies of orthography, etc., but the differences between *PV* and *BB* and the constancy of the meter are unmistakable.

Max Erik[98] holds *PV* to be "incomparably higher" than *BB* and the poet's "technique to be more natural." Yisroel Tsinberg,[99] following Erik almost verbatim, alludes to the musicality and the technical level of the stanzas (obviously: they suited his ears, trained on a.-s. meters). But neither author so much as attempts to explain this impression. The aesthetic principles of ottava rima, its unique combination of similarity and variety and similarity again, create an everyman's sonnet, its simplicity compensated for by a move into length and narrative. Levita stretched his wings and unraveled his casual yarn, the Yiddish chitchat about the unbelievable courtly lives.

In Italy ottava rima had been "the exclusive meter of epic and other narrative"[100] (Polizino, Pulci, Boiardo, Tasso, and others). From Italy it spread to other languages and came to be widely used in Camoëns's "Lusiades," in

Byron's *Don Juan,* in various works by Lope de Vega, Goethe, A. W. Schlegel, Zhukovsky, Pushkin, Yeats ("Sailing to Byzantium" and "Among School Children"), and A. Leyeles (in his Yiddish book of poetry, *Fabius Lind*). The form made its debut in Germany in a translation of Tasso's "Gerusalemme Liberata" (1626), while Byron first introduced it in his rendering of Pulci. According to one opinion, this stanza "verleitet zu isolierter Schilderung und kommt voll zur Geltung nur bei subjectiver, ironisch-lyrischer Distanz gegenüber den Stoffen, während ihre lyrisch-romantische Form für gegenständlich-objektive epische Themen wie etwa Tassos 'Befreites Jerusalem' weniger geeignet erscheint."[101] This subjective ironic-lyrical detachment indeed prevails in Byron's *Don Juan,* and it is evident as well—though in a more naive and less personal manner—in Levita's epics. Now, in its classic form, the ottava rima requires not merely a rhyme scheme (*abababcc*) but also a constant meter, viz. the endecasyllabic line (*endecasilabo,* consisting of eleven syllables with a required stress on the tenth). In this transformation it was also used in Hebrew, beginning with the work of Levita's contemporary Joseph Tsarfati, a native of Rome who died in 1527. Although Italian poetry certainly had iambic tendencies, its rule was merely syllabic. But when the form was translated into German, English, and Russian poetry, where the a.-s. meter predominated, and from these languages into modern Yiddish[102] and Hebrew, it naturally became an iambic pentameter, i.e. a five-stress line of ten syllables (the tenth is stressed, and additional unstressed syllables are allowed; it may have eleven or twelve syllables in a line, depending upon whether the rhyme is ultimate, penultimate, or dactylic).

But Levita uses the pentameter only in the couplet (*cc*).The lightness of his style, his folksy tone, and the rhetorical effectiveness of his verse are carried in the main by an iambic tetrameter, i.e. a four-stress line of eight syllables (or nine or ten, depending on the rhyme gender).

This meter has been extolled by Tomaševskiy for fitting the natural length of a prosaic phrase and thus representing natural speech well. Tomaševskiy considers it a lively, spoken, elastic line of verse.[103] H. S. Bennet, too, speaks of the merits of octosyllabics: "It is an excellent verse for a quick-moving, conversational type of poem. It is not so well adapted to convey emotion as it is to convey information or description, and the line nowhere seems long enough to allow much freedom to the writer, or any undue elaboration."[104] In this respect *PV* merely crystallizes a rhythmic-syntactical pattern found in *BB*.

This meter became the dominant form of Russian poetry, and it was from this source that it reached the modern epic works in the Jewish languages, e.g. those of David Shim'oni (Šimonovich) in Hebrew and Emanuel Kazake-vitsh in Yiddish. Here are two examples of this pattern in *BB*—one a normal stanza, the other a dactylic version (the examples are "regular"; on deviations see Chapter 8):

> Fïl lōyt dï ŏfnd
> dï āl mŏl pflēgň zāyn gŏr rēydïg.
> Un shvetsn oft in eynem fund
> oyf unzer bruder fun Veneydig.
> Zi shprokhn vi zi zayn im grund
> un troylikh zer un nit gineydig.
> Keyn fremdn menshn zi on zehen kenen
> nun merk vi zi im guts nokh heyl zayn genen.
>
> > (39r.i)

> Dŏlfïn dĕr shprōh: "Vï shtēyt ĕz drōyf,
> dŏs īr măyn lāyd vŏlt hāynt dĕrvāytĕrň?
> Vi volt ir kumen do heroyf:
> volt ir mit zayl, volt ir mit laytern?
> Drum, libe brider, merkt vol oyf
> dos ir nit drunter gingt tsu shaytern.
> Ey volt ikh do for brengen al mayn tegn,
> ey dos ir het ayn layd fun maynen vegn."
>
> > (61v.v; punctuation partly supplied)

All the traits of these stanzas have been mentioned before: the alternation of rhyme and of rhyme gender; the symmetrical tetrameter; the distinctive pentameter of the couplet and the finality of its form. The order of the rhyme gender—whatever may have been its reason in *BB*—is now explainable: only in this way can two lines, of which the first is ultimately stressed, be read as one rhythmical unit, without interruption of the iambic flow. This link of each pair of lines is further emphasized by the dominant syntactic structures and by the punctuation of *PV*: a period after every second line (as shown in our first example).

Levita frequently introduced syntactic and other variations into this pattern. But the meter is unmistakably present.

The headings and closings of the chapters, as well as the captions to the illustrations, are written in non-iambic rhyme pairs. Though most of these could be considered normal four-beat lines in an accentual framework (as in *BB*), here, against the iambic background, they serve as a kind of prosaic counterpoint to the meter.

There remains the problem of Levita's priority in the discovery of accentual iambs. This question is not of decisive importance to our study, considering the evidence of the author's own internal development. But in view of the previous historians of German versification, Levita's priority on a European scale seems uncontestable. There might be only one other contender to the title of pioneer: Sebastian Brant, whose "Narrenschiff" was printed in 1494 and popular thereafter. His meter contains eight syllables and displays a strong iambic tendency. But, as Heusler has demonstrated,[105] 11.5 percent of the lines have palpable accent deviations ("fühlbare Tonbegung"); moreover, this number does not include deviations permitted in the German a.-s. system after Opitz, e.g. when verbal prefixes are unstressed: *nachsètzten*), and the ultimate rhyme pairs are monotonously used by Brant without alternation.

Levita avoided such violations of the language. It is clear, too, that he did not continue with the syllable-counting tradition and did not always maintain the count of syllables. His pattern grew out of his own development and is in many details closer to the so-called folksong tradition.[106] It is indicative of Brant's position in the history of German metrics that his followers again moved away from his iambicity; in other words, they did not understand it.

Of course, iambic tendencies were in the air, in certain folksongs too (e.g. the Yiddish "Shabes-lid"), but Levita was the first to regularize and canonize the meter. He did this not by directly transferring it from semi-iambic folksongs but by using quite free folksong patterns and then applying to them the Italian strict syllabic principle.

PROBLEMS OF DEVIATION AND SPELLING IN *PARIZ UN VIENE*

This chapter was written based on parts of *PV* before a new edition was published in Hebrew in Jerusalem.[107] Chone Shmeruk says in his introduction that "the transformations of the strophic structure in Yiddish until their final crystallization in *Pariz un Viene* were described in detail by Benjamin Hrushovski (Harshav). His findings about the process of creation of this strophe in Yiddish are precise, though now we can be more exact in some of the details, based on the complete text of the book."

A formal analysis will disclose numerous deviations from the metrical pattern of *PV*, although most of them do not range beyond a single syllable in either direction. The text was printed after the author's death. In this unique text many words appear in variant spellings, the orthography is not always consistent, some features of pronunciation have no spelling equivalents, and misprints as well as possible "corrections" occur. Hence, it is not always easy to distinguish between a spot requiring correction and an admitted variation.

My analysis of the text shows that all deviations from an ideal scheme are explicable, especially when, instead of considering an abstract norm, one takes into account the conventions of poetry in all periods.

(1) Some sextets display iambic pentameters instead of the normal tetrameters. The additional iamb proves that the movement of the poem was primarily iambic rather than a matter of syllable counting (as in *Knittelvers*) or stress counting (as in folksongs and in *BB*). The addition makes such a line similar to a line of the couplet.

In the 116 stanzas of chapter X there are 25 such lines, i.e. an average of one in each 28 lines. In many of them the change in length is syntactically or stylistically motivated. In every case the change provides rhythmical variation without breaking the iambic flow. For example: "Der mönkh hob on un tröstet in / un shprokh: 'zayt frölikh nun un nit meyn zorgn!'" (61v.iv). The second line is a pentameter, but the monk's words make up an extraneous tetrametric phrase, as if the introduction to speech, "un shprokh," were a mere external guidelines. Here is a stanza in which the content motivates a dynamic rhythm that is underlined by the syntactical play to vary the standard pattern:

> Do shtos fun land, do knipf, do bind,
> do vaz der zegel oyf getsohen,
> un got—der shiket in ayn gutn vind
> herob fun zaynen himel hohen.
> Zi furn ob dohin geshvind,
> zi furn nit—ikh halt zi flohen!
> Glaykh az oyz ayner biksn flikht ayn kugel,
> azo geshvind zakh ikh ni forn hi tsu mugel.
>
> (63v.ii)

To the pentameter of the third line is added a strong, unusual enjambment breaking up immediate constituents (*vind* and *herob*). The long phrase contrasts with the short enumerations of the beginning, and the entire passage is underlined by the rhetorical figures.

On the other hand, we also find, though rarely, lines consisting of three iambs each (42r.ii and elsewhere).

(2) Here and there, formal scanning will find words which seemingly contradict the stress pattern. At the maximum, even supposing that the place of the stress in each word was the same then as it is today, we will have in chapter X an average of one such case in every fifteen lines of the sextet. This, however, is not the "Tonbeugung" of the German *Meistersang*, for here the number of syllables is not as strict (as we saw in point 1 above), there is hardly ever more than one such deviation per line, and those which occur are explainable in a rhythmical reading. The majority of these cases occur in the first and third iambs, i.e. in the symmetrically weaker stresses, or else they come at the onset of the rhythmical movement, in a beginning of a verse. Such phenomena are quite common in modern poetry, in Russian and English respectively (cf. the qualifications of the rule of §13). Most of these words are secondary in the phrase and can be read with a hovering accent, while the major word is stressed more strongly. For example "ŏbēr Păriź dĕr vór dĕr gründ"(63v.iv) The weakness of this position is demonstrated by large-scale statistical studies in Russian, where iambic tetrameter is widespread. According to Tomaševskiy, 57 percent of the third iambs are unrealized (i.e. have no language stress). In Levita's verse, the rhythmical role of the unstressed parts of long words in Russian (and in later Yiddish) poetry is fulfilled by the weaker word:[108] "măn fint ŏbēr zăyns gláykhn zéltn" (61v.ii); and "der vór unter den tish gezunken" (62v.ii), as if *ober* and *unter* had a hovering stress. It is as if "man fínt ober" and "unter den tísh" were considered one word each; the requirement of overlapping metrical accent and major word stress is then fulfilled. "Ober" is usually in a position like this, which leads one to suspect that it was accented ultimately: but this conclusion is unnecessary. The history of English prosody is full of similarly needless assumptions, as when, in connection with Wordsworth's "Protrácted amŏng éndless sólitùdes," one wonders if "among" did not have initial stress in Wordsworth's day. A non-mechanical reading may simply hover over a word which has some relatively weak stresses in a phrase or is located in a relatively weak stress position (or both) and subdue it accentually to its neighbors. In modern poetry there are many parallels, e.g. in a poem written

in Yiddish in the same meter: "Es klapt a tsug unter di shtern, / un s'klapt dayn harts un s'klapt mayn harts" (E. Kazakevitsh, "Tsug numer 42"). The word "ŭntĕr" seemingly contradicts the meter, but it stands in a weak position (the third iamb)[109] and is a syntactically subordinated word. Another solution is calling such a weak word and the following iamb an "ionic" foot |— ∪ ∪ —|, but that would change our assumption that all feet in a line are equal. Otherwise, any prosaic text can be divided into various Greek feet.

This group of deviations also includes some independent words (ten in the whole of chapter X), but all of those appear in the first or third iamb of the respective line. Moreover, most are infinitives; they may even be residues of the habit of rhyming "shtelén–reydén."[110] The others are part of close syntactical groups, e.g. "tut yederman voz im iz lib / *orum un raykh,* un yung un altn" (61r.v) or "foter un muter" (70r.ii). This is quite usual in English poetry, though it is not often found in Yiddish verse after Levita.

Special mention might be made of the words "Pariz" and "könig." Misstressing here may be a means of emphatic reading. Thus Viene cries out, "den shprokh zi mit eyn shray eyn grosn: 'O Páriz, Páriz, māyn hĕrts līb!'" (66v.i), whereas in normal conditions the name is stressed as "Paríz."

All in all, the number of deviations, though of several subtypes, is incomparably smaller than in modern poetry, where the long word and unrealized stresses come into their own.

(3) In the couplet, throughout the book, the deviations are relatively more numerous. (Wyatt, too, had clearer meters in his short lines; cf. §10). There is a tendency toward a caesura after the third iamb, though it is not consistent. In chapter X a word is misaccented in the couplet on the average of once in nine lines. There too, however, the misaccented words are mostly syntactically weak ones, and they stand primarily at the beginnings of lines or in comparatively weak positions.

(4) We sometimes find, as a parallel to the additional iambs in the sextet, a couplet with four iambs instead of five. This is, again, a pattern familiar in the poem. It serves expressive purposes. Consider the shortening of the last line of stanza 68r.i, motivated by Viene's happy meeting with Pariz: "Un drikt in mit den orem ale beydn / un kont für freyd eyn vort nit reydn." "As if she could not speak any more" is expressed in the shorter line.

Rhythmically expressive, too, is the drastic change in the following couplet (66v.i), where it serves as a kind of counterpoint. Here is the whole stanza:

Der könig glaykh for tsorn brand,
für grosn laydn, für grosn shrekn.
Er zakh für im di shmokh un shand
un vust nit vi ers zolt tsu dekn.
Un az er shtund oyf dizem shtand,
do hort man zer in aln ekn
yukhtsn, shrayen, griln mit grosn freydn:
"Es kumt, es kumt dem königs eydn!"

The trochaic chain in the seventh line is unknown in sextets. It is explainable as a direct continuation of line 6 (which ends unstressed), owing to the surprising enjambment. The shortening of the final line may be a simple misprint where the normal pattern of 3+2 iambs would give "Es kumt, es kumt, es kumt dem königs eydn."

(5) As is common in poetry, particularly when it is based on the spoken language, Levita's work displays numerous contractions or expansions of words by one syllable in suitable positions and regular forms.[111] The following categories emerge:

(a) There are numerous shortened enclitics: "du hosts for shuld un mogsts derkene" (69r.i); "un bald az zis hot in der hant" (64v.iii); etc.

(b) The situation is similar for proclitics ("ir ver mir nit für kern *n*toyer"; 67r.iii), but the abbreviations are not yet represented in the modern orthographic manner. Nevertheless, the meter shows unequivocally that many words fully spelled out, such as *dos, iz, es, ikh, er,* are actually apocopated; the process is also applied to some words which in modern literary Yiddish are not subject to apocopation. But when "dos shif" is read as "s shif" and "ven zi vert" is read as "ven z'vert," the meter is above reproach.

(c) Levita also elides some word-final vowels before words with vowel onset (thus, "di mü, di angst, di Odardo hot" is read as "d'Odardo"; 61r.iii) and occasionally ignores the *shewa* before final *n* in verbs, especially before vowels ("zĭ vērn ăntvākhn"; 62v.ii). Similarly, the derivative of Hebrew *de'ah* appears once as *dēy* and once as *dēyĕ*.

(d) Frequently the spelling implies a syllable added for metrical purposes, mostly through the introduction of a *yud* indicative of a *shewa: hinvēk' vāndeln, hinōys' forn, oyb'ikhōb, er zōgĭt nūn makh't, tsil't.*

(e) Much less frequent are the cases in which one syllable is missing or in which a completely extraneous one is added. By using Levita's own devices, as outlined in (a)–(d), these can easily be compensated for. Our right to do so is supported by the printer's inconsistencies and by his possible misunderstanding of the metrical principle.

(6) There are certainly also misprints which can be corrected. Although corrections for metrical reasons are dangerous,[112] and although they are not truly necessary (since a long poem can easily overcome deviations of all kinds), some nevertheless seem quite safe. These are either printer's mistakes, casual misreadings, understandable pitfalls of parallelism, or corrections of grammar. Thus on page 27r. we twice find "vor gevest" (in two different spellings) where the original probably had simply "vor" ("[da]s zǐ bāy děn fōtěr vōr gǐvēst ǐn zāyněr krānkǎyt": a most unusual six-iamb line in the couplet).[113] The accentual violation in dǐ ālt mǔtēr" (7or.iv) can be straightened out by means of a less simple order: "dǐ mǔtěr ālt," which is supported by the parallel "děr fōtěr ālt" in the same stanza. In many cases the sense of line is saved by slight metrical corrections. Whether all irregular lines are due to misunderstanding is, however, a matter of unresolved and unnecessary speculation.

ON LEVITA'S PLACE IN THE DEVELOPMENT
OF YIDDISH VERSE

In the history of Hebrew grammar Levita was an important intermediary between the Spanish Hebrew tradition and the modern, Ashkenazi period, as well as between the Jewish tradition and Christian Hebrew studies. But how did his work influence or change the course of Yiddish literature? I should not presume to attempt an answer to this question here, but I shall set down a few remarks about the place of his verse in the development of Yiddish poetry.

Somewhat similar was the lot of Hebrew iambs, developed in Italy (as an interesting result of the crossbreeding of two other metrical systems, the syllabic and the quantitative, which—in the conditions given by the language and the meter—paradoxically caused the overlapping appearance of a third system, the accentual-syllabic one). Italian Hebrew poetry strongly influenced the poetry of the Ashkenazic Enlightenment in Germany and Russia in the nineteenth century. In spite of the a.-s. metrical systems in the surrounding languages, the Haskalah poets had "finger-joint aches" (according to one of them) from counting the syllables in every line. Moreover, in continuing the Italian-Hebrew rhyming tradition many of the Enlightenment poets of northern Europe availed themselves of a small portion of the language (only about 8 percent of the vocabulary) in making their rhymes. In the "Sephardic" pronunciation of Hebrew in Italy this was more understandable, since few words were available for penultimate rhyming. But because of the different pronunciation of the Ashkenazic poets, they did not notice the iambs and had to rediscover them in Russia around 1890.

Yiddish verse in Italy did not live much longer than Levita himself. Its subsequent "low" existence elsewhere was not conducive to the maintenance of sophisticated forms. *PV* was forgotten altogether, while the numerous editions of *BB* culminated in a prose version with only a few vestiges of rhyme. Since, in folklore, verse continued to be connected with song or recitative, the constancy of syllable numbers did not matter. Any "iambic" tendency in the Yiddish or Hebrew-Yiddish short poems of the fifteenth and sixteenth centuries found its climax in Levita; folksong did not as a rule continue the development in this direction. On the contrary, in folksong the average number of syllables between stresses grew. The meter of folksongs and historical poems thereafter was accentual, primarily with four- or three-beat lines of two major varieties: (1) the more "usual" line, with fewer slacks between stresses (one or two), especially in lyrical songs, and (2) the longer, multisyllabic four-beat line (primarily in narrative poems).[114] All strophic forms, too, tended in folksong to become uniformly simple.[115] This situation did not change in principle in the Age of Enlightenment. Only in the 1880s, with the revival and fresh absorption of nineteenth-century European culture, was the a.-s. principle reintroduced into Yiddish and Hebrew.[116] The decisive, immediate conclusion was apparently the Yiddish verse of Shimon Frug, who came to Yiddish verse after being a Russian poet (this necessarily implied an experience with a.-s. meters) and who was extremely influential in his day.

In Italy there was at least one attempt to write purely syllabic verse in Yiddish—the kind of verse which Levita might have attempted if he had not known better than that. This was the introductory poem to the Yiddish Pentateuch printed in Cremona in 1560. The author was Yehuda ben Moshe Naftali from Crem, called Leyb Bresh. Characteristically the poem is written in the Hebrew "Merubah" form, rhyming *aaa bc cc b ddd b* . . . , etc. Every small verse-unit had four syllables (quatrain). Concomitantly, the rhyme disregarded stress but did consider the preceding consonant, exactly as in Hebrew: "rú-fen, tri-fen, hóf-fen," etc.

This is the example mentioned by Wagenseil. Another wave of syllabic meter in Yiddish, short-lived and quite unnatural (considering the background of folksong and surrounding European a.-s. poetry), came directly before the second revival of a.-s. meters, in the 1880s. The source was obviously the obsolete convention of Hebrew Haskalah poetry in its last days.[117]

Yiddish poetry before Levita was characterized by a preponderance of masculine rhymes. Although this pattern ran counter to the state of the language, it was a powerful German convention and made its impact on Yiddish poetry. According to L. Landau, in German epics penultimate rhymes constituted no more than about 10 percent of all rhymes.[118] In Yiddish epics, the proportion was slightly higher: a partial count finds that such rhymes are about 17 percent of the rhymes in the book of Esther and 15–20 percent in the *Shmuel-bukh*. The undeveloped stage of penultimate rhyming is evident from the repetitiousness of a few standard pairs: on two facing pages (2–3) of the *Shmuel-bukh*, out of eleven penultimate rhymes we find "tragn–zagn–geschlagn" six times; on another page (21), the same triplet occurs seven times among a total of twelve rhymes. But in Yiddish the majority of words were fit for penultimate rhyming because they were penultimately accented. Thus in the *Shmuel-bukh* masculine words make up only about 20 percent of all words in caesura, where rhyming requirements are not imposed. Another 10–20 percent consist of words of Hebrew origin. This fact seems to support the notion that the Hebrew stratum was already then penultimately stressed. The *Doniel-bukh* (Basel, 1557; Cracow, 1588), professedly written on the pattern of the *Shmuel-bukh*, makes the caesura exclusively penultimate and has many words of Hebrew origin in this position, although words with a Hebrew component are avoided in rhyme position. This dominance of masculine rhyming was supported by the freedom to rhyme final syllables even when they were unstressed, especially in words of Hebrew origin ("Mitspo–do"). The rhyming of words with antepenultimate stress ("glaykh–kinigraykh") is generally tolerated in regular iambic poetry, too, although moderns dislike even this relaxation of the rhyme-stress correlation.

The ultimate convention was overthrown by Levita, no doubt under Italian influence. Hebrew poetry in Italy had become exclusively penultimate at the ends of lines, although the pronunciation remained "Sephardic," so the language of the rhymes was seriously strained by the primarily ultimate accentuation. But the Italian poetic convention in this case accorded well with the accentual form of the majority of Yiddish words. Thus the rhyming possibilities were vastly enriched.

The sound element of rhyme was enriched at the same time. In the Yiddish epics the rhyme was extremely limited, since a minority of words had to cover a majority of rhymes. In Hebrew, on the other hand, every word could contribute its final syllable to a rhyme, so it was natural to "raise" the sound requirement and to include an extra consonant on a mandatory basis. In Hebrew, in fact, the pattern of the "supporting consonant" was consistently maintained until the nineteenth century, and it prevailed in bilingual poems, too. In Yiddish, on the other hand—as in other Germanic languages—the corresponding enrichment had to await the removal of the decisive rhyming place from the last to the second-to-last or even the third-to-last but stressed syllable. This increased the choice of rhyming words and the length of the rhymeme (the repeated sound segment). In masculine rhymes, as in terminal rhymes, the sound segment of Hebrew words is longer, and the rhyme in Hebrew texts is thus richer than in Yiddish texts because of the additional consonant. But after the introduction of penultimate rhymes the opposite became true. Thus the Hebrew text of *Megiles Vints* rhymes, still in terminal fashion, "gdoLA–seLA"and "layLA–hatsaLA," but in the Yiddish half of the poem, we find two-syllable rhythms of Hebrew origin: "tfILE–kehILE"and "IzbELE–sELE" (in *PV*).

Another possible source of feminine rhymes and of alternating rhyme gender was the Yiddish short poem, which was close in form to the German folksong. Unfortunately, few texts of this genre have survived.

Whatever the reasons, we see that the Yiddish *Artushof* in its ottava rima version, professedly patterned after *BB*, has 15–20 percent of its sextets in purely penultimate rhymes, while the others, as in the bulk of *BB*, are alternating ultimate/penultimate rhymes. The Yiddish half of the bilingual *Megiles Vints* has one-third of its half-stanzas ending in purely penultimate rhymes, while the balance is again ultimate/penultimate (masculine/feminine): only a negligible proportion have other rhyming patterns. The usual order of alternation in modern ottava rima stanzas in Yiddish, as in German and Russian, is the opposite, namely penultimate/ultimate (feminine/masculine). Here the principle of the two lines functioning as one unit has been replaced by the rule of the diminishing second line.

Another piece of evidence for Italian influence in the predominance of penultimate rhymes is the long poem *Akeda* ("The Sacrifice of Isaac"); the version stemming from Germany has about 25 percent penultimate rhymes, but an Italian manuscript contains some additional stanzas with 75 percent penultimate rhymes. On the basis of various aspects of this additional part, Chone Shmeruk surmises that it was added by Levita. Characteristically, although many words of Hebrew origin appear in the text, this long poem does not have a single rhyme between two such words. But the small additional part, mostly penultimate rhymed, has three stanzas rhyming *aaaa* with all Hebrew-origin words in rhyming position: in two of them all four rhyming words are of this component of the language, and in one of them two Hebrew-origin words are rhymed with one of Germanic origin and one of Italian origin.[119] This tendency was clearly further strengthened in Yiddish folksong and poetry in the Slavic domain.

Thus Levita's rhyme marks a turning point in the history of Yiddish verse. The predominance of ultimate rhymes, with vestiges of the old concept of terminal rather than stress-bound rhyme, is replaced by an abundance of penultimate (feminine) rhymes (with an admixture of dactylic ones) conforming with the language stress and organically incorporating words of non-German stock (Hebrew, Italian, later also Slavic) in their normal Yiddish pronunciation.

Because of the erratic existence of Yiddish literature through history, Levita's creation was doomed to be forgotten. But the pattern of his growing discovery of a.-s. meters, unsophisticated though it may seem to us; the mechanics of his individual insight, which enabled him to utilize and combine the conditions given to him into a creation that was rigorous and supple at the same time— being typical of the manner in which a.-s. meters were created elsewhere— present a singular case of the intricate dynamics of poetic language, a case in which one person can be seen traversing the whole way in his own work. Levita sensed the road to the second prosodic possibility, without which accentual poetry in modern times is unthinkable.

Basic Forms of
Modern Yiddish Poetry

Meter and sound orchestration are central to Yiddish verse to more of an extent than a contemporary reader of English poetry might be prepared to encounter.[1] The "magic" of repeated metrical patterns, symmetry and parallelism, puns and deviations, reinforced by sound play and rhythmical variation, does to the simplest words what music does to the elementary words of popular songs. In Russian poetry, the poetic quality of the text is invested in sound patterning no less than in original imagery, metaphor, paradox, complexity of meaning, surprising language, and fictional worlds—aspects that are more crucial to the dominant poetry and criticism in English.

The central poetry-making function of meter and sound in most of Yiddish poetry is the legacy of Russian Modernist poetics, which exerted a major influence on modern Yiddish verse. Like Baudelaire, who combined "Modernist" themes and images with classical verse forms and rhyme patterns, Russian Modernist poets—Mandelshtam, Mayakovsky, Pasternak, Tsvetaeva—molded their Futurist metaphors and surreal compositions in consciously crafted rhythms, dense sound patterning, and conspicuous rhyme innovations. The language of poetry promoted neologisms and what I call "focusing sound patterns,"[2] such as T. S. Eliot's *"word–Word–world–whirled"* ("Ash-Wednesday"), which do not imitate any sounds in nature but focus the reader's attention on some interrelated words, encased in memorable sound configurations. This was also true for early German Modernist poets, such as Stefan George and R. M. Rilke, at the beginning of the twentieth century. In Yiddish, as in Russian, using such sound patterns remains a strong tendency to this day, as can be seen in the "neoclassical Modernism" of the last great Yiddish poet, A. Sutzkever (1913–2010).

In English poetry, on the other hand, Modernism is identified by and large with free verse. Sound patterning often does play a conspicuous role in the texture of the poetic language but not in predictable, symmetrical molds, such as meter and rhyme. In the history of English poetry, the break between the metrically oriented Romantic and Edwardian verse of the nineteenth and the beginning of the twentieth century and what followed was so radical that the very sense of what in the meters and metrical variations so enchanted the poets and readers has been lost. T. S. Eliot's early poetry, published in his student years in the *Harvard Crimson* and never collected in a book in his lifetime, was written in agile and precise "Edwardian" meters.[3]

This difference in emphasis in the cultural perceptions of what is essential to poetry is reflected in the diametrically opposed poetic theories promoted by representatives of both cultures. Roman Jakobson, a Futurist poet and linguist raised in the Russian avant-garde tradition who had a decisive impact on modern Structuralism, derived his concept of "poetic function"[4] mainly from the study of meter and sound patterns. His Anglo-American "meaning"-oriented contemporaries, the New Critics and their followers, on the other hand, indulged in metaphor, ambiguity, and paradox and disregarded versification even while interpreting the well-formed strophic poems of Keats, Shelley, and Wordsworth.

Apart from this functional difference between the two poetic cultures, there are more subtle but crucial differences between the English and the Russian traditions. Typically, the most widespread English poetic meter was an iambic pentameter, i.e. an asymmetrical line composed of five iambic feet that are unequally divided into two or more syntactic-rhythmical units (cola). Such asymmetrical groups of feet change their boundaries differently in different lines. The scanning regularity (five iambs per verse line) is further overshadowed by the irregular patterning of syntactical units with their enjambments and long periodical sentences, as in Milton's *Paradise Lost* (see Chapter 1), where the first sentence spreads over sixteen lines. On the other hand, the major metrical form in the Russian tradition is Pushkin's symmetrical four-iamb line, variations of which contribute great flexibility and rhythmical interest and invite the reader's involvement in the poetry. Here, tension and variety are achieved by the great variety in the structure of the Russian words and their lengths and places of stress. Yiddish and Hebrew poets in the modern age absorbed their metrical sensibilities largely from this tradition.

Furthermore, since regular accentual-syllabic meters were so new in Yiddish poetry—they were introduced as the dominant form only in the late 1880s—their very use was exhilarating. They sounded so mellifluous and musical and set off poetry from the vulgar spoken language. They reigned in Yiddish poetry for such a short period that there should not have been any sense of saturation, any need for programmatic revolt. Yet the very use of regular, "classical" meters was a revolt. If such a feeling gripped Yiddish poets in the 1920s, it was under the impact of a general European "battle-cry of freedom" in verse, as T. S. Eliot put it, and, in particular, under the influence of Anglo-American Modernist taste, which had to overcome four hundred years of almost automated, routine metrical verse in English. When A. Leyeles, the New York Yiddish *Inzikhist* (Introspectivist), talked of liberating words from traditions and conventions, it was a general European-American rather than a particular Yiddish tradition that he revolted against, since, for him, Yiddish poetry and his own intellectual world were part of general culture.

One basic, inherent reason for the different perceptions of the same meters in English versus Russian or Yiddish lies in the different sound-structures of the languages. The vocabulary of traditional English poetry is 80 percent monosyllabic, with 17 percent of the words having two syllables and 3 percent being long words of three or more syllables,[5] whereas Yiddish and Russian have many polysyllabic words variously stressed: in the beginning, the end, or the middle of the word. This variety can create interesting counterpoints between the words and the feet of the regular meter. Such a simple Yiddish word as אַרױפֿגעטשעפּעטע **a-ROYF-ge-tshe-pe-te** (hooked onto)[6] has six syllables, with four syllables coming after the stress and carried by it—"in the air," as it were. In a versification favoring predominantly rising feet (iambs and anapests, $| \cup -|$ and $| \cup \cup -|$) stressed toward the end, the effect of such a word, stressed close to its beginning, creates a rhythmical counterpoint between the language and the meter: *aróyfgetshépete*. In an iambic line it would have three iambs a-**róyf**-ge-**tshe**-pe-**te**, while only the first is realized in language.

The main idea of this argument is that *meter* and *rhythm* are two different constructs. Meter takes up an abstract and regular grid, while rhythm is the result of interaction between several factors in reading or constructing the specific poem. In meter, all feet are identical; in rhythm we consider expressive reading that changes throughout. The readings can vary, but the horizons are the metrical scanning, on the one hand, and the actual units of the spoken language, on the other. The size and placement of words in a poem are different from the metrical scheme and from each other's size and placement. Tensions and counterpoints between elements of the two systems (verse and language) provide life and variety, and there are rules of correlation between the two asymmetrical systems. Similar tensions arise between the units of verse and the units of sentences. The meanings of the text or constructs of interpretation provide direction for the reader's orientation in interpreting the rhythm.

Let us observe several strophes from a poetic cyle by H. Leivick (Leyvik), "In shney" (In Snow), written in a meter of four trochees. This cycle, light as the snow, evokes the poet's flight from exile as he traveled through Siberia to America. I did not capitalize the beginnings of verse lines in Yiddish in order not to confuse those capitalizations with stress. An arrow indicates the direction of reading.

איז דער וועג מאָנאַטן לאַנג,

ציט זיך ווי אַ זילבער שנור.

פֿאָר איך מיטן זילבער שנור,

מורמל עפּעס אַ געזאַנג.

→

IZ der VEG moNAtn LANG,	— ∪ — ∪ — ∪ —
TSIT zikh VI a ZILber SHNUR.	— ∪ — ∪ — ∪ —
FOR ikh MItn ZILber SHNUR.	— ∪ — ∪ — ∪ —
MURml Epes A geZANG.	— ∪ — ∪ — ∪ —

[Like a silver string unfolding / For months, the road is long— / I travel with the silver string, / Murmuring a song.][7]

This is a perfectly executed metrical scheme with four language stresses to each line, matching the metrical accents of the trochaic grid, and with an unfinished last foot.

Now let us look at the opening strophe of the same cycle, "In Snow"; here we again have four trochees. We can scan it mechanically thus:

לאַנגע ווינטערדיקע נעכט

→

LANge VINterDIke NEKHT	— ∪ — ∪ — ∪ —

The actual stresses given in the language, however, are fewer than four. We imposed a secondary accent on DIke.

I shall now mark only such accents that are actually realized in the language. A vertical bar (|) indicates boundaries between words or word-groups that can be pronounced separately, as in an expressive (rather than scanning and mechanical) reading.

לאַנגע װינטערדיקע נעכט,

װײַסע שטראַלנדיקע טעג.

האָב איך אײַנגעשפּאַנט מײַן פֿערד

לאָזן זיך אין װײַטן װעג.

→

LANge VINterdike NEKHT, | — ∪ | — ∪ ∪ ∪ | — |

VAYse SHTRAlndike TEG. | — ∪ | — ∪ ∪ ∪ | — |

hob ikh AYNgeshpant mayn FERD | ∪ ∪ — ∪ ∪ | ∪ — |

LOzn zikh in VAYtn VEG. | — ∪ ∪ | ∪ — ∪ | — |

[Long winter nights. / White, radiant days. / I harnessed my horse / To go far away.]

In this presentation, the trochaic metrical scheme persists in the background and we can scan it precisely, with a metronome if we wish. But when the strophe is read expressively, according to the units of the language, only the first two lines are identical; no regular metrical line appears. We get two or three actual stresses per line and several widely differing rhythmical units (containing two, four, one, five, or three syllables), juxtaposed to each other. After the first trochaic word (**LANge**) comes a long, hyperdactylic word: **VIN-ter-di-ke**; it, too, is initially stressed and begins as a repetition of the first trochee, but after the stress it goes up in three unstressed syllables, creating a strong melodic effect in Yiddish. After this long unit, we rest on one stressed syllable, closing the line, which seems, in this context, to underline the matter-of-fact reality.

This pattern, repeated in the first two lines, creates a "melodic" opening of the strophe. The third line shifts into a different rhythm, announced at the outset by subduing the stress of the first syllable: instead of a trochee, we have an anapestic line opening with auxiliary words. A long rhythmical unit of five syllables dominates the line. The last line is again different in effect. We can explain it by observing the places of actual stress in the trochaic tetrameter: in the first three lines, the second and fourth trochees are stressed; i.e. every even trochee is stronger than the odd ones, creating a double symmetrical wave in the Russian tradition.

Defying this regularity, the last line skips the second stress, thus avoiding symmetry and sounding prosaic; then it ends in two "iambs," which, again, have a prosaic effect, especially when defying the strong trochaic beginning of the poem.

The underlying formal trochaic meter is preserved in all those rhythmical variations, but the use of long and short words creates rhythmical dynamization of the text. After this opening, the second strophe begins with an entirely regular trochaic line—both in language and in meter—which is surprising and effective as a counterpoint to the first, variegated strophe:

הײ און ברויט און ווײַן געקויפֿט

→

HEY un BROYT un VAYN geKOYFT   — | ∪ — | ∪ — | ∪ —

[I bought hay, bread, wine.]

The simple practicality of this statement is underlined by the exact scanning, with full four stresses; by the monosyllabic stressed words; and by the shift from the trochaic meter to iambic word-units. A reading of the three examples side by side will show the range of rhythmical variety available to masters of Yiddish verse even in the confines of one rather simple and trite meter. These possibilities—of juxtaposing short and long, variously stressed words; of juxtaposing the words to the metrical feet; and of juxtaposing neighboring lines of a poem to each other—were exploited to the full for the whole gamut of poetic tones by the Yiddish American poets who emerged with the melodic achievements of *Di Yunge,* the "Young Generation," in New York in the second decade of the twentieth century. According to the theory of rhythm promoted by the Russian Symbolist Andrey Bely, any change of the patterns from line to line has a rhythmical value apart from the independent precision of the meter itself.

A. Leyeles opens his virtuoso sonnet garland "Autumn"[8] thus:

אַ לויב דיר, האַרבסט, סעזאָן פֿון רײַפֿן גאָלד,

פֿון דורכזיכטיקע, בענקענדע קריסטאַלן.

→

a Loyb dir, HARBST, seZON fun RAYfn GOLD,

|∪ — | ∪ — | ∪ — | ∪ — ∪ — |

fun DURKHzikhtike, BENkende kriSTAln. |∪ — ∪∪∪ | — ∪∪ | ∪ — ∪ |

[I praise you, autumn, season of ripe gold, / cold, translucent, and nostalgic crystals.]

The first line sets the tone of a precise iambic pentameter, placing this garland of sonnets in the European sonnet tradition. The second line provides only three out of five possible stresses, introducing a strongly changed rhythm on the same metrical base and seeming to underline all that longing in its endlessly drawn-out dactylic and hyper-dactylic words: **DURKH-zikh-ti-ke** ($-\cup\cup\cup$), **BEN-ken-de** ($-\cup\cup$). Sometimes Leyeles even manages to skip two consecutive stresses of the trochaic meter, creating a long, five-syllable unstressed stretch, as in his poem "Tao" (*AYP*, 85):

שלאָס פֿון קאַלטע, בלישטשענדיקע כריזאָפּראַזן

SHLOS fun KALte, BLISHTshendike khrizoPRAzn

→

$$|-|\cup-\cup|-\cup\cup\cup|\cup\cup-\cup|$$

[Castle of cold, sparkling chrysoprase]

Five unstressed syllables in a row: this is created by conjoining two long words, one initially and one terminally stressed (in our case, the conjoining is supported by the strangeness of this glittering world to Jewish immigrant ears). There is no doubt that Leyeles knew what he was doing in seeking this effect, which was praised in Russian Symbolist prosody and re-created in pentons (five-syllable measures) about the same time in Ashkenazi Hebrew by Saul Chernikhovsky.

This rhythmical figure in "Tao" is counterpointed by the concise last line of the four-line strophe in two short, stressed words:

→

IKH – aLEYN. $-|\cup-|$
[I-alone]

H. Leivick made memorable use of dactylic words in his self-proclaimed "first" poem, famous for its musicality:

ערגעץ וויַיט, ערגעץ וויַיט
ליגט דאָס לאַנד דאָס פֿאַרבאַטענע,
זילבעריק בלאָען די בערג
נאָך פֿון קיינעם באַטראָטענע;
ערגעץ טיף, ערגעץ טיף
אין דער ערד איַינגעקנאָטענע

וואַרטן אוצרות אויף אונדז

וואַרטן אוצרות פֿאַרשאָטענע.

→

ergets VAYT, ergets VAYT	| ∪ ∪ — | ∪ ∪ — |
ligt dos LAND dos farBOtene,	| ∪ ∪ — | ∪ ∪ — ∪ ∪ |
ZILberik BLOen di BERG	| — ∪ ∪ |— ∪ | ∪ — |
nokh fun KEYnem baTROtene;	| ∪ ∪ — ∪ | ∪ — ∪ ∪ |
ergets TIF, ergets TIF	| ∪ ∪ — | ∪ ∪ — |
in der ERD ayngeKNOtene	| ∪ ∪ — | ∪ ∪ — ∪ ∪ |
vartn OYtsres oyf UNDZ	| ∪ ∪ — ∪ | ∪ — |
vartn OYtsres farSHOtene.	| ∪ ∪ — ∪ | ∪ — ∪ ∪ |

[Somewhere far, somewhere far away / Lies the land, the forbidden land. / Silvery blue the mountains / Never trod by man; / Somewhere deep, somewhere deep inside, / Kneaded into the earth, / Treasures are waiting for us, / Treasures covered with dirt.][9]

An anapestic meter is established in the first line, subordinating even two-syllable words (*ergets, vartn*) to its strong stresses: ערגעץ ווײַט **ergets VAYT** \| ∪ ∪ — \|, ערגעץ טיף **ergets TIF** \| ∪ ∪ — \|. But suddenly each pair of what started as anapestic units culminates in its opposite, a dactyl: פֿאַרבאָטענע **far-BO-te-ne** \| ∪ — ∪ ∪ \|. This dactylic ending is strengthened by the fourfold repeated dactylic rhyme and by the pervasive parallelism: **farBo-te-ne—baTRO-te-ne—ayngeKNO-te-ne—farSHO-te-ne**. The effect of the dactylic words is reinforced by several intersecting devices: the dactyls are juxtaposed to their opposite, the anapest meter; they are made conspicuous by the dactylic rhyme; they are prominent as a minority layer in the Yiddish language; and they evoke the effects of dactylic endings in Russian lyrical poetry, which are especially strong when attached to non-dactylic meters, as in Byron's canto I of *Don Juan*. In addition, each dactylic word here ends in three open syllables, making it easy to draw them out in reading or singing: **far-bo-o-o-te—ne**. And these dactyls are juxtaposed to the earthy, strongly stressed monosyllabic key nouns of the poem: **VAYT, LAND, BERG, TIF, ERD**.

A similar effect is achieved by the sudden reversal of the meter in the dactylic opening of the third line: **ZIL-be-rik**. All this is reinforced by a network of anaphores and parallelisms. The basic rhythmical tension is repeated: the pairs of lines are parallel to each other and create a "musical" effect.

FREE VERSE

After World War I, Yiddish poetry evolved, deviating variously from this European metrical tradition. At first, the meter stayed close to the traditional meter but deformed its effects of regularity. For example, in Moyshe-Leyb Halpern's "Our Garden," each strophe establishes a perfect meter of four trochees, repeated in two rhymed couplets and introduced by an initial refrain "aza gortn aza gortn." The basic four-line strophe is:

אַזאַ גאָרטן וווּ דער בוים
האָט זיך זיבן בלעטלעך קוים,
און עס דאַכט זיך אַז ער טראַכט :
ווער האָט מיך אַהער געבראַכט?

אַזאַ גאָרטן, אַזאַ גאָרטן,
ווי מיט אַ פֿאַרגרעסער-גלאָז
קאָן מען זען אַ ביסל גראָז,
זאָל דאָס אונדזער גאָרטן זײַן
אָט אַזאַ אין מאָרגנשײַן?

→

aza gortn vu der boym   — ∪ — ∪ — ∪ —
hot zikh zibn bletlekh koym,   — ∪ — ∪ — ∪ —
un es dakht zikh az er trakht: — ∪ — ∪ — ∪ —
ver hot mikh aHER geBRAKHT?[10] — ∪ — ∪ — ∪ —

aza gortn, aza gortn,   — ∪ — ∪ — ∪ — ∪
vu mit a farGREser-gloz
kon men zen a bisl groz,
zol dos undzer gortn zayn
ot aza in morgnshayn?

[What a garden, where the tree is
Bare, but for its seven leaves,
And it seems it is amazed:
"Who has set me in this place?"

What a garden, what a garden—
It takes a magnifying glass
Just to see a little grass.
Is this garden here our own,
As it is, in the light of the dawn?][11]

But this regular, elementary pattern is suddenly subverted by an additional, unrhymed long line (line 5), with a provocative, "Jewish" conversational manner:

אַוודאי אונדזער גאָרטן. וואָס דען, ניט אונדזער גאָרטן?

aVAde undzer gortn. vos den, nit undzer gortn?

[Sure, it's our garden. What, not our garden?]

Halpern breaks out of the symmetrical mold with a gesture of defiance. In fact, surprisingly, this line can be read as a precise, six-foot iambic line, but the context of trochaic inertia makes it feel like free rhythmic spoken language.

In many poems, especially when using a ballad tone (e.g. "Kol-Nidre"), Halpern abandoned the regular meters by turning to the free-syllable meter of folksong, based on lines with four or three stresses. When he employed his personal voice in his long monologues, however, he favored an irregular iambic flow, locating the irregularity in the free and changing length of mostly long prosaic lines and avoiding parallelism, thus creating a non-poetic narrative effect. This conversational iambic flow, often prefiguring the monologues of Allen Ginsberg, is usually harnessed in rhyming pairs in payment of a kind of sloppy duty to a folkloristic and children's conception of poetry as rhymed language.

A more radical departure from regular meters was effected in "free rhythms," as advocated by the Introspectivists in New York. See J. Glatshteyn's book *Fraye ferzn* (Free Verse).[12] Since the handling of syntax and the tone of a poem may be decisive in the rhythmical impact, the variety of individual rhythms seems, indeed, much wider than in the metrical tradition. The two main directions of such free verse may be called "dynamic" and "conversational" rhythms.[13]

"Dynamic" rhythms are irregular; there is no single metrical pattern for the whole poem. But the patterns are more rather than less rhythmically structured, using local rhythmical configurations strongly deviant from prose or else an interplay of changing metrical segments, heightened sound effects, and internally inverted rhymes. An English example for one kind of "dynamic" rhythm can be seen in T. S. Eliot's "Ash-Wednesday." The Yiddish theoretician of poetry A. Leyeles claimed that Yiddish free verse, though influenced by the general principle of free verse, as pronounced in Anglo-American Imagism, developed a richer gamut of rhythmic expression than its English counterpart. Indeed, Yiddish poets combined the Russian sensibility for heightened sound patterning in poetry with the Anglo-American "battle-cry of freedom," with freedom representing the individuality of the artist, the individuality of the single poem, and the individuality of the particular line or image. Such intense rhythmical texture may seem affected or artificial to a contemporary English-speaking reader, but it was at the heart of the poetic impulse of many Yiddish and Russian poets in the 1920s and 1930s. Naturally, such effects are intimately tied up with a feeling for the language and should be conveyed to Yiddish readers, orally if possible. A reading of such a poem by A. Leyeles, "January 28," can be seen in Chapter 7 in this book.

At the other pole, we have "conversational" rhythms, especially as developed by Halpern, Glatshteyn, and Leyeles. Leyeles used rhythms of both types, even in one poetic cycle, "The Diary of Fabius Lind," where we have highly structured as well as conversational poems. The rhythms introduce the intonations and interjections of a Yiddish speech situation, suppressing meter as well as any tendency toward parallelism of adjacent lines. The continuity of an advancing monologue rather than equivalences of verse determine their rhythmical impact. The rhymes are convenient for bringing out the full flavor of Yiddish conversation, verbal gesture, and characterization in poetry. See, for example, Halpern's long, rambling monologue "This I said to my only son at play—and to nobody else,"[14] written when his son was two years old. As Glatshteyn wrote (in Yiddish) in 1947: "Whitman went far away from Shelley and Keats—from song to the rhythm of human speech. Free verse is the measured human breath of speaking, shouting, or solemn recitation . . . but free verse could not cover the wise prosaic smile of the clever tongue."[15]

RHYME AND STROPHIC FORMS

The same tendency that favored free verse rather than precise meters in contemporary English poetry worked against the conventional "square" use of rhyme in strophes. It was part of the loss of confidence in the traditional matrix of the strophic poem, which molds the size of thematic units in advance— in favor of free segmentation of the poetic text, dictated by the rhythm of individual lines, their syntax, and their poetic content and supported by the English tradition of free syntactic units modifying the monotony of regular meters. But it also reflected the higher degree of attrition of English conventional rhymes compared to their attrition in such languages as Russian and Yiddish. In English, where most words are monosyllabic and most rhymes are both monosyllabic and masculine, it is hard to provide large numbers of new and rich rhymes, which normally would use several syllables or imprecise or disharmonic endings, spread back deep into the line. Lord Byron used them and produced a comic effect. Neither is it easy to provide conspicuous contrasts between the rhyming and the non-rhyming sounds of the final words. On the other hand, inventive rhymes flourished in Russian Modernism, where long words are abundant, and became one of its central markers.

Influenced by Russian Modernist poetics, Yiddish and Hebrew poetry also luxuriated in inventive rhymes. Innovation in this domain was enhanced by the open-minded enlargement of the Yiddish vocabulary—both in so-called Internationalisms, multilingual concepts of modern civilization, and in slang and dialect expressions (the High and the Low)—and its heightened component-consciousness of the eclectic language, Yiddish. This is obvious in the verse of such masters as Yehoash, Perets Markish, Eliezer Shteynbarg, A. Leyeles, and A. Sutzkever. It was a major reason for the plethora of strophic patterns—with the exceedingly difficult form of multiple and intertwined rhyme members—developed by such a sworn verslibrist as A. Leyeles. For him, free verse at one pole and complex metrical strophes at the other were both departures from the conventional quatrain—i.e. the implied inventive effort, rhythmical variety, and illusion of individuality of each poem. Such is, for example, the rich fourfold rhyme in Leyeles's poem "Herod," where he conjoins disparate semantic fields and juxtaposes words from several stock dialects of Yiddish:

הורדוס-האָרדעס-מאָרדעס-דערמאָרד עס

HORdes–HORdes–MORdes–derMORD es

The meaning needs to be deciphered: *Hordes* ("Herod," from Hebrew and Greek); the almost homonymous *hordes* (hords—Internationalism, via Polish or German); *Mordes* ("mugs" or "animal faces"—a coarse word, conspicuously Slavic); *dermord es* ("murder it"—a compound rhyme, from German).[16]

In free verse as well, especially in the poetry of Leyeles and Glatshteyn, rhyme plays an important role as a sporadic focusing device. A special form of internally inverted, unexpected rhymes was developed by the Introspectivists; in it the end of a line is echoed in the beginning or the middle of a following line, with the traditional stopping effect often overruled by the continuing syntax. In this form, rhyme gave up the compositional function which it had in the strophic poem, along with the pleasure of fulfilled expectations, and acquired a function—similar to that of unfolding metaphors—of punctuating the text with surprising, self-contained sound units. In Leyeles's words, "It comes suddenly. A halt in mid-leap. The leap into the unknown. For us, rhyme is preparation, not rest."[17]

At the other pole, Leyeles's sonnet garland "Autumn" may serve as an example of a European form re-created in Yiddish. It has fifteen concatenated Italian sonnets written in iambic pentameter. Each sonnet employs the difficult Italian rhyme pattern: the first eight lines are bound with only two rhymes in an inverted order, *abba baab cdcd ee,* and the Shakespearean couplet is used as an aphoristic closure. In addition, the individual sonnets are concatenated: the last line of each sonnet is repeated as the first line of the next sonnet (often with ingenious syntactic variations). The fifteenth sonnet is composed of all the first lines of the preceding fourteen sonnets, again using the same difficult rhyme pattern. As a result, a dense rhyme grid embraces the whole structure, creating innumerable echoes between the various sonnets and their topics. Two key rhymes occur twenty-eight and twenty-six times, respectively; others occur fourteen times (with no rhyming word repeated). This musical magic is impossible to reproduce in translation.

FORMAL CONFINEMENT OF EVIL

The horrors of Dante's Inferno would remain unalleviated horrors, the raptures of his Paradiso would be visionary dreams were they not molded into a new shape by the magic of Dante's diction and verse.[18]

האָרכט מײַן וואָרט דורך אײַער זוכן, לײַדן, האָוועו,

אין געצוימטע און געמאָסטענע אָקטאַוון.

ווען קיין גרענעץ איז נישטאָ פֿאַר די יסורים,

ווייטיק-אויס אַ סיאָג פֿון שטרענג-געצוימטן פֿורעם.

horkht mayn vort durkh ayer zukhn, laydn, haven,
in geTSOYMte un geMOStene okTAvn.
ven keyn grenets iz nishTO far di yeSUrim,
veytik-oys a syog fun shtreng-geTSOYMtn furem.

> (A. Leyeles, "To You, Yiddish Poets,"
> in "A Dream among Skyscrapers")

[Through your searching, suffering, frenzy, hear my word / In restrained and measured octaves. / When there is no limit to your anguish, / Build your pain into a fence of rigorous form.]

At about the same time, in the late 1930s or early 1940s, Leyeles wrote three poems with a surprisingly similar perception of the soul as a battlefield of madness, of irrational drives that possess a person. The points of view in the poems, however, are cardinally different and so, appropriately, are the rhythmical conceptions of the poems. The poems are "Foreign Fencers" (*AYP,* 174–177), "Shlomo Molkho Sings on the Eve of His Burning" (*AYP,* 176–179), and "Herod" (*AYP,* 178–185). (All three were published in Yiddish after the Holocaust, in his book of poetry *A yid oyfn yam* [New York, 1947].)

"Herod" is the brutal king and paranoid madman who slaughtered everyone in sight, a Stalin out of Jewish history, breeding hatred and fear and himself a "slave to a curse," moved by powerful internal forces he cannot control. "Shlomo Molkho on the Eve of His Burning" presents an intriguing historical figure with a messianic vision and daring arrogance, a redeemer in dark times in Jewish history, a leader who carries the masses with him in a utopian vision only to pay for it with his own isolation and inevitable destruction. (The historical Molkho was burned at the stake after an attempt to enlist the Pope in his cause.) Leyeles's drama on this topic had its world premiere in Vilna ghetto in 1943, before its annihilation.

In the poem, Molkho also has a Stalinist streak; he is the Messiah, the Redeemer, enjoying the blind submission of the crowd; he, too, is gripped by vanity, by the narcissist aggrandizing of his "I," which breeds loneliness and fear of himself. But historically, from a "messianic" point of view, Molkho is a positive hero, and Leyeles presents his tortured self-understanding. Night, "the metamorphoser of forms," piles doubt on him in darkness, on the eve of his execution, and extorts his real, personal confession; his transformation makes him "humble and silent with joy," relieved to exchange the "redeemer's poison" within him for the pure breath of the flame of the auto-da-fé.

Though the poem about Herod sees him from the outside, it reveals the king's internal psychotic drama and incorporates his own point of view in Free Indirect Style. Herod's position is formulated in rhetorical, aphoristic summaries. The tone—that of a solemn, concise, and nervous recitation—is underlined by the formal strophic structure and declamatory rhetoric. The poem about Molkho is the internal monologue of a mystic transformed and liberated by embracing the exalted vision of his own burning; its rhythm is as free as his liberated mood. It is, however, not a prosaic free verse; rather, the mood is conveyed in the festive tone of an ode to the night that is gradually transformed into the passionate confession that leads up to the dramatic gesture.

The third poem, "Foreign Fencers," presents the sleepless nights of Leyeles's own arrogant and lonely "I"—a resigned, latter-day Fabius Lind (the poet's alter ego from the 1930s) in sophisticated introspection, in the grip of overpowering drives and contradictions. Though no leader, redeemer, or slaughterer, he, too, is a battlefield of madness; within him, too, in the battlefield of his psyche, there are "masters of evil," devious demons descending "from a spider-webbed attic" (*boydem*) and devastating his "authentic image." (Is this attic his subconscious? Or should we say "superconscious"? Or is it a collective subconscious like a Jewish *boydem*, an attic filled with antiques?) But Lind manages to externalize the battlefield, the whole "foreign fencing" that goes on inside him and from which he has no escape; he stands like an observer outside himself and smiles. The rhythm is also free, following the fluctuating observations but underlining the ironies almost from the beginning and lacking the long periodical sentences and exclamation points of Molkho's ode.

The evil of the most individual Introspectivist and the introspection of the most evil figure of the century—transposed into the repetition of history—are two poles of one scale. There is an affinity between Messiah and tyrant, between inhuman history and the frail humanity of the poet himself. According to the poet's theory of "bipolarity" (see "Chronicle," no. 22), "the most dedicated verslibrists will suddenly turn to the most confined, classical forms." The superformal and the hyper-prosaic are two sides of the same coin. As befits this book, I shall concentrate on the formal principles of "Herod."[19]

"Herod" has a fixed, consistent meter and rigorous strophic structure invented by the poet, enriched by free sound orchestration and rhythmical variation. There are nine strophes of nine rhyming lines each, with a tenth line as an unrhymed, defiant closure. Thus, the first stanza of the translation reads as follows (the reader is invited to scan the dactylic pattern, artificial as it sounds in translation):[20]

→

∪∪ — 0 ∪ — 0 ∪ — ∪∪ — ∪
Herod is old. His face, anointed with ointments,
∪∪ — ∪∪ — ∪∪ — ∪∪ —
Balsams and makeup from Egypt, looks young. But his gaze—

Restlessness, fear and grim clouds in the darkening folds,
Monstrous two halves side by side—an abyss:
Roman—and Semite; despair—and good fortune;
Patron of strange little swallows,

Breaker of a nation's neck;
Slave on a throne,
King in the yoke
Of unsated desires, of sickly and stealthy suspicions.

Below, capital letters indicate all accented syllables. The original reads:

הורדוס איז אַלט שוין. זײַן פּנים, געריבן מיט זאַלבן,
מיצרישע שמירעכצן, קוקט נאָך אויס יונג, נאָר זײַן בליק —
אומרו און פּחד און כּמאַרעס אין טונקעלע פֿאַלבן.
אָפּגרונט וווּ ס׳לויערן מאָנסטרישע האַלבן :
רוימער — סעמיט ; האַלב פֿאַרצווייפֿלונג, האַלב גליק ;
זאָרגער פֿאַר ווילד-פֿרעמדע שוואַלבן,
ברעכער פֿון אומהס געניק,
קנעכט אויף אַ טראָן,
קיניג אין קאָן
בײַ אומלעשבאַרער דאָרשט, בײַ פֿאַרדאַכטן געהיימע און קראָנקע.

HORdos is ALT shoyn. zayn POnim, geRIbn mit ZALbn
MITSrishe SHMIrekhtsn, KUKT nokh oys YUNG, nor zayn BLIK—
UMru un PAkhed un KHMAres in TUNkele FALbn,
OPgrunt vu S'LOyern MONstrishe HALbn;
ROYmer—seMIT; halb farTSVEYflung, halb GLIK;
ZORger far VILD-fremde SHVALbn
BREkher fun Umes geNIK
KNEKHT oyf a TRON
KINig in KON
bay umLESHbarer DORSHT, bay farDAKHtn geHEYme un KRANke.

We may now abstract the metrical scheme:

Meter	Rhyme	Ending
— ∪ ∪ — ∪ ∪ — ∪ ∪ — ∪ ∪ — ∪	a	feminine
— ∪ ∪ — ∪ ∪ — ∪ ∪ — ∪ ∪ —	b	masculine
— ∪ ∪ — ∪ ∪ — ∪ ∪ — ∪ ∪ — ∪	a	feminine
— ∪ ∪ — ∪ ∪ — ∪ ∪ — ∪	a	feminine
— ∪ ∪ — ∪ ∪ — ∪ ∪ —	b	masculine
— ∪ ∪ — ∪ ∪ — ∪	a	feminine
— ∪ ∪ — ∪ ∪ —	b	masculine
— ∪ ∪ —	c	masculine
— ∪ ∪ —	c	masculine
∪ ∪ — ∪ ∪ — ∪ ∪ — ∪ ∪ — ∪ ∪ — ∪	x	feminine

The meter begins with the solemnity of a dactylic pentameter; the line is an almost epic. Unlike the iamb, the dactyl—with its stress at the opening of each line and foot—is a very pronounced meter in Yiddish, requiring a solemn, even artificial reading. The length of the lines systematically recedes, from five dactyls down to two, the rhythmical units becoming more and more concise and tense.

Against this background of the long-winded, forward-pulling, ever-narrowing dactylic rhythms, there is the unexpected break of the last line: its meter is the opposite—an anapest, it has no rhyme, and after the couplet of short-breathing exclamatory verses, it sounds like an endlessly long line, a cry of madness breaking out of confinement. The rhyme patterning does not coincide with the patterns of length but rather creates a counterpoint to them until the last couplet where they fall together. In the couplet, each of the short lines creates an arch, leaning on two stressed syllables at its ends, reinforced by rhyme and often by alliteration as well:

קנעכט אויף אַ טראָן,

קיניג אין קאָן

→

KNEKHT oyf a TRON,	— ∪ ∪ —
KINig in KON	— ∪ ∪ —

The long-winded dactylic lines leading up to short lines help create their strong rhetorical effect, which is reinforced by the alliteration: out of four stresses, three have the sound cluster K + N which dominates the last line— with the word *kinig* (king) also mirroring the earlier rhyme, *genik* (neck).

An additional device uses the two periods inside the first two lines to break up the forward-moving rhythm. At the end of line 2, however, a phrase opens up ("But his gaze—") which requires completion and for which no verb is supplied in the long, periodic, tense sentence, which continues relentlessly to the end of the strophe. But this long-winded forward movement is also filled with obstacles and broken up into small autonomous segments, framed by the rhymes and by rhetorical pairs of oppositions ("Roman—and Semite; despair—and good fortune"), though a final stop is not permitted until all rhymes are completed and the flow issues into the final long and unrhymed phrase. Thus, a tension between the ever-continuing, ruthless forward drive, in ever shorter and tenser units and the stalling, local dams constitutes the rhythmical character of this poem. Leyeles's original strophic matrix is its indispensable base.

A great deal of what was going on in Yiddish poetry in this period—in the Soviet Union and in the West—was invested with such intensive attention to the texture of sound and language in a poem.[21]

7

THE CONSTRAINTS OF FREEDOM
IN MODERN YIDDISH POETRY

Vers libre . . . is a battle-cry of freedom, and
there is no freedom in art.

—T. S. Eliot

The tasks of world theater serve us as the tasks of
our theater, and only language distinguishes us
from others.

—A. Granovsky, director of the avant-garde
Moscow Yiddish Theater

This study was conducted in 1953, after World War II, when there still were many Yiddish poets aware of their craft around the globe, when there was a living memory of their age of glory, and when there was a fresh dream of humanistic science and international structuralism. The study emerged from a similar investigation of Modern Hebrew free rhythms, published in part as a brochure, *The Rhythm of Largeness* (1964).[1]

Free rhythms are not simply prose chopped up into arbitrary verse lines.[2] Though those verses are free in comparison with their predecessors in precise meters, freedom never comes without limits or constraints unless it is really prose (is there such a thing?). As our structural description of free rhythms advances, the boundary of prose recedes. In this chapter, I try to define the limits of that freedom and observe different kinds and categories of free rhythms. I do so using a corpus of literature that is mainly Yiddish modern poetry. We may observe that Yiddish poetry—coming from the Russian orbit—has much more flamboyant rhythmical expressions than does English poetry, where the poet must be shy about overly conspicuous sound play.

CULTURAL CONTEXTS

Most of Yiddish poets in the twentieth century have undergone the influence of at least two from among a variety of literatures: Russian, German, English, American, Polish, French, and Hebrew, including Biblical and Ashkenazi Hebrew. Some of the Yiddish poets wrote poems in Hebrew as well, and vice versa: many Hebrew poets from eastern Europe wrote some poems in Yiddish (Shteynberg, Fichman, Bialik). In a single generation and often on the same few geographic and sociocultural bases all these interacting influences have flowed, like so many tributaries, into the pool of a common, barely surviving Yiddish literature.

Moreover, for reasons of cultural history, Yiddish literature had not shared the intellectual development of its European neighbors for hundreds of years. Yiddish poets in New York were cobblers and wall painters rather than children of clergy. It was a different social class that wrote and cherished poetry. Consequently, when the young east European Jewish intelligentsia, in one grand leap, landed in the twentieth century, Yiddish poetry undertook to catch up with Europe's deepened appreciation of the classics and the Modernist trends of recent generations. Eclecticism it was, but demonstrative eclecticism, as in Chagall's paintings[3] or in the Yiddish language itself. As I argue elsewhere,[4] Yiddish is not only a language of *fusion* between its components, as Max Weinreich pronounced (which was good for the claim that it was an independent language), but an *open* language that could freely use any number of words from its source languages (German, Hebrew, Polish, Russian, American, plus international political vocabulary to describe the modern world). As Wallace Stevens said, all French words are part of the English language. If you read an orthodox Yiddish newspaper today, you see that all Hebrew words are part of the Yiddish language.

As a result, modern Yiddish poetry, apart from its intrinsic value in Jewish culture, may serve as an extraordinary source for the understanding of general literary processes, literary trends, and literary forms. We can learn here about the crisscrossing of "influences" and the degree of their absorption; the significance of a cultural heritage peculiar to the group and the problem of giving it expression in new forms; the role of the sociocultural base in deciding the amount and types of influences admitted; and, on the other hand, the degree of inertia of conservative forms and patterns and the possibilities of an organic evolution to cultural forms of an entirely different mode. We can witness the relative roles of the early environment of a writer vis-à-vis his milieu during his subsequent development, especially against so striking a background as the sudden transition of an entire culture and an entire nation from small towns to cities, from one country to another—even across an ocean. Yiddish poetry was comparative literature par excellence.

Let us keep in mind, too, that despite the eclecticism of these cross-influences and the clashes of cultures and trends, it is thanks to the power of a specific Jewish culture and a separate Yiddish language, supported by a reinvigorated organized society and the creative personalities of many poets, that a good deal is original, including unique literary trends and patterns of expression which are not a copy of any extrinsic trend: *Di Yunge* (the "Young Generation") in New York around 1910; *Inzikh* ("Inside Yourself"; Introspectivism) in New York in 1919; *Khalyastre* (Happy Gang), in Warsaw-Berlin-Paris in the early 1920s; *Yung Vilne* (Young Vilna), in Vilna, Poland, in the late 1930s.

B. R. Lewis wrote: "Poetry is the rhythmic expression in rhythmic language of rhythmic poetic emotions."[5] Hence, an authentic poet's treatment of rhythmic forms reveals his adherence to a literary-cultural trend. Thus, Fritz Strich, in his book *Deutsche Klassik und Romantik* (Bern, 1954), distinguished between the two trends Classicism and Romanticism in German literature according to their essentially different approaches to man, nature, subject matter, language, and rhythm and rhyme. In this perspective, only an upheaval in the whole human and poetic perception of the world produces changes in the obstinately conservative forms of poetic structure.

In sum: (a) the general human foundations of rhythm—biological, psychological, and cultural—and (b) the interaction of traditional and foreign influences (c) on the basis of the specifics of the Yiddish language and in the conditions of its concrete prosodic structure—all those have created unique forms of free-rhythm poetry.

By "free rhythms" I have in mind: freedom from the prevalent metric system, which in Yiddish, as in English, was accentual-syllabic (a.-s.). An a.-s. meter determines both the number of syllables per verse line and the number and order of stressed and unstressed syllables. At the same time, the term "free rhythms" implies not just form but a poetic language which gives the reader the impression of rhythmical discourse, irrespective of meter and in contrast to prose.

Unlike Andreas Heusler,[6] I include as free rhythms poems that have a fixed number of stresses in a verse line and a free number and order of unstressed syllables. With the number of stresses the same, such poems nevertheless may have an altogether different rhythmical impact, depending on the changing number of free syllables between the stresses and on the type and limits of freedom. In this respect, Heusler is mistaken because of his strictly isochronistic, musically determined doctrine, which literally assumes equal time to any distance between two stresses. We can stretch or squeeze the unstressed syllables for any result we want, but language is not music.

On the other hand, metrical lines of unequal length were a form widespread in Yiddish metrical poetry, even in the era of purely a.-s. meters, e.g. in the fables of Eliezer Shteynbarg (1880–1932), written in iambs with changing length of lines. We will call such a.-s. poems "free verse"—to differentiate them from "free rhythms"—since the length of their verses is not predetermined, having no fixed number of feet, but the number and place of syllables in a foot is constant. The term "measure," or "tact," is the textual distance between two stresses (including one of them). It is the musical term for what in metrics is called a "foot." A foot includes one stressed and one or more unstressed syllables, repeated a number of times in a verse line.

In regular a.-s. meters there are areas of flexibility, or *licentia poetica*, when both ends of the line are relatively free, e.g. in the end of a verse line determined by the rhyme. Hence an iambic pentameter could have ten or eleven syllables, provided the tenth syllable is stressed and the eleventh not. Poems may have a free anacrusis (accretion or subtraction of the opening syllables of a verse line), or addition or subtraction of unstressed syllables in the caesura. Whether all those are still allowed in precise meters depends on the perception of meter in a specific poem: the meters may be precise in the interior of the line but free on its margins. Hence "free verse" refers to freedom in the number of feet; "free rhythm," in contrast, refers to freedom in the number of syllables in the interior of a rhythmical wave.

In free rhythms, the best way to assess the measure of freedom taken in the poem is to transcribe the numbers of syllables as if the meter were regular and observe the deviations from a regular abstract scheme.

In the following, all metrical diagrams are to be read from left to right, according to the direction of the English transcription, unless otherwise indicated. The direction of reading is marked by an arrow.

For example, here is a poem by Eliezer Grinberg:

און אַ געהיימע האַנט באַשיט

די קעפּ פֿון ביימער \ מיט יונגן צוויט.

אָוונט קומט, \ שלאָפֿט מען איין

באַרוישט פֿון שטילן \ שטערנשיין.

→

ŭn ā GĔHĒYMĔ / hānt băshīt //	∪ — ∪ — ∪ | — ∪ —
dĭ kēp fŭn BĒYMĔR / mĭt yūngn tsvīt. //	∪ — ∪ — ∪ | ∪ — ∪ —
Ōv̆nt kūmt, / shlōft mĕn āyn //	0 — ∪ — | 0 0 — ∪ —
Bărōysht fŭn shtiln / shtĕr̆nshāyn.	∪ — | ∪ — ∪ | — ∪ —

[And a secret hand pours / young blossoms over the heads of trees. / Evening comes, and one falls asleep / intoxicated by the cool starlight.][7]

(Vertical bars mark the borderline of a word or a colon. All translations of poetic texts in this chapter are rendered in prose.)

The first and fourth lines have four regular iambs each. The second line has an accretion of two weak syllables in the caesura, marked by zeroes.

A sense of symmetry predominates in every line, enhanced by the internal rhyme in the first two lines. By means of deviations from a schematic meter, excessive melodicity is avoided and a certain prosy narrative tone is attained, encouraged by the scene and mood of the poem. Except for the middles of lines (caesura), two stressed or two unstressed syllables do not meet head on. That is, the poem is basically written in binary feet: iambic and trochaic. In the third line, on the contrary, most weak syllables disappear. Hence the second line has nine syllables, while the third has only six, yet the meter is the same: four iambs. The proportion is unusual: the third line has two unstressed to four stressed syllables. The length of the lines is different, but structurally justified, as the zeroes show.

The borderline cases include also poems which are written ostensibly in an a.-s. meter but carry several stronger stresses, which are not distributed at equal syllabic intervals. A higher rhythmical wave dominates the reading, as in the poem "Oyf di fayern" by H. Leivick (1888–1962):

אויף די פֿײַערן אין לופֿט די טאַנצנדיקע קוק איך,

און די אויגן מײַנע

ווערן ווי די פֿײַערן אין לופֿט די טאַנצנדיקע.

The following diagram shows the sizes and boundaries of words. Double accents indicate a stronger stress:

→

Ŏyf dĭ fâyĕrň ĭn lūft dĭ tāntsňdīkĕ kūk ĭkh,

$$\cup\cup{-}\cup\cup\,|\,\cup{-}|\,\cup{-}\cup\cup\cup\,|{-}\cup$$

ūn dĭ ōygň māynĕ $\cup\cup{-}\cup\,|{-}\cup\,|$

vērň vī dĭ fâyĕrň ĭn lūft dĭ tāntsňdīkĕ.[8] ${-}\cup\,|\,\cup\cup{-}\cup\cup\,|\,\cup{-}|\,\cup{-}\cup\cup\cup$

[I look at the fires dancing in the air, / and my eyes / become like the fires dancing in the air.]

Formally these are trochees (seven or eight trochees in the long lines), $|{-}\cup{-}\cup{-}\cup{-}\cup{-}\cup{-}\cup{-}\cup|$. But to limit the number of stresses in a line, we shift from trochees into double trochees or paeons. In reality, four major stresses dominate every long line in the poem. In order to decide about the mode of reading we have to invoke the lofty mood and observe the high number of long words. The pressure to not have more than four major stresses per line exerts its power to emphasize the coda in major stresses: $|\cup\cup{-}\cup$ $\cup\,|\,\cup{-}|\,\cup{-}\cup\cup\cup\,|{-}\cup\,|$. The number of trochees is not the same in every line. And the distances between major stresses change: sometimes five syllables to one stress, sometimes only two or merely one. Precise meters have been liberated from the metronome.

Here is another strophe from the same poem:

שינערעטצעניפ רעטכידעג ריאָוורעטש רעביאָונָפיול סע יוו —

די אויגן מײַנע —

צו די ווײַטעלֿפֿעּיעערןושנײַדן זיי זיֿדּודורך דער פֿינצטערניש.

→

Vī ĕs lōyfň|ĭbĕr shtērň|ĭn gĕdīkhtĕr|fĭntstĕrnīsh—

$$|\cup\cup{-}\cup\,|\,\cup\cup{-}\cup\,|\,\cup\cup{-}\cup\,|{-}\cup\cup|$$

dĭ ōygň māynĕ— $|\cup{-}\cup\,|{-}\cup\,|$

tsū dĭ vāytĕ|fâyĕrň||shnāydň zēy zĭkh|dūrkh dĕr fĭntstĕrnīsh.

Between any two stresses we have one up to four syllables.

Large rhythm:[9] $|\cup\cup{-}\cup\,|{-}\cup\cup\,|{-}\cup\cup\cup\,|\cup\cup{-}\cup\cup$

The same in *trochees:* ${-}\cup{-}\cup\,|{-}\cup{-}\cup{-}\cup{-}\cup{-}$

[As the stars run across the dense darkness / these eyes of mine / cut through the darkness to the distant fires.]

The pressure toward large rhythms is supported by the four super-accents, an optimal size in the culture. The result is a two-story rhythmical structure: the mechanical effect of pedestrian trochees, like the warp in the base of a carpet, overruled by a pattern of major stresses in free distances. We can scan the mechanical meter or express the "rhythm of largeness" in the free, wide steps.

The stronger stresses may lie regularly on every second metric stress, and then a paeonic impact (four-syllable foot) is created. It may, however, result in unequal word groups, which are sensed as rhythmically free, but which have not yet dared to liberate themselves from the formally accepted underlying a.-s. infrastructure. In some readers, this may evoke a scanning trochaic reading, which deadens both the dactylic line endings and the entire organic mood of the poem. But the tension and competition on two levels is effective.

The true unit of rhythm is not a foot but a "syntagma," or "colon" (a term revived by the Russian Formalists)—i.e. a syntactic-rhythmical unit with often ambiguous boundaries that appears as a word with its auxiliary words grouped around one major stress. This group can be pronounced without an interruption in breathing even in slow reading. The division of the line into cola, over-riding the metrical units and counteracting with those, is the true rhythmical force of verse. This became possible when Yiddish poetry (under Russian influence) promoted the especially long words, dactylic rhymes and so on.

In reality, we may distinguish two major groups of free rhythms:

a) *Accentual rhythms,* which retain an equal or equivalent number of feet and accents per line but have changing numbers of syllables. Accentual rhythms are often "folk-like" in a modern way in their tone and language and usually preserve a strophic structure. (On the folksong, see Chapter 8.)

b) *New free rhythms,* which are free both in the length of their feet and in the number of feet per line. New free rhythms are chiefly found in free-rhythmic texts. Their rhythmic impact is closely related to the expression of the atmosphere or mood of a poem or a poet and therefore differs widely, depending on the author and the subject matter of a specific poem. New free rhythms fluctuate between highly rhythmicized big-city dynamics, on the one hand, and mundane, terse statements on the verge of prose, on the other.[10]

HISTORICAL SURVEY OF YIDDISH VERSE

The history of Yiddish verse can be sketched as having four main stages.

THE LATE MIDDLE AGES

In the secular Yiddish epic or biblical narrative poem (e.g. *Shmuel-bukh,* fifteenth century), under German influence, yet written with Hebrew/Yiddish letters, the meter is free-accentual.

Was there a coherent Yiddish literature after the earliest rhymed text appeared in the thirteenth century (in the Cairo Genizah)? The Yiddishist movement after World War I wanted a pedigree and constructed such a history. The first history of Yiddish literature was written in English by Professor Leo Winner at Harvard University. Max Erik, Max Weinreich, and Israel Tsinberg contributed their own histories of Yiddish literature. Chone Shmeruk renewed the project after the Holocaust. But actually the so-called history consisted of individual texts, disconnected from each other, without a network of schools, writers unions, publishing houses, political parties, and other unifying institutions that emerged at the end of the nineteenth century.

THE NINETEENTH CENTURY IN EASTERN EUROPE

This was the flourishing period of the briefer lyrical and balladic folksongs in Yiddish.[11] Both the sophisticated and the popular Yiddish poetry of the Haskalah (Enlightenment) was free-accentual under the influence of the folksong and in turn influenced the folksong thanks to its wide dispersion. The filling of feet grows in diversity in proportion to the literariness of the songs: sometimes the lyrics of entire song seem nearly to be in iambs, and even more frequently they tend toward amphibrachs.

On the other hand, the prosody of "High" Hebrew in the Haskalah is syllabic, as prescribed in the Italian tradition, demanding a fixed number of syllables per line and no constraints on stresses (except at the line end). It was in this way, in syllabic meters, that the Haskalah poets wrote in Hebrew, and Shloyme Etinger (1801–1856) wrote in Yiddish. Yet all this goes against the strongly accentual quality of their own daily speech (Yiddish). In Hebrew the syllabic pattern (of Hebrew Italian heritage) persisted until the 1890s. Patently, the *read* language needed above all a meter for the eye. But *spoken* Yiddish needed a meter for the ear. Therefore the same poets who wrote Hebrew poems syllabically wrote their Yiddish poems accentually. No wonder that Avrom-Ber

Gotlober (1811–1899), the first of the bilingual Jewish poets in the Haskalah, was also the first in eastern Europe to attempt to write a Hebrew poem in a.-s. meter. Subconsciously this was supported by the folksy type of language of these authors. But the Yiddish songs were written to be sung to a melody— hence their syllabic freedom in contrast to the printed poetry in Russian or German read by the same poets, which was entirely a.-s.

Characteristically, Shloyme Etinger, a man of fine literary tastes, could construct complex strophes, but he counted the syllables in translating Schiller's "Das Lied von der Glocke." Another Hebrew poet in the Vilna Haskalah, Adam HaCohen, complained that his fingers ached when he wrote poetry (because he had to count thirteen or eleven syllables in every line). The poems do not have an immediate emotional impact. Even in translating a free-accentual ballad ("Walheid" by Theodor Körner), Etinger set himself a uniform syllabic pattern according to one of the strophes of the original. And Gotlober, who was influenced by folk patterns, *weighed* the same "Glocke," retaining only its stress count. Though he already knew what an a.-s. meter was in Russian and in German poetry, he tried it out in some of his own poems but did not use it consistently to the end.

Even Yehuda-Leib Gordon (YaLaG; 1831–1892), the major Russian Haskalah poet, who lived in St. Petersburg in his later life and was influenced thematically by Russian poetry—even he wrote syllabic poems in Hebrew and spoke against accentual meter. Yet in Yiddish he wrote only accentual or purely a.-s. poems. The tendency to lapse into a.-s. meters may be due to the fact that the poets *wrote* their poems; that is, in abstracting themselves momentarily from the melody, they needed the inner balance furnished by an a.-s. meter in order to feel the isochronism, lost with the music. Such poems also lack the effects of being digested, simplified, and transformed by the folk culture into an assimilated folksong.

Even the works of the most folk-like of the poets are distinguished from folksong, if by no other feature than by the almost constant rhyming of all lines: the wandering bard Berl Broder used a strophe rhyming **abab**—that is, the first line rhymes with the third, the second with the fourth—and not, as in the genuine folksong **mana**, where only the even lines (a) rhyme. The folksong does not want to break the sentence, which usually covers two lines with no rhyme in the middle.

This criterion permits us to detect individual songs of this period in collections of folksongs (subsequently their sources may be located or other literary features discovered). The rhymed couplets with unequal numbers of measures practiced by the *badkhonim* (wedding jesters) continue the free line-length of the recitative. Their verbose, sermonizing language often lacks an inner rhythm and internal cohesion, and since no rules are observed, we often have simply rhymed prose, with changing lengths of lines and with rhymes as appended jokes. The *badkhn* improvises and "tells" the songs only at the wedding. His songs can therefore be separated from wedding occasions and become regularly sung pieces only if they are pressed into the framework of lines of up to four measures and of uniform strophes, as was done by Eliyokum Tsunzer (Zunser; 1836–1913), a *badkhn* turned poet. Tsunzer, to be sure, was unable to express a thought in four lines—his rhythmical impulse was longer than that—yet his long strophes are each composed of several quatrains with folk rhymes.

THE CLASSICAL PERIOD

The classical period of Yiddish literature came at the end of the nineteenth century. In poetry, there was a brief transitional period of scant artistic value. But it did prepare a mass reader for a.-s. meters and supported the development of a poetic-rhetorical technique in song and declamation.[12] In the 1880s and 1890s, in Yiddish as in Hebrew, poetry all at once became a.-s. For decades the *maskilim*, the Hebrew purists, had been reading a.-s. poems in German and Russian, but it was a silent, bookish, and passive reading: they were not fully at home either in German or in Russian and did not hear the sounds of the poetry in a deeper sense. If they understood it, they could not actively absorb the greater poems or even their subject matter. Therefore their few attempts to approach this read poetry in sound and to write a.-s. poems themselves remained isolated. Only as a wider stratum of the young Jewish intelligentsia joined the general culture could the experiencing of Russian literature in an active, creative sense begin. This led to an upheaval in all the fundamentals of Jewish poetry in both Yiddish and Hebrew simultaneously—i.e. the upheaval was socioculturally determined; the leap was to a new artistic level, in rhythm as well as in other respects.

A contributing factor was the decisive turn from the sung poem to the poem for reading, teaching, and recitation, which needs substantial isochronical features in the text itself in place of the melody. But the new doctrine penetrated even the song: Tsunzer, the folk bard, who could do without equal numbers of syllables and leave the music to preserve the rhythms, nevertheless began to sing a.-s. songs as early as the 1880s. The iambs that had been invented in

Venice in the sixteenth century—and all but forgotten—finally were accepted in the whole culture at the end of the nineteenth.

Since rhythm is experienced only accentually, in this period even Heine's works were interpreted and adapted in Yiddish in an a.-s. pattern (just as previously the a.-s. poetry of Schiller was reinterpreted either only syllabically, in Hebrew, or only accentually, in Yiddish). Avrom Reyzin (1876–1953), H. N. Bialik (1873–1934), Sholom Aleichem (1859–1916), Itzhak (Yitzhok) Katzenelson (1886–1944), even the folk singer Mordkhe Gebirtig (1877–1942), and many others, created folksongs which are genuine as to their content but take the form of the 4 + 3 trochees of the Russian *častuška*.

AFTER WORLD WAR I

At the beginning of the twentieth century Jewish poetry was exposed to classical European literature; the upset of the First World War finally cast it into the stream of problematic contemporary Modernist trends. The previously isolated attempts ceased to be peripheral. A new language, new imagery, new art, new subject matter, new rhythms appeared on the scene.

With respect to rhythmics there was a sharp reaction against the metallic character of the impressionistic, symbolically colored poems of the beginning of the century (e.g. poems by *Di Yunge*, the "Young Generation" in America). These poems were an expression of the time: even the representatives of the earlier trend, such as H. Leivick and Moyshe-Leyb Halpern, opened themselves to free rhythms and were accepted by the Modernists (Glatshteyn) as genuine poets.

We can mark the dates exactly. In the works of H. Leivick in New York, poems in free verse first crop up in his book *In keynems land* (In No-Man's-Land; written in 1916–1920). His poem "Oyf di fayern" (1916), quoted above, is his only free-rhythm poem prior to *In keynems land,* but it, too, was meant to be a.-s. Thus, in M. Basin's comprehensive anthology of Yiddish poetry of 1917,[13] inspired by the poetics of *Di Yunge,* free rhythms do not yet occur. Moyshe-Leyb Halpern's (1886–1932) *In Nyu-york* (published in 1919) is still purely a.-s. But his second book, *Di goldene pave* (The golden peacock; 1924), is almost entirely free-rhythmic. In a span of just five years the free rhythm revolution occurred!

It is notable that true Expressionism in Yiddish in Poland in the 1920s did not import from Germany liberation from the a.-s. meter. The Yiddish *Mefisto* (Lemberg, 1921) by Uri-Zvi Grinberg (1894–1981) is purely a.-s., but his general rhythm is closely related to his later free rhythms. Polish poetry traditionally was syllabic. The Expressionists made their revolution in rhythmics within the old framework by exploding the symmetric and uniform limits of line and strophe, by giving an extraordinarily dynamic character to the sentence, by developing metric contrasts, and by executing a stirring paeonization of the iambs and trochees. Grinberg, when he shifted in 1924 to writing in Hebrew, called it "the rhythm of Largeness" (in Hebrew: *ritmus harakhavut;* see my Hebrew book *Omanut HaShira* [The Art of Poetry]). Storms rather than melodies were forged from the iambs. Similar was the "solemnly fervent" (in Yiddish: *patetish*) poetry of Ukrainian Yiddish "revolutionary" lyricism.

Yiddish Expressionism tore down the uniformity in the number of feet per line (lines could be shorter and much longer as well). The square four-line strophe structure, on the one hand, and the folk-like trend, on the other hand, dispensed only with the equality within measures. Hence, the specific Yiddish Introspective trend (*Inzikhizm*) in the United States joined both these tendencies and created truly modern expressions of free rhythm, differing as the several Introspectivist poets differed from each other. These expressions were created—i.e. they were not written automatically—as free prose, but great attention was paid to the constructive devices of the poem, other than the meter, which shape its specific rhythmical impact.

Free rhythms did not prevail in the main body of Yiddish poetry, although the influence of the new rhythmic sensibility went far beyond the borders of free rhythms. Only some poets refrained from a.-s. metrics, notably women poets. The Introspectivist A. Leyeles (1889–1966) wrote both the most formal and the most compact free forms, beyond prose, ostensibly dictated by the thematic unfolding of the text. He renewed in Yiddish the most rigorous Romance strophic forms (rondeau, villanelle, sonnet ring, ottava rima). Like his free rhythms, this return to strict forms reflected his reaction to the monotony of the poems of the preceding generation, which seemed little differentiated from one another in form, in which the words were blurred in a fluid euphonious gentle tunefulness. Critics who are astonished at such inconsistency on the part of a poet should realize that his rhythmic innovations were reactions to a previous prevalent rhythm, not to meters as such. Meter is a mere scheme, while the rhythm of a poem is the linguistic expression of a particular "life rhythm." Consequently the free-rhythm patterns of A. Leyeles in New York are akin to M. Kulbak's big-city rhythms in Berlin or Perets Markish's in Paris.

The difference between this post-metrical period and the free rhythms preceding the a.-s. meters (e.g. in the Hebrew Bible and in the Yiddish folksong) consists in the fact that the modern poets and their readers had experienced the a.-s. order even before the new freedom. The new free rhythms were supported by this perception; they based themselves on the a.-s.-metric inertia, utilized its proportions as a background, and emphasized contrasts and their violation of these patterns.

ACCENTUAL FREE RHYTHMS

Among the great variety of trends in the general category of free rhythms, we can distinguish several groups with changing global principles.

The free-accentual rhythms keep a bound number of accents in the model grid of a line with free numbers of unstressed syllables. The most widespread form of Russian poetry in the second decade of the twentieth century was the so-called *dolnik* (Akhmatova, Tsvetaeva, Esenin, Mayakovsky). This rhythm, on the borderline of exact meters and on the threshold of free syllable numbers, had several names in Russian, such as *udarnik* (accentual), Štokmar's "net," and *dolnik,* the term accepted today. According to Vladimir A. Pyast, it was no less widespread than the four-iamb line in nineteenth-century Russian poetry.[14] The *dolnik* is essentially a triple amphibrachic line in which unstressed syllables are occasionally skipped, thus breaking the smooth flow of the verse—this would normally not have been done by Pushkin or other Russian poets before Modernism. There is no regular number of syllables per line, but the proximity of regular a.-s. meters is obvious. If the meter is seen as a *net,* the skipped syllables make "holes" in the net, as in the following diagrams.

איך ווייס ניט מיט וועלעכע שלעסער
פֿאַרשליסט מען אַ האַרץ פֿון פּיַין,
נאָר אפֿשר, נאָר אפֿשר איז בעסער
וואָס אומעט איז היַינט מיַין פֿריַינד.

→	
Ikh veys nit mit velekhe shleser	∪ — ∪ ∪ — ∪ ∪ — ∪
Farshlist men a harts fun payn,	∪ — ∪ ∪ — 0 ∪ —
Nor efsher, nor efsher iz beser	∪ — ∪ ∪ — ∪ ∪ — ∪
Vos umet iz haynt mayn fraynd	∪ — ∪ ∪ — 0 ∪ —

(Aaron Kushnirov, "Raseya")[15]

[I don't know with what locks / you lock a heart full of anguish, / but perhaps, perhaps it is better / that sadness today is my friend.]

Aaron Kushnirov (1891–1949) uses the stretched form *VE-le-khe* instead of the standard *vel-khe* and achieves another dactyl.

After the reader has become used to the amphibrachic net, where a syllable or two are missing, metric inertia supplies a pause in its place. A reading either stretches or emphasizes the remaining syllables, depending on the content and the concrete syntactic construction. Schematically this is represented by 0 (a hole in the net) in order to preserve the accustomed time interval from stress to stress. The syllabic pauses occur unpredictably, without a set order; this yields a pleasant variation, making it possible to avoid a stirring anapestic flow, break the flow of the sentence and separate individual words for the purpose of illuminating them, interrupt the breathing, and create a mood. The characteristic emotional lyrical tone in the poem may be varicolored, according to the number and place of the interruptions.

וועמען בעטן, צו וועמען זיך וועכדן
אין היימלעכקייט פֿון צימערן שטילע —
האַרץ אַזאַ פֿאַרשייטס אוכ נישט שטענדיקס
האָט היַינט פֿאַרבענקט זיך נאָך פֿרילינג.

→

Vemen betn, tsu vemen zikh vendn	∪ ∪ — ∪ | ∪ — ∪ | ∪ — ∪
In heymlekhkayt fun tsimern shtile—	∪ — ∪ ∪ | ∪ — ∪ ∪ | — ∪
Harts aza farshayts un nisht shtendiks	0 — 0 | ∪ ∪ ∪ — | ∪ ∪ — ∪
Hot haynt farbenkt zikh nokh friling.	∪ — 0 | ∪ — ∪ | ∪ — ∪

[Whom to ask, to whom to turn / in the privacy of quiet rooms— / Heart so wanton and inconstant / has been seized by a longing for spring.]

In the schematic net we have one syllable missing in line 4 and two in line 3. We also get the opposite, three slacks between stresses (instead of one) in lines 2 and 3.

The preserved amphibrachic ternary net forces the reader to fit into the pattern by speeding up the breathing or by interrupting it according to the reconstructed intention of the writer, i.e. in a way that resembles the writer's breath fluctuations and gestures during the composition and performance of the poem. The word *harts* (heart) at the onset of the third line is emphasized both because it alone occupies a place equivalent to four syllables and because an interruption is necessary after it in order to pass to the unstressed trisyllabic sequence without violating the metric feeling. But no less significant rhythmically is the lack of an article or adjective, which elevates the noun *harts* to a generic symbol.[16] It was this prominence of the word *harts* in the feeling of the poet which created the rhythmic devices, and they now work back on the reader in leading him to reproduce in his sensibility the original structuring of the poet's experience.

The interruptions are not always functional, bound to a specific word. Their purpose is also to create the general atmosphere of the poem. The interruptions focus our attention on individual words—as opposed to the flow of sentences. The several syllabic accretions accustom us to separating every colon as a unit of rhythm and content, in contrast to the net of feet on which the new image is projected. The differences in the lengths and endings of the colon are thus sensed more vividly and create a lively rhythmic nuance (compare, for instance, the effect of the dactyl in *hĕymlĕkhkĕyt* |— ∪ ∪ |).

Similarity rather than identity, equivalence rather than equality, are characteristic not only of meter but also of the widespread assonant rhyme. In other words, the entire feeling of writer and reader has become freer; there is a tendency to use contrasts and tensions even with the most elementary structural principles, and the emphasis shifts from the regularity of feet to the diversity of cola.

In Yiddish poetry, this form is rather rare even among the writers of Russia, with the exception of Kushnirov. But in Hebrew it is widespread among poets influenced by the same Russian poetry, such as N. Alterman (1900–1970; especially in *Simkhat aniyim*), Rachel (Raḥel; 1890–1931), and I. Bat-Miriam (1901–1980).[17] Although in the free-accentual patterns of the Bible the number of slacks was quite free within a fixed number of feet, Modern Hebrew offered no direct stimulus for such freedom; the Yiddish ear, on the other hand, experienced the liberating effect of the still-living folksong.

In Hebrew it was only a Jewish folk-like Diaspora subject-matter that occasionally brought with it a comparable freedom, e.g. for the Hebrew poet David Šimʾoni (Šimonovich; 1886–1956) in poems on the catastrophe (the Holocaust) and, in a different manner, for U.-Z. Grinberg in his Hebrew works—and he was a poet not influenced by the above-mentioned Russian moderns.

A more authentic folk-like poet was Itsik Manger:[18]

יעקבֿ אבֿינו זיצט אַלט און מיד
אויף דער גראָזבאַנק פֿאַרטראַכט.
ער פֿילט די ביינער טוען אים וויי
נישט פֿאַר קיין שום ייד געדאַכט.

→

Yankev ovinu zitst alt un mid	$-\cup\cup-\cup\,|\,0\cup-\,|\,0\cup-$
Oyf der grozbank farnakht.	$-0\cup-\cup\,|\,\cup-$
Er filt di beyner tuen im vey	$\cup-0\,|\,\cup-\cup\,|\,0-\cup\cup-$
Nisht far keyn shum yid gedakht.	$\cup\cup-\cup\,|\,0-\,|\,0\cup-$

[Jacob our Patriarch sits old and tired / on the bench of grass in the evening. / He feels his bones aching, / may all Jews be spared (such pain).]

Manger easily produced iambs and sonnets but in *Medresh Itsik* (Itsik's Midrash, Paris, 1951 = *Khumesh-lider*, 1935) he strives to stay quite close to the folk feeling, to persuade the folk reader of the naive truths of his characters. All poems in that book are composed in the symmetric folk strophe **mana**. The sole exception—the rhymed couplet "Lid funem loyfer" (**aa bb . . .**)—does not belong to the period described, but is an intrusion from the time of writing. Manger is aware of how strange or ornate a fully rhymed *abab* pattern strikes the folk ear. If only lines 2 and 4 are rhymed, then lines 1 and 3 fulfill a constructive function, but to rhyme all lines is a luxury.

The even lines mostly have three stresses each and are in lively alternation with four-foot lines. But with all this freedom, the observance of inner laws is characteristic. Most of the rhymes are ultimate (masculine), with a few exceptions in the *megile* poems, even though in Yiddish, penultimate (feminine) rhymes are easier to find; they firmly terminate the strophe (a function formerly served by the melody). In one group of poems (on the biblical Hagar) all lines have three feet, but then the first and third lines never have ultimate terminations. This interdiction seems, on the one hand, to be due to the alternation with the ultimate even lines and, on the other, to be a vestige of the folksong of the same type, where the unstressed last syllable bears the fourth stress of the melody. (In the German folksong, too, the masculine three-measure line does not occur in the odd lines.)

The freedom within the measures represents an attempt to avoid any order and keeps us from becoming accustomed to one pattern. But since there is no isochronic melody, Manger keeps within the limits of two unstressed syllables per foot.

So, too, in Manger's book *Briv fun Velvl Zbarzher tsu Malkele di sheyne* (Letters of Velvl Zbarzher to Malkele the Beautiful; 1937). Although Zbarzher, the real-life bard who is the prototype for these poems, came close to such a limitation (which governed the love lyrics of folksong), he often failed to sustain it because his hearing lacked an a.-s. orientation. Coming from high literature, Manger has the a.-s. ear, hence his quantitatively limited freedom. Though a melody is absent, he essentially transmits the same folk rhythm. An excess of unstressed syllables would disturb the perception of the fixed number of stresses in the line; i.e. the similarity of the lines and the poem's rhythm as a whole would be obscured. The nearly rigid order causes every disturbance to produce a dramatic tension between itself and the drawn-out meter. Here the deviations are not perceived as "disturbances," because no such order is present. No sooner do we get accustomed to the trisyllabic pattern than we lapse into disyllables, and vice versa. There is thus no tension but an easygoing flow.

The whole construction of the strophe forces us into an isochronic perception of measures without making us feel all syllables as equal time units; that is, our reading is less forced, the syllables being—in an expressive reading—of various durations, as in direct narration.

The framework of the same four-foot line puts into prominence various thematically conditioned manners of feeling the rhythm. For example, the lines of the quietly lyrical poems have fewer syllables, which are very close to forming iambs, being interrupted only occasionally by an extra syllable, in a way resembling Heine's love lyrics. So it is in the poems "Khaves viglid," "Neomi zogt 'Got fun Avrom,'" "Neomi geyt shlofn," and the Avishag poems. The foot is unlike the interrupted anapest, because there the missed syllable is filled by a syllabic pause, while here, the normal iambic flow is disturbed by an extra "burdening" with occasional additional syllables. Thus seeming prosaicness and simplicity are created by the lyrical, somewhat excited mood.

Against this background the stark contrast of Manger's "Avishags troyer" (Avishag's Grief) is apparent. This poem exceeds the bounds of the book with its long heavy lines as well as with its measures of more than three syllables, the antisymmetric contrast between sentence and line, the enjambment, and the sharp line cuts, which, in a free reading, not only obliterate the last symmetric basis of the poem—the equal lines—but even blur the rhyme.

Here is a strophe from a different poem, "Avishag," which is in keeping with the rest of the book (though more markedly iambic). If not for slacks in the third and the fourth lines, the meter would be purely iambic:

זי לייגט צוויי פֿינגער צו צום מויל
און פֿײַפֿט די שאָף צונויף ;
צײַט אַהיים, ווײַל מאָרגן פֿאַר טאָג
פֿאָרט זי אין מלכס הויף.

→

Zĭ lēygt tsvĕy fingĕr tsū tsŭm mōyl   ∪ — | ∪ — ∪ | — ∪ — |

ŭn fāyft dĭ shōf tsŭnōyf;   ∪ — | ∪ — | ∪ — |

tsāyt ăhēym, văyl mōrgń făr tōg   0 — ∪ — | ∪ — ∪ | ∪ — |

Fōrt zĭ ĭn mēylkĕhs hōyf.   0 — ∪ | ∪ — ∪ | 0 — |

[She puts two fingers to her mouth / and whistling, gathers her sheep; / time
to go home, for tomorrow before dawn / she is going to the king's court.]

The spicy element here is the last line, which mentions the ominous prospect of offering her body to the impotent old king, and is written not from the points of view of the king or the Bible narrator but from the point of view of the peasant girl. The naïveté of the rhythm is done with.

And now, here is an excerpt from the very different "Avishags troyer":

אַז לכבֿוד אים די גאָלדענע אוירינגלעך

אין מײַנע אויערן. \ און דאָס געבלימלטע שבת-קלייד

וואָס כ‹טראָג אין דער וואָכן. \ און דאָס רייטלען זיך

פֿון אַלע מײַנע רויזן אויף דער בעט.

→

Ăz lĕkōvĕd īm dĭ gōldĕnĕ ōyrĭnglĕkh

    | ∪ ∪ — ∪ — | | ∪ — ∪ ∪ | — ∪ ∪ |

ĭn māynĕ ōyĕrń. / Ŭn dŏs gĕblīmltĕ shābĕs-klĕyd

    | ∪ — ∪ — ∪ ∪ | | ∪ ∪ ∪ — ∪ ∪ | — ∪ ∪ |

vŏs kh'trōg ĭn dĕr vōkhń. / Ŭn dŏs rēytlĕn zĭkh

    | ∪ — | ∪ ∪ — ∪ | | ∪ ∪ — ∪ ∪ |

fŭn ālĕ māynĕ rōyzń ŏyf dĕr bēt.

    | ∪ — ∪ ∪ ∪ | — ∪ ∪ ∪ — |

[. . . that in his honor (are) the golden earrings / in my ears. And the
flowery Sabbath dress / which I wear on weekdays. And the blushing / of
all my roses in the flowerbed.]

Here the net of four or three stresses is preserved, but the sentences overrule the verse lines. The break in the middle of the line is stronger than at its end. If we rearrange the text according to the syntactical division, we get a prosaic sequel:

az lekoved im di goldene oyringlekh in mayne oyern.
un dos geblimlte shabes-kleyd vos kh'trog in der vokhn.
un dos reytlen zikh mit ale mayne royzn oyf der bet.

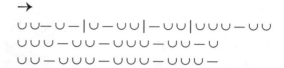

$$∪∪—∪—|∪—∪∪|—∪∪|∪∪∪—∪∪$$
$$∪∪∪—∪∪—∪∪∪—∪∪—∪$$
$$∪∪—∪∪∪—∪∪∪—∪∪∪—$$

The result is one–five slacks and four–five stresses per line, a rhythm close to prose. In addition, a prose intonation is established, and the leveling of stresses is canceled.

Two paths lead from the last example. One of them, taken here by Moyshe-Leyb Halpern,[19] permits full syllabic freedom in a fixed number of measures (4 + 3):

ס׳איז אמת, איך בין טאַקע ווייַט פֿון דיר

נאָר דײַנע צערטלעכקייטן \ אין די בריוו צו מיר

דערמאָנען גאַנצע טשאַטעס מיט זומער-פֿייגל

וואָס זוכן בלומען-האָניק צווישן קראָפּעווע.

→

S'ĭz ēmĕs, ĭkh bīn tăkĕ vāyt fŭn dīr

$$|∪—∪|∪—∪∪|—∪—|$$

Nŏr dāynĕ tsērtlĕkhkăytň / ĭn dĭ brīv tsŭ mĭr

$$|∪—∪|—∪∪∪|∪∪—∪—|$$

Dĕrmōnĕn ŏn gāntsĕ tshātĕs mĭt zūmĕr-fĕygl

$$|∪—∪|∪∪—∪|∪—∪—∪|$$

Vŏs zūkhň blūmĕn-hŏnĭk tsvīshň krōpĕvĕ.

$$|∪—∪|—∪∪∪|∪∪—∪∪|$$

[It is true, I am indeed far from you / but your tendernesses in your letters to me / recall whole hosts of butterflies / seeking flower nectar among nettles.]

This pattern avoids the frequent oscillation between iambic and anapestic lines. One to five slacks is the widest gap possible.

The other path breaks open the symmetrical folk strophe. Only the equal number of measures (in poetry, feet) in most lines remains to transmit a connected feeling. But the sentences overflow the line boundaries, and what is most important, the lines are not symmetrically paired. In the last example the rhyming in the strophe's interior was already blurred.

The rhythmic value of rhyme is most significant. Even a four-line strophe sounds quite different—not like a poem at all—if the rhymes are not in the folksong pattern. In a poem by Ber Horovits,[20] the rhyming *oygn-gefloygn* in the beginning and end of the strophe almost hide the rhyme:

בײַ נאַכט פֿאַרמאַך איך די אויגן \ אויף מײַן שלאָף-געלעגער,\

פֿלאַטערנדיק, רוישנדיק קומען \ מלאכים פֿון

הימל געפֿלויגן

→

Bay nakht farmakh ikh di **oygn** / oyf mayn shlof-geleger,

$\cup - | \cup - \cup | \cup - \cup | \cup \cup - \cup - \cup |$

flaterndik, royshndik kumen / malokhim fun himl gefl**oygn**

$- \cup \cup \cup | - \cup \cup | - \cup | \cup - \cup | \cup - \cup | \cup - \cup |$

[At night I close my eyes / in my bed, / flutteringly, noisily there come / angels flying from heaven.]

The poet makes three-measure lines that rhyme anti-traditionally: **amna**. While his patterns vary, Horovits is in general closer to the folk narrative and to the overall spirit of folklore than to the folksong.

Moyshe-Leyb Halpern approaches folksong effectively in his typical five-line strophe **manao**. Only the second and fourth lines rhyme. This is, in fact, a folksong strophe **mana** with an accretive line. The rhyme has an almost unnoticed effect, like that of internal rhymes. He continues this later in freely rhymed non-strophic poems which are based only on an equal number of feet per line, i.e. on freedom within the fixed folk verse but without the perfection of the symmetric folk strophe.

Thus the folksong, having influenced first the strophic structure in a.-s. meters and then the general rhythmic configuration, now inspires a form of poetry which keeps only the verse structure, with all its freedom, while violating the strophic matrix.

THE YIDDISH LANGUAGE AS A RHYTHMICAL FACTOR

There is one type of Yiddish folksong which is unknown in German. To Heusler's four-cadence types we must add, for Yiddish, the four-measure line with a dactylic ending, which is characteristic of the Russian song:

איך האָב מיך פֿאַרליבט \ אין אַ שײן ייִנגעלע

→

ʻĭkh hōb mĭkh fărlībt / ĭn ă shĕyn yīngĕlĕʼ $\cup - \cup \cup - | \cup \cup - | - \cup \cup$

[I fell in love with a handsome boy.]

The dactyl (— ∪ ∪) or hyperdactyl (— ∪ ∪ ∪) permits the voice to sweep over the beat and allows an arch of unstressed syllables (as in the Russian *bylina*—a narrative poem about ancient heroes).

The external Slavic influence on Yiddish poetry came rather late (coinciding with the adoption of a.-s. metrics). But from the spoken culture, the strong effect began earlier, particularly in the non-artificial folksong. The formal framework obstinately remained old Germanic, i.e. purely accentual, but the distance from one stress to the other increased in Yiddish as a result of the widening phrasal wave under the influence of the East Slavic environment.

The average interval between two stresses in present-day Russian use is 2.8 syllables, which is equivalent to 1.8 unstressed syllables for every stressed syllable. Štokmar observed that in order to change this average (his term is *koefitsient slogoudarnosti*, "coefficient of syllables per accent") by as much as 0.1, a distinct change in vocabulary is necessary. In Russian syllabic poetry he found the average still as high as 3.2.[21] This average was even greater in Old Russian (according to Štokmar, 4.0, or at least 3.8); it is also greater in Ukrainian, by which Yiddish was considerably influenced, while in German this interval is far smaller (closer to 2.0 than to 3.0). In Yiddish the phrasing patterns have in this respect come under the complete sway of Slavic. Several phenomena have accompanied this development in Yiddish and are reflected in poetry.

Since the number of stresses per line in the folksong did not change, the number of syllables can serve as evidence of that broadening of the phrasing pattern. Within Yiddish proper the change is clear. The *Bovo-bukh* (1508) actually has iambic lines (2.0 syllables). In the narrative *Vints-Hans-lid* (1616) there is, ostensibly, complete freedom of measure length (up to five syllables), yet the real average is still only 2.5 syllables per stress. In the more recent narrative Yiddish folksong, in comparison, the average exceeds 3.0 syllables, with a definite tendency toward the paeonic (four-syllable meter):

אַ מאָטיוו, מעֶנטשן, וועֶל איך אײַך זינגעֶן

→

a motiv, mentshn, vel ikh aykh zingen   ∪∪ — | — ∪ | — ∪∪ | — ∪

[Folks, I will sing you an air.]

In Y. L. Cahan's collection,[22] the section "Ballad-Like Songs" yields the following averages:

Song no. 1 has an average of 3.0 syllables per stress.

Song no. 15 has 3.5.

Song no. 8 (written in the characteristic narrative style) has as many as 3.7.

In the long song no. 16, the first four strophes (a dialogue) have 2.7.

The last four lyrical love songs have 2.6.

But the typical narrative strophe rises to an average of 3.5

Here is an example of the last:

אַזוי ווי לייבעלע איז אין שטוב אַרײַנגעקומע

→

Azoy vi Leybele iz in shtub arayngekumen

$$\cup - \,|\, \cup - \cup \cup \,|\, \cup \cup - \,|\, \cup \cup \cup - \cup$$

[As soon as Leybele entered his house.]

A range of two to three syllables describes the findings based on this book: two (including the stress) means iambs, three means anapests, and free verse operates in the space between them.

Furthermore, in some poems the swing of the pendulum may be smooth or dramatic (moving between one and four). The German folksong, like the older Yiddish song, tends toward the prevalence of iambs; i.e. it contains fewer syllables per stress. Comparing a German free-accentual song with a Yiddish transformation of it (or one in a related style), we find:

→

Es war einmal ein junger Knabe	$\cup - \cup - \cup - \cup - \cup$
der liebt sein SHÄTZLEIN sieben Jahr	$\cup - \cup - \cup - \cup -$
und als der Knab in die Fremde kam,	$\cup - \cup - \cup \cup - \cup -$
da ward ihm sein Schätzlein krank.	$- \cup - \cup - \cup -$

[There was once a young lad / he loved his sweetheart for seven years, / and when the lad left home, / his sweetheart became sick.]

The German song, with one exception, is iambic.

איך האָב געליבט אַ מיידעלע פֿון אַכצן יאָר,
געליבט האָב איך איר אַ דרײַ-פֿיר יאָר.
איך האָב געוואַלט וויסן צי זי האָט מיר ליב,
בין איך אַוועקגעפֿאָרן פֿון שטוב.
ווי דער יונגער קנאַבע איז אַפּגעפֿאָרן
אַזוי איז די געליבטע קראַנק געוואָרן.

→

Ikh hob gelibt a MEYDELE fun akhtsn yor,	∪ — ∪ ∪ ∪ — ∪ ∪ ∪ — ∪ —
gelibt hob ikh ir a dray-fir yor.	∪ — ∪ ∪ — ∪ — ∪ —
Ikh hob gevolt visn tsi zi hot mir lib,	∪ — ∪ ∪ — ∪ ∪ — ∪ ∪ —
bin ikh AVEGEFORN fun ir shtub.	— ∪ ∪ — ∪ ∪ ∪ — ∪ —
Vi der yunger KNABE iz opgeforn	∪ ∪ — ∪ — ∪ ∪ — ∪ — ∪ —
azoy iz di gelibte krank gevorn.	∪ — ∪ ∪ ∪ — ∪ — ∪ — ∪

[I loved a girl of eighteen, / I loved her for three or four years. / I wanted to know if she loved me, / So I left her house. / As soon as the young fellow left, / His beloved fell ill.]

According to Alfred Landau,[23] in the German text the syllable/stress ratio is 2:1, while in the Yiddish text, we have a 2:7 ratio, and the multisyllabic measures are prominent. One could argue that I included multisyllabic measures, however: stressing every second syllable gives us seven iambs. But the genre does not allow for more accents than four. The difference may be symbolized by a passage from the disyllabic *Schätzlein* in German to a trisyllabic מיידעלע *meydele* in Yiddish: *meydele* (girl) uses German suffixes with a Russian profusion of dimunitives.

Thus modern Yiddish makes possible greater rhythmic diversity by alternating the number of syllables in a given number of measures. The same is true of modern free rhythms: in English they display a strong bent for the iambic, while in Yiddish, the number of syllables per measure ranges quite widely, as we will show below, and in a text which is normally "prosaic" the meter is, on average, amphibrachic (three syllables), with many paeonic leaps (four syllables deriving from two iambs). This tendency in the spoken language has supported the following phenomena:

(a) *Yiddish has a multiplicity of long words, particularly with dactylic and hyperdactylic terminations.*

(1) In the folksong, we are struck by the frequency of the dactylic diminutive with the disyllabic suffix: יינג-עלע *yīng-ĕlĕ* (boy), אַלט-יטשק-ע *ālt-ĭtshk-ĕ* (old), and יונג-ינק-ע *yūng-ĭnk-ĕ* (young) are all diminutives. The number generally exceeds the modern German equivalent by a whole syllable.[24]

(2) In Yiddish there are markedly longer suffixes and prefixes, with the stress often falling on the first or second syllable; these have spread to roots of Slavic origin:

באַ-רעד-עװדיק-ע	bă-rēd-ĔVDĬK-Ĕ	| ∪ — ∪ ∪ ∪ |	(talkative)
גליװער-דיק-ע	glīvĕr-DĬK-Ĕ	| — ∪ ∪ ∪ |	(jelly-like)
לײַכט-נ-דיק-ע	lāykht-n̆-DĬK-Ĕ	| — ∪ ∪ ∪ |	(shining)
שטיינ-ער-יק-ע	shtēyn-ĔR-ĬK-e	| — ∪ ∪ ∪ |	(stony)
טרויער-יק-ע	trōyĕr-ĭk-ĕ	| — ∪ ∪ ∪ |	(mournful)
צונויפֿ-לייג-ן	TSŬNÖYF-lĕyg-n̆	| ∪ — ∪ ∪ |	(to put together)
אָפּ-לייקענ-ען	öplĕyKĔN-ĔN	| — ∪ ∪ ∪ |	(to deny)
פֿאַרמעט-ענ-ע	pārmĕt-ĔN-Ĕ	| — ∪ ∪ ∪ |	(of parchment)
אַנדער-ער	āndĕr-ĕr	| — ∪ ∪ |	(the other)
קוטשער-אַװע	kŭtshĕr-ĀVĔ	| ∪ ∪ — ∪ |	(curly)
קודלע-װאַטע	kŭdlĕ-VĀTĔ	| ∪ ∪ — ∪ |	(shaggy)

(b) *Yiddish does not have the German requirement of a secondary stress
on the syllable of a long word second back from the primary stress.* At least
such secondary stresses are much weaker in Yiddish[25] and are therefore
not necessary in poetry. Even when the primary stress is on the prefix of a
long word, the lexical root does not receive a stress. Witness the folksong
passages:

דו האָסט מיר דאָך צוגעזאָגט בריװעלעך צו שרײַבן

→

dŭ hōst mĭr dŏkh TSŬGĔZŌGT brīvĕlĕkh tsŭ shrāybn̆

\| ∪ — ∪ ∪ \| — ∪ ∪ \| — ∪ ∪ \| ∪ — ∪ \|

[you have promised me, after all, to write letters]

ראָזשינקעס מיט מאַנדלען

→

rōzhinkĕs mĭt māndlĕn   \| — ∪ ∪ ∪ — ∪ \|

[raisins and almonds]

בין איך אַװעקגעפֿאָרן פֿון איר שטוב

→

bīn ĭkh ĀVĔKGĔFŌRN̆ fŭn ĭr shtŭb

[so I traveled away from her home.]

\| — ∪ \| ∪ — ∪ ∪ ∪ \| — ∪ — \|

In rhyming position the stress sometimes continues to fall on the root of
the complemented verb:

ווי אַזוי וועל איך עס קענען איבערשטיין

 vǐ ăzōy vĕl ĭkh ĕs kēnĕn ībĕrshtēyn

[how will I be able to bear it]

Here the end word rhymes with *shteyn*. Occasionally, however, the proper primary stress is completely overshadowed by the prominence of the rhyming ("second-ary") stress: אָנקלינגען *ŏnklĭngĕn* ("to ring the bell") rhymes with זינגען *zīngĕn* (instead of the standard *ōnklĭngĕn*). In dialect אויסקומען *ŏyskīmĕn* (rather than *ōyskĭmĕn*) rhymes with שווימען *shvīmĕn*. But diminutives remain dactylic even in rhyming position; and so are enclitic combinations at the end of unrhymed lines:

און היַינט בין איך באַרעדט געוואָרן \ דורך אַ פֿאַלשן יינגעלע

ŭn hāynt bĭn ĭkh BĂ-RĒDT GĔVŎR | ∪ — ∪ ∪ ∪ | — ∪ ∪ |
dūrkh ă fălshň yīngĕlĕ

[Today I was slandered / by a faithless lad][26]

וועסטו פֿליִען אין דער וויַיט אַהין *vestu flien in der vāyt ăhĭn* (you will fly there, into the distance) is also in a song in which every remaining odd line termi-nates in a dactylic word.[27]

(c) *The same law is manifested in the collocations of "small words" and in idioms:*

קען איך ניט *kēn ĭkh nĭt* "and so I can't"
וויל איך ניט *vĭl ĭkh nĭt* "and so I don't want to"
וויפֿל איז דער זייגער *vĭfl̆ ĭz dĕr zēygĕr,* | — ∪ ∪ ∪ — ∪ | "what time is it?"

The last represents a paeonic arch without a stress on *iz*.

(d) *There are additional minor phenomena, such as the lack of the Ger-man-type preterite for expressing the past tense.* Instead, Yiddish has only the compound tense (frequent in narrative folksong) with a single stress in the participle. Compare the German *ĕr gīng wēg* | ∪ — — | with the Yiddish ער איז *ĕr iz ăvĕkgĕgăngĕn* | ∪ ∪ ∪ — ∪ ∪ ∪ |, which has six syllables on two sides of the stress and an extended prefix to boot. (In everyday German speech, the equivalent perfect participle would have two stresses correspond-ing to the single stress in Yiddish, despite the greater number of syllables.)

Expressionism brought a new manner of feeling rhythm into Yiddish poetry. It was a new feeling for the general language as well. Leyb Naydus (1890–1918) could still rhyme בורשטין *bŭrshtīn* ("amber") with ke-ni-**gin** in a four-iamb line:

דעם קלענסטן באַנד פֿון קעניגין

→

dĕm klēnstň bānd fŭn kēnĭgīn | ∪ — ∪ — ∪ — ∪ — |

[the smallest ribbon of the queen][28]

But Modernist Yiddish poetry does not tolerate a secondary stress in a dactylic ending like **ke**-ni-gin | — ∪ ∪ |), and this type of rhyme, ke-ni-**gin**, is interdicted. Along with the wide use of long and composite words with single stresses in their paeonized iambs, Expressionism has introduced many new enclitic combinations. The paeon in general became a favorite in this period— for example, Mordkhe Gebirtig's folk-like song (melodically supported): *shlōf zhĕ mĭr shŏyn / Yānkĕlĕ mă̆yn shēynĕr / dĭ ēygĕlĕkh dĭ shvārtsĭnkĕ mă̆kh-tsū* (Go to sleep now, my handsome Yankele, / close your dear dark little eyes).[29] Here is the metrical pattern:

→

paeons | — ∪ ∪ ∪ | — ∪ ∪ | ∪ — ∪ // ∪ — ∪ ∪ | ∪ — ∪ ∪ | ∪ — |
iambs   — ∪ — ∪ — ∪ — ∪ — ∪ // ∪ — ∪ — ∪ — ∪ — ∪ —

Instead of full iambs (ten times), we have six paeons. The long words, even in iambic poems, are so spaced that only every other iamb is stressless (pyrrhic), resulting in paeons overall.

This was achieved by inversions of former proclitic combinations, as in a poem by the young Perets Markish (1895–1952) in his book *Nakhtroyb* (1922):

און קלאַנגען ברעקלען זיך פֿון טײַכן אויס

און װינטלעך אין עק-װעלט מיט זײ נאָך אָװנטיקן טוי גייען

Ŭn klāngĕn brēklĕn zïkh FŬN TĀYKHŇ ŌYS | ∪ — ∪ ∪ |

ŭn vīntlĕkh ïn ĔK-VĒLT MĬT ZĚY nŏkh ŏvňtïkň tōy gĕyĕn

[טוי גייען *tōy gĕyĕn* rhymes with פֿאַרצויגן *fărtsōygň*!] | ∪ — ∪ ∪ ∪ — ∪ ∪ |

[and sounds crumble out of rivers / and breezes go with them after dew to the end of the world]

קומען זיי פֿון אַלע זײַטן טאָג אין איינעם שטיל אָן

KŬMĔN ZĔY FŬN ĀLĔ ZĀYTŇ TŌG in ĕynĕm SHTĬL ŎN [rhymes with

Dlīlĕn] | — ∪ ∪ ∪ — ∪ ∪ ∪ — ∪ ∪ ∪ — ∪ |

[they arrive quietly together from all ends of the day]

כ׳זאָל אַרויסשטעקן דעם צונג זיך

אַז פֿרײַ זאָל אַ שטויביקע שוועל זײַן

kh'zōl ărōys-shtĕkn DĔM TSŪNG ZĬKH |∪∪ — ∪∪|∪ — ∪|

ăz frāy zŏl ă shtōybĭkĕ SHVĔL ZĂYN [rhymes with *rēlsň*]

|∪ — ∪∪—∪∪ — ∪|

[that I may stick out my tongue at myself, / that a dusty doorstep may free be]

An inversion of this sort brackets the whole end of the sentence in one single-breathed expression. As the New York poet and satirist Moyshe Nadir (1885–1943) put it:

אַזעלכע ברײַטע איך-וועל-אַײַך- נישט-לאָזן-כאַפּן-דעם-אָטעמדיקע לידער!

→

azelkhe brĕytĕ ĭkh-vĕl-ăykh-nĭsht-lŏzň-khăpň-dĕm-ōtĕmdĭkĕ lĭdĕr!

|∪∪∪ — ∪|∪∪∪∪∪∪∪∪ — ∪∪∪|— ∪|

[such broad I-won't-let-you-catch-your-breath poems!]

And as Der Nister (1884–1950) wrote even of prose that it was:

אַ מעשׂה מיט איינעם, וואָס האָט גרויסע אויגן געהאַט

→

A mayse mit eynem, vos hot grŏysĕ ōygň gĕhăt

|∪ — ∪∪ — ∪∪∪∪ — ∪∪ — |

[literally, "A story of one who big eyes had"]

On the whole, the long words and the general rhythm of broadly spaced major stresses (which are consequently all the stronger) produce a large-breathed tone in the paeonized metric framework of Yiddish Expressionism, while the free rhythms make for momentum, agitation, dynamism (Leivick, Leyeles, and others) and not necessarily "solemn fervor" (pathos). To put it more exactly, only what was perceived as the solemn fervor of the content prevents paeons from decomposing into iambs or trochees, while the lack of a constant iambic net in the free rhythms permits large unstressed arches ("paeonic" and even "pentonic").

A study of the vocabulary of the poetry of Milton, Pope, Tennyson, and other English poets[30] showed 17 percent disyllabic words and 80 percent monosyllables, i.e. only 3 percent trisyllables and longer words. In Yiddish the percentage of long words is incomparably greater; the proportion of four- and five-syllable words is particularly great, although, the precise calculations are still lacking.

In Moyshe Kulbak's (1896–1940) folk-like line

אַז די באַעבעשי די אַלטיטשקע איז אויסגעגאַנגען

Ăz dĭ bōbĕshĭ dĭ āltĭtshkĕ ĭz ōysgĕgängĕn

$|\cup\cup-\cup\cup|\cup-\cup\cup|\cup-\cup\cup\cup|$

[When dear old grandmother passed away][31]

the meter is paeon II (four syllables, and the second is accented).

Words of three and more syllables constitute 21 percent of the words in the quoted verse (of which 68 percent have dactylic and hyperdactylic terminations). In his poem "Vilne" (1926), the corresponding proportion of longer syllable words is 13 percent (of which 53 percent have dactylic and 22 percent hyperdactylic terminations, mostly because they are descriptive adjectives). This, together with the many compounds, prevents us from feeling that the poem is written iambically, which it is in fact. For this reason, too, the number of iambs per line is not fixed. But a "solemn fervor" is avoided because it is not necessarily every second iamb that is stressed. Here the percentage of long words is normal. In Leivick's linguistically "normal" poem, "Der volf," the long words also amount to 13 percent.

The number of long words is not in itself decisive for the rhythm. In analyzing one of the most solemnly stirring passages in the German Expressionist anthology *Menschendämmerung,* I found 27 percent long words, but an average of only 2.9 syllables per stress. In contrast, in the beginning of H. Leivick's "Der volf" (p. 180)[32] we have an average of 3.9 syllables per stress,[33] though the long words constitute no more than 13 percent of the total words. In Yiddish, one-base words of up to five syllables are frequent, e.g. the plural adjectives ŌPgĕrĭsĕnĕ $|-\cup\cup\cup\cup|$ ("torn off"). In the lines below, capital letters indicate the stressed syllables, and all read as single-stressed:

$\rightarrow$

באַרעדעוודיקע	băRĒdĕvdĭkĕ	$\|\cup-\cup\cup\cup\|$	(talkative)
אויסגעליידיקטע	ŌYSgĕlĕydĭktĕ	$\|-\cup\cup\cup\cup\|$	(emptied)
פֿאַראַיאָריקע	făräYŌrĭkĕ	$\|\cup\cup-\cup\cup\|$	(last year's), and
שטערנגאָלד even	SHTĒRňgöld	$\|-\cup\cup\|$	(star gold)
וועלטנאַכט	VĒLtnăkht	$\|-\cup\cup\|$	(world-night)

(U.-Z. Grinberg)

אַלטשוואַרצער	ĀLTshvărtsĕr	| — ∪ ∪ |	(old-black)
			(Kulbak)
ליכט-געבּוירענע	LĪKHT-gĕbŏyrĕnĕ	| — ∪ ∪ ∪ ∪ |	([of] light born)
וועלט-פֿאַרשטאַנדיקע	vēlt-fărsSHTĂNdĭkĕ	| ∪ ∪ — ∪ ∪ |	(with an understanding for the world)
שווער-אָטעמדיקער	shvĕr-Ōtemdĭkĕr	| ∪ — ∪ ∪ ∪ |	(heavy-breathing)
			(A. Leyeles)

A big role in the rhythmic impact is also played by the character of word composition. In "Di bobeshi oleho-hasholem is oysgegangen" → \| ∪ — ∪ ∪ \| ∪ ∪ ∪ — ∪ \| ∪ — ∪ ∪ ∪ \| by M. Kulbak, in the songs of Gebirtig, and in folksongs of a similar type, the paeonicity is "smooth" because all cola are constructed in the same manner. In other poems, however, long words create great tensions thanks to the contrast with preceding lines or with the surrounding types of word composition.

In Yiddish poetry, significance is attached to the opposition between *descending* long words (from stress to unstressed) and *ascending* word collocations (from unstressed to stressed). These are usually proclitic in Yiddish. The broad distance between stresses, like the penchant for dactylic word types, has apparently been adopted from East Slavic, but the old Slavic tendency to enclitic combinations (NĒ ză čtŏ \| — ∪ ∪ \|, NĒ bўlŏ \| — ∪ ∪ \|) has not been emulated; cf. Yiddish נישטאָ פֿאַר וואָס nĭshtŏ făr vōs \| ∪ ∪ ∪ — \| ("not at all," a rejoinder to "thank you"), נישט געווען nĭsht gĕvĒN \| — ∪ — \| ([has] not been).[34] Yet the Yiddish Modernist writers, particularly those of the Russian sphere, have for the sake of variation formed new enclitic combinations. If, for example, a dactylic word is followed by an anapestic proclitic formation, a polysyllabic arch is formed; even the simplest case, like אָפּגעברענט מײַנע ליפּן ŌPgĕbrĕnt măynĕ lĭpň \| — ∪ ∪ ∪ ∪ — ∪ \| (burned my lips), is already a "penton" (five-syllable measure) if it is metrically sustained. The opposite leads to a sudden clash of two strong centerlike stresses, each carrying many unstressed syllables. The following line almost demands a dash between the two stresses, and the descent following the clash is also highly effective:

←

אין דײַן האַלדז אײַנשטשעמען זיך

ĭn dăyn hāldz āynshtshĕmĕn zĭkh   \| ∪ ∪ — — ∪ ∪ ∪ \|

[to claw your throat]

Because of its specific linguistic features, certain important findings of the general science of rhythm are inapplicable to Yiddish. Friedrich Jünger[35] finds that the maximum length in excess of which it is difficult to retain a line as an organized verse is six feet or seventeen syllables. And this is understandable: in German it is nearly impossible to have a syllable-to-stress ratio in excess of 3.0. In Yiddish, however, there are much longer lines which hold up well and are not even split into two parts by a fixed caesura. Consider, for instance, this twenty-one-syllable line:

און מיט אונטערגעבראָכענע קני זיך צוגעשלעפּט צו די טרעפּ פֿון אָרון־קודש

ŭn mĭt ŭntĕrgĕbrŏkhĕnĕ knī zĭkh tsŭgĕshlĕpt tsŭ dĭ trēp fŭnĕm ŏrn-kōydĕsh

→ | ∪ ∪ — ∪ ∪ ∪ ∪ ∪ |—| ∪ — ∪ ∪ | ∪ ∪ —| ∪ ∪ ∪ — ∪ |

[and with collapsed knees pulled (him)self to the steps of the (synagogal) Holy Ark][36]

It contains five feet (i.e. a syllable-stress ratio of 4:4!) in an environment of mostly long, four-foot lines. Such a verse is possible because it is the number of stresses that is decisive, not the number of syllables. The resulting possibility of forming unusually long lines without transgressing the limitation on the number of stresses endows Yiddish with a definite advantage from the point of view of rhythmic impact. The Yiddish response to Homeric hexameter is transparent. More broadly streaming than hexameter are these lines from Leivick's "Ferzn":[37]

מיט אַן אויסגעשטרעקטן קאָפּ צום הימל הייב איך זיך אַרויס פֿון אונטער דעם
באַפֿאַלנדיקן וואָרעם,
טרייסל אָפּ פֿון זיך דעם ריח פֿון די אָנגעקלעפּטע שטיקער רויען ליים,
און העכער פֿון מײַן קאָפּ אַריבער שטרעקט זיך צו דער הייך מײַן ווײַסער אָרעם,
און שפּרייט זײַן ווײַסע ליכטיקייט אויף מענטש און חיה, גראָז און בוים.

Mit an oysgeshtrektn kop tsum himl heyb ikh zikh aroys fun unter dem bafaln-dikn vorem,

→ | ∪ ∪ — ∪ ∪ ∪ | — | ∪ — ∪ | ∪ ∪ ∪ — | ∪ ∪ ∪ ∪ | ∪ — ∪ ∪ ∪ | — ∪

treysl op fun zikh dem reyekh fun di ongeklepte shtiker royen leym,

→ | ∪ ∪ — ∪ ∪ | ∪ — ∪ | ∪ ∪ — ∪ ∪ ∪ | — ∪ | — ∪ | — |

un hekher fun mayn kop ariber shtrekt zikh tsu der heykh mayn vayser orem,

un shpreyt zayn vayse likhtikayt oyf mentsh un khaye, groz un boym.

[With head stretched to the sky I lift myself from under the attacking worm, / shake off the odor of the glued-on chunks of clay, / and above my head my white arm stretches upward, / and spreads its white brightness over man and beast, grass and tree.]

In the first line, there are as many as twenty-six syllables. Yet it holds together; and the rhyme, too, which demands that it be reached, encourages us to read the line in one breath.

Heusler and Jünger both believed that the length of one colon was restricted to a maximum of six syllables. But in Yiddish, the long words make possible the existence of longer monopodic cola:

$$\rightarrow$$

ער איז איבערגעבליבן	ĕr ĭz ibĕrgĕblĭbn̆	| ∪ ∪ — ∪ ∪ ∪ ∪ |	(he remained)
אין אַן אויסגעהרגעטער	ĭn ăn ōysgĕhărgĕtĕr	| ∪ ∪ — ∪ ∪ ∪ ∪ |	(in a slaughtered)
מיט אַ צונויפֿגעפרעסטן	mĭt ă tsŭnōyfgĕprĕstn̆	| ∪ ∪ ∪ — ∪ ∪ ∪ |	(with a clenched)

These are especially perceptible in long lines. We must conclude that this restriction, too, is not linguistically universal but is linguistically conditioned. In this respect, Yiddish has definitely left the Germanic sphere behind it.

DYNAMIC FREE RHYTHMS

This group of poems in free rhythms includes poems (a) which have no predetermined ordering device (meter) but (b) whose rhythmic impact is conspicuous and unlike that of normal spoken language. It does not follow that they contain no such devices at all; quite the contrary, their effect is usually rather strong. But we do not know in advance when the shifts from one metrical segment to another will appear and how long it will last, hence their integral interaction with their context. As in the Bible, there is no single metrical rule and no clear-cut separation of meter, meaning, rhyme, and other sound devices. Sentence and period structure, length of lines, internal rhymes, word collocations and repetitions, extraordinary aggregations of syllables in a foot, metrically similar groups, parallelism or contrast of devices of the same type or of different types—all these together produce the rhythm. There are as many peculiarities as there are genuine poems, but the general character of the poet is quite prominent in each of them. We will analyze examples from the works of several modern Yiddish poets with only an outline of commentary.

Here is an excerpt from A. Leyeles's "In sobvey, II," plus the three lines that precede it:[38]

פלוצלונג ווייזט פֿון באַלקן זיך אַ האַנט
און נעמט שטראָמען גאָלדענע דאָלאַרן
אויף דער לעבעדיקער וואַנט אין דעם קאָשמאַרענעם
טונעלן-לאַנד – אַראָפּ.
די לעבעדיקע וואַנט –
אַ ציטער.
די וואַנט אַ ציטער –
מענטשן-געווייטער.
הענט ווייסן וואָס צו טאָן.
הענט קלאַפּן.
הענט שפּאַרן.
הענט טאַפּן.
הענט שאַרן.

כאַפּן הענט!
ברענט!
אַ שינאהדיקער, מענטשעדיקער קנויל.
אויגן, אוירן – גאָרן.
און די דאָלאַרן
שטראַלן,
פֿאַלן,
שאַלן
אויף אַ ליגנדיקער, ראַגנלענדיקער,
האַסנדיקער וואַנט
פֿון דער האַנט אויפֿן באַלקן
אַראָפּ.

In Table 7.1, the numbers indicate the syllable-to-stress ratio. They show that instead of one regular meter, we have here a span from one extreme to the other: from one stressed syllable (staccato) to five stressed syllables (paeon or penton).

Here is a translation:

> Suddenly—from the ceiling—a hand
> Pours streams of golden dollars
> On the breathing wall in nightmare tunnel-land.
> The breathing wall—
> A tremor.
> Human blizzard.
> Hands hurt.
> Hands push.
> Hands search.
> Hands shuffle.
> Hands catch!
> A hating human tangle—
> Ablaze,
> Eyes, ears—crave, race.
> And the dollars
> Radiate,
> Roar,
> Fall
> Upon a sprawling, struggling hating wall—
> From the hand on the ceiling
> Down.

Table 7.1. Metrical Analysis of A. Leyele's "In sobvey, II" and Three Preceding Lines

Introductory Lines 3.2	Description 3.8 (paeon)	Plŭtslĭng vāyzt fŭn bālkň zĭkh ă hănt ŭn němt shtrōměn gōlděně dŏlārňě ŏyf děr lēbědĭkěr vānt ĭn děm kŏshmārěněm tŭnēlň-lănd— ărōp.	
	Preparation 2.7	Di lebedike vant—	∪ — ∪ ∪ ∪ —
		a tsiter.	∪ — ∪
		Di vant a tsiter—	∪ — ∪ — ∪
		mentshn-geviter	— ∪ ∪ — ∪
	Action 1.5 (almost nothing but stresses)	Hent veysn vos tsu ton.	— — ∪ — ∪ —
		Hent klapn.	— — ∪
		Hent shparn.	— — ∪
		Hent tapn.	— — ∪
		Hent sharn.	— — ∪
		Khapn hent!	— ∪ —
		Brent	—
	Description 3.3	A sinediker, mentshediker knoyl.	∪ — ∪ ∪ ∪ — ∪ ∪ ∪ —
	Counteraction 2.25	Oygn, oyern—garn.	— ∪ — ∪ ∪ — ∪
		Un di dolarn	— ∪ ∪ — — ∪
		shtraln,	— ∪
		faln,	— ∪
		shaln	— ∪
	Description 3.75 (paeon)	oyf a ligndiker, ranglendiker, hasndiker vant	∪ ∪ — ∪ ∪ ∪ — ∪ ∪ ∪ — ∪ ∪ ∪ —
	Counteraction 3.0	fun der hant oyfn balkn arop.	∪ ∪ — ∪ ∪ — ∪ ∪ —

A big-city tempo. Short, choppy sentences. No articles, no auxiliary verbs; mythical reality. Remarkable are the dramatic, thematically determined shifts from long paeonic lines to the staccato of almost nothing but stressed syllables. Each short segment has its own meter, and only the sharp differences can emphasize the effect.

Instead of one regular meter, we have a flowing movement, sweeping many short metrical fragments created ad hoc by the rhythm rather than by the content. We encounter radical shifts from one end to another and back, from one-syllable to five-syllable feet. This is not the self-image of free verse but rather a complex, shifting mosaic of metrical fragments—"dynamic rhythm."

The hymnal—even daemonic—treatment of the big city is effected by long-breathed lines of many syllables with stirring, short-lined terminations. Here is a hymn to Manhattan Bridge ("Manhetn-brik"):[39]

זאָל איך באַזינגען דיַין נאַכט, \ ווען מיט דער ענדלאָזער שורה פֿון באַלוירכטענע אויטאָס

און טראָאַקס \ מיט די עלעקטרישע בליצן ביַי דיַינע ריפן פֿון שטאָל \ פֿינקלסטו, רייצסטו,

ווי אַ רינג פֿון מאָנסטער ברילייאַנטן, \ דו פֿאַרקנסערין פֿון די צוויי זיך יאָגנדיקע שטעט?

Zol ikh bazingen dayn nakht, / ven mit der endlozer shure fun baloykhtene oytos
un troks / mil di elektrishe blitsn bay dayne ripn fun shtol / finklstu, reytsstu, vi
a ring fun monster brilyantn, / du farknaserin fun di tsvey zikh yogndike shtet?

[Shall I sing your night, / When in the endless chain of illuminated cars and
trucks, / In the electrical lightnings at your ribs of steel / You sparkle, tease, like
a ring of monster-diamonds, / You, matchmaker of two speeding cities?]

The rhythm of the metropolis is transmitted chiefly by the multifarious staccato. The short sentences themselves—and the aggregation (not symmetry!) of parallel linguistic units of whatever type—produce the movement, the abrupt shifting of the situation, the diversity; it is one of the ways of expressing the *kaleidoscopic* poetics of the *Inzikhists*.

In "In sobvey, I"[40] there is more action than in the above example, and it is rendered without the use of a single verb. Alone among all the words, the three verbs in the introduction describe no real motion. Instead of verbs we have verbs made into nouns: *rir-rir* (move-move), participles, comparatives, interjections; their order and rhythm transmit the movement to us; that means that the deviation from the normal (as well as its character, its density, its extremity) is more important than the material of the deviation.

A similar big-city rhythm, from the energy and nervousness of the short, staccato sentences, is felt not only in descriptions of the city itself. Big-city "impulses of emotion" were introduced by Leyeles into the formerly melodic accentual-syllabic metrics as well. In the early sonnet "Vinklen" (*Yungharbst* [Warsaw: Kultur Lige, 1922]) we read: "Trepn. Masn. Shtaygn. Faln. Fintster. Nakht." (Stairs. Masses. Ascend. Fall. Dark. Night.), etc. In just 14 lines, we have 43 punctuation marks and 37 sentences; the traditional a.-s. meters rarely have a period in the middle of a line.

With time, the rhythm of the metropolis became internalized and multi-dimensional; metropolitan rhythms became a metaphor for the individual consciousness, for state of mind. Such is the poem "January 28" from the "Diary of Fabius Lind" (Leyeles's alter ego), in *Fabius Lind*.[41] Let us look at the English translation before turning to the original:

January 28

Darkness.
Thick, lumpy,
Primeval, uncanny, gaping darkness.
Suddenly—white sparks, bright stripes.
Magnesium-flare—white, white.
A knee—warm, soft, tight.
A hoop around me, like the ring around Saturn.
Tight around me. White. Motherly nocturne.
Somber excitement.
Brain-flood. Fall—fly. Fall—fly.
Knee. Magnesium-glow. And again—
Lumpy, coal-black darkness.
Abyss.[42]

The poem does not have a single verb. No direct action is narrated. Only nouns, including nouns of action, with many adverbs and adjectives, "furnish" the fictional space, as it were. All this is presented in abrupt, discontinued, often elliptic short sentences: neither telling nor moralizing, nor smart Yiddish chitchat. The experience is kaleidoscopic, with flashes of direct images from disjointed domains rather than similes (similes were opposed in early Introspectivism). Though the function of the images is metaphorical in relation to the created mood, they are motivated as associations in the perceiver's stream of consciousness. No basic situation is mentioned, except for the "darkness," i.e. a negative scene for the sense of seeing. The readers have to reconstruct for themselves the situation and some hypothetical events from which the mood emerges. There may be an unclear yet intense erotic climax ("knee"), or a death experience, or a reciprocal metaphor between those two. The rest is left to the readers' interpretation or re-creation: extreme erotic experience as a metaphor for death and death as a metaphor for erotic climax, as in English metaphysical poetry.

The last word, "farFAlenish," is a neologism. It indicates falling in an abyss; literally it also means "lost cause" or "fallingness" in general: "getting lost in the abyss." The poem is articulated in Leyeles's staccato rhythm. Almost all continuity is broken up. In 13 lines, in a text of only 55 words, we have 17 periods and 36 punctuation marks. The internal rhymes, too, cutting across adjacent sentences, enhance the autonomous presentation of each separate word and highlight its echoing of the words of previous lines rather than direct—logical or syntactic—connections to its neighbors.

This structure is supported by a dense rhythmical texture. There is no consistent meter for the whole poem, no regularity can be expected in advance, but the stressed and unstressed syllables are organized in changing metrical segments and configurations, echoing each other throughout the poem. Since the flow of the sentence or of a metrical scheme is largely subverted, the importance of the individual word ("word-image") or of the small rhythmic-syntactical unit (colon) becomes prominent. The repetition and juxtaposition of such units create the rhythmical shifts of the poem.

Internal rhymes and echoing sound patterns enhance or make a counterpoint to the rhythmical structures. Here is the original Yiddish followed by a transcription:

28יאַנואַר

פֿינצטערניש.

געדיכטע, קנוילידיקע,

אוראַלטע, גרוילידיקע, אומהײמלעכע, מוילידיקע.

און פֿלוצלונג – פֿונקען וויַיסע, גאַנצע פֿאַסן.

מאַגניום-גלי – וויַיס, וויַיס.

אַ קני – וואַרעם, וויַיד און שטיַיף.

אַ רײף אַרום מיר, ווי דער רינג אַרום סאַטורן.

שטיַיף אַרום מיר. וויַיס. מוטערלעכער נאַקטורן.

סומנע רײצעניש.

מאַרך-פֿאַרפֿלייצעניש. פֿאַל – פֿלי. פֿאַל – פֿלי.

קני. מאַגניום-עלי. און ווידער –

קנוילידיקע, קוילידיקע פֿינצטערניש.

פֿאַרפֿאַלעניש.

→

fintsternish.	—∪∪|
gedIKHte, koylike,	∪—∪|—∪∪|
uralte, groylike, umHEYMlekhe, moylike,	—∪∪|—∪∪|∪—∪∪|—∪∪|
un plutslung—funken vayse, gantse pasn.	∪—∪|—∪|—∪|—∪|—∪|
magniym-gli—vays, vays.	—∪∪|—|—|—
a kni—varem, veykh un shtayf.	∪—|—∪|—|∪—|
a reyf arum mir, vi der ring arum saTURN.	∪—∪∪—|∪∪—∪∪∪—∪|
shtayf arum mir. vays. muterlekher nokTURN.	—∪∪—|—|—∪∪∪—∪|
sumne reytsenish.	—∪—∪∪|
markh-farFLEYtsenish. fal—fli. fal—fli.	—∪—∪∪|—|—|—|—|
kni. magniyum-gli. un vider—	—|—∪∪—|∪—∪|
knoylike, koylike fintsternish,	—∪∪|—∪∪|—∪∪|
farFAlenish.	∪—∪∪|

The main metrical configurations used in this mosaic are:

1) Dactyl:

>   fintsternish, knoylike, uralte, groylike

>   → |—∪∪|—∪∪|—∪∪|—∪∪|

2) Trochees:

>   funken vayse, gantse pasn   → |—∪|—∪|—∪|—∪|

3) "Stress meter" (single stressed syllables, following each other, nonexistent in regular meters):

>   fal—fli. fal—fli. kni.   → |—|—|—|—|—|

4) A rhythmical "arch," i.e. a double dactyl stressed on or close to both ends (with optional additional syllables on the margins):

> |magniyum-gli.|shtayf arum mir.|a rayf arum mir.|

>   → |—∪∪—||—∪∪—||∪—∪∪—|

5) A "super-arch," with stresses on both ends and two and more syllables in between:

> |muterlekher nokturn.|ring arum Saturn.|

>   → |—∪∪∪∪—∪|—∪∪∪∪—∪|

6) A "rising" double unit, opposite to the two former ones and ending in an open dactyl. Where the arch has the effect of a closure, resting on its final stress, here we have a double rising move, more emphatic in the end:

> |sumne reytsenish.|markh-farfleytsenish.|

>   → |—∪—∪∪|—∪—∪∪|

The chart below gives a summary. The x's indicate markers of temporal transition, "suddenly" and "again," which are not part of the stream of consciousness itself; they can be shown, however, as metrical transitions.

Syllables per Foot	Metrical Base
3	Dactyl
3 3	Dactyl
3 3 3 3	Dactyl
(x) 2 2 2 2	Trochee
(3 + 1) 1 1	Arch; stress
2 2 1 2	Stress
(3 + 1) (4 + 2)	Arch; super-arch
(3 + 1) 1 (5 + 2)	Arch; stress; super-arch
(2 + 3)	Rising
(2 + 3) 1 1 1 1	Rising; stress
1 (3 + 1) (x)	Stress; arch
3 3 3	Dactyl
3	Dactyl

As we see from the chart, the first three lines almost approach a dactylic meter, with three syllables to each stress; but the possibility of reading the lines in one continuous flow is broken up by small deviations—for example, an extra syllable in the middle of line 3 which forces us to break up the flow and then resume the dactyl again. Thus, after the first single-dactyl line, which sets the tone, we have three double-dactyl segments that rhyme with each other: *fintsternish|gedikhte, knoylike|uralte, groylike|umheymlekhe, moylike|*.

After the dactylic opening, a regular trochee emerges in the fourth line. But since the reader's inertia was guided by a three-syllable meter, the reader will try to accommodate the fourth line in the same manner, giving both syllables the time of three or adding a silent interval after each trochee:

$$\rightarrow$$

funken vayse, gantse pasn. $- \cup 0 - \cup 0 - \cup 0 - \cup$

When the line is independent, those are four trochees, but in this dactylic context, the words sound very different from the same words in a poem with regular trochaic meter, because the inertia of three-syllable feet encourages the addition of a "missing" syllable.

Then the quasi-dactylic frame is counterpointed by the single, stressed syllables, which often compose a whole sentence or independent syntactic unit (*vays. vays. kni. fal—fli. fal—fli. kni.*)—quite contrary to the rhythmical flow of spoken Yiddish. Against these monosyllabic units, we get the opposite: long, double-stressed rhythmical configurations ("arches" and "rising" feet). Indeed, the monosyllabic "stress meter" and the hyperdactylic arch represent the two extremes in the Yiddish language and Yiddish poetry. Strengthened by rhyme, these repeated configurations make conspicuous rhythmical leitmotifs in the poem. Thus, rhythmical awareness is heightened rather than slackened, and the internal tensions between the "word-images" are foregrounded.

In this poetry, metrical disorder signals not a prosaic tone but individual attention to specific lines and words. Rhythm becomes as unpredictable and intense as metaphor. The rhymes between words in one line or in parallel lines support their rhythmical values.

A further example by A. Leyeles:[43]

אין ווייַסע קרייַזן פֿון נייַגעריקייַט

פֿאַרש איך אַ שווייַגיקער דייַן לויטער געזיכט.

אַ העלזיכטיקע ליכטיקייַט שפרייַט זיך מיט מיסטישקייַט

פֿון דיר

איבער דער וויסטעניש פֿון מייַן וועלט.

ביסטו נישט אַלץ פֿאַר מיר?

דאָך באַהאַלטסטו פֿון מיר דייַן וואָרע געשטאַלט.

איך קען גאָרנישט דיך.

ביסט ניט אויסברענגעריש

מיט דייַן געגאַד.

נאָר פֿון דייַנע צופֿעליקע שטראָלונגען

ווער איך, דער פֿאַרפֿאַלענער, געטרייַסט און געלייַזט.

אַ מינוטן זעלטענע,

ווען פֿון זייער באַהעלטעניש

לייַכטן אַרויס די שטראַלן פֿון דעם סוד,

וואָס האַלט אונדז, באַוועלטיקטע, מיסטיש צוזאַמען.

דאַן וויקלען אויך דיך ספֿיראָלן פֿון נייַגעריקייַט.

דאַן ברענען צוזיייַגיקער, ברענען דורכזיכטיקער

די קנאָספן פֿון דייַן ליכטיקייַט,

און ווילסט מיך דערקעננען —

ווי איך דיך.

We get chains of internal rhymes with open dactylic endings: **mÍSTIShkayt–vÍSTENISH–bÍSTu NISH.** Here, capital letters indicate the words involved in the internal composite rhymes, not just the rhymeme.

> In VÁYSE KRÁYZN fun NÁYGERIKAYT
> Forsh ikh a SHVÁYGIKER dayn lóyter GEZÍKHT.
> A HÉLZIKHTIKE LÍKHTIKAYT shpréyt zikh mit MÍSTISHKAYT
> Fun dir
> Iber der VÍSTENISH fun mayn vélt.
> BÍSTU NISHT ÁLTS FAR MIR?
> Dokh BAHÁLTSTU FUN MÍR dayn vóre geshtált.
> ikh KÉN GORNISHT díkh.
> Bist nit OYSBRÉNGERISH
> Mit dayn genód.
> Nor fun dayne tsúfelike SHTRÁLUNGEN
> Ver ikh, der FARFÁLENER, getréyst un geléyzt.
> O minutn ZÉLTENE,
> Ven fun zeyer BAHÉLTENISH
> Laykhtn aróys di shtráln fun dem sód,
> Vos hált undz, bavéltikte, místish tsuzamen.
> Dan víklen oykh díkh spiráln fun NÁYGERIKAYT.
> Dan brénen TSVÁYGIKER, brenen DÚRKHZIKHTIKER
> Di knóspn fun dayn LÍKHTIKAYT,
> Un vílst mikh derkénen—
> Vi ikh dikh. → | ∪ — — |

[In white circles of curiosity / I study in silence your pure face. / A clairvoyant brightness diffuses with mysticity from you / over the wastes of my world. / Are you not everything for me? / Yet you hide from me your true shape. / I know not you at all. / You are not extravagant / with your grace. / But by your accidental emanations / I, the lost one, am consoled and saved. / O minutes rare / when from their hiding / the rays emanate from the secret / which keeps us, overcome, mystically together. / Then the buds of your brightness burn more branchily, translucently / and you want to know me thoroughly / as I want to know you.]

The poem is announced as an "Etyud" (Étude), as in painting: an exercise in internal rhyme-making. It is an achievement in its own right, especially the proclitic rhymes (i.e. of words subordinated to a previous major stress), yet also as a love poem. It is saturated with, composed of, rich internal rhymes. The rhymes are concatenated; they do not terminate lines but, on the contrary, occur inside the lines, leaning over the full stops. It is the actual end of the line which remains without a rhyme. Out of 60 cola, 36 participate in the rhymes and assonances.

Similarly in the poem "Dos lid" (The Poem):[44] in the first two strophes, 39 out of the 47 cola participate in sound relations, including rhymes and rich alliterations. Characteristic is the fact that the rhyming there is more adjoining than concatenating; that is, internal rhymes occur in every line. In this poem we also find almost pure amphibrachs, and their disturbances creates syntactic pauses.

The rhyme causes a kind of metric, non-syntactic cut in the verse line, thanks to which the pattern in all segments is amphibrachic almost throughout. According to F. Strich, the love of rhymes is a distinct trait of Romanticism, and if such historical parallels can be made, it is the Romantic principle in Leyeles that mixes with the idea of the avant-garde. Rhyme is characteristic, too, of his mystically colored love poems, but the character of the rhymes varies. They can also be grotesque, as in "February 29" (*Fabius Lind*). The rhymes produce proclises of short words: ביסטו / ניש אַלץ פֿאַר מיר bĭstŭ nĭsh[45] ălts făr mĭr | — ∪ ∪ — ∪ ∪ | rhymes doubly with וו̆יסטעניש vīstĕnĭsh and with băhăltstŭ fŭn mĭr | ∪ — ∪ ∪ — |;איך קען גאָרניש אויסברענגעריש ĭkh kēn gŏrnĭsh | ∪ — ∪ ∪ | with ŏysbrēngĕrĭsh | ∪ — ∪ ∪ |.

Of the words, 22 percent are long (compared with the 3 percent in English poetry), and of those, 77 percent are dactylic and hyperdactylic; the dactyls take up 35 percent of all cola. This is a great deal if we consider that most short words are connected proclitically with others. The average is three syllables per stress.

Rather than representing concatenations of sound (as in rhyme), the poetry of A. Leivick is characterized by a concatenation of phrases moving from one line to the next. Every second hemistich is repeated in the first half of the next line as a magical incantation. By this device he creates a uniform, religiously lyrical, mood-expressive atmosphere:

אַהינטער ניו-יאָרק פֿאַרקײַקלט זיך די זון,
פֿאַרקײַקלט זיך די זון און לאָמפּן צינדן זיך אָן.
אַז לאָמפּן צינדן זיך אָן פֿאַלט אַ געל-ווײַסע שײַן,
פֿאַלט אַ געל-ווײַסע שײַן אויף אַלעמען אָן.

Ahinter Nyu-vork farkayklt zikh di zun,
farkaylt zikh di zun un lompn tsindn zikh on.
Az lompn tsindn zikh on falt a gel-vayse shayn,
falt a gel-vayse shayn oyf alemen on.[46]

[Beyond New York the sun rolls down, / the sun rolls down and the lamps
light up; / When the lamps light up, falls a yellow-white glow, / A yellow-
white glow falls on all of us.]

Instead of terminal rhymes, we have chiastic parallelism of half-verses. But
as a primary device this is relatively infrequent in the work of either poet, nor
is it entirely sufficient, in the absence of a fixed strophe, especially where an
organic wholeness of the poem is desired. Hence it is unified by means of the
internal repetition of sounds and words. Note the all-pervasive *f* alliterations.

פֿאָהאַנגען פֿון צימערן – װי פֿונאַנדערגעריסענע פֿליגלען,
װי פֿונאַנדערגעריסענע פֿליגלען פֿון דערקױלעטע פֿײגל –
און דער טאָג איז נאָך ליכטיק, און דער טאָג איז נאָך פֿרײלעך –
פֿאַר װאָס פֿאַרגײט ער נישט? פֿאַר װאָס פֿאַרגײט ער נישט?
דינע פֿינגער ציִען זיך נאָך דינער,
דינע פֿינגער פֿרירן אױף געפֿרױרענע פֿעלדער –
װײַסע בעטן – װי געפֿרױרענע פֿעלדער –
בלױע פֿינגער אױף געפֿרױרענע פֿעלדער.

Forhangen fun tsimern—vi funandergerisene fliglen,
vi funandergerisene fliglen fun derkoylete feygl—
un der tog iz nokh likhtik, un der tog iz nokh freylekh—
far vos fargeyt er nisht? Far vos fargeyt er nisht?
Dine finger tsien zikh nokh diner,
Dine finger frirn oyf gefroyrene felder—
vayse betn—vi gefroyrene felder—
bloye finger oyf gefroyrene felder.[47]

[Curtains in rooms—like wings torn apart, / Like torn-apart wings of slaughtered
birds— / And the day is still bright, and the day is still gay— / Why doesn't it set?
Why doesn't it set? / Thin fingers grow thinner, / Thin fingers freeze in freezing
fields— / White beds—like freezing fields— / Blue fingers in freezing fields.]

The last sentences, emphasized here, are perhaps the most powerful expres-
sion of sexual starvation in Yiddish poetry. The alliterative spell of *f* throughout
the poem (25 *f*'s), repetitions, symbolically detached images—the unsaid wants
to develop and receives a new, unsaid symbol: a mystic mood results. The lofty
tone is due to the high syllable-stress ratio (on average, 3:4). A wholeness of
strophe (or rather, of a free line-group) is thus also achieved. All lines have
four feet. Yet because of the lack of end-rhymes and the many-syllabled feet,
this is not felt directly but through the internal caesura which divides every
line into two parallel parts.

From the extreme *concatenation*—the tying of each new syntactic period to a preceding central word or colon—we have passed on to the *ring*, which encloses a newly created line-group into a homogenous whole or brackets line-groups as parts of a complete, coherent poem. Consider Leivick's "Iber di shlofndike oygn" (Over the Sleeping Eyes; p. 132):

איבער די שלאָפֿנדיקע אויגן פֿון אַלע מענטשן,

פֿרעמדע מענטשן אין פֿרעמדע הײַזער,

טראָגט זיך דורך דער באַריר פֿון מײַן האַנט,

פֿון מײַן האַנט, וואָס דעקט צו מײַנע אייגענע אויגן.

אָנגעגליטע פֿײַערדיקע רינגען

קײַקלען זיך אין געדריי

און מײַנע אויגן ווערן נישט מיד

פֿון צו קוקן אויף זיי.

זע, מענטשן ליגן זיך אין די הײַזער און שלאָפֿן.

ï˘běr dĭ shlōfňdĭkĕ ōygň|fŭn ālĕ mēntshň,

　　　　　2 paeons + 3 iambs　　∪ ∪ ∪ — ∪ ∪ ∪ — ∪ | ∪ — ∪ — ∪ —

fremde mentshn in fremde hayzer,

　　　　　2 + 2 trochees　　　　— ∪ | — ∪ | ∪ — ∪ | — ∪

trogt zikh durkh der barir fun mayn hant,

　　　　　3 anapests　　　　　— ∪ | ∪ ∪ — | ∪ ∪ —

fun der hant, vos dekt tsu mayne eygene oygn.

　　　　　4 anapests

Ongeglite fayerdike ringen

　　　　　3 paeons　　　　　　— ∪ ∪ ∪ | — ∪ ∪ ∪ | — ∪

kayklen zikh in gedrey

　　　　　1 "penton"　　　　　— ∪ ∪ ∪ | ∪ —

un mayne oygn vern nisht mid

　　　　　1 paeon + 3 dactyls

fun tsu kukn oyf zey.

　　　　　2 dactyls

Ze, mentshn lign zikh in di hayzer un shlofn.[48]

　　　　　　　　　　　— | ∪ ∪ — ∪ ∪ | ∪ ∪ — ∪ | ∪ — ∪

[Over the sleeping eyes of all the people—/ Strange people in strange houses—/ Hovers the touch of my hand, / Of my hand that covers my eyes—/ Glowing rings of fire / Are wheeling around, / And my eyes are not tired / From gazing spellbound. / See, people lie in their houses and sleep.]

We will not dwell on the construction of thematic motives and word threads. Thanks to the syntactic suspense (e.g. the late arrival of the main sentence units), we cannot interrupt our reading until the end of the fourth line (the following strophes have even longer periods).

It is notable that the *metric segments* wind and grow gradually (in pure metric groups) from disyllabic to pentasyllabic feet and start anew. The transitions are easy; the same meter is sustained and is continued in the thematically most closely related lines (first and second, third and fourth, seventh and eighth). The two instances of transition from one meter to another in the middle of the line are connected with an emotional pause: in both cases it follows the central word, *oygn*. It is this internal order which makes so acute the contrast with the isolated, prosaic last line (*ze, mentshn . . .*), in which *every* foot is of different length (one, two, four, three, and two syllables). The line recurs thrice as a leitmotiv. Another example is Leivick's "Der geviksiker tate" (p. 144), where all stanzas begin with a certain variation of the heading.

In this rhythmic type, it is not the concluding sentence alone, but the arch-like syntactic periods, which create the closed circles. The periods stretch from line to line, with an inner suspense which is rhythm-building. The suspense is produced both by leaving important syntactical units unsaid at the beginnings of sentences and by the interspersion of mutually parallel sentence parts. Stacatto rhythm, when rigorously applied, has one syllable per foot.

As one passes from staccato (one or two syllables per foot)—through the concatenated patterns—to the syntactical periodic arch which is closed like a strophe—the internal stresses become more widely spaced. If the smaller circles are successfully broken in the process and periodic sentence is piled on periodic sentence, as in the flowing, "musical" poem, while the stress intervals increase (i.e. the number of syllables grows) and the long-breathed epic lines are maintained—a *streaming rhythm*[49] results.

There is no Yiddish hexameter, and the width of the feet would not create a particularly lofty effect in this language. The corresponding streambed of Yiddish poetry therefore consists of chiefly polysyllabic feet and secondarily of long, many-foot lines with multi-line sentences. The impression is of free rhythm, or solemn prose, yet the structure is close to traditional strophes (3 × 4 lines, mostly with four major stresses per line). The epic, biblical style is underlined by the frequent use of "and" at the beginning of many lines or sentences.

... אוּן עס איז געווען אויפֿן דריטן פֿרימאָרגן,

ווען די זון איז אויפֿגעגאַנגען אין מיזרח-זײַט

איז פֿון דער גאַנצער שטאָט שוין נישט געבליבן קיין זכר.

אוּן די זון איז געשטיגן אַלץ העכער אוּן העכער.

ביז וואַנען זי איז צוגעקומען צום מיטן הימל,

אוּן אירע שטראַלן האָבן זיך באַגעגנט מיט דעם רבֿס אויגן.

אוּן דער רבֿ איז געלעגן אויף אַ באַרג אַש אוּן שטיינער,

מיט אַ צונויפֿגעפרעסטן מויל אוּן אויסגעגלאָצטע שוואַרצאַפלען,

אוּן אין זײַן נשמה איז געווען שטיל אוּן פֿינצטער אוּן מער גאָרנישט

אוּן ווען זײַנע אויגן האָבן דערפֿילט אויף זיך די הייסע שטראַלן

האָבן זיי זיך פֿונאַנדערגעשפּרייט אוּן געקוקט אוּן געקוקט,

ביז וואַנען זײַן גוף האָט אָנגעהויבן זיך רירן אוּן אויפֿקומען.

	Number of Stresses
... ŭn ĕs ĭz gĕvēn ŏyfñ drītñ frĭmōrgñ,	4
vĕn dĭ zūn ĭz ŏyfgĕgāngĕn ĭn mīzräkh-zǎyt	4
ĭz fŭn dĕr gāntsĕr shtōt shŏyn nĭsht gĕblībñ kĕyn zēykhĕr.	4
Un di zun iz geshtign alts hekher un hekher	4
biz vanen zi iz tsugekumen tsum mitn himl,	4
un ire shtraln hobn zikh bagegnt mit dem rovs oygn.	4
Un der rov iz gelegn oyf a barg ash un shteyner,	4
mit a tsunoyfgeprestn moyl un oysgeglotste shvartsaplen,	4
un in zayn neshome iz geven shtil un fintster un mer gornisht.	4
Ŭn vĕn zǎynĕ ōygñ hŏbñ dĕrfīlt ŏyf zĭkh dĭ hēysĕ shtrālñ	4
hŏbñ zĕy zĭkh fŭnāndĕrgĕshprēyt ŭn gĕkūkt ŭn gĕkūkt,	4
bĭz vănĕn zǎyn gūf hŏt ōngĕhŏybñ zĭkh rīrñ ŭn ōyfkŭmĕn.	4

[... And it was on the third day in the morning, / When the sun rose in the East / Not a trace was left of the city. / And the sun rose higher and higher, / Till it reached the center of the sky, / and its rays met the eyes of the Rov. / And the Rov lay on a mountain of ashes and stone, / His mouth clenched and his eyes glazed, / And in his soul, silence and darkness and nothing more. / And when his eyes were touched by the hot rays / They opened wide, peering and probing, / Till his body began to stir and rise.][50]

In the last line, there are 17 syllables to 4 stresses, giving a foot of over 4.0 syllables per stress.

Because of the great differences in the order of stressed and unstressed syllables, the poem is not "melodic." There is no compositional factor like rhyme.

And yet this is not prose but lofty epic poetry, for the sentences spread over several lines, the syllable-stress ratio is high (3:9), and the epic language devices avoid minor secondary stresses by requiring this lofty tone; note the frequent *un . . . , un az . . . , un ven . . .* (and, and as, and when). The line terminations are mostly penultimate, and the number of feet per line remains fixed.

For more numerous feet, see the "streaming rhythm" example from Leyeles, but note that a line of more than five feet is decomposed by a caesura (as in Leivick's "Volkns hintern vald," p. 411).[51] A streaming rhythm is also realized in ostensibly metric poems if their linguistic construction allows a reading with a reduced number of principal stresses. The long line stimulates the reader to reduce the number of feet, i.e. to emphasize the number of main stresses (rather than any stresses). This occurs, for example, in Kulbak's long poem "Vilne." But if the main stresses form a new metric net (paeons), the streaming rhythm is lofty in a solemnly fervent rather than an epic way.

FREE "SPOKEN" RHYTHMS

Since the preceding two groups dispense with any predetermined organization, the rhythm is produced mainly by linguistic means; that is, linguistic expression is called upon to solve the rhythmic problems at each concrete spot. Thus the center of attention shifts to language.

On the whole, linguistic expression in the third group creates effects with marked deviations from the rhythms of the spoken language. The deviations of Group Two went principally in two directions:

a) departure from the normal speech flow by an increase in the stress intervals

b) modification of normal sentence structure and erection of artificially sharp rhythmic differences between sentences, both by the use of abrupt, very short sentences and by the construction of tense, inversive, long syntactic periods to hold a chain of lines together, thus producing the impact of a streaming strophe by linguistic rather than prosodic structures (meter)

In the "spoken" rhythms we may consider a syllable-stress ratio of somewhat less than 3:0 (about 2:8) as normal. On the other hand, in the dynamic rhythms, this ratio always exceeds 3:0 (i.e. it is above normal; about 3:4). It may be different in different parts of the poem. Furthermore, it may be affected by special diction or by special contrasts produced between the several portions of one poem in terms of syllable-stress ratio. The speech-like rhythms ordinarily form parallel or continuing parts of a sentence; we can interrupt at the end of almost any line without being left in syntactic suspense. But there must be continuity. If the lines are not interconnected, the poem does not give a rhythmic effect even if a formal meter exists. Thus J. Glatshteyn's "Eybik":[52]

פֿופֿצן קנויטן אָנגעצונדן, \ אַ מיטוואָך פֿאַריום-טובֿט. \ אַלע רעדער אָפּגעשטעלט. \ אַלע
רוישן אײַנגעשטילט. \ אַלע גאַסן אויסגעצירט – \ פֿאַר וועמען מאַכט איר חגא? \ פֿאַר
מיר, וױיל איך בין אײביק. \ וױ פּעטרישקע איז אײביק. \ וױ מאַראַנצן-שאָלעכץ, \ וױ אַ
שטויבעלע, \ וױ אַ פֿונק, \ וױ אַ וינטלבלאָז, \ וױ אַ וואַסער-טראָפּן . . .

fuftsn knoytn ongetsundn, / a mitnvokh faryontevt. / ale reder opgeshtelt. / ale royshn ayngeshtilt. / ale gasn oysgetsirt- / far vemen makh ikh khoge? / far mir, vayl ikh bin eybik. / vi petrishke iz eybik. / vi marantsn-sholekhts, / vi a shtoybele, / vi a funk, / vi a vintlbloz, / vi a vaser-tropn . . . etc.

[Lighted fifteen wicks / turned a weekday into a feast. / Stopped all wheels. / Subdued all noises. / Adorned streets— / For whom am I making a profane holiday? / For me, because I am eternal. / As parsnips (in Yiddish, a symbol of triviality) are eternal. / Like orange peel, / like a particle of dust, / like a spark, / like the blow of a breeze, / like a water drop.]

Does anyone feel that these are mostly pure trochees, the "same" trochees as those of the so melodic poems of the preceding generation? (Glatshteyn is not supposed to write in meters.) There is no billowing forward movement here, just a mere, deliberately monotonous list. The forms, of course, are mixed, the boundaries vague.

A more moderate form of language has been given rhythmic expression in this group with its unexaggerated tempos. The poets, by virtue of their temperament and, in particular, their folk-like language style, came under the influence of the folksong; the dividing line between them and the poets of Group One is often vague with respect to word flow. This is not so, however, with regard to foot construction: the lack of fixed strophes in Group Three is closely connected with the lack of a fixed line length. The stresses are not particularly prominent because they are not set apart as a constructive device of the line. All in all, the "singable" poem has come to an end with the elimination of pure isochronism; only in minor syllabically organized groups does isochronism continue to be perceptible.

The group under discussion is quite widespread in various forms. The Yiddish poets in the United States, especially, under the liberating influence of modern American poetry, have avoided "songiness" by violating all symmetric forms, avoided "solemn fervor" (pathos) by eschewing polysyllabic gallops, and avoided dynamism by employing a language style which requires everything to be calmly said rather than "made conscious" (*bavustikn* was Kushnirov's term) in an epically lofty manner or mystically hinted. Their syllable-stress ratio is low.

In the work of Jacob (Yankev) Glatshteyn (Glatstein; 1896–1971)—the other major *Inzikhist* (the first was Leyeles)—we find different forms, depending on the period of his development and the particular poem. Since to him the individual verse is important, his language segments are accentually-syllabically measured. There is a great deal of calm iambicity, but it is broken, now by a disturbing accretion, now by a segment of another a.-s. meter which we are hindered from perceiving as such by our metric inertia induced by the preceding segment. In the truly speech-like poems in the name of Rebbe Nakhman of Bratslav (a speaker within a speaker) even the segments are not metric.

In his new period, Glatshteyn created speech-like, maximally non-melodic rhythms heavily laden with folk locutions; his principal device was his synthetic, intensely Jewish style: "reboyne dealme hayitokhn, davay a bisele nakhes" (Lord of the Universe, please, let's have a little satisfaction): the words are derived from four languages that are components of Yiddish—Aramaic, generic "Slavic," German, and Ashkenazi Hebrew—and yet a phrase is profoundly Yiddish. His poetry is tantamount to slow, weighty, well-considered, wise speech; the phrasing of it is governed not just by the language but by the length of his lines (which are also his sentences). His characteristic rhyming pattern connects the end of one line with the beginning or the middle of the next line (a form often used by Leyeles), yet the line-initial rhyme is not the end of an expression, but a beginning, and is thus blurred. However, the close rhymes are a mainstay of his poem and, additionally, a means of arranging words of neighboring lines in a metrically parallel way and of eliding from one line to the next.

In narrative poets such as Berish Vaynshteyn (Weinstein; 1905–1967) or Eliezer Grinberg (Greenberg; 1896–1977), a single a.-s. background (ordinarily trisyllabic) is felt in entire poems. Connected with this is their tendency to strophic form. The free tone is achieved by disturbances in the trisyllable net, which are ordinarily related to syntactic or reading pauses; and by the intercalation of "iambic" segments, mostly in the interior of lines, to cancel the metrical impact.

פֿאַנצערס פֿון שיפֿן צעשלאָגן די כוואַליעס אין שוים און צערודערן די באָרטנס.
שטריק מיט געאַנקערטע שיפֿן רירן די ברעגן.
האַפֿנס רוישן מיט אָפּגעריסענע קלעצער פֿון הילצערנע ווענט.
אויף די קלעצער שוימיקער מאָך גרינט ווילד און קיל.

→

Pāntsĕrs fŭn shīfň tsĕshlōgň dĭ khvlāyĕs ĭn shōym ŭn tsĕrūdĕrň dĭ bōrtňs.

$$— \cup\cup — \cup\cup — \cup\cup — \cup\cup — \cup\cup — \cup\cup\cup — \cup$$

Shtrīk mĭt gĕānkĕrtĕ shīfň rīrň dĭ brĕgň. $— \cup\cup — \cup\cup — \cup| — \cup\cup — \cup$

Hāfňs rōyshň mĭt ōpgĕrĭsĕnĕ klētsĕr fŭn hĭltsĕrnĕ vēnt.

$$— \cup — \cup\cup — \cup\cup\cup\cup — \cup\cup — \cup\cup —$$

Ŏyf dĭ klētsĕr dĕr shōymĭkĕr mōkh grĭnt vīld ŭn kĭl.[53]

$$\cup\cup — \cup — \cup\cup — | \cup — \cup —$$

[Armor of ships smashes the waves into foam and agitates the coast. / Ropes with anchored ships move the shores. / Harbors hum with beams torn from wooden walls. / On the beams the frothy moss greens, wild and cool.]

There are syllable omissions which are connected with thematic or phrasal breath interruptions. A few "detached" words like *opgerisene* in line 3 suffice to cancel the regular metric wave. In comparison with the previously cited streaming poetry, Vaynshteyn's spoken yet epic work is calmer; his syllable-stress ratio is only 2:9.

The third subgroup comprises lyric poems, individual and mostly brief ones (e.g. the free lyricism of Y. L. Teller [J. L. Teller; 1912–1972], Ber Horovits, Aba Shtoltsenberg, several women poets), which do not maintain a fixed number of feet in the line but whose shorter lines permit the reader to feel the feet more vividly and contribute to the creation of atmosphere. The frame of the poem and of the strophe is often linguistically rigid. Here is an example by Malke Kheyfets Tuzman (1896–1987):

נעם מיך אַרום, מיין ליבער,
נעם מיך אַרום.
מיט דאָרנס אין די פֿינגער נעם מיך אַרום.
מיט שטאָלשפּליטערס אין די אָרעמס
נעם מיך אַרום.
מיטן פֿינצטער פֿון דיין אויסגעהאַקט אויג,
מיט דיין גאָר צעוווּנדיקט לעבן,
נעם מיך אַרום.

Nēm mǐkh ărŭm, măyn lībĕr,
nēm mǐkh ărŭm.
Mǐt dōrn̊s īn dǐ fingĕr nēm mǐkh ărŭm.
Mǐt shtōlshplǐntĕrs ǐn dǐ ōrĕms
nēm mǐkh ărŭm.
Mītn̊ fīntstĕr fŭn dăyn ŏysgĕhăkt ôyg,
mǐt dăyn gōr tsĕvūndǐkt lēbn̊,
nēm mǐkh ărŭm.[54]

[Embrace me, my dear, / embrace me. / With thorns in your fingers embrace
me. / With steel splinters in your arms / embrace me. / With the dark of
your knocked-out eye, / with your entire life, all wounds, / embrace me.]

The reiteration also acts as a rhythmic leitmotiv, which is prominent against
the background of differently ordered lines.

The boundary between this form and prose is not always clear, especially
where there are no terminal rhymes. Thus Ber Horovits composed a free-rhyth-
mic poem in which the rhyme does not come until the end of the exceedingly
long periods.[55] The very vagueness of the stress distribution, the subjective
perception of unequal semi- or quasi-stresses, is a sign of proximity to prose.
But this type of text is not prose, not even in its most unorganized passages.
The poem's typographical arrangement makes us read it as a poem, with a
special suspense in each line, with a will to compare the lines and equate them
with a uniform stressing. According to Andrey Bely[56] the line determines our
breath load. That is, a great deal depends on its length alone. Every line is an
aural image (Arno Holz, *Revolution der Lyrik*, 1899), and only genuine poets
know, or rather feel, how it should be constructed, especially in the difficult
conditions of full freedom. As another contemporary wrote,

> Free verse . . . is an additional instrument . . . but its scope, I think, will never be
> otherwise than very restricted, both because it is only suited for certain moods
> and certain subject matter, still more because to write successfully without meter
> needs stronger inspiration, more mastery of rhythm, and a severer sense of form,
> not less discipline, but a greater discipline than to write in meter.[57]

The absence of meter has the advantage of creating more immanent rhythms
for the poem in an age which no longer believes in the suggestive possibil-
ity of metrically and phonically rocking the reader into a lofty or romantic
mood. Now that the content of the word is in the center, the word must not
be smoothed over by melodic undulations.

Jünger indicates that in Hölderlin's hexameters there are already many tro-chees (rather than dactyls), i.e. instances of slowed down movement in which all parts of the verse strive toward independence. But rhythmical mediocrity can also be broken simply by passing from one group of meters to another in the middle of a line, i.e. simply by breaking the inertia. Quite "prosy" is the appearance of the following lines by Leyeles (from his poem "Lodzh"):[58]

צו זען די ערשטע זון פֿון עלעקטרישער פּראַכט

האָט אין אַ פֿרײַער נאַכט נאָך מײַן טאַטע געפֿירט מיך.

דעם ערשטן עלעקטרישן טראַמוױי – וווּנדער, חלום, שד –

בין איך אין דער זעט פֿון צען-יאָריקן נײַגער

אַליין געלאָפֿן זען.

Tsŭ zēn dĭ ērshtĕ zŭn fŭn ĕlēktrĭshĕr prākht   ∪ — ∪ — ∪ — | ∪ ∪ — ∪ ∪ — |
hŏt ĭn ă frāyĕr nākht nŏkh măyn tātĕ gĕfirt mĭkh.

                       ∪ — ∪ — ∪ — | ∪ ∪ — ∪ ∪ — ∪ |
Dĕm ērshtň ĕlēktrĭshň trāmvăy—vūndĕr, khōlĕm, shēd—

                      ∪ — ∪ ∪ — ∪ ∪ ∪ — | — ∪ — ∪ — |
Bĭn īkh ĭn dĕr zēt fŭn tsĕn-yōrĭkň nāygĕr   ∪ — ∪ ∪ — ∪ ∪ — ∪ ∪ — ∪
ălēyn gĕlōfň zēn.   ∪ — ∪ — ∪ —

[To see the first sun of electric splendor / my father on a night off took me. / The first electric streetcar—miracle, dream, demon— / I, in the satiety of my ten-year-old curiosity / myself ran to see.]

Schematically, the first two lines may look like a compilation of pure iambic and pure anapestic segments, even of similar length and order, but because of the break, the feeling is free-rhythmic and anti-melodic. The internal order-ing has its effect, but it is subtly induced, and the reader is enticed into the rhythmic pattern through the back door, as it were. The metric nature of every thematic segment attracts attention to it and helps it stand out independently.

But a unique wholeness must be created which does permit the replace-ment of the poem by prose. Besides the arrangement in short lines, the dif-ference between such unmetered poetry and prose consists of unusual speech movement, rhythmically governed word order, and a partial, nonsubduing a.-s. feeling. Characteristic of the "freedom" of this rhythmical group is Ber Horovits's manifesto (to be read vertically):

אומגעבונדן,   וער ס‹האָט ליב

נישט געקאָװעט   גערעגלטע װאַסערן –

שװים מײַן געזאַנג!   איך האָב ליב

וויַ אַ באַרגוואַסער שוויַם   פֿרײַע, ראַשע

אין ווילד-אײַגענע ברעגעס!   . . . רײַסנדיקע באַרגוואַסערן

věr s'hŏt līb ŭmgěbūndň,
gěrēgltě vāsěrň—nīsht gěkōvět
īkh hŏb līb shvīm măyn gězāng!
frāyě, rāshě vǐ ă bārgvǎsěr shvīm
rāysňdǐkě bārgvǎsěrň . . . ĭn vǐld-ēygěně brēgěs![59]

[Some people like regulated waters— / I like / free, rapid / gushing mountain streams . . . / Untied, / unshackled, / swim, my song! / Like a mountain stream, swim / within savage banks of your own!]

A glance at the scheme shows the a.-s. feeling to be so strong that from meter to meter we glide into pure anapests. A similar declaration by U.-Z. Grinberg in Hebrew (in his book *Kelev bayit*) against "foreign iambs" lapses itself into precise iambs or trochees.

To be sure, the short line helps.

RETROSPECTIVE REMARKS

The differentiation between rhythm and beat by the German psychologist Ludwig Klages[60] is followed in the study of free verse by Hans Hellenbrecht.[61] However, if one sees rhythm as connected with experience (*Erlebniss*), and beat (*Takt*) as connected with consciousness, it is difficult to understand the appearance of strong beats in the behavior of small children and the free-rhythmic flow of intellectual poetry of the twentieth century. From the pure beat, which is most precise in a machine, through the scanned verse which dominates a poem, to the poem of pure flowing rhythm, where only the sentence prevails, as in prose, there is a wide range of intermediate combinations. On the whole, it can be said that the folksong is sung flowingly, such approaches to order as do occur being blurred; the dance song, on the other hand, and even more so the children's song, underscore the beat. In a.-s. meters, "melodic" impressionistic poems are separated in this way from the declamatory and political poems and marching songs. In the truly free rhythms, the content is decisive, and the rhythmic effects, too, are achieved above all on a content basis.

According to syllabic relations, poems can be divided into the following types:

(a) The first type has a single a.-s. metric net covering the whole poem but interrupted by syntactic or emotional pauses. Here an important role is played by the limits of freedom.

(b) In the second type, one prevalent meter is inside most of the major word groups but not at their boundaries. Emphasis is usually on continuity, and there are no fixed strophes or line dimensions. The prevailing dimensions are furnished by the fixed number of unstressed syllables between every two stresses in each colon and content-determined word-group; however, the homogenous pattern does not necessarily exceed the boundaries of content groups. For example, in "Dos lid" by Leyeles, trisyllabicity prevails, but among the individual deviations we find strophe beginnings such as the following: *in ōnhĕyb ĭz dĕr nĭgň* | ∪ — ∪ | ∪∪ — ∪ | (in the beginning is the melody) and *in ōnhĕyb vĕkt zĭkh dĕr nĭgň* | ∪ — ∪ | — ∪∪ — ∪ | (in the beginning the melody awakes). It is evident that the author makes a significant breathing pause after *in onheyb* (that is, associating it with the biblical "In the beginning"), although there is no comma. The prevailing trisyllabic foot forces us in reading to reproduce the same pause in order to avoid having a single utterance-segment contain more than two unstressed syllables between every two stresses. Freer instances in the same group are Leyeles's "Etyud" and the above-mentioned fragment by Vaynshteyn.

(c) In the third type, one rhythmic leitmotif (i.e. occasional cola of a fixed rhythmic group) permeates the entire poem or an entire strophe. Occasionally there also occurs a manifest struggle between two rhythmical leitmotifs or—in the case of highly distinct individual strophes—of a leitmotif with an opposing net.

(d) The fourth type has concatenated a.-s. metric groups that change their basis from one instance to the other, but in such a way that in passing from line to line in one sentence, there is no interruption; either the end and the beginning of a line are segments of a single net or they grow naturally into each other. This occurs in concatenated rhythms when the poet has difficulty in freeing himself from the a.-s. sensibility at every concrete instant and cancels the a.-s. pattern as a poem-building principle.

It is rare—except in strongly agitated streaming rhythms—for any a.-s. metrical background to be absent. (We are speaking of modern poetry, not of folk-like literature in which the number of feet is retained.) The implicit a.-s. schema provides a grounding effect which does not reach the surface. Only where an extensive a.-s. order is present does it dominate the line; only then, too, can it be perceived and perhaps act as a disturbance, forcing more frequent stresses than the content would require.

און רויִקער פֿון אַלץ איז דאָך דאָס אָנקומען פֿון אונטערגאַנג

ŭn rūĭkēr fŭn ālts ĭz dōkh dŏs ōnkŭmēn fŭn ūntĕrgāng

$$| \cup - \cup \cup - \cup \cup \cup - \cup \cup \cup - \cup \cup |$$

[and calmer than anything is after all the approach of downfall]

This is a paeon II and is liable to slip into an iambic beat; that is, by inertia it forces superfluous secondary stresses onto the long words: $| \cup - \cup \cup |$ $- - \cup \cup | \cup - \cup \cup | \cup - \cup \cup |$.

However, Leivick himself in "Der volf" removes one syllable that is inserted (the word *dokh*) and places this verse line in a frame where every line is interrupted by a metric caesura and the second part is suddenly anapestic. The result is paeonicity; that is, the preservation of the widely spaced stresses of the long words becomes a requisite (at most, perhaps, the word רויִקער rūĭkēr receives a secondary stress in the poem):

און אַז איך זאָג נאָר אַרויס דאָס וואָרט – ווערט מיר גוט

ווײַל רויִקער פֿון מיר איז דער קאַלטער קלאַנג פֿון וואָרט

און קעלטער פֿונעם קלאַנג פֿון וואָרט איז דאָס פּנים פֿון גאָרנישט

און רויִקער פֿון אַלץ איז דאָך איז דאָס אָנקומען פֿון אונטערגאַנג.

→

Un az ikh zog nor aroys dos vort—vert mir gut

$$| \cup \cup \cup - \cup | \cup - \cup - | \cup \cup - |$$

Vayl ruiker fun mir iz der kalter klang fun vort

$$| \cup - \cup \cup \cup - | \cup \cup - \cup - \cup - |$$

Un kelter funem klang fun vort iz dos ponim fun gornisht

$$| \cup - \cup - \cup - \cup - | \cup \cup - \cup \cup - |$$

Un ruiker fun alts iz dos onkumen fun untergang.

$$| \cup - \cup - \cup - | | \cup \cup - \cup \cup | \cup - \cup \cup |$$

[And as soon as I utter the word, I am relieved / because the cold sound of the word is calmer than I / and colder than the sound of the word is the face of nothing / and calmest of all is the approach of downfall.]

The schema is, according to my reading, carefully constructed down to the last details. (Note the missing syllable in the middle of each line.) The effect of the entire configuration is one of genuine free rhythm, in spite of the stretches of metrical segments.

In Kulbak's "Khanke—a fayerdike kale," the syllable-stress ratio of the first nine lines is 3:4, but without the first line it is 3:7. The difference is due to the many stresses in that first line:

חנקע, איי, חנקע, קום צו מיר פֿאַר נאַכט

Khānkĕ, ĕy, Khānkĕ, kūm tsŭ mīr fǎr nākht

[Khanke, hey, Khanke, come to me in the evening]

But this is the result only of a formal syllable count. The time intervals between stresses here are no smaller than in the many-syllabled sequel. And conversely, the relative lack of unstressed syllables helps to create a feeling of sentence interruption.

The effect of syllable order in the subconscious becomes manifest during sharp transitions from net to net. In "Shotns" (Shadows),[62] Leyeles writes:

פֿאַר מײַן פֿענצטער שטייען ביימער

ערנצט, שוויגיק, פֿאַרטראַכט.

זײערע יונגע צווײַגן, פֿלעפֿערישע בלעטער

רירן זיך, רעגן זיך

וויגן זיך, באַוועגן זיך,

אין די פֿלירטנדיקע ווינטלעך

פֿון דער פֿרילינגדיקער נאַכט.

far mayn fentster shteyen beymer	$\|-\cup-\cup-\cup-\cup\|$
ernst, shvaygik, fartrakht.	$\|-\cup-\cup0\cup-\|$
zey(e)re yunge, tsvaygn, pleferische bleter	$\|\cup\cup-\cup-\cup\|-\cup\cup\cup-\cup\|$
rirn zikh, regn zikh	$\|-\cup\cup-\cup\cup\|$
vign zikh, bavegn zikh,	$\|-\cup-\|\cup-\cup\cup\|$
in di FLIRtnDIKE vintlekh	$\|\cup\cup-\cup\cup\cup-\cup\|$
fun der FRILingDIKER nakht.	$\|\cup\cup-\cup\cup\cup-\|$

[Before my window trees stand / serious, taciturn, absorbed in thought. / Their young branches, stupefying leaves / stir, start, / sway, move / in the flirtatious breezes / of the spring night.]

The capital letters indicate sound patterns. We can see that the special rhythmic effect of this formally nonmetric passage is achieved by the gradual and plain increase in stress intervals: from a precise trochee, through disyllabicity in every colon, a formal pattern of trochees, dactyls, trisyllabicity in the cola—up to full four-syllable paeons. Only the preceding dense net can so impressively emphasize the airy, buoyant effect of the last two paeonic lines (and of the next-to-the-last lines of dactyls). A paeon is a four-syllable foot, stressing only one of the four syllables; in a paeon III the stress falls on the third syllable, $| \cup \cup - \cup |$; paeon I has the stress on the first, $| - \cup \cup \cup |$.

In this connection it is important to realize that the avoidance of secondary stresses in long words is made possible first and foremost by the fact that the paeons occur, not next to iambs (which would "iambicize" the paeons, too), but next to longer, trisyllable feet. If, in reading, we wish to compare the new feet with the already established feet intervals, we cannot do it by splitting a foot into two pieces; the foot becomes more heavily loaded—for an instant this is unusual—and then the net widens from three to four syllables.

This effect of metric inertia is the main factor requiring a single meter in an entire a.-s. poem. The strict form of the Greek odes—precisely fixed in each line, though irregular—had a liberating influence on German poetry because of their non-uniform pattern.[63] In Yiddish poetry, too, mixed (but predetermined) meters make them essentially closer to free-rhythm than to metric poems.

In another strophe from Leyeles's *Rondeaux and Other Poems*:[64]

בלאָס-געלבלעכע רויז. אַראָמאַט

פֿון שטילע, פֿײַערלעכע ריטואַלן,

פֿון גאָטדינונג אין װײכע זײַד-סאַנדאַלן,

פֿון גלויבן מיט װײַזהײַט שוין זאַט

blas-gelblekhe royz. Aromat / fun shtile, fayerlikhe ritualn, / fun gotdinung in veykhe zayd-sandaln, / fun gloybn mit vayzhayt shoyn zat

[Palely-yellowish rose. Aroma / of quiet, solemn rituals, / of divine service in soft silk sandals, / of faith already sated with wisdom.]

The verse lines are written in a strict form: the first and last lines are amphibrachs, while the middle two lines are iambs (and so on throughout the poem):

$$| \cup - \cup \cup - \cup \cup - || \cup - \cup - \cup - \cup - \cup - \cup |$$

Truly paeonic poems do not stick to pure a.-s. meters. We are speaking only of a tendency to paeonization; a slight iambic (or trochaic) secondary stress is always present. But in the free rhythms, paeonic lines are rather strong, especially after a trisyllable preparation.

Even as many as five unstressed syllables can be maintained after an appropriate preparation, one which does not permit the reader to fall into a denser net. In Kulbak's "Khanke—a fayerdike kale," quoted above, we read:

איך בעט עס ביַי דיר, חנקעלע, קום צו גייַן.

אַ שטילינקער וועל איך ליגן.

אָט אַזוי שטיל ווי אַ שעפסעלע.

דו וועסט זיצן אָט דאָ אויפֿן שוועל.

איך – אויף דער ערד וועל איך ליגן אויסגעצויגן.

מיטן קאָפּ אויף די הענט וועל איך ליגן.

אָט אַזוי.

איך וועל דיר פֿרעגן : חנקעלע, האָסטו שוין אויסגעמעלקן די בהמות דײַנע?

→

Ĭkh bēt ĕs bǎy dīr, Khānkĕlĕ, kūm tsŭ gēyn. | ∪ — ∪ ∪ ∪ | — ∪ ∪ | — ∪ — |
Ă shtīlĭnkĕr vĕl ĭkh līgň. | ∪ — ∪ ∪ | ∪ ∪ — ∪ |
Ōt ăzŏy shtīl vĭ ă shēpsĕlĕ. | — ∪ ∪ — | ∪ ∪ — ∪ ∪ |
Dū vĕst zītsň ŏt dō ŏyfň shvēl. | ∪ ∪ — ∪ ∪ | ∪ — | ∪ ∪ — |
kh—ŏyf dĕr ērd vĕl ĭkh līgň ōysgĕtsŏygňĬ | — ∪ ∪ ∪ | ∪ ∪ — ∪ | ∪ ∪ — ∪ |
Mĭtň kōp ŏyf dĭ hēnt vĕl ĭkh līgň. | ∪ ∪ — | ∪ ∪ — | ∪ ∪ — ∪ | — ∪ — |
ōt ăzŏy. | — ∪ — |
Ĭkh vĕl dĭr frēgň, Khānkĕlĕ, hŏstŭ shŏyn ōysgĕmŏlkň dĭ bĕhēymĕs dăynĕ?
| ∪ ∪ ∪ — ∪ | — ∪ ∪ | ∪ ∪ ∪ ∪ ∪ — ∪ | ∪ ∪ — ∪ ∪ ∪ |

[I ask it of you, Khanke, come to me. / I will lie still. / As still as a lamb. / You will sit here on the doorstep. / As for me—I'll lie stretched out on the ground / With my head on my hands will I lie. / This way. / I will ask you: Khanke, did you milk your cows yet?]

The syllable-stress ratio of the last line goes all the way to 5:0! And yet, in another frame, it could be read iambically and monotonously. The reader has a choice: ten iambs (with their monotony) or four major stresses in a line. The context encourages the reader not to go beyond four stresses, even if that creates high syllabic ratios in a two-story rhythmical grid. The trisyllabic net with its several skipped syllables forms the preparation for the swing. The long word אויסגעמעלקן *ōysgĕmŏlkň* | — ∪ ∪ ∪ | accustoms us to the hyperdactylic and makes possible the enclisis: די בהמות דײַנע *dĭ bĕhēymĕs dăynĕ* | ∪ ∪ — ∪ ∪ ∪ |. When we read the line detached from the poem, we usually find more stresses, especially since the possibility of iambic order is so natural.

Only by taking into account the interaction factors can a poet create an impact through the selection of long words. Thus, in a poem composed on an iambic net, if we were to insert the phrase זײַ שעפֿערישע דרייַסט *zay sheferishe drayst* (be creative boldness), it would mostly be read as an iamb, but when several phrases so constructed come in parallel, and, in addition, the first violates the iambic pattern, there results a free-rhythmic fervor as in the following:

וער האָפֿנדיקע פֿאַרגעבונג! זײַ אײביקע באַנײַונג!

זײַ שעפֿערישע דרײַסט! און דו הערסט

וער אײביקע באַלעבונג. יערסט

זײַ אָטעם פֿון גײַסט! און ווערסט!

וער ליכטיקע באַפֿרײַונג,

Ver hofndike fargebung!   zay eybike banayung!

Zay sheferishe drayst!   Un du herst

Ver eybike balebung.   yerst

Zay otem fun gayst!   un verst!

Ver likhtike bafrayung,

[Become hoping forgiveness! / Be creative boldness! / Become eternal animation. / Be breath of spirit! / Become bright liberation, / be eternal renewal. / And you hear / ferment / and become!][65]

Only the preceding many-syllabled arches (due to the long Yiddish descending words) allow such a bold emphasis of the three energetic stresses-cum-rhymes at the end.

When it exists, the a.-s. meter prevails over the cola in the line. Similarly, when the number of feet in the line is fixed, the line is usually a stronger unit than the syntactic group. On the other hand, when the syntactic groups become stronger, they cancel the line symmetry, and the stresses are weakly felt because of their irregularity; consequently, the number of stresses is also less perceptible even if fixed. Given a free number of stresses, there are two possibilities: (a) regularity of line, with the line frequently containing up to four stresses, with few deviations from four or three; the number then does not exceed five, yet—in the case of six—the line is divided by a fixed, permanent caesura or else it ceases to be a line of a poem; (b) tangible differences in line length; in that case, lines with a great many stresses also occur.

Similarly, Hellenbrecht notes that "the number of rises usually fluctuates between one and six."[66] When the line becomes excessive in length, we lose our sense of the poetic rhythm. Even when the line is written in trochees, like N. B. Minkov's long rhymed periods in "Der letster tsug,"[67] it is hard to feel the feet. The rhythmic value of the rhyme also goes almost entirely to waste.

The more regular the number of stresses, the more apparent the deviations. An extraordinarily long line usually produces heaviness, while a short line adds weight to its words, as in these lines from Leyeles:[68]

בלאָטיקע, בלוטיקע באַלאַדע פֿון באַלוט –
קעמערלעך דלד אויף דלד, וועבשטול, בעטן, קינדער,
מיט אָרעמקייט בלינדער, מיט אַזאַ עשירות נויט,
מיט אַזאַ שמאַלצגרוב נויט –
לאָדזש

Blotike, blutike balade fun Balut—
kemerlekh daled ofy daled, vebshtul, betn, kinder,
mit oremkayt blinder, mit aza ashires noyt,
mit aza shmaltsgrub noyt—
Lodzh.

[Muddy, bloody ballad of Balut — / cubicles four (feet) by four, weaving loom, beds, children, / with blind poverty, with such a wealth of want, / with such a gold mine of want— / Lodz.]

The alliteration of the first line—with *blt* occurring four times—emphasizes the poetic text in counterpoint with the poverty of the Jewish Balut, the lower-class section of Lodz where the ghetto was established under the Nazis. Our tendency toward equilibrium and toward unexaggerated dimensions inclines us, on the one hand, to give greater force to the stresses of the short lines and, on the other hand, to read as few main stresses as possible in a long line, provided it is felt as a line.

Therefore, a relatively small proportion of long words suffices to create loftiness—for example, in a streaming rhythm as in Leivick's poem "Unter di trit fun mayne fis" (Under the Tread of My Feet):

אונטער די טריט פֿון מיַינע פֿיס,
אין די טיפֿע טיפֿענישן פֿון דער ערד,
הער איך דאָס אומאויפֿהערריקע גערויש-געזאַנג פֿון מיַין לעבן
שטראָמענווייז-אָדערנווייז.

ŭntĕr dĭ trīt fŭn māynĕ fĭs,
īn dĭ tīfĕ tīfĕnīshň fŭn dĕr ērd,
Hĕr ĭkh dŏs ŭmŏyfhĕrĭkĕ gĕrŏysh-gĕzăng fŭn măyn lēbň
Shtrōmĕnvăyz-ōdĕrňvăyz.

[Under the tread of my feet, / In the deep bowels of the earth, / I hear the unceasing clamor of my life / in currents—in arteries.][69]

The emphasis on the proximity of the same-sound stresses in *tīfĕ tīfĕnīshň* | — ∪ | — ∪ ∪ ∪ | makes an excellent (iambicizing) backdrop for the strongly contrasting third line. We see an interaction of all principles: syntactic suspense (the main clause not occurring until the third line); long, hyperdactylic words in a long line; and a chord in the two parallel (almost rhyming) dactylic single words which bear the main sense of the sentence: *shtromenvayz* | — ∪ ∪ | and *odernvayz* | — ∪ ∪ ∪ |. The real syllable-stress ratio is 3:8.

Therefore, too, those lines occur in which it is difficult to determine the number of stresses we hear as prose. Too many stresses destroy a line as a (comparable) unit, and only an a.-s. meter allows an alternate ordering principle. Hence the accepted rule: in poetry the stresses are more uniform than in normal language.

In all this, one thing is clear: we are intent on perceiving a short line much the same way we perceive the preceding long line. But this does not mean equating the two—it only means pressure in that direction. The same applies to the syllables. Isochronism, too, does not necessarily mean equal duration of measures, merely similar duration that can be experienced by the human interpreter as equivalent. But the tendency to equate (especially with the last established point of inertia) is always present and causes the preceding text to affect the manner of reading a line in a poem.

On the whole, two principal forces contribute to the creation of rhythm in a poem: order and contrast. The greater the order, the more metric the pattern and the more basis there is for the contrasts to have effect. But while "in a work of art, a rhythm *is* only by its constants," at least in the ordered segments, "it *lives* only by its variables,"[70] that is, by contrast with the normal. The contrasts with order create the suspense of the poem. In free rhythms, where the order is not predetermined, the rhythmic effect is achieved by contrast with the surrounding and preceding context and by opposition to ordinary linguistic utterances. Therefore word order and inversion are vital in this type of poetry. The linguistic specificness consequently plays a larger role than in metric writing.

On different bases, certain devices produce similar effects, depending on the total structure. For example, the emphasis of words and intensification of cuts between them can be carried out in three ways: (a) by syntactic pauses; (b) by breaks in the metric net—for example in A. Leyeles's "Februar-nakht,"[71] where, after a series of precise anapests, the last line divides words in a strongly emotional way,

און די פֿעברואַר-נאַכט איז צו שײן \\ אַפֿילו צו זײַן צערטלעך

un di februar-nakht iz tsu sheyn / afile tsu zayn tsertlekh

[and the February night is too beautiful / even to be tender]

—and (c) by internal rhymes (which often accompany breaks in the net and support it). Thus, after lines of pure disyllabic net, we find in Leyeles's "February 27" (*Fabius Lind*):[72]

אַלע שפֿיל-פּאַמאַליעס און געזאַנג-קאַפּאַליעס – שפֿילט טרילט טרעלט קװעלט פּױקט און אױגט

un iz tu
ālĕ shpīl-pămălyĕs ŭn gĕzāng-kăpălyĕs— / shpīlt trīlt trēlt kvēlt pōykt ŭn ōygt

[all playing hosts and singing ensembles—a grotesque distortion of the normal *kapelyes*— / play trill warble swell drum and act like 'Og.]

Kapelyes are groups of musicians. 'Og is from Deuteronomy 3:11, or it is a neologism from "eye"–"eyes"?

A clash of two adjacent stresses is almost impossible in the flow of speech; a break is demanded between the stresses. If the Greeks combatted the molossus, three subsequent stresses ($\acute{-}\ \acute{-}\ \acute{-}$), it was retrieved again by this poet's style of manifesto-like phrasing (to cite A. Bely), that is, a style of free dynamic rhythms which allow themselves to be read with a highly marked phrasing. But a basic rhythmic law remains unavoidable in the poem; the constant stresses are made possible only because, in this style, interruptions between stresses in reading are actually made. This is accomplished either by a break in content atmosphere or—especially where stresses are numerous—by auxiliary devices of interruption, such as commas or internal rhymes.

Commas are unnecessary: every syllable is stressed, every word is separate. Two rhymed cola are felt as rhythmically parallel. In the trisyllabic net of Leyeles's "Dos lid," there is another deviation:

אַ נישט-דײַטלעכער אױפֿשפֿיל, אַ װײַטלעכער צונױפֿשפֿיל

ă nĭsht-dāytlĕkhĕr ōyfshpĭl, ă vāytlĕkhĕr tsŭnōyfshpĭl

$$| \cup \cup - \cup \cup | - \cup | | \cup - \cup \cup | \cup - \cup |$$

[an indistinct striking-up, a rather distant playing together]

But owing to the rhyme, no imperfection is felt.

Incidentally, the same poem shows how an exaggerated piling up of rhymes, especially when symmetrically grouped, can be an excellent device for achieving grotesqueness; it was also used by Glatshteyn, as in "Shir—a gezang,"[73] in contrast to the asymmetrical interwoven abundance of complex rhymes in Leyeles's seriously lyrical "Etyud."

Jünger has observed that the rhyme delivers the solution to the verse-sentence conflict into the hands of the verse. But this is true only of the terminal rhyme. Leyeles's internal rhymes, in blurring and cutting up both the verse and the sentence, assign the dominant role to the colon—to the word meanings—as well as to the non-predetermined, ever-sudden rhyme itself, which is the transcendent power of the poet's rhythmic impulse (inspiration). Jünger has further stated that the rhyme lifts symmetry above rhythm (i.e. above the forward flow). As far as the terminal rhyme is concerned, this is doubtless true. But in Leyeles's work the question is solved in each spot, and often the decision is not in favor of symmetry. That means a genuinely free-rhythm approach to rhyming.

Experience with Russian, a language containing many long words, has shown that the more syllables, the stronger the pauses between words (Bely). But clearly the converse is also true: the stronger the pauses between the words, as in dense rhyming, the greater the number of syllables that can be read at once, or (if there are few syllables) the greater the weight that is given to the existing stress and the more strongly underscored is the emphasized colon, for a strengthening of the pause leads to an increase in the potential energy of the phrasing proper (in Bely's terminology), and as a result, the intonation (the kinetic energy) is also strengthened.

Generally the opposition between rhyme and logic[74] is manifested in Yiddish poetry both in the dense rhymes of children's songs and in the impulsive rhyming of A. Leyeles (as one expression of his mystifying approach to the wonder of poetic experience), but not in the symmetrical, terminal rhyme, which is abundant in the most judicious metric songs of the day.

BETWEEN LANGUAGES AND LITERATURES

All in all, Yiddish free rhythms stand between the East Slavic model, with its many enclitic and proclitic combinations, and denser stressing and thus differentiation of stress levels. The interaction of these two bases makes possible the great elasticity of Yiddish free rhythms in contrast to both the uniformity of phrasing of the Russian *bylina* (at one pole) and the nearly prosaic disrupted iambicity of modern English free rhythms (at the other pole). Yet we often feel that Yiddish free rhythms lean in one direction or the other, not only because of personal rhythmic or thematic inclinations but also because of the influence of surrounding ways of feeling the language. In a most general sense—other factors aside—this is the cause of the conversational and iambic character of more recent Yiddish free-rhythm poetry in the United States. For the same reason, the influences of the Russian language multiplied the number of dactylic endings in Yiddish poetry in the Russian sphere. In both cases, the statement applies mainly to the period between both world wars, specifically to Yiddish writers rooted in the respective languages of the non-Jewish environment.

Concerning the manner in which the influence of foreign literatures was experienced, we should add that the stimulus which upset the old melodic equilibrium did indeed come from German Expressionism and Russian Modernism. But true free rhythms were created in Yiddish to a significant degree primarily in the United States. The influence of the Anglo-American moderns is strongly in evidence, especially in the work of the younger generation of poets, both in content and in means of expression, and even more perhaps in the manner of poem construction with the free rhythms.

In addition to direct personal influence, general atmosphere is also important. It was only in the United States that the Yiddish poem freed itself of counted measures and came to require equal strophes. It is interesting that, in the same environment, American Hebrew poetry, written by poets of the same eastern European background, retained the a.-s. system. The poets drew inspiration from English classical poetry (especially Romantic poetry, notably that of Tennyson and Shelley), not from the contemporary environment. The reason is inherent in differences of language and cultural history.

We must remember, in this connection, that Polish and Russian poetry, after a short period of ferment between the wars, mostly went in the direction of a.-s. metrics (or something close). In Russia, a factor contributing to this development (besides the official line) was the possibility of rich alternation of language rhythm in the same metric framework. In Poland, the a.-s. system was still felt to be a fresh contrast to the syllabic pattern of classical Polish poetry. And this development was joined by the principal Yiddish poets in those countries. Thus, the *Yung Vilne* group was completely a.-s. in their poetry and only sometimes free-accentual (Elkhonon Vogler), while the same generation in America was free-rhythmic.

The influence of Hebrew in this domain is quite feeble, because Hebrew was not a living territorial language. The Hebrew features in Yiddish are basically an addition within the framework of the general metrics. Their impact is either linguistic or conscious rather than directly aural: this is true especially of the various acrostically concatenated lines. It is interesting, however, that the environment penetrated even into the "Hebrew" devices themselves.

For example, in a double-acrostic song, we read under the letter *tav:*

ניט קיין תּורה, ניט קיין געלט \ וואָס זשע טויג מיר גאָר די וועלט

nit keyn Toyre, nit keyn gelt / vos zhe Toyg mir gor di velt?
[Neither learning nor money, / what good is the whole world to me?][75]

Toyg, though spelled with a *tet,* has entered into an alliterative combination with *Toyre,* spelled with *tav:* hearing triumphed over an alphabetic device.

It was only modern poetry which could, with its conscious approach, adopt biblical rhythmics, for the genuine free rhythms sought not the formal metrics but deeper inner rhythmic properties. Leivick (in "Der volf") and Leyeles (in, e.g. "Ruvn"—*A yid oyfn yam,* 85) each displayed their peculiar individualities with biblical material, but in the works of both we also detect the biblical rhythm in their linguistic expression. On this point Leyeles, who is metrically further removed from the Bible, is closer to it in essence thanks to his Hebraizing diction, sentence structure, and parallelisms.

The same goes for the Russian *bylina:* the area of its lingering existence was far from the Jewish Pale of Settlement and did not affect the poetry directly. But the deepened appreciation of the structure of rhythmic configurations enabled Yiddish poets to penetrate even into rhythms that were historically passé and to revive them in Yiddish, too. Leyeles writes in "Di almone un er" (*Fabius Lind*):[76]

נישט קיין שוואַרצע כמאַרע אויפֿן הימל רײַט,
נישט קיין דונערבליץ די הייך צעשנײַדט.
ס‹ליגט די גאָרע ערד איצט אַ פֿאַרטײַעטע,
די מענטש-געטרעטענע – אַ צעטומלטע,
אַ צעטומלטע, אַ צערודערטע, ערבֿ ציטערניש, ערבֿ שוידערניש.

Nisht keyn shvartse khmare oyfn himl rayt,
nisht keyn dunerblits di heykh tseshnaydt.
S'ligt di gore erd itst a fartayete,
Di mentsh-getretene—a tsetumlte,
A tsetumlte, a tseruderte, erev tsiternish, erev shoydernish.

[Not a black heavy cloud rides the sky, / not a thunderflash cuts the high. / The whole earth now lies concealed, / the man-trodden one lies confused, / confused, upset, on the verge of quaking, on the verge of shuddering.]

The organic rendition of rhythm, diction (dactyls), sentence structure, and mythological figures of the Russian *bylina* (as formerly of the Bible) creates the desired impact on the reader; and its effectiveness is all the greater if the Yiddish reader knows the model according to which the poem was created and reads it as this rhythmic atmosphere requires.

8

FREE RHYTHMS IN YIDDISH FOLKSONGS

After Herder, there was intense interest in folklore and ethnic folk poetry in Europe—especially in the folk culture of stateless minorities—including Jewish folksongs in the spoken language, Yiddish. Many collectors published songs and large collections.

The Bible as well as the folksongs were written in free rhythms. The number of unstressed syllables between two stresses in both is indeterminate and fluctuating, so the modern concept applies. The folksong did not know that it was composed in free rhythms. The music provided the rhythm, rhyme provided the strophic framework, and the number of syllables could be adjusted, stretched, or condensed to accommodate the music.

I shall consider the rhythm of the texts alone, without their melodies,[1] for several reasons:

1) Within the framework of one and the same musical rhythm, diverse language rhythms—i.e. various ways and speeds of filling the melody with syllables—have arisen, differing especially according to the thematic genre.
2) The same basic language rhythms govern love songs, folk proverbs, and children's counting-out rhymes, even those which have no melodies.
3) Prose, too, can be set to music. We know of prayers with prose texts. Another example is Prokofiev's opera to Lev Tolstoy's prose text of *War and Peace*. It is therefore necessary to see whether, and in what way, the text on its own is a poem. If it is, the choice of words is constrained by certain restrictions. Without those restrictions we could not turn prose into poetry even by forcing a musical rhythm onto it.

4) Rhyme is not necessary to melody, although rhyme is an indispensable device of strophic construction in the folksong lyric.

5) Folksong has influenced the rhythms of subsequent art poetry principally through the rhythm of its lyrics. The musical stresses are not always identical with the linguistic ones. Moreover, a gap in the full number of syllables may be filled by the melody but not by the language alone.[2]

6) There are songs whose language rhythm is distinctly Germanic (in that it retains the general conservative feeling of the folksong) while the melody is Slavic.

7) Only the uniform rhythmic system of the texts permits the easy transfer of melodies from song to song, as well as the contamination of text fragments and the transfer of conventional locutions and formulas. The Russian scholar M. P. Štokmar[3] demonstrated that the whole rhythmic system of the texts of Old Russian songs was essentially different from the rhythm of their later melody and conformed to the historical specificity of the sound structure of the Old Russian language.[4]

The characteristic strophe of the folksong is constructed in the simplest manner. It is basically symmetrical and uniform: four lines rhyming *mana*. The letters *a*, *b*, *c*, etc., indicate separate rhymes; *m*, *n*, etc., indicate non-rhyming line endings. Every two lines form a syntactic unit, concluded by a rhyme, and the break between the lines is identical to the strongest break in syntax and content of the strophe. Every line contains four accents, which are usually divided by a caesura into 2 + 2, unless there are only three stresses, which often creates a "lightening" effect and a pleasant contrast to the full lines.

Thus, for example:[5]

מײַנע שבתים און מײַנע יום-טובֿים

זײַנען מיר געוואָרן פֿאַרשטערט;

זינט איך האָב דײַן ליבע דערקענט

ליגט מיר מײַן פּנים אין דער ערד.

→

Mayne shabosim un mayne yontoyvim	$\vert - \cup \cup - \cup \cup - \cup \cup - \cup \vert$
zaynen mir gevorn farshtert;	$\vert - \cup \cup \cup - \cup \cup - \vert$
zint ikh hob dayn libe derkent	$\vert - \cup - \cup - \cup \cup - \vert$
ligt mir mayn ponim in der erd.	$\vert - \cup \cup - \cup \cup - \vert$

[My Sabbaths and my holidays / have been ruined; // since I recognized your love / my face lies in the ground (i.e. I am downhearted; "der erd" is probably pronounced as one syllable: drerd).]

Both sentences are constructed in parallel and form one whole, closed and emphasized by the rhyme. Additional rhymes (on the first and third lines) would be a luxury and would break up the sentences, since they would run counter to the folk conception of rhyme as a concluding force. In our example, the Introspectivist A. Leyeles understood this when he emphasized that "for us [. . .] rhyme comes not as an expectation but as a surprise. It comes suddenly. A halt in mid-leap. The leap into the unknown. For us, rhyme is preparation, not rest. For us, it is not denial but confirmation of belief in ever newer and broader possibilities of the world, of a world of which we can only have pre-monitions but which is not yet opened to our senses."[6] The first line gets us into the inertia of the normal line length of four measures, so we want to give the second line the same time interval. We render a pause after the second line, similar in length to a measure, and this underscores the syntactic pause. Through the use of this and other devices of this type, the strophic structure helps absorb and retain the content of the poem with a minimum strain.

This is the oldest German strophic form. Its source is a rhymed pair of Old German long verses of 4 + 3 stresses (Langzeilen). Eventually the first line splits into two, creating a shorter basic line; for that reason, the principal rhymes are in the second and fourth lines. This strophe fits the general rhythmic feeling that human beings have when faced with accentual language material; the form originated not only in Germany.

Among German folksongs (in the early New German period, from the beginning of the fourteenth century to the beginning of the seventeenth), Andreas Heusler finds strophes of more numerous lines and of different rhyme patterns.[7] These were no doubt induced by the constant stream of artistic forms of the German *Lied* (including the musical *Lied*) into the folk domain.[8]

In Yiddish, however, an artistic poetry with sophisticated or deviant forms arose relatively late; it had little time to be digested by the folk culture and was all the less capable of causing a change in the uniform and conservative folk patterns from the inside. What is more, the four-line strophe remained the main form of the Yiddish literary poem almost until the revolution of Expressionism.

Full cross-rhyming *abab* is rare in Yiddish folksong and is of late literary origin. It is remarkable that where the content of a literary poem has been altered in folksong, the full rhymes of the poem have also been discarded. For a clear-cut example, see Y. L. Cahan (Kahan).[9] Two poems by Sholem Bern-shteyn rhymed *abab*, but when folklorized, had their rhyme scheme changed almost without exception to *mbnb*. The rhyme scheme *abab* indicates two alternating rhymes; every line rhymes with another one. The rhyme scheme *mana* shows rhyming only with the second and forth lines; *m* and *n* indicate a rhyming position without a second rhyme pattern. The short lines have been lengthened by filling them with additional syllables, in accordance with the traditional folk line. Consequently it is not true that "a folksong can more easily be recognized by its internal thought or spiritual [*gedanklekh oder gaystik*] content than by external, formal features."[10]

Couplet rhymes of the type *aabb* are also infrequent, occurring only in full four-measure lines (mostly complete sentences) and, even then, only in certain thematic forms; there, too, it is the melody which keeps them in the traditional four-line framework.

The Yiddish folksong does not know an independent strophe of more than four lines. It seems that such a strophe could not be remembered as a fixed form in which the content is subject to alteration. Whenever we find longer strophes, they get reshuffled into quatrains[11]—unless the form is a pattern poem (inherited from the Hebrew piyut fifteen hundred years earlier) in which only two (!) words are changed from strophe to strophe. This is the case with the only strophic song recorded by Cahan which was not originally made up of quatrains: the popular seven-line rhythmical song, known in many versions:

→

Yome, yome,	x′ x′	[Yome, yome,
hpil mir a lidele	x′ x′	play me a song
vos dos meydele vil	x′ x′ x′	that the girl wants.][12]

In the published collections of Yiddish folksongs, the norm is a four-line strophe. The few deviations from that pattern fall into three categories.

1) The notation is incorrect; e.g. the extra lines do not appear in all strophes of a poem, or they represent an accidental accretion, as when the melody repeats the last two lines of each strophe, the repetition being a variation. In one song,[13] instead of its twice having the line

דער ציגײַנער, דער טאָטער, \ ער האָט מיך אומגליקליקלעך געמאַכט

der tsigayner, der toter, / er hot mikh umgliklikh gemakht

[the Gypsy, the Tatar, / he ruined me]

we find a variation in the repetition:

דער ציגײַנער, דײַן פֿאָטער, \ דאָרטן זיצט ער און לאַכט

der tsigayner, dayn foter, / dortn zitst er un lakht

[the Gypsy, your father, / there he sits and laughs]

This is the germ of a six-line stanza, but the four-line source is apparent.

2) A single four-accentual line is recorded as two lines with two stresses each. Sometimes this notation supposedly records an internal rhyme. But internal rhymes—a result of the mid-line caesura—are not sustained throughout a folksong. Furthermore, in the resulting new stanza rhyme scheme *aacbbc*, each *a* and *b* line has only two measures (*c* usually has three). That is to say, with regard to diachronical metrics, it is still the original strophe of 7, namely: 4 + 3, 4 + 3. Nevertheless, the rhythmic form does make a different impression.

3) Whatever exceeds four lines constitutes a refrain or a group of several additional lines which recur (exactly or with small variations) throughout the song.

4) Quite rarely, there is a song that is not in strophic form but is constructed on a single cumulative or expanding pattern, as exemplified by the "Chad Gadya" (Song of the Kid) sung on Passover: 1, 5, 6, 7.[14] In recent times, these have no longer represented a sung form of great dispersion outside the Passover Seder.

All of the deviations from the principal strophic structure are forms of address, repetitions of words, refrains, and the like—playful ornamentations[15] which add life, emphasis, and atmosphere but do not serve the development of the song's content.

Songs by literary poets, too, are interpreted in the folksong context as constructed according to the quatrain principle, and if they are assimilated in the folksong repertoire, they are so treated and even so reconstructed. An interesting example—"Di mashke" by Mikhl Gordon (1823–1890), containing 13 six-line strophes *aabbcc*—is recorded by Sh. Bastomski erroneously as a folksong containing 19 four-line strophes (*aabb*).[16] It is evident that the majority of changes connected with the folklorization of the song, changes of content included, were conditioned by the reconstruction of the form.[17]

Conservatism in the field of form is also reflected in the character of the specific song groups. The Yiddish children's play-song has retained the specific two-measure form of the Old German children's saying. This is true textually also, as Cahan confirms: "A large part of the play and counting-out verses sung by [Jewish] children, certain riddle and wishing songs, were already known in Germany in the fifteenth and sixteenth centuries."[18]

The Yiddish proverb, within a four-measure framework, often contains only three measures, and there are also some of two measures.[19]

In the Slavic domain in the nineteenth century, trochees prevailed. Nevertheless, songs which are adaptations of explicit translations of Slavic accentual-syllabic (a.-s.) folksongs retain only that which is acceptable to the old (Germanic) rhythmical sense: the number of stresses. The number of syllables in the interior of the measure is, however, set free.[20] The famous soldiers' song is an example:

בעסער צו לערנען חומש מיט רשי \ איידער צו עסן די סאָלדאַטסקע קאַשע

beser tsu lernen khumesh mit rashe / eyder tsu esn di soldatske kasha

The meter is almost a precise dactyl:

→

$- \cup \cup - \cup \ | - \cup \cup - \cup$

$- \cup \cup - \cup \ | \cup \cup - \cup \ | - \cup$

[It is better to study the Pentateuch with Rashi's commentary / than to eat soldiers' pap]

The venerable Bible commentator RaSH"I is domesticated by rhyming his name with the mundane *kashe*, cooked cereal. Furthermore, the song plays on the two homonyms of *kasha*: the first from Talmudic Aramaic קשיא, "a method of advancing an argument by asking questions"; the second from Russian קאַשע, "cereal."

Such changes are made even in those bilingual folksongs in which the original Slavic stanza alternates with a Yiddish translation. Here, the Polish

gdzīe těn chłŏpiěc cō mniě chciāł | $- \cup - \cup - \cup -$ |

becomes

ווי איז דאָס בחורל וואָס האָט מיך געוואָלט!

vū ĭz dŏs bōkhěrĭ / vōs hŏt mĭkh gěvōlt?

→

| $- \cup \cup - \cup \cup \ | \cup - \cup \cup -$ | (a quasi dactyl)

[where is the fellow who desired me?][21]

At least the trisyllabic diminutive *bokherl* did not have to be there. (The base form, בחור *bokher*, is disyllabic, like the Polish model *chłopiec*.) However, the Slavic folksong in the nineteenth century was predominantly trochaic (it was a *chastushka*—a dance quatrain in trochaic tetrameter). Yiddish has one syllable more than the Slavic!

The folk alterations are not accidental; they are intended to attenuate march-like or urban rhythms in the spirit of folk informality and the old free narrative style. Thus the tempo of the amphibrachic stanza of the revolutionary song by M. Sore-Rives (pseudonym of Khaim Miller [Alexandrov]; 1869–1909) is softened by the folk culture[22] through the inclusion of additional syllables in the same melody. The song by Sore-Rives (as sung as a folksong) runs as follows:

בריִדער, מיר האָבן געשלאָסן
אויף לעבן און טויט אַ פֿאַרבאַנד
מיר שטייען דאָ אין שלאַכט ווי גענאָסן,
די פֿאָנע די רויטע אין האַנט.

→

Brīděr, mĭr hōbň gěshlōsň	0 — ∪∪ — ∪∪ — ∪
ŏyf lēbň ŭn tōyt ǎ fǎrbānd.	∪ — ∪∪ — ∪∪ —
Mĭr shtěyěň[23] dŏ ĭn shlākht vĭ gěnōsň,	∪ — ∪∪∪ — ∪∪ — ∪
dĭ fōně dĭ rōytě ĭn hānt.	∪ — ∪∪ — ∪∪ —

[Brothers, we have concluded / a pact for life and death. / We stand as comrades here in battle, / the red flag in our hands.]

Now the completely folklorized version:[24]

בריִדער, אויב גאָט וויל אונדז ניט העלפֿן,
לאָמיר זיך באַפֿרײַען אַליין.
לאָמיר זיך צערײַסן פֿון די קייטן
און לאָמיר אַליין צוזאַמען גיין.

Brīděr, ŏyb gōt vĭl ŭndz nĭt hēlfň,	— ∪∪ — ∪∪∪ — ∪
lōmĭr zĭkh bǎfrāyěn ǎlēyn.	— ∪∪∪ — ∪∪ —
lōmĭr zĭkh tsěrāysň fǔn dĭ kēytň	— ∪∪∪ — ∪∪∪ — ∪
ŭn lōmĭr ǎlēyn tsŭzǎměn gēyn.	∪ — ∪∪ — ∪ — ∪ —

[Brothers, if God does not want to help us, / let us liberate ourselves. / Let us tear ourselves from the chains / and let us go together on our own.]

In the folk adaptation there are several accretions with three syllables between the stresses and several feet reduced to one weak syllable. The metronome records $\flat$ = 166 in the first case and $\flat$ = 72 in the second. What a difference in tempo! Yet it is created principally by a slightly increased syllable load in the measures. Since for the content to be conveyed, the words cannot be slurred, the long line must have more time to be read or sung. Herein lies the one difference between meter and rhythm. Even when the meter permits a free number of syllables (and even with the same musical rhythm), the precise number is significant in creating the tempo and the general rhythmic impression of a song; it depends upon the very heart of the poem or the song.

The melody of the folksong retains the isochronic nature of the measures and permits freedom in the number of syllables. That is to say, if a measure consists of a single syllable, that syllable is stretched in performance, while if it consists of many syllables, the notes are split in order to allot to them smaller segments of time. But too many syllables are not tolerated in a measure, because then each syllable would be too short to be heard accurately. The folksong strives above all to give clear expression to the content. The rest is orchestration. In deference to the content, the melody may be altered; if it is not, the language text is changed.

For example, in the song "Vigndik a fremd kind" (To Cradle a Stranger's Baby), every musical 2/4 measure equals two textual measures (four textual measures per line).[25] At the termination of lines a single syllable occurs alone in a measure, occupying a quarter note all by itself (normally a syllable takes up only an eighth note). At the most this song has four syllables in a single measure, at a sixteenth note each. If the liberty of a fifth syllable was taken, its duration would have to be a thirty-second; that is, it would be slurred in pronunciation, being eight times shorter than another syllable. Therefore איז *iz* would be abbreviated to *z*:

דײַן מאַמעשי 'ז געגאַנגען אין מאַרק אַרײַן

dayn mameshi 'z gegangen in mark arayn | ∪ — ∪ ∪ | ∪ — ∪ | ∪ — ∪ ∪ |

[your mommy's gone to the marketplace]

This shortening takes place in spite of the tendency of folksongs to re-expand, for clarity's sake, the abbreviations of poets, even at the expense of a.-s. regularity. Thus the poet Dovid Edelshtat (1866–1892) writes in amphibrachs,

איר פֿרויען וואָס שמאַכטן אין הויז 'ן אין פֿאַבריק

ir froyen vos shmakhtn in hoyz 'n in fabrik

[you women who languish at home and in the factory],

but the recorded folksong expands the abbreviation: און אין פֿאַבריק un in fabrik.[26]

The collectors of Yiddish folksongs have not always taken sufficient heed of this phenomenon. The contradictions between text and musical notation are often evident. Heusler notes that in German folksong a single measure encompasses from one to five syllables. The described melodic requirements limit the measure to four syllables. Thus a line of the same four-stress meter may contain from four syllables (e.g. מײַן זיס ליב קינד máyn zís líb kínd "my sweet dear child")[27] up to sixteen syllables. Both extremes are rare. As a rule, all lines of a song are similar in structure.

A precise count of syllables in volumes of Yiddish folksong collections leads to interesting observations concerning the manner in which limitations upon the permitted range create specific forms and devices in consonance with the tone of the content. The most important groups in Yiddish folksong are these:

(1) *Lyric love songs.* These have a maximum of three syllables in one measure, which produces an iambic-anapestic movement. For example:

זאָל איך אַזוי לעבן: וו אוי, וואָס כ›האָב געוואָלט האָב איך אויסגעפֿירט,
האָט מיר גאָט געגעבן וו כ׳האָב געוואָלט אַ שיין יִינגעלעוו

→

öy, vös kh'höb gĕvölt höb ĭkh öysgĕfirt,	— ∪ ∪ ∪ — ∪ ∪ — ∪ —
zöl ĭkh äzöy lēbň:	— ∪ ∪ ∪ — ∪
kh'höb gĕvölt ă shēyn yīngĕlĕ	∪ ∪ — ∪ ∪ — ∪ ∪
höt mĭr göt gĕgēbň	∪ ∪ — ∪ — ∪

[Oh, what I wanted I attained, / may I live so (as this is true): / I wanted a handsome boy / and God gave me one][28]

A major subgroup sticks to a pattern of two syllables per measure (i.e. iambic flow), with the exception of long dactylic words (mainly diminutives), which create three-syllable measures. A song published by Cahan (A 22) is so constructed down to the last syllable (here the dactylic words are in caps):

טיף אין וועלדעלע שטייט אַ ביימעלע
און די צוויַיגעלעך בליִען;
און ביַי מיר, אָרעם שניַידערל,
טוט דאָס הערצעלע ציִען.

→

tif in VELDELE shteyt a BEYMELE	— ∪ — ∪ ∪ │ — ∪ — ∪ ∪
un di TSVAYGELEKH blien;	— ∪ — ∪ ∪ │ — ∪

un bay mir, orem SHNAYDERL   — ∪ — | ∪ ∪ — ∪ —

tut dos HERTSELE tsien.   — ∪ — ∪ ∪ — ∪

[Deep in the forest stands a tree / and its branches are blooming; / and in me, poor tailor, my heart is drawn]

The diminutive is not just to indicate small size or a child. It also indicates an endearment, showing the emotion of the writer or singer toward the object or person described.

The long dactylic words give rise to three-syllable dactylic measures.

(2) *Narrative folksongs.* These have a maximum of four syllables per measure, that is, freedom up to the limits of melodic acceptability. The linguistic expressions are characteristic of a narrative tone, as here:

הערט נאָר אויס, מענטשן, וואָס ס'האָט זיך געטראָפֿן

→

Hert nor oys, mentshn, vos s'hot zikh getrofn | — ∪ ∪ — ∪ ∪ — ∪ ∪ — ∪ |

[Listen, folks, to what happened]

אַזוי ווי מען האָט

azoy vi men hot | ∪ — ∪ ∪ — |

[as they . . .], etc.

In general, Heusler observes, "the (mostly more voluminous) historical and political folksongs, as well as the saga-like narrative songs ('folk ballads and romances') stand out on this account. They incline above all to a longer anacrusis (up to five syllables before the first stress) and to heavy internal measures."[29]

Here, too, there is a distinct subgroup (consisting mostly of symbolic or ballad-like songs) marked by a maximum of three syllables per measure, except for measures containing dactylic words which are tetrasyllabic,

אַ מיידעלע אַ קליינינקע

→

ă mēydĕlĕ ă klēynĭnkĕ   ∪ — ∪ ∪ | ∪ — ∪ ∪

[a little girl (or "sweet girl")],

or dactylic/enclitic combinations, as in the first part:

קריגט מען נישט צו קויפֿן

→

KRĬGT MĔN NĬSHT tsŭ kŏyfň   — ∪ ∪ ∪ — ∪

[is not to be had for sale].

(3) *Children's songs and rhymes.* The majority of children's songs and counting-out rhymes stick to a maximum of two syllables per measure. These texts would be pure trochees and iambs if not for the existence of one-syllable measures containing the stress only. The playfulness of the children's songs has brought about close rhymes. In most children's games and counting-out rhymes, the regular four-stress line has split into two-stress lines, just like the lines of German children's games. Frequently it is precisely the two-measure form which has retained the accumulation of unstressed syllables typical of German. Yet by and large, the Slavic trochee had already penetrated German, especially in texts transplanted from Slavic languages.

(4) *Yiddish narrative songs.* The German five-syllable freedom is rarely utilized in Yiddish and appears only in Yiddish narrative songs where the event related bears a rather concrete, local or group character (e.g. in the thieves' songs from Warsaw, which concern particular heroes).[30] Here is an example from one song:

"דאָנערשטיק אין דער פֿרי בין איך מיר אין גאַס אַרויסגעגאַנגען"

→

Donershtik in der fri bin ikh mir in gas aroysgegangen

— ∪ ∪ ∪ ∪ — ∪ | ∪ ∪ ∪ ∪ — ∪ ∪ ∪ — ∪

[Thursday morning I casually went out into the street]

The four stresses in this line prevent the text from splitting it into further, smaller measures. The inclusion of the song and its events in the common stock of folksongs leads to a blurring of its local or incidental character (i.e. group 2: narrative folksongs). Five-syllable measures force the slurring of syllables or an imprecise filling of the melody; it is so difficult to feel a song rhythm in them that they border on the prose recitative.

No theoretical framework has been set up by the ordinary singers of folksongs; even scholars, because of their musically influenced theories of the song, have not paid proper attention to the rhythms of the lyrics. Nevertheless, the general thematic character of the song has determined the stream of its language:

· Heavy narrative epics have been rendered in long lines.
· Lyricism has been treated lightly.
· Short verses approach metric uniformity.
· Children's songs have stressed the beat and neither the flow of language nor the content, so rhyme and sound and a minimum of syllables are important.

In short, a firm tradition of rhythmic types (not only of metrics) developed in the folksong, supported by peripatetic versions of established songs.[31]

Among other formal properties of the Yiddish folksong, the following are also pertinent to the present topic. Despite syllabic freedom in the interior of the line and at the line end, as when two parallel lines have, respectively, a masculine and a dactylic ending, certain strict limitations are sometimes observed. Heusler notes them without interpreting them, yet they are quite significant. Here is one example out of many. In the song Cahan (A 212), which formally has three stresses per line in the text, every odd line is feminine, every even line masculine. The reason is clear: the first line must have an additional syllable on which the missing fourth stress could be placed; and the second line, according to the feeling of those enjoying it, must deviate from the first and must usually be shorter in order to create a sense of pausing at the end of the sentence. A masculine three-measure line is the only possible length.

The distribution of short and long measures is also important. Thus Cahan (A 194):

אַ שם האָב איך גֶעהאַט פֿאַר אַן ערלעך מיידל
דער שם איז מיר גֶעווען טײַערער פֿון געלט.
יעצט בין איך אָרעם, עלנט און באַליידיקט . . .
אײַ, דורך דיר האָב איך פֿאַרשפּילט מײַן וועלט.

→

A shem hob ikh gehat far an erlekh meydl	∪ — ∪ ∪ ∪ — | ∪ ∪ — ∪ — ∪
der shem iz mir geven tayerer fun gelt.	∪ — ∪ ∪ ∪ — | — ∪ ∪ ∪ —
yetst bin ikh orem, elnt un baleydikt.	— ∪ ∪ — ∪ | — ∪ ∪ ∪ — ∪
ay, durkh dir hob ikh farshpilt mayn velt.	— ∪ — | ∪ ∪ ∪ — ∪ —

[I had the reputation of a respectable girl, / this reputation was worth more to me than money. / Now I am poor, lonesome, and humiliated . . . / You have caused me to lose my world.]

Narrative folksongs are characteristically laconic. The breath pause at the caesura is conspicuous. According to Andrey Bely, the length of the line determines the breath load. This song is not long-winded (see Cahan A 148, 150, 170, 214, etc.). Instead of a wave flung forward, the basic movement is that of an arch, *ă shēm hŏb ĭkh gĕhāt* $\cup - \cup \cup \cup -$, resting on two stresses at each end of the colon, with as many unstressed syllables as possible in the interior of the measure. The full measure preserves the narrative content. But the short line is light and lyrically agitated, its playful tone (the text is playful, too: the seducer is called ייִנגעלע *yingele*, "little boy," with "blue little lips") conveys the levity of the song, and the tension between the long measure and the short line—or the tension of the arc—emphasizes the tragic content.

(איך האָב געשפּילט אַ ליבע \ כ'האָב געפֿירט אַ ראָלע;

\ כ'האָב צוגעזאָגט אַ ייִנגעלע \ אַז איך וועל זײַן זײַן כּלה . . .).

$\rightarrow$

(Ĭkh hōb gĕshpĭlt ă lībĕ / kh'hōb gĕfĭrt ă rōlĕ

$$\cup - \cup \cup \cup - \cup \mid - \cup \cup \cup - \cup$$

kh'hŏb tsūgĕzŏgt ă yīngĕlĕ / ăz īkh vĕl zăyn zăyn kālĕ . . .)

$$\cup - \cup \cup \mid \cup - \cup \cup \mid\mid \cup - \cup \cup \mid \cup - \cup$$

[I carried on a love affair / I acted my part / I promised a boy / that I would be his fiancée]

Midway between this paeonic arc and the trochaic pattern of the children's game with respect to both technique and the tone of the content lies the dactylic arc of the game song of adults. Note the structure of the characteristic closure of a Purim play:

הײַנט איז פּורים, \ מאָרגן איז אויס, \

גיט מיר אַ גראָשן \ און וואַרפֿט מיך אַרויס

$\rightarrow$

hăynt ĭz pūrĭm, / mōrgn̆ ĭz ōys,	$- \cup - \cup \mid - \cup \cup -$
gīt mĭr ă grōshn̆ / ŭn vārft mĭkh ărōys	$- \cup \cup - \cup \mid \cup - \cup \cup -$

[Today is Purim, / tomorrow it will be over, / give me a penny / and throw me out.]

The "Gazlen-shpil" (Robber Game) recorded by Lehman is similar:[32]

קוקט איִך נאָר אום \ אין די אַלע פֿיר זײַטן, \

דער גזלן וועט באַלד \ קומען צו רײַטן

→

kūkt ăykh nŏr ūm / ĭn ālě fĭr zāytň, /   — ∪ ∪ — | ∪ — ∪ ∪ — ∪

dĕr gāzlĕn vĕt bāld / kūmĕn tsŭ rāytň   ∪ — ∪ ∪ — | — ∪ ∪ — ∪

[Come, look around you / on all four sides, / the robber will soon / come riding]

The rhythm of many dance songs is similar, as here:

שפּיל מיר אַ סעמענע , \ ניט קיין קאָזאַצקע, \

איך בין אָן אָרעמע \ אָבער אַ כוואַצקע

→

Shpīl mĭr ă sēmĕnĕ, / nīt kĕyn kŏzātskĕ, /   — ∪ ∪ — ∪ ∪ | — ∪ ∪ — ∪

īkh bĭn ăn ōrĕmĕ / ōbĕr ă khvātskĕ   — ∪ ∪ — ∪ ∪ | — ∪ ∪ — ∪

[Play me a *semene* (kind of dance), / not a *kozatske*, / I am poor / but snappy.][33]

None of these inner forms, however, carried the Yiddish folksong to a.-s. metrics. Even the big city had no such effect: most of the Warsaw thieves' songs were also constructed in the old manner. The old strophic pattern was more subject to change: deviant rhyme schemes (mainly *abab* and *aacbbc*) penetrated the folksong from the theatrical hits and the popular literary songs. But the rhythm resisted change. Even the Slavic environment did not transmit its a.-s. patterns to Yiddish directly, despite the adoption of Slavic motifs in content and melody. It was through the Yiddish children's song, which took in sequences of Slavic sounds as such, that a.-s. metrics first penetrated into Yiddish folksong. See, for example, the first of the "Two Foreign-Language Counting-Out Rhymes of Jewish Children of Samogitia."[34]

This group of songs was then expanded to include a.-s. refrains and couplets (in particular from the theater repertoire). Again these segments in which pure sound played a dominant role were the channels for a.-s. importation.

The Yiddish folksong experienced a new and stricter ordering in its content-laden segments under the influence of the political mass song, principally the socialist-anarchist mass song. The anthem, the marching song, and the chorus song require that their strict general organization be heard. The thematic influence of the Russian workers' political song also made itself strongly felt. Thus M. Beregovski's anthology of Yiddish folksongs contains many that are nearly a.-s. songs, even if they are of a local narrative type.[35]

Only when the Yiddish speakers began to sing a great many songs by their own new poets did their collective ear become accustomed to the requirements of amphibrachs and syllable order, and they gradually introduced these elements into the old song stock. A similar change took place in the Russian folksong in the nineteenth century under the influence of the literary poem. Even the irrepressible rhymester—the potential first creator of a folksong—began to write a.-s. poetry. At the last stage, during the tragic disappearance of the folksong together with its singers, a.-s. forms were the most widespread type.

The a.-s. meters prevail in the hundreds of Yiddish folksongs of the German ghettos and concentration and extermination camps of World War II.[36] This may be evidence for the influence of Yiddish cultural poetry, which folklorized the new poems. A similar phenomenon can be observed in the Soviet domain, especially folkorization by soldiers in the war. In Sh. Goldshmid's collection of Soviet Yiddish World War II songs, all texts are a.-s, as required by the commissars.[37] There is no doubt in my mind that this book contains some real folksongs, quite remote from the official style of Soviet poetry. The narrative strophe has four primary stresses per line, just as it used to in the old folksong, but the completely paeonized lines have decomposed into seven precise trochees, 4 + 3, divided by a caesura:

פֿון דער הײַנטיקער מלחמה וועל איך לידער זינגען,

אַז סע זאָל די גאַנצע וועלט מיט די לידער קלינגען,

ווי ס׳איז פֿאַרגעקומען דאָרט מיט יאַשקע דעם אָדעסער,

אַז ער האָט געשלאָגן זיך מיטן דײַטש אויף מעסער

→

fun der hayntiker milkhome vel ikh lider zingen,

$$| - \cup - \cup - \cup - \cup | - \cup - \cup - \cup |$$

az se zol di gantse velt mit di lider klingen,

$$| - \cup - \cup - \cup - | 0 - \cup - \cup - \cup |$$

vi s'iz forgekumen dort mit Yashke dem odeser,

$$| - \cup - \cup - \cup - | \cup - \cup - \cup - \cup |$$

az er hot geshlogn zikh mitn daytsh oyf meser.

$$| - \cup - \cup - \cup - | 0 - \cup - \cup - \cup |$$

[I shall sing songs of the present war, / so that the whole world may resound with these songs, / how it happened there with Yashke the Odessan, / he fought the German at knife's point.]

In terms of style this is the old Odessa. As the preface makes clear, the heroes were already named in the song in 1905; except for the name Hitler, the images and locutions are traditional (ווי ער האָט דערזען . . . *vi er hot derzen* [as he noticed . . .]), etc.; yet one misses the flexible and direct, free language of the folksong not forced into the frame of an official Soviet a.-s. meter.

APPENDIX A

Perception, Rhythmical Groups, and the Bible (1959)

This is the second part of my paper "On Free Rhythms in Modern Poetry," read at a landmark conference (1959) in Bloomington, Indiana, which started the Structuralism and Semiotics trend in the United States. The paper was published in *Style in Language,* edited by Thomas A. Sebeok, a year later. I was then a graduate student under René Wellek at Yale and a friend of my mentor Roman Jakobson at Harvard. The two parts of the paper—changed over time and presented here in reverse order, as Appendix A and Appendix B—stand as a document of my engagement in this topic.

Usually a verse line is a perceptible group of stresses (two, three, or four) or a dipody (or tripody) of such groups. Thus (1) verse lines are correlated units, and (2) within the line the stresses are conspicuous as the main constituents of the unit. Their conspicuous position leads to a leveling of differences between stresses and to an equalizing of the syllable distances between them whenever possible, especially in reading. Although the principles of this overall rhythmic organization of relationships require a special argument, I shall try to state the main notions that should be understood as a basis for a discussion of any type of free rhythms.

It has been observed many times that not every possible metrical arrangement, length of line, etc., is commonly used in poetry.

As implied by Gestalt psychology, the organization of perceptibly similar elements into groups, similar groups into higher groups, and so forth, is a major tendency of human perception. The rhythmic organization of a poem does not provide any ready order or hierarchy of groupings; it provides merely a *possibility* for a certain organization, which is realized by the reader. The reader realizes it in part by habit or agreement (tradition, knowledge of conventions)

and in part by a feeling for regulated human rhythmic features (rhythmic iner-
tia, rhythmic impulse). Only on this basis can we speak about "expectations"
or "frustrated expectations"; only on the basis of a rhythmic impulse, created
by a partial order, does a meter exist; only thus can we understand rhythmic
"disturbances," "deviations" or parallels, rhythmic "leitmotifs," etc.

Of course, the tendencies of perception are highly flexible, they are regu-
lated by the enormous variety of structural variations and shades of emphasis
on meaning, and practically, they provide for what seems to be an unlimited
range of expressive possibilities.

Therefore, I do not propose to explain rhythm from the rules of Gestalt
psychology; rather, I shall analyze the structures of a text and ask, What kind
of reading does this text require? or What are the ways of reading that can
bring to life the language of this poem in all its aspects?

Nevertheless, psycho-physiological limitations (or faculties) persist; for
example, the average distance between two stresses is limited. This does not
mean a precise regularity, as the "musically" minded theorists supposed. But
we cannot dismiss the limitations when great differences occur: a great num-
ber of slacks (non-stressed syllables between stresses) tends to provide for a
faster reading than do concentrations of stressed syllables, which invite spac-
ing between them or, at least, are strikingly conspicuous because of the wide
departure from the normal.

In the field of groupings, it seems to me that the evidence of poetry in all
different rhythmic systems suggests an overall rule that we organize language
material whenever possible into hierarchies of simple groups. Variations of
similar units allow for this grouping of structures; symmetry and asymmetry,
length at different levels, interplay or overlappings between metric groups and
language groups—all those are responsible for the different rhythmic effects.
By a simple group I mean a group of two or three smaller units (since a group
of two or three is not divisible into smaller groups) and perhaps also of four,
which is an innerbalanced composite unit (usually 2 + 2 but sometimes 1 +
3). Every constant organization must be built on these principles; only local
variations may deviate.

On the lowest level the matter is clear: our metrical feet consist of two or
three syllables (or dipodies of such groups). A paeon (four-syllable unit) tends
to be read as an iambic or trochaic dipody, unless very strong factors coun-
teract it. Greater numbers of slacks occur only if they are not regular, that is,
in free rhythms or in prose.

I cannot here go into a discussion of the highest level, the structure of stanzas, but it is clear that even on this level a regular stanza can be kept in mind (and perpetuated) only when the rhyme variations are organized so that the same group is not repeated more than thrice (e.g. in ottava rima we have three groups of *ab* rhymes and then, to sum up, a couplet, *cc: abababcc*).

There can be several intermediate levels, and this is also true of the structure of the verse line. It has often been observed that a line of more than four stresses cannot be kept as a single unit and splits inevitably into two or more groups.[1] The usual explanation is that eight or nine syllables (or so) are the normal syntactical unit (colon or syntagma).[2] But although this may be true, it seems clear to me that the factor of grouping is decisive:

→

$|\cup-\cup-\cup-\cup-\cup-\cup|$

Yet not all pentametric lines (of five iambs) split inevitably into two; some can be read as a single unit—for example, "And smóoth as Monuméntal Alábaster" (*Othello*), but this undivided pentameter

→

$|\cup-|\cup\cup\cup-\cup|\cup\cup-\cup|$

(*pace* Kayser) occurs only when a line can be conceived as a group of three stresses (and not five), even if these are only major stresses.[3]

Whether this is the case in every line is unimportant. The fact remains that major rhythmic differences between poems depend largely on the respective length of the line. Two or three stresses, being essentially a single unit, cannot create a line balanced inwardly and are only a part of greater groupings. The preference for four stresses in different systems, especially in folklore, is obvious. The English iambic pentameter enables the poem to carry content, especially in longer poems, by a constant variation of its inner groupings, avoiding the monotony of a symmetrical unit; whereas the Russians used for the same purpose a four-iamb unit, avoiding monotony by the great variation in the use of word boundaries which is possible in Russian.

Great as the differences may be, no unit can be kept in mind as a constant norm unless it is grouped in a perceptible way. We do not remember or "feel" any constant number (say, sixteen syllables) unless it is so grouped. It has been shown (by P. Servien and others) that in the French classical

6 + 6 (Alexandrine) verse the organization of stresses in every verset tends to be regular, iambic or anapestic, though changing from line to line and from verset to verset. So the poet (and the reader) does not have to count six syllables. He can feel such a unit as a simple group of simple groups of syllables (2 × 3 or 3 × 2). Such a simple group of stresses usually overlaps with the smallest rhythmic-syntactical unit, the colon.

To be sure, these remarks need a great deal of elaboration. For our purposes the fact is useful that perceptibility is more important than constant numbers. This was probably in Tomaševskij's mind when he considered meter merely as an auxiliary device, the measure of equivalence of verse lines.[4]

The poetry of the Hebrew Bible—a "natural" free-rhythmic system—is built, basically, on this principle. A "line" consists of two (or, seldom, three) simple groups (versets), usually parallel, or partially parallel, in their syntactic and semantic structure. These basic units are not equal; all attempts to correct the text in order to achieve strict numbers make no sense from any textual point of view. (The same is true of attempts to reconstruct exact strophes in the Bible.) But there is no need for this. The rhythmic impression persists in spite of all "irregularities." The basic units almost never consist of one stress or more than four stresses, which can be symbolized as *lim 4*. The stresses are strong, being major stresses of words (in a synthetic language) and being reinforced by the syntactic repetition. Thus the groups can be felt as similar, simple, correlated units. As the number of stresses in such a unit is small, they become conspicuous, giving special weight to the individual words.

Although no regularity of syllables is needed, the distances between stresses are made to be within a limited range by excluding two adjacent stresses in one syntactic phrase and providing secondary stresses for long words.

Although modern poetry is far more complicated, the length of the line is limited here too. W. Kayser complains that the long lines of the Expressionist German poet Stadler (even when metrical) are incapable of being perceived as single units. But we must suppose that at least in the poet's perception they made sense, since Stadler's long lines, like Marianne Moore's or Whitman's (with a few explicable exceptions), do not exceed a simple group of simple groups of stresses, that is, $lim\ 4^{lim\ 4}$. But these are the longest lines in poetry; usually we have one or two, or fewer than two, groups of different length and structure. The number of stresses in each of the correlated groups is small and thus conspicuous, which contributes to the leveling of the stresses and to a tendency toward the characteristic emphasis of each word and a bringing of the local elements into prominence and into relative, temporary independence and isolation from the long linear flow of a sentence.

Under these conditions, when stresses become conspicuous they tend to have a relative order, and the syllable distances between them tend to be correlated, which is one of the major tools of local rhythmical expression.

Of course, this can be done only if the meanings and syntagmatic relations of the words support it—for example, if the weight of single words is more important than the statement of a whole sentence and sufficiently independent to resist intonational subordination (the cutting off of the long waves chiefly contributes to this tendency).

As the rhythm of the poem stresses the "density" of the poetic language (Tynjanov), so does the density of an elliptical poetic language underline the poetic rhythm. It is obvious that modern poetry has explored new ways not only in the field of syllable relations but in almost all fields of poetic language. Free rhythms are only a part of these new media and can only be studied as such.

APPENDIX B

Toward a Critical Theory of the Structures
and Functions of Modern Poetry (1959)

This is the first part of my paper "On Free Rhythms in Modern Poetry." For the second part, and an explanatory headnote, see Appendix A.

I. PLEA FOR A STRUCTURALISM OF FREE RHYTHMS

There are two possible ways of facing the fact of the existence of free verse:[1] one is to exclude free rhythms from poetry (since their "form" is supposed not to be "detectable"[2]); the alternative, if we cannot afford simply to dismiss important parts of modern poetry (as well as parts of Goethe, Heine, Hölderlin, the Bible, and so forth), is to revise thoroughly our old notion of poetic rhythm (as we did for the "ornamental" theories of poetic language) and then to come back to a structural and meaningful description of free-rhythmic phenomena.

We are not saying that such a revision has not yet been attempted, but that it has not yet gone the long way from the happy chaos of ingenious insights to a sound and specific body of knowledge.

Anyone attempting to proceed in this field faces the ungrateful job of plunging into an enormous variety of metrical theories,[3] many of which are estranged from the practice of modern literary criticism, and vice versa. Karl Shapiro—who knows the English writings in this field better than many in his generation—wrote:

One of the most distressing aspects of the study of English prosody, whether as theory of forms or as versification, is the necessity of beginning with absolute fundamentals and working up through an enormous copia of *unscientific scholarship*, analyses which have not even premises in common, and the prejudices of the poets, critics and students of the past three and a half centuries. I do not mean that I have done all this, or intend to, except as an amateur, but I want to point out at the start that if there is any one certainty in this field of study it is that dissension has been the rule from beginning to end.[4]

I am quoting at length, identifying myself with both parts of these—probably too sharp—statements, since it is easier than undertaking the task of proof. But a similar pessimism was heard recently from a more significant source, the "New Critic" J. C. Ransom, who wrote retrospectively:

It is strange that a generation of critics so sensitive and ingenious as ours should have turned out very backward, indeed phlegmatic, when it comes to hearing the music of poetry, or at least, to avoid misunderstanding, to hearing its meters. The only way to escape the sense of a public scandal is to assume that the authority of the meters is passing, or is past, because we have become jaded by the meters; which would mean that something else must be tried.[5]

Precisely this is the point: "Something else must be tried." The lack of interest in prosody in literary circles was due to the correct feeling that the mere naming of a meter is as insignificant to the understanding of poetry as classification according to the 250 rhetorical figures and tropes.[6] A generation which knew so rightly to stress (if not overstress) the organicity of a complex poetic structure could not be interested in what is actually an abstraction, a "prosaic," "scientific," "rational," extremely poor paraphrase of the "music of poetry." On the other hand, we cannot dismiss prosody as an irrelevant, merely "formal" or secondary question. Generations of poets attested to the central, poetry-making significance of rhythm. It is an illusion that poetic language alone—metaphoric, ambiguous, or otherwise—can, without its peculiar rhythmic embodiment in the structure of a poem, account for the semantic and "ontological" specificity of poetry. The question is how to translate the feeling of poets and critics into precise, many-sided and distinguishable observations. When so subtle a critic of poetry as R. Blackmur feels that "it is when words sing that they give that absolute moving attention which is beyond their prose powers";[7] that "Style is the quality of the act of perception but it is mere play and cannot move us much unless married in rhythm to the urgency of the thing perceived";[8] when he judges according to these principles, saying, for example, about Wallace Stevens, Marianne Moore, and E. E. Cummings (as compared to Yeats, Eliot, and Pound) that "none of them could ever so penetrate either their prosody or their words that their poems become their own music or their own meaning,"[9] since "it is by prosody alone—by the loving care for the motion of meaning in language—that a poet may prove that he 'was blessed and could bless,'"[10] he hits at the central points of our problem, although he does not support his metaphoric statements by the kind of concrete analysis he employs in the case of poetic language.

If metaphor is "inevitable in practical criticism,"[11] we have to admit also that it is different from metaphor in poetry, at least in its objective of conveying a less relative order of truth. And in this objective it must base itself on a body of carefully analyzed facts within the structures of poems, which are responsible for the gamut of different rhythmical impacts and functions in poetry, even when we feel that a mere description of a structure does not convey the unique impact of an individual poem. To sum up: "Es ist schon heute nichtssagend, einen Rhythmus lediglich als schön, angenehm, kräftig, weich, markant und wie auch immer zu bezeichnen, ohne dass man die objektiven Gegebenheiten erfasst und darstellt."[12] (Today it says nothing any longer if we describe rhythm merely as beautiful, pleasant, strong, soft, remarkable or whatever, without grasping and describing the objective data.)

Many of the greatest achievements of world poetry are created in free rhythms.[13] A series of the most interesting movements in modern poetry did their worst and their best without strict meters: some are now curiosities of literary history, some turned from revolutionary movements almost into classic ones. Questions of rhythm were central in their arguments as well as in their endeavors.[14] The greatest diversity of rhythmic expression ever seen was tried out in almost one generation. And we cover all this with one negative term, *free verse,* a term created by poets as a slogan against a former literary convention but meaningless as a single positive description of poets as diverse as Eliot and Cummings, Brecht and Trakl, Mayakovsky and Stramm, Rilke and Marianne Moore, H.D. and Wallace Stevens.

Poets knew that the concept was not merely negative. H. de Regnier's remark of 1891 is still a challenge for criticism: "La liberté la plus grand: qu'importe le nombre de vers, si le rythme est *beau?*"[15] And so are T. S. Eliot's aphorisms: "No verse is free for the man who wants to do a good job. . . . *Vers libre* is a battle-cry of freedom, and there is no freedom in art."[16] He is stressing the inner responsibility of the artist in organizing his word material, which is—according to much evidence—more difficult without the support of a metrical framework. In 1942, in retrospect, Eliot wrote: "Only a bad poet could welcome free verse as a liberation from form or the renewal of the old; it has an insistence upon the inner unity which is unique to every poem, against the outer unity which is typical."

But a criticism, which was so valuable in understanding the "inner unity which is unique to every poem" in the field of meaning or the language of poetry, achieved—if we may generalize—rather poor results in the field of rhythm as soon as a set of traditionally presupposed rules failed to appear.

Despite many valuable insights (often mixed with naive notions on basic matters), there exists no systematic critical analysis of our problem.[17] Some attempted solutions are very poor; for example, the latest German book in this field (A. Closs's *Die freien Rhythmen in der deutschen Lyrik*);[18] see Feise[19] for a critique) is chiefly a description of poems and poets who have happened to write in free rhythms. There is a serious literature in German on "classic" free rhythms (e.g. on Hölderlin).[20] But the quite different problems of Expressionist poetry are almost untouched, except in generalizations. A serious German tradition of trying to see in free rhythms a kind of genre,[21] "die Form der Begeisterung" (Kommerell), or the like, breaks down when confronted with the variety of the Modernists. The prominent Anglo-American "New Critics" did not go into the problem (save for essayistic purposes), with one exception, Yvor Winters,[22] who is limited in his scope and achievements. The gap between criticism and scholarship, the mistrust for "exact" measurement, the lack of continuity of accumulated observations, and the lack of a broad and comparative study of minutiae (which the Russian Formalists did carry out) may account for this.[23]

The most detailed studies on free verse were written in French,[24] where the problems of rhythm are very much alive in the general theories of literature, and the awareness of rhythmic complexity, even in metrical verse, is commonly known, or at least has been since the studies of Servien (e.g. P. Guirard[25]). But there the problem is somewhat different, being a freedom from syllabic norms, as opposed to accentual-syllabic norms, with which I am dealing now (as in English, German, or Russian).

The Russian Formalists,[26] whose greatest achievements were in metric verse, were stopped in their work too early to be able to solve descriptively the contemporary questions of free rhythmic structures. (Besides, Russian "free" rhythms were not as free as many in German or English.) Moreover, in concrete metric analysis, some of them lost contact with the whole and individual poem. They were less interested in a single poem than in tendencies of generations and looked, therefore, for the dominant rule rather than for local hierarchies of structure (Jakobson's term), which meant—for free rhythms—too vague generalizations. But a few ventures, revealing broader interests than careful syllable counting, are among the most valuable writings in our field, notably Jakobson's analysis of the contribution of semantic elements to Mayakovsky's rhythms,[27] Tynjanov's analysis of the relations of rhythm and poetic language, done with a keen understanding of free rhythms,[28] Brik's remarks on "rhythm and syntax,"[29] Tomaševskij's penetrating essay on "rhythm and verse"[30]—these, as well as the authors' statistical studies revealing the complexities of metrical verse may serve as a departure for a close structural analysis, which is bound to bring concrete, valid, and meaningful results if carried out in a broad, comparative way within the framework of a modern understanding of poetry and the complexity and "organicity" of its language (as revealed in "New Criticism" or in writings inspired by German phenomenology).[31]

The best start of a renewed argument would be in a series of thorough analyses of different poems—but only when carried out in a careful, critical perspective. This will reveal the artful organization in what seems to be a matter of indescribable feeling. But since such an analysis must operate with heavily contaminated concepts, I shall try at first to state a few generalizations, which—though far from exhausting the needed clarifications—seem to be obvious conclusions from any broad inquiry into the rhythms of poetry. Such a procedure—revealing, I hope, something of the complexity of our problem—must be at the expense of a supported and well-developed argument.

II. METER AND RHYTHM

We have to distinguish between the concept of meter and the concept of rhythm.[32] Although meter has the value of a traditional norm and appears as a permanent impulse in the reading of a poem, it is rather an abstraction, one never realized precisely, whereas the rhythmical aspect of a poem implies the whole impact of the movement of the language material in the reading of a poem. By making this distinction, we, on the one hand, save the concept of meter from destruction by exact measurement and, on the other hand, avoid confusing the systematization of meters (which is important in itself) with an understanding of the contributions of rhythmical effects to the whole poem as a work of art.[33]

Poems with the same metrical scheme may have entirely different rhythms and can be rhythmically less alike than poems with different schemes—for example. those written by one author. The reason for this is that meter, being a central rhythmical factor, is not necessarily the most important or the most distinctive one. A sonnet by Rilke written in one extremely inverted sentence can be understood as different from a classical sonnet in terms of syntactic structure as a central rhythmical factor in poetry. The revolution here is not less than, and not far removed from, certain syntactical trends in modern free rhythms. But the problems of syntax in its poetic—and, in our case, rhythmic—functions are almost untouched by research, although they involve linguistic elements no less than the number of stresses.[34]

To make a good poem, meter is not enough. This was one of the chief motives in the opposition of free-verse poets to the practice of their predecessors. As Blackmur points out, "This is the chief indictment against that aspect of our poetry which we call verse. Syllable and stress are not enough to make a metric into a style, although they are quite enough to make a doggerel."[35] It is not only the "resistance of the language material" (as the early Žirmunskij thought) or certain allowances for *licentia poetica* which account for deviations from a smooth metrical order. The difference between poetry and music in this respect is not to the disadvantage of poetry, as it was commonly assumed. Just as we freed ourselves from the fallacy of *ut pictura poesis* to see the peculiar poetic figurative combinations of sensuous—and not only sensuous—elements, so we are to stress the positive values of the many-leveled expressive variety of rhythm which can be achieved in poetry, with elements of meaning playing a significant role. And, of course, there are poetic rhythms without any meter, as there are poems without any metaphor.

Therefore, a mere naming of the meter is as meaningless for the interpretation of an individual poem as the naming of its general idea: both are abstractions. The matching of form types and theme types on so abstract a level—as has often been done[36]—is largely futile.

A poem cannot be exhaustively decomposed into separate elements, rhythmic, semantic, etc. To describe the poem we must look at it as a whole from different aspects, the aspect of meaning, the aspect of rhythm, etc. Each of them is but a certain function of the totality of elements of the poem. To use a simplifying comparison: a poem is like a many-sided crystal; we can observe its inner properties only from one side at a time, but its whole structure appears through each particular face, showing different emphases in different directions.

If, in reading a poem, we try to listen to its rhythm, we cannot fail to see the participation of the meaning in its creation, nor rhythm's role in the creation of meaning. Thus we can avoid the old fallacy of a form-content dichotomy and yet not give up an approach to poetry through its different aspects. But with one condition: we have to deal with a whole aspect and not merely with a certain a priori known element of it, such as an idea or a meter. We have to understand not the mechanical relations of syllables but the dynamic properties of rhythm.

Rhythm is an "organic" phenomenon and can be appreciated fully by a phenomenological approach to the poem, that is, by going within it and moving in a hermeneutic circle from the whole to the parts, and vice versa.[37] Nevertheless, factors contributing to its intersubjective character are detectable. Moreover, we can find characteristic features by which it is possible to describe the rhythmical style of a poem or a poet, or—with more flexibility—of a period or a genre.

We can observe many rhythmical factors: metrical sequences and deviations from their ideal norms; word boundaries and their relations to the boundaries of feet; syntactic groups and pauses and their relation to metrical groups (line, caesura); syntagmatic relations, word order, syntactic tensions; repetitions and juxtapositions of sound, meaning elements, etc. Practically everything in the written poem can contribute to the shaping of the rhythm—the words in their multidimensional organizations as well as aspects of the whole which arise implicitly from the lines, such as tone, ethos, atmosphere, *Stimmung* ("mood"—a central term in contemporary German literary criticism), or whatever we call them—although each element may, and does, have other functions in the poem too.

Inasmuch as elements of meaning or, for example, syntagmatic relations take part in shaping the rhythm, we have to describe them as real structural elements existing in the written poem. If rhythmic forms and the rhythmic impact are influenced by the feeling of a general ethos or tone, we can detect the choice of words, syntactic patterns, and thematic elements which shaped it. Moreover, there are mutual interrelations of structure, meaning, and function on all levels and between all levels. Structures exist only under these conditions. Stress patterns come to life; decisions about where and how to stress, where and how to "feel" a pause, etc., are made on the basis of a reading of the poem as a whole. In this organization of the language material, rhythmic factors in the narrow sense (as the ways of Gestalt perception) take part, as do factors of meaning, tradition, and the like.

Not all the existing elements have the same value in each concrete case. We have to determine not only what the distinctive elements are but also how they work together in their concrete configurations in different poems.[38]

We cannot do this by recording readings of poems (1) because there are subjective elements in a reading; (2) because a recording shows the physical and not the psychological facts, the sounds and not their significations; (3) because a full realization of the rhythm by voice reading is often impossible, just as it is often impossible to make a full pictorial realization of the figurative language in a poem. There are tensions that are not realized in a single reading (such as the tension between the factual reading and the metrical norm created during the same reading), as well as "rhythmical oxymorons" or "rhythmical ambiguities," although their rhythmical role is obvious. But, of course, a rhythm exists only as an "auditory imagination" (even meter does not exist in the text itself, but as a potentiality). We have to analyze the clues which the text provides for the readers for grouping, pausing, emphasizing, breathing, etc., looking not for their possible physiological realizations but for their significance in a context and within a tradition.

Moreover, statistical evidence is not enough, although it may help to distinguish certain expressive tendencies in great numbers of poems, as has been shown especially by the Russian Formalists. It may be misleading to show similar numbers for different reasons; or, the more we move away from the normative element, the more we might disregard local variations or local significances.

A style is created not by majorities but by certain conspicuous uses of elements; sometimes one metaphor means by its individual value or function more than ten other "formal" metaphors. And in our field, where the very decision about what is used as an accent must be made in each case (since literary significance is not equal to linguistic significance), the hierarchy of elements, as well as the role of statistical facts, must be judged according to their particular functions.[39] A critical approach is necessary to select and to weigh the effects of possible factors within a given framework. Therefore, a rhythm analysis can be only a part of the "art of interpretation," although it can—and should—be described in exact terms based on the written text.[40]

The foregoing remarks do not imply that a rhythm analysis has to deal with all the problems of the poem, but rather that it has to keep them in mind and take them into consideration.

Systematizations of elements are helpful. But easily made systematizations should not prevent us from seeing what the rhythm is[41] or lead us to mistake the description of significant elements for the real effect of the whole poetic phenomenon. But, on the other hand, a phenomenological approach has the dangers of an uncritical relativism and impressionism or mystification in description if it does not use structural terms and comparative methods.[42] The latter way is the task of rhythmology (as distinct from "metrics"), and this is possible even in free rhythms, where we can always detect the underlying structures if we are not bound by pseudo-classical superstitions.

III. WHAT ARE FREE RHYTHMS?

By free rhythms I mean poems which (1) have no consistent metrical scheme—that is, those in an accentual-syllabic system have freedom from the prevalent, predetermined arrangement of stressed and unstressed syllables— but which (2) do have a poetic language organized so as to create impressions and fulfill functions of poetic rhythm.

I prefer the German term "free rhythms" to the French *vers libre,* since the latter implies freedom from the norms of a syllabic system, freedom primarily in the length of the verse line rather than in the relations of stressed to unstressed syllables.

No doubt the first modern impulse toward freedom from metric norms came from France[43] and spread all over Europe. This impulse fits with the inner logic of the different "ideologies" of Modernist movements. But, as close analysis shows, this influence was rather confined to slogans, which were even less concrete than figurative language. The use of concrete structural devices—not formulated in any rational way—was initiated and developed in each language according to its peculiar resources and by each artist according to his habits and poetic needs.

In the search for a feeling for concrete syllable relations, word grouping, intonations, etc., poets of each language went to their own contemporary speech habits, as well as their own revised poetic traditions (although the new free rhythms are not identical with, and in their range exceed by far, everything known in the past).

Nevertheless, these local developments show similar tendencies, owing to their relation to the common European cultural heritage, the common functional tendencies of the Modernist movements, and certain general human rhythmic properties and limitations. In this area, a comparative study can be much more illuminating than observations of what seems to be "natural" within one language.

The proclaimed tendencies of free rhythmic poetry ranged from a search for more "speech-like," "prosaic" expression to an effort to create individual structures rhythmically more organized than is possible in metrical verse, with preference for local effects rather than for the overall unity of the poem. Often these polar tendencies appear in the rhythm as well as in the diction of a poem. Both can be an attempt to escape "musical" fluidity and to regain the value of the single word, even at the expense of—or, rather, by means of—cutting off the stream.

Many misunderstandings—rationalistic views as well as those that detach form from content—stem from a simplified view of the function of meter in poetry. By such standards, meter is indispensable. But if we analyze its contributions to the meaning and the "world" of the poem, we see that its functions may be many-sided and vary from one poetic system to another. An important contemporary observation holds that "the influence of meter is . . . to actualize words: to point them and to direct attention to their sound. In good poetry, the relations between words are very strongly emphasized."[44] According to my previous distinctions, I should say that meter, by itself, does not cause this "actualization of words"; meter can have the opposite effect (as in "musical," impressionistic poetry). Here "good poetry" means poetry in which the rhythmical factors perform this central, poetry-making task; and this is often what free rhythms aim at. "'The unity and compression of the verse line' brings words closer to each other, makes them interact, overlap, crisscross, and in so doing, reveals the wealth of their 'lateral' potential meaning."[45] The variety of ways of actualizing words makes it impossible to speak about free rhythms as one type in any concrete way. In the following, I shall outline a few major principles of free rhythms, keeping in mind that their actualizations follow this variety and are more complex and rich in implications than any all-inclusive principles.

The phenomenological evidence is that free rhythms may have a more "rhythmical" and less "prosaic" impact than many metrical texts. It is possible to show in detail that they are often highly organized and by no means constitute a border area between prose and poetry. There is a misunderstanding—going back to the Greeks—which requires strict numbers as the only differentia of poetry. Strict numbers are not only insufficient (meter without rhythm) but also unnecessary. They can easily limit the flexibility and variety of expression. Moreover, although the numerical relations in free rhythms are a distinctive rhythmical factor, it remains a fallacy to say that the less strict the numbers are, the closer we are to prose. As studies in prose rhythm show, it is possible to find prose that is numerically more "regular"—on all levels—than are many poems. Furthermore, prose approaching regularity sounds more "musical" and often more monotonous than many poems approaching prose.[46]

Iambic pentameter may sound "prose-like," whereas irregular numerical relations can themselves be a rhythmical factor merely by being different from those in regular prose. Thus modern poetry uses as conspicuous rhythmic devices maximal numbers of slacks, on the one hand (Mayakovsky), and adjacent stresses, on the other (Stramm, Mayakovsky, Williams, often Eliot). Similarly, juxtaposition of a long line and a very short one is a rhythmical factor, although it is the opposite of numerical regularity, and so on.

Purity of principles is not a feature of poetry (at least when we consider its minutiae). There are many factors that are characteristic of the pole of poetry as opposed to the pole of prose. There are characteristic features of poetic language. But it is impossible to name a differentia which will appear in all poetry and which cannot appear even in greater numbers in certain prose texts. The same applies to numerical relations of groups of syllables or words if they are not strict. Nevertheless, the rhythmical difference is obvious, and it is first of all an ontological one. For example, much has been written about the "ü"-sound of Goethe's poem "Über allen Gipfeln" as a poetry-making factor; prose is full of such sounds or repetitions of sounds, but their mere number does not mean much if we do not consider their function and the different ontological systems. The same is true of ambiguities, connotations, or any multiplicity of meanings evoked in words of poetry which do not usually function in works of prose. The differentia of poetry is the verse line; it is hard to overestimate its importance in creating the poetic rhythm and the very being of the poem.

When we rewrite a poem and arrange the lines in a new way, we see a striking difference, and when we write a poem as prose, we often lose not only the specific rhythm but the poem as a work of art itself. Only careful, close analysis—far beyond syllable counting—reveals the subtle differences that account for this phenomenon.[47]

In the framework of the poem, rhythmic and figurative elements, which appear in other frameworks, too, are restressed, reorganized, and reinterpreted in our perception, according to their relative locations and functions; they get another perspective and specific gravity and then play an important role in shaping the world of the poem. Our very confidence in the signification of the words depends on these conditions. The mark of this ontologically different framework is the verse line.

Moreover, the verse line can, and does, also fulfill concrete rhythmical tasks. If it is not identical with the syntactic grouping, we have a tension between the two factors that creates or deforms some other factors (especially intonation) and can lead to the restressing of words at both ends of the line, as compared with words in prose positions.[48] If the sentence is long, the verse segments lead to a leveling of phrase divisions and stress gradations in the sentence, in addition to the leveling of stresses and stress distances, and to a breaking of the sentence intonation and a restructuring of consecutive parts into parallel-related units.

APPENDIX C

A List of Spanish Hebrew Meters

There are six basic regular meters. These can be illustrated by using the list of all meters and variants which appear in the classical anthology edited by J. Schirmann (Hayim Shirman): *Hebrew Poetry in Spain and Provence* (Berlin: Schocken, 1938).

Marginal Meters

PC binary initial	PC PC PC PC	המתקרב	*ha-mitkarev*
CP binary final	CP CP CP CP		
CC binary neutral	CC CC CC CC	משקל התנועות	*mishkal ha-tenuʾot*
PCC ternary initial	PCC PCC PC	המרובה	*ha-merubbeh*
	PCC PCC	המרנין	*ha-marnin*
CPC ternary medial	CPC CPC CP	הקלוע א׳	*ha-kaluʾa* (a)
	CPC CPC	הקלוע ב׳	*ha-kaluʾa* (b)
CCP ternary final	CCP CCP CCP	השלם א׳	*ha-shalem* (a)
	CCP CCP CC P/C*	השלם ב׳	*ha-shalem* (b)
	CCP CCP CCC	השלם ג׳	*ha-shalem* (c)
	CCP CCP CPC	השלם ד׳	*ha-shalem* (g)
	CCP CCP CPCC	השלם ה׳	*ha-shalem* (h)
	CCP CCP CP	המהיר א׳	*ha-mahir* (a)
	CCP CCP CC	המהיר ב׳	*ha-mahir* (b)
	CCP CCP C	השלם ד׳	*ha-shalem*
	CCP CCP [d, c]	השלם ה׳	*ha-shalem*
	CCP CCP C	השלם ו׳	*ha-shalem*

*The rhyming position is changing in the two halves of the hemistich; it is either a peg or a cord, thus making a last foot of three cords: CCC.

All the differences between meters are variants in the third foot. Variations of feet in verse endings are of several kinds:

1) The last foot is short (catalectic), PCC → PC, CPC → CP; CCP → CC. This change occurs nearly always in ternary meters, where it is the usual case (unless it is the last peg which is shortened, as in the final *ha-shalem*).

2) The last foot is hypercatalectic: CCP → C, which is very rare.

3) A peg is replaced by a cord: CCP → CCC; CP → CC, which occurs quite often since so-called short syllables are scarce in Hebrew;

4) Two cords are replaced by a peg: CCP → PP; PPC → PP. This is a rare variation, occurring in changing meters, especially in the second foot.

5) A peg is advanced: CCP → CPC (or CP), e.g. in *ha-shalem* (g).

The most widespread changes are a catalectic foot (1) or a substitute by a cord (3). (See the lists of regular ternary meters.)

NOTES

CHAPTER 2. DO SOUNDS HAVE MEANING?

1. The first version of this essay was published in Hebrew in 1968 with examples from English and Hebrew poetry: Benjamin Harshav [Hrushovski], "Do Sounds Have Meaning? The Problem of Expressiveness of Sound-Patterns in Poetry," *Ha-Sifrut*, 1 (1968): 410–420. See also Harshav, "Principles of a Unified Theory of the Literary Text," in Ziva Ben Porath and Benjamin Hrushovski, *Structuralist Poetics in Israel* (PPS 1; Tel Aviv: Porter Institute for Poetics and Semiotics, 1974).

2. Nathan Alterman, "Geshem sheni ve-zikaron" [Second Rain and Memory], in *Kokhavim ba-khutz* (Tel Aviv: Hakibbutz Hameukhad Publishers, 1972). Used with permission from Hakibbutz Hameukhad publishing house.

3. Aleksei Kruchonykh, "Dyr bul shchyl," widely quoted, was first mentioned in the Russian Futurist manifesto, "Slovo kak takovoe" [The Word as Such] (1913), signed A. Kruchonykh and V. Khlebnikov. For the published manifesto, see "Samovitoye Slovo," in *Literaturniye Manifest ot Simbolizma do Nashih Dnei*, ed. S. B. Djimbinova (Moscow: Izdatelskii Dom XXI–Soglasie, 2000), 144.

4. James R. Kreuzer, *Elements of Poetry* (New York: Macmillan, 1955), 67.

5. I. A. Richards, "Science and Poetry," in *Criticism: The Foundations of Modern Literary Judgment*, ed. Marc Schorer, Josephine Miles, and Gordon McKenzie (New York: Harcourt, Brace, 1948), 507.

6. Roman Jakobson and Linda Waugh, *The Sound Shape of Language* (Bloomington: Indiana University Press, 1979), esp. chapter 4, "The Spell of Speech Sounds." Roman Jakobson's "Six Lectures on Sound and Meaning," read in New York at a meeting attended by Claude Lévi-Strauss, influenced the foundation of Structural Anthropology.

7. Maurice Grammont, *Les vers français* (Paris: Delagrave, 1967); Paul Delbouille, *Poésie et sonorités* (Paris: "Les Belles Lettres," 1961).

8. See R. Jakobson, *Six Lectures on Sound and Meaning*, trans. John Mepham (Cambridge, Mass.: MIT Press, 1978). See also David I. Masson, "Thematic Analysis of Sounds in

Poetry," in *Essays on the Language of Literature,* ed. Seymour Chatman and Samuel R. Levin (1960; Boston: Houghton Mifflin, 1967).

9. Kreuzer, *Elements of Poetry,* 67.

10. Ibid., 68.

11. T. S. Eliot, "The Waste Land," in *Collected Poems, 1909–1962* (New York: Harcourt Brace, 1963), 65, 66.

12. T. S. Eliot, "Ash-Wednesday," in *Collected Poems,* 92.

13. See W. K. Wimsatt, Jr.'s "The Structure of Romantic Nature Imagery," in *Verbal Icon: Studies in the Meaning of Poetry; and Two Preliminary Essays Written in Collaboration with Monroe C. Beardsley* (New York: Noonday Press, 1964).

14. On the key concepts of mirroring and asymmetry, see Benjamin Harshav, *Language in Time of Revolution* (Stanford, Calif.: Stanford University Press; Cambridge, England: Cambridge University Press, 1999).

15. See my essay on metaphor, "Poetic Metaphor and Frames of Reference," in Benjamin Harshav, *Explorations in Poetics* (Stanford, Calif.: Stanford University Press, 2007), chapter 2.

16. W. H. Auden, "A Voyage," from *Collected Poems of W.H. Auden,* ed. Edward Mendelson (New York: Modern Library, 2007), 176.

17. Maurice Grammont, *Traité de phonétique* (Paris: Delagrave, 1933).

18. See Roger Brown, *Words and Things* (New York: Free Press of Glencoe, 1958), esp. chapter 4, "Phonetic Symbolism and Metaphor."

CHAPTER 3. RHYTHMS OF THE BIBLE REVISITED

1. My earlier ideas on the rhythms of the Bible appeared in an often-quoted survey of the history of Hebrew versification: Benjamin Hrushovski, "Prosody, Hebrew," *Encyclopedia Judaica* (1972). Since then, several versions of the survey have appeared, including in my Hebrew book *Toldot ha-tsurot shel ha-shira ha-ivrit min ha-tanakh ad ha-modernizm* [A History of Hebrew Versification from the Bible to Modernism] (Ramat Gan: Bar-Ilan University Press, 2008). John F. Hobbins, summarizing recent scholarship, wrote: "The most fitting description of ancient Hebrew verse known to the present writer is that of B. Harshav [Hrushovski] as summarized by R. Alter" (John F. Hobbins, "Regularities in Ancient Hebrew Verse: A New Descriptive Model," *Zeitschrift für die Alttestamentliche Wissenschaft* 119, no. 4 [2007]: 564). I am grateful to Pastor John Hobbins, who thought along similar lines in his own work on the Hebrew Bible.

2. "Frame of reference" (*fr*) and "projection" are terms from my theory of the literary text; see Benjamin Harshav, *Explorations in Poetics* (Stanford, Calif.: Stanford University Press, 2007).

3. For my early ruminations on the psychology of natural rhythms, see Appendix B in this book.

4. See my discussion of Whitman's *Song of Myself,* Song 33, in *Omanut haShira* [The Art of Poetry] (Tel Aviv: Porter Institute for Poetics and Semiotics; Jerusalem: Carmel Publishing House, 2008), 124–125.

5. "Line" is a metaphor, borrowed from written texts.

6. See Benjamin Harshav, "The Jerusalem Windows in the Perspective of Chagall's Poetics of Art," in *Marc Chagall: Hadassah from Sketch to Stained Glass* (Paris: Musée d'art et d'histoire du Judaïsme, 2002).

7. See Roman Jakobson's analysis of the election slogan "I like Ike," where "I" is included in "Ike" and "Ike" is part of "like."

CHAPTER 4. THE SYSTEMS OF HEBREW VERSIFICATION

1. This chapter is an expanded version of my theory of Hebrew versification systems. My first comprehensive survey of Hebrew versification from the Bible to the present was published in English in *Encyclopedia Judaica*: Benjamin Hrushovski, "Prosody, Hebrew" (1972). This was followed by a more precise but shorter version: Benjamin Hrushovski, "Note on the Systems of Hebrew Versification," in *The Penguin Book of Hebrew Verse*, ed. T. Carmi (London: Penguin, 1981). An expanded version appeared as two books in Hebrew: Benjamin Harshav, *Toldot ha-tsurot shel ha-shira ha-ivrit min ha-tanakh ad ha-modernizm* [A History of Hebrew Versification from the Bible to Modernism] (Ramat Gan: Bar-Ilan University Press, 2008); and *Mishkal ve-ritmus ba-shirah ha-ivrit he-ḥ adasha* [Meter and Rhythm in Modern Hebrew Poetry] (= *Selected Writings: Studies in Literature and Culture*, vol. 7) (Jerusalem: Carmel Publishing House; Tel Aviv: Porter Institute for Poetics and Semiotics, 2008). Chapters 3 and 4 in the present volume cover some of the same territory. For studies on specific issues see the list of my publications on prosody—both general and Hebrew—at the end of this book.

2. On Base Languages, see Benjamin Harshav, *Language in Time of Revolution* (Stanford, Calif.: Stanford University Press; Cambridge, England: Cambridge University Press, 1999).

3. See Benjamin Harshav, ed., *Shirat ha-Tekhiya ha-Ivrit* [Poetry of the Hebrew Revival: A Critical and Historical Anthology], 2 vols. (Jerusalem: Mosad Bialik; Tel Aviv: Open University, 2000). See section on Ephraim Lissitsky, vol. 2, p. 65.

4. I wish this "weaker" line had the opposite history, starting with a simple rhyme and developing the complex Kallirian forms at the end, without going back and forth, but the question must be left in the hands of the piyut scholars.

5. The poems in this section were selected from Carmi, *Penguin Book of Hebrew Verse,* and are cited by page number.

6. There are many places in the piyut where the word *Elohim* (God) does not count, especially since an epithet of God appears right away. It may be a later addition. The reading would have been: אזכיר גבורות / נאדרי בכח // יחיד ואין-עוד, / אפס ואין-שני.

7. *Sefer Ben Sira ha-shalem,* ed. Moshe Tsvi Segal (Jerusalem: Mosad Bialik, 1958), 302.

8. Menahem Zulay, introduction to *Piyutey Yanay* (Berlin: Schocken, 1938).

9. John Crew Ransom rhymed PlATO–PotATO (in the poem "Survey of Literature"). But this was only a stray discontinuous rhyme, not a norm.

10. This is a good example of the similarity in the pronunciation of Hebrew in Palestine then and now.

11. Ezra Fleischer, *Piyutey Shlomo ha-Bavli,* 79: "B. Hrushovski [Harshav] will undoubtedly dwell on the details of this issue in his research in this field."

12. See Saadia ibn Denan's little book *Seifer ha-Shorashim,* the first attempt to analyze the Hebrew meters by a systematic comparison with their Arabic models. In J. Schirmann [Hayim Shirman], ed., *Hebrew Poetry in Spain and Provence* [in Hebrew] (Berlin: Schocken, 1938), vol. 2, p. 665.

13. Charles Lalo, *Notions d'esthétique* (Paris: Presses universitaires de France, 1960), 61.

14. For details, see Appendix C.

15. See Appendix C.

16. See a list of marginal meters in Appendix C.

17. See J. Schirmann (Hayim Shirman), *Anthology of Hebrew Poetry in Italy* (Berlin: Schocken, 1934).

18. This may be a nice idea, but perhaps the historians of that period should rethink the chronology. I use here the accepted order of events.

19. See Chapter 5 in this book.

20. Yet see my study of free rhythms in modern Yiddish poetry in this book, Chapter 7.

21. In the original there is an "h," but it is not pronounced.

CHAPTER 5. THE DISCOVERY OF ACCENTUAL IAMBS IN EUROPEAN POETRY

1. Some theoretical ideas on free rhythms can be found in my essay (written under the name Benjamin Hrushovski) "On Free Rhythms in Modern Poetry," in *Style in Language,* ed. Thomas A. Sebeok (New York and Cambridge, Mass., 1960), 173–190. For a classification of such phenomena in one literature see an earlier study: Benjamin Hrushovski, "On Free Rhythms in Modern Yiddish Poetry," in *The Field of Yiddish: Studies in Yiddish Language, Folklore, and Literature,* ed. Uriel Weinreich, vol. 1 (New York, 1954), 219–266.

2. The first section of the original paper remains as first published in 1964.

3. In the past I used the widespread abbreviation **t.s.,** (tonic-syllabic, as used in Slavic literatures), but have settled on "stress" in language versus "accent" in verse—hence "accentual" rather than "tonic," and "accentual-syllabic" (**a.-s.**) for the meter.

4. V. M. Žirmunskij, *Vvedenie v metriku,* trans. C. E. Brown; ed. Edward Stankiewicz and W. N. Vickery (Leningrad, 1925), 88 f.

5. W. Kayser, *Das sprachliche Kunstwerk* (Bern, 1984), 242; for parallel statements cf. A. Heusler, *Deutsche Versgeschichte (mit Einschluss des altenglischen und altnordischen Stabreimverses),* 3 vols. (Berlin-Leipzig, 1925), vol. 1, p. 7; K. Shapiro, "English Prosody and Modern Poetry," *ELH,* 14 (1947): 77.

6. Karl Vossler, *Dichtungsformen der Romanen* (Stuttgart, 1951), 8, 19.

7. L. Benoist-Hanappier, *Die freien Rhythmen in der deutschen Lyrik* (Halle, 1905), 75.

8. M. Weinreich, *Shtaplen* (Berlin, 1923), 151.

9. I have argued this in somewhat greater detail in Hrushovski, "On Free Rhythms in Modern Poetry"; see appendixes A and B in this book. The field has not yet been explored from a structural point of view, although some basic insights have been contributed by interpretive critics.

10. H. W. Wells, *New Poets from Old* (New York, 1940), 138; H. E. Holthusen, "Vollkommen sinnliche Rede" [Fully Sensuous Speech], *Akzente*, 4 (1955): 346–355. Similar ideas were widespread, particularly among German scholars—even among men of such stature as Andreas Heusler and Oskar Walzel and even before the Hitler period.

11. Andreas Heusler, "Deutsche Verskunst" [German Art of Versification], in *Kleine Schriften* (Berlin, 1943 [!]), 8. The paper was printed in 1925 and reprinted in a thirty-three-page booklet in Berlin in 1951 from his 1943 *Kleine Schriften*.

12. Ibid., 9, 23.

13. W. Kayser, *Geschichte des deutschen Verses* (Bern, 1960), 17.

14. M. Platel, *Vom Volkslied zum Gesellschaftslied . . .* [= *Sprache und Dichtung*, no. 64] (Bern, 1939), 37.

15. F. Dostoevsky, *Russkie pisateli o literaturnom trude*, vol. 8 (Leningrad, 1955), 159.

16. Heusler, "Deutsche Verskunst," 3, 4, 5, 7.

17. Cf. the recent argument in W. K. Wimsatt, Jr., and M. C. Beardsley, "The Concept of Meter: An Exercise in Abstraction," *Proceedings of the Modern Language Association*, 74 (1959): 585–598.

18. Heusler, *Deutsche Versgeschichte*, vol. 3, p. 121.

19. C. S. Lewis, *English Literature in the Sixteenth Century* (= *Oxford History of English Literature*, vol. 3) (Oxford, 1954), 225.

20. Further details are presented in the following section. Characteristically enough, the Netherlands, a border country, also preceded Germany in the reform of its metrics and played the role of an intermediary. See Heusler, *Deutsche Versgeschichte*, vol. 3, p. 63.

21. It is significant that in Polish, where the place of the stress is fixed (always on the penultimate syllable) and the possibilities of variation are consequently limited, syllabic meters (counting of the number of syllables) prevailed and a.-s. meters did not gain ground until the nineteenth century (M. Długska, "Sylabotonizm," *Sylabotonizm* [Wrocław, 1957]).

22. In Hebrew, a sensitive poet and critic, J. Fichman (Y. Fikhman), did catch the almost-iambic meter in Luzzato's sonnets.

23. Cf. Vossler, *Dichtungsformen der Romanen;* Długska, "Sylabotonizm."

24. Vossler, *Dichtungsformen der Romanen*, 160.

25. K. R. Ruprecht, *Einführung in die griechische Metrik* (Munich, 1950), 9.

26. J. T. Shipley, ed., *Dictionary of World Literature* (New York, 1953), s.v. "English Versification."

27. H. S. Bennett, "Chaucer and the Fifteenth Century," in *Oxford History of English Literature* (Oxford, 1954), vol. 2, part 1, p. 93.

28. Kayser, *Geschichte*, 24.

29. Heusler, *Deutsche Versgeschichte*, vol. 3, p. 1.

30. Heusler, "Deutsche Verskunst," 19; cf. also 17.

31. Cf. the summary in ibid., 5.

32. Heusler, *Deutsche Versgeschichte*, vol. 2, p. 154.; see the summary in Heusler, "Deutsche Verskunst," 9 f.

33. G. Bullett, *Silver Poets of the Sixteenth Century* (London, 1947), ix.

34. R. Lamson and H. Smith, eds., *The Golden Hind* (New York: Norton, 1956); Lewis, *English Literature in the Sixteenth Century*, 225. Cf. also §11.

35. Cf. Heusler, *Deutsche Versgeschichte*, vol. 2, p. 53; and W. Kayser's criticism, *Geschichte*, 23. But Heusler, too, is aware that "das Tonverdrehen [*sic*], das häuft und steigert sich nun bei diesen handwerklichen Meistern bis zu grundsaetzlicher Missachtung der Sprache" (*Deutsche Verskunst*, 13).

36. See my study of Hebrew rhyme, its theory, and its history: Benjamin Harshav, *Toldot ha-tsurot shel ha-shira ha-ivrit min ha-tanakh ad ha-modernizm* [A History of Hebrew Versification from the Bible to Modernism] (Ramat Gan: Bar-Ilan University Press, 2008).

37. Heusler, *Deutsche Versgeschichte*, vol. 3, p. 97.

38. Heusler, *Deutsche Verskunst*, 10.

39. Cf. E. Schroeder, *Das historische Volkslied des dreissigjährigen Krieges* (Marburg, 1916), 142.

40. Cf. B. O. Unbegaun, *Russian Versification* (Oxford, 1956), 21.

41. J. Minor, *Neuhochdeutsche Metrik* (Strasbourg, 1893), 431; Žirmunskij, *Vvedenie v metriku*. On the difference between Italian and French, see the important paper of the late H. Peri: "La versificationà accents fixes dans les langues romanes," *Actes du Xe Congrès International de Linguistique et Philologie romanes* (April 1962).

42. B. Tomaševskij, *O stixe* (Leningrad, 1929), 312, 320.

43. In the period between 1600 and 1750, called by Heusler "der Opitzische Zeitraum," 95 percent of all written German poetry was binary (*Deutsche Versgeschichte*, vol. 3, p. 64 f).

44. Lewis, *English Literature in the Sixteenth Century*, 225.

45. Kayser, *Geschichte*, 32 f.

46. Ibid., 28.

47. Tomaševskij, *O stixe*, 332 f., 358 f.

48. Vossler, *Dichtungsformen der Romanen*, 8, 19.

49. Bennett, "Chaucer and the Fifteenth Century," 87.

50. I use the signs "ŏ" and "ŏ" for syllables accented and unaccented by the meter; and the sign "ó" for language stress (or for schematized "actual" reading).

51. A comparative assessment of such differences in poetic rhythm due to differences in tradition and the traits of a particular language is made in R. Jakobson, *O česskom stixe* (Berlin, 1923); cf. also Žirmunskij, *Vvedenie v metriku*, 81–86. Some points, especially in connection with English poetry, have been demonstrated in H. Lanz, *The Physical Basis of Rhyme* (Stanford, Calif., 1931), 207 ff.

52. I owe the impulse for the treatment of this topic, as well as numerous suggestions and access to copies of rare books and manuscripts of Yiddish and Hebrew medieval poetry, to my friend the late Chone Shmeruk.

53. The most important descriptions of his work in Yiddish are: M. Weinreich, *Bilder fun der yidischer literatur-geshikhte* (Vilna, 1928); Max Erik, *Vegn alt-yidish roman un novele* (Warsaw, 1926); and Erik, *Geshikhte fun der yidisher literatur* (Warsaw, 1928). There is also a relatively popular critical book by N. B. Minkoff.

54. Ch. Shmeruk, *Belehrung der jüdisch-teutschen Red und Schreibart* (Königsberg, 1699), Für-tragB. A good example of the bilingual tradition is provided by the collection of poems written down by Menakhem Oldendorf around 1516 and published by L. Löwenstein: see "Jüdische und jüdisch-deutsche Lieder," *Festschrift Israel Hildesheimer* (Berlin, 1890), 126–144.

55. *Lieder des venezianischen Lehrers Gumprecht von Szczebrshyn,* ed. Moritz Stern (Berlin, 1922).

56. See Chapter 3 in this book.

57. *Megiles Vints,* 2nd ed. (Amsterdam, 1648), reprinted by the Hebrew University in 1962; cf. M. Weinreich, *Shtaplen,* 140–192.

58. Ch. Shmeruk, "Which Holiday Is the Best? A Versified Dispute between Hanukkah and Other Holidays," *Di goldene keyt,* no. 47 (1963): 160–176.

59. Löwenstein, "Jüdische und jüdisch-deutsche Lieder," 134 f.

60. Steinschneider, Cat. Bodl. 3682 (M. Steinschneider, *Catalogus librorum hebraeorum in Bibliotheca Bodleiana* [Berlin, 1852–1860; rpt., 1932, 1964]).

61. Similarly in other passages (*Das Schemuelbuch des Mosche Esrim Wearba,* ed. L. Fuks, 2 vols. [Assen, 1959–1961]).

62. On Yiddish, cf. U. Weinreich, "On the Cultural History of Yiddish Rhyme," in *Essays on Jewish Life and Thought* (New York, 1959), 423–442 (on Levita, 426, 439); and U. Weinreich, "On Multisyllabic Rhyme," *Yidishe shprakh,* 15 (1955), 97–109.

63. In the *Shmuel-bukh* I noticed only five such cases, e.g. *makher–mer* and *shrayber– dar* (stanzas 579, 902, 967, 1668, 1714). But these are merely permitted cases; there are also numerous stress-bound penultimate rhymes, whereas in Hebrew there were no penulti-mate rhymes, since terminal rhyme was the rule.

64. L. Fuks, ed., *The Oldest Known Literary Documents of Yiddish Literature* [c. 1382], 2 vols. (Leiden, 1957).

65. I use a new academic edition published in Jerusalem by the Israel Academy of Sciences and Humanities: Elia Levita, *Pariz un Viene,* ed. Chone Shmeruk with Erika Timm (Jeru-salem, 1996).

66. The *Bovo-bukh* is photographically reproduced in book form, with some errors corrected, and with an English introduction, in *Elia Bachur's Poetical Works,* vol. 1, ed. Judah A. Joffe (New York, 1949).

67. On the parallel case in German, cf. Heusler, *Deutsche Verskunst,* 11.

68. In Russian syllabic poetry, too, all rhymes were penultimate, under Polish influence (as shown by Tomaševskij, *O stixe,* 323).

69. W. Kayser, *Kleine deutsche Versschule* (Bern, 1946), 46.

70. N. B. Minkoff, *Elye Bokher un zayn Bovo-bukh* (New York, 1950), 30.

71. Elia Levita, *Bovo-bukh* (Buenos Aires, 1962).

72. At Trinity College, Cambridge, I made use of the photocopy in the possession of Ch. Shmeruk. Now *PV* is published in full in a critical edition edited by Ch. Shmeruk, cited above.

73. M. Weinreich, *Bilder,* 189.

74. There are only two exceptions: 41r.iii and 43v.iv. In this numbering, the Arabic numerals refer to the leaves; *r* and *v* stand for recto and verso, respectively; and the Roman numerals identify the stanzas.

75. Erik, *Geshikhte*, 196.
76. Cf. Y. Shatski, in *Filologishe shriftn* (YIVO), 1 [1926]: 191.
77. M. Weinreich, *Bilder*, 189.
78. L. Landau, *Arthurian Legends* (Leipzig, 1912), xxxviii f.
79. M. Weinreich, *Bilder*, 190.
80. Landau, *Arthurian Legends*, 15, and English introduction, 9.
81. Cf. Schroeder, *Das historische Volkslied*, 149. I employ the term *Volkslied* as it is used by German scholars, i.e. as a description of the genre rather than of the origin.
82. Heusler, *Versgeschichte*, vol. 3, p. 148.
83. Cf. U. Weinreich, "Stress and Word Structure in Yiddish," in Weinreich, *Field of Yiddish*, 1–27.
84. Cf. Heusler, *Deutsche Versgeschichte*, vol. 3, p. 141.
85. Since this study deals with syllable numbers and stress, I did not go into the complex problems of sound quality and Yiddish dialects. The transcription is approximate and does not claim to reflect the pronunciation accurately. There is evidence that the text wavers between diachronically or dialectically differentiated pronunciations, notably in the matter of *a* (*á*) vs. *o*. In cases of doubt, my transcription leans toward the modern Standard Yiddish state of the vocalism.
86. Since the word for "tears" elsewhere appears without *h*, as *trern*, I take this letter *h* (in *trĕhĕrn*) as a sign for an extra syllable. Such syllables are frequent in *PV*; see Chapter 7.
87. The sound quality of Levita's rhymes remains to be studied in detail, especially in relation to the problem of the author's pronunciation. On the effect of rhyming Yiddish words from several stock languages and on the dactylic rhyme, see U. Weinreich, "Stress and Word Structure in Yiddish."
88. Regnart was born in the Netherlands. This account follows Platel, *Vom Volkslied zum Gesellschaftslied . . .* , 29–35.
89. See Appendix A for an early suggestion of the idea of simple groupings.
90. Kayser, *Kleine deutsche Versschule*, 17.
91. Žirmunskij, *Vvedenie v metriku*; cf. also B. Tomaševskij, *Teorija literatury* (Moscow, 1925).
92. R. Freiherr von Lilienkron, ed., *Deutsches Leben im Volkslied um 1530* (Berlin-Stuttgart, 1884).
93. Cf. Heusler's example of five possible readings—all in conformity with the laws of meter—of one line by Klopstock, and of seven different metrical readings of one line by Schiller (*Deutsche Versgeschichte*, vol. 1, p. 84).
94. I therefore fail to understand what M. Schüler meant by his statement that "die Zeile hat in der Regel 10 Silben" ("as a rule, the verse line has 10 syllables"; "Das Bovo-Buch," *Zeitschrift für hebräische Bibliographie*, 20 [1917]: 87).
95. Schroeder, *Das historische Volkslied*, 136.
96. The table is not precisely to scale, since from no. 300 onward I marked every 100 instead of every 50 stanzas. In every group I counted all the syllables of the first two stanzas in each set of ten (i.e. stanzas 1, 2; 11, 12; 21, 22; 31, 32; 41, 42). But in the later groups (of 100 stanzas) I checked only the first 50 stanzas, since the changes did not seem significant. On the other hand, as far as rhyme is concerned, I counted *every* item.
97. Kayser, *Kleine deutsche Versschule*, 47.

98. Erik, *Geshikhte*, 168.
99. Yisroel Tsinberg, *Geshikhte fun der literatur bay yidn*, vol. 6 (Vilna, 1930), 91, 97.
100. J. T. Shipley, ed., *Dictionary of World Literature* (New York, 1953), 295.
101. G. von Wilpert, *Sachwörterbuch der Literatur* (Stuttgart, 1959), 592.
102. For a Yiddish example, see Leyb Naydus, "A poeme on a nomen (oktavn)," written in iambic pentameters with penultimate-ultimate rhymes (the opposite of Levita's rule).
103. B. Tomaševskij, *Stilistika i stixoslozenie* (Leningrad, 1959), 360, 364; Tomaševskij, *Teorija literatury*, 82.
104. Bennett, "Chaucer and the Fifteenth Century," 86.
105. Heusler, *Deutsche Versgeschichte*, vol. 3, p. 51.
106. Besides the aspects already discussed, especially the irrelevance of the number of syl-lables and the consideration given to language stress in the text as well as in rhyme, mention should be made of the distinction of a two-part structure of a folksong stro-phe, as opposed to the three-part pattern of Meistersang (cf. Kayser, *Geschichte*, 20). Moreover, the poem of the Meistersinger had an *"Atempause"* (breathing pause) after each line, whereas Levita tries to overflow such a pause.
107. Levita, *Pariz un Viene*.
108. E. A. Sonnenschein, *What Is Rhythm?* (Oxford, 1925), 93.
109. On this "alternation of strong and weak downbeats" (i.e. metrical accents), see R. Jakob-son, "Linguistics and Poetics," in Sebeok, *Style in Language*, 362.
110. A large number of Brant's cases belongs to this group; cf. Heusler, *Deutsche Versge-schichte*, vol. 3, p. 51.
111. Similar patterns were used in German folksong in the seventeenth century; cf. Schroeder, *Das historische Volkslied*, 143 ff.
112. Cf. Vossler, *Dichtungsformen der Romanen*, 92 f.
113. A similar case is the six-iamb line of stanza 62v.ii, where "zi vorn flegn" should be simply "zi flegn." The same comment applies to the added double negation in 69r.i. But as I said, the iambic flow remains, even in the uncorrected text.
114. See Hrushovski, "On Free Rhythms in Modern Yiddish Poetry" (now re-edited and included in this book as Chapter 8).
115. Ibid., 225 f.
116. Ibid., 234.
117. See D. Hofshteyn and F. Shames, *Teorye fun literatur* (Kharkov, 1930), 115.
118. L. Landau, "A Hebrew-German Paraphrase of the Book of Esther of the Fifteenth Cen-tury," *Journal of English and Germanic Philology*, 18 (1919): 1–59.
119. Cf. MS Sorbonne 158 (Bibliothèque Nationale, Paris) vs. MS Hamburg 209.

CHAPTER 6. BASIC FORMS OF MODERN YIDDISH POETRY

1. This essay (originally written c. 1990) is placed here as a background for Chapter 7.
2. See Chapter 2.
3. T. S. Eliot's first volume of poetry, *Prufrock and Other Observations* (London: The Ego-ist, 1917), represents this overcoming of metrical constraints by the use of meter and its deformations.

4. Roman Jakobson, "Linguistics and Poetics," in *On Language and Literature,* ed. Linda R. Waugh and Monique Monville-Burston (Cambridge, Mass.: Harvard University Press, 1990).

5. Josephine Miles, *Style and Proportion: The Language of Prose and Poetry* (Boston: Little, Brown, 1967).

6. Most Yiddish examples in this chapter are included, in the original and in an English translation, in Benjamin and Barbara Harshav, *American Yiddish Poetry: A Bilingual Anthology* [AYP] (Berkeley: University of California Press, 1986; Stanford, Calif.: Stanford University Press, 2007); copyright © 1986, 2007 Benjamin and Barbara Harshav. All rights reserved. Used with permission of Stanford University Press, www.sup.org. The current example is from Glatshteyn's poem "1919," in *AYP,* 208–209.

7. *AYP,* 680–681.

8. *AYP,* 113–125.

9. *AYP,* 678–679.

10. In Yiddish, most words are stressed on the first syllable; in all other cases here, the stressed syllable is capitalized. This rule may change for other purposes, depending on context.

11. *AYP,* 394–397.

12. J. Glatshteyn, *Fraye ferzn* [Free Verse] (New York: Grohar-Stadolski, 1926).

13. I discussed these forms in detail in my paper of 1953, "On Free Rhythms in Modern Yiddish Poetry," in *The Field of Yiddish: Studies in Yiddish Language, Folklore, and Literature,* ed. Uriel Weinreich, vol. 1 (New York, 1954), now in this volume as Chapter 8.

14. *AYP,* 491.

15. See Chronicle, no. 27, in *AYP,* 302–303.

16. Uriel Weinreich pointed out this trend in his classic paper "On the Cultural History of Yiddish Rhyme," in *Essays on Jewish Life and Thought, Presented in Honor of Salo W. Baron* (New York: Columbia University Press, 1959), 423–442.

17. A. Leyeles, no. 19, in "Chronicle of a Movement: Excerpts from Introspectivist Criticism," in *AYP.*

18. Ernst Cassirer, *An Essay on Man* (New Haven: Yale University Press, 1944), 155.

19. For a more detailed study of the poem, see B. Harshav, *The Polyphony of Jewish Culture* (Stanford, Calif.: Stanford University Press, 2007), 113–117.

20. In the translation of this poem, Barbara Harshav and I gave up the rhymes altogether in trying to convey the metrical scheme precisely, skipping, however, a syllable here and there to avoid what would be too mechanical an impression or too easy a forward flow in English when uninhibited by the rhymes.

21. For a more detailed reading of specific poems, see Chapter 7.

CHAPTER 7. THE CONSTRAINTS OF FREEDOM IN MODERN YIDDISH POETRY

1. This study of Yiddish verse, written in Jerusalem in 1953, was commissioned by the linguist Uriel Weinreich in New York for the first volume of *The Field of Yiddish: Studies in Yiddish Language, Folklore, and Literature* (New York, 1954). The paper was translated into English by Uriel Weinreich and thoroughly reedited by me in 2010–2011.

2. The first two sections of this essay are almost verbatim from the first edition of Weinreich, *Field of Yiddish.*

3. See Benjamin Harshav, *Marc Chagall and the Lost Jewish World* (New York, 2006).

4. Benjamin Harshav, *The Meaning of Yiddish* (Stanford, Calif., 1999).

5. B. Roland Lewis, *Creative Poetry: A Study of Its Organic Principles* (Stanford, Calif., 1931), 315.

6. Andreas Heusler, *Deutsche Versgeschichte (mit Einschluss des altenglischen und altnordischen Stabreimverses)*, 3 vols. (Berlin-Leipzig, 1925–1929).

7. Eliezer Grinberg, *Di lange nakht* (New York: Lipkaner Besaraber Sosayeti, 1946); translated by Benjamin Harshav.

8. H. Leivick [Leyvik], "Oyf di fayern," in *Ale verk*, vol. 1 (New York: H. Leivick Yubiley-Komitet, 1940), 67. Used with the permission of the estate of H. Leivick. All my quotations from Leivick are from this volume unless otherwise indicated.

9. On the "rhythms of largeness," see my study in the Hebrew volume *The Art of Poetry* (= *Selected Writings: Studies in Literature and Culture*, vol. 2) (Jerusalem and Tel Aviv, 2000).

10. The section on free rhythms in Yiddish folksongs, which was here in the original essay, is now Chapter 8.

11. On free rhythms in Yiddish folksong, see Chapter 8.

12. Tsunzer's poem "Shives-tsien" (Return to Zion) of 1884 was already in iambs.

13. M. Basin, ed., *Finf hundert yor yidishe poezye* [Five Hundred Years of Yiddish Poetry] (New York, 1917).

14. Vladimir A. Pyarst, *Sovremennoe stikhovedenje* (Leningrad, 1931).

15. Aaron Kushnirov, "Raseya," in *A Shpigl oyf a Shteyn: An Anthology of Poetry and Prose by 12 Soviet Writers* (Jerusalem: Magnes Press, Hebrew University, 1987), 312.

16. August Closs, *Die freien Rhythmen in der deutschen Lyrik* (Bern, 1947), writes (85): "We would like here to point again at the nouns without articles, by which the word gains force and personification."

17. See my book *Mishkal ve-ritmus ba-shirah ha-ivrit he-ḥadasha* [Meter and Rhythm in Modern Hebrew Poetry] (= *Selected Writings: Studies in Literature and Culture*, vol. 7) (Jerusalem: Carmel Publishing House; Tel Aviv: Porter Institute for Poetics and Semiotics, 2008).

18. Itsik Manger, "Yankev ovinu zitst alt un mid . . ." in *Medresh Itsik* [Itsik's Midrash] (Paris, 1951). "Avishag," and "Avishags troyer," quoted below, also come from *Medresh Itsik*. Used by permission of Arthur Gottesfeld, executor, estate of Itsik Manger.

19. Moshe-Leyb Halpern, *Di goldene pave* (New York, 1924), 69. Used with permission of Isaac Halpern. Our tendency to feel the lines as equal makes possible the accumulation of unstressed syllables. A secondary stress disturbs us because it would raise the normal number of stresses.

20. Ber Horovits, *Fun mayn heym in di berg*, vol. 1 (Vilna: Kletskin Publishers, 1929), 41.

21. See M. P. Štokmar, *Issledovaniia v oblasti russkogo narodnogo stikhoslozheniia* (Moscow, 1952), part 3, chapter 1.

22. Y. L. Cahan, *Shtudyes vegn yidisher folksshafung* (New York, 1952), vol. A.

23. Alfred Landau, ["Notes on Yiddish Folklore"], *Filologishe shriftn* (YIVO), 1 (1926): 18 f.

24. On the German dialectical basis of some Yiddish diminutives, see Alfred Landau, "The Diminutive in Galician Yiddish" [in Hebrew], *Yivo-bleter*, 11 (1937): 155–172. But there remain the questions about whether in German the suffixes were not stressed, and why it was precisely the disyllabic diminutive suffixes which were accepted in Eastern Yiddish. From the standpoint of rhythmic effect, it is sufficient to compare the Yiddish with the later German folksong.

25. Uriel Weinreich was of the same opinion.

26. Cahan, *Shtudyes vegn yidisher folksshafung,* vol. A, p. 196.

27. Ruth Rubin, *A Treasury of Jewish Folksong* (New York, 1950), 28.

28. Leyb Naydus, "Dos lid fun shklaf," in *Lirik* (Warsaw, 1926), 118.

29. Mordkhe Gebirtig, *Mayne lider* (Cracow, 1936), 21.

30. See Josephine Miles, *Style and Proportion: The Language of Prose and Poetry* (Boston, 1967); and Lewis, *Creative Poetry,* 301.

31. Moyshe Kulbak, "Raysn," in *A Spiegel oyf a Shteyn,* editor in chief, Chone Shmeruk; poetry editor, Benjamin Hrushovski [Harshav]; and others. All cited Kulbak poems can be found in this source.

32. Used with permission of the estate of H. Leivick. See also Leivick, "Der volf," in Benjamin and Barbara Harshav, *American Yiddish Poetry: A Bilingual Anthology* [AYP] (Berkeley, Calif., 1986; Stanford, Calif., 2007), 699. The English translation is from *AYP.* Copyright © 1986, 2007 Benjamin and Barbara Harshav. All rights reserved. Used with permission of Stanford University Press, www.sup.org.

33. Or, at a minimum, 3.5. See also the figures for the epic folksong and for the following examples.

34. See also Štokmar, *Issledovaniia v oblasti russkogo narodnogo stikhoslozheniia.*

35. Friedrich Georg Jünger, *Rhythmus und Sprache im deutschen Gedicht* (Stuttgart, 1952).

36. Leivick, "Der volf," in *AYP,* 180.

37. Leivick, *Ale verk,* 144. Used with permission of the estate of H. Leivick.

38. A. Leyeles, *Rondos un andere lider* [Rondeaux and Other Poems] (New York: M. N. Mayzel, 1926], 43. The translation that follows is from *AYP,* 101 (Copyright © 1986, 2007 Benjamin and Barbara Harshav. All rights reserved. Used with permission of Stanford University Press, www.sup.org). *Sobvey* is "subway" in a New York Yiddish accent.

39. A. Leyeles, *Rondos,* 39; *AYP,* 97 (Copyright © 1986, 2007 Benjamin and Barbara Harshav. All rights reserved. Used with permission of Stanford University Press, www.sup.org).

40. *AYP,* 97.

41. A. Leyeles, "Fabius Linds Togbukh," in *Fabius Lind* (New York: Inzikh, 1937), 14; *AYP,* 139.

42. *AYP,* 138–139 (Copyright © 1986, 2007 Benjamin and Barbara Harshav. All rights reserved. Used with permission of Stanford University Press, www.sup.org).

43. A. Leyeles, "Étude" ["Etyud"], in *Rondeaux and Other Poems* (New York: Inzikh, 1926), 77.

44. A. Leyeles, *A yid oyfn yam* (New York: Tsiko, 1947), 7; also *AYP,* 169.

45. *Nish,* "not," is spelled with *sh* and without *t:* so Leyeles reads as is shown by all his rhymes.

46. A. Leivick, "Di gel vayse shayn" [The Yellow-White Glow], in *Ale verk,* 112; used with permission of the estate of H. Leivick; *AYP,* 687 (Copyright © 1986, 2007 Benjamin and

Barbara Harshav. All rights reserved. Used with permission of Stanford University Press, www.sup.org).

47. A. Leivick, "Nisht gezetikte tayves" [Unsatiated Passions], *in Ale verk,* 133; used with permission of the estate of H. Leivick; *AYP,* 689 (Copyright © 1986, 2007 Benjamin and Barbara Harshav. All rights reserved. Used with permission of Stanford University Press, www.sup.org).

48. Used with permission of the estate of H. Leivick; *AYP,* 693 (Copyright © 1986, 2007 Benjamin and Barbara Harshav. All rights reserved. Used with permission of Stanford University Press, www.sup.org).

49. With respect to this concept, I am close to Wolfgang Kayser: *Das sprachliche Kunstwerk* (Bern, 1948), 260; and *Kleine deutsche Versschule* (Bern, 1946).

50. *AYP,* 699.

51. *AYP,* 735.

52. Jacob Glatshteyn, "Eybik," in *Kredos* (New York: Idish lebn, 1929), 64. Used with permission of the Estate of Jacob Glatshteyn.

53. Berish Vaynshteyn, "Inem borten" [On the Docks], in *Brukhshtiker* [Broken Pieces] (New York: Haveyrim-komitet, 1936).

54. Used with permission of the Estate of Malke Kheyfets Tuzman. The English translation from *AYP,* 595 (Copyright © 1986, 2007 Benjamin and Barbara Harshav. All rights reserved. Used with permission of Stanford University Press, www.sup.org).

55. Ber Horovits, *Reyakh fun erd,* vol. 2 (Vilna, 1930), 83.

56. Andrey Bely, *Ritm kak dialektika . . .* (Moscow, 1929).

57. L. Binyon, *Tradition and Reaction in Modern Poetry,* The English Association, Pamphlet no. 63 (1926), 13.

58. A. Leyeles, *A yid oyfn yam,* 220.

59. Ber Horovits, *Fun may heym in di berg,* vol. 1 (Vienna, 1919), 5.

60. Ludwig Klages, *Vom Wesen des Rhythmus* (Zurich, 1934).

61. Hans Hellenbrecht, *Das Problem der freien Rhythmen mit Bezug auf Nietzsche,* Sprache und Dichtung, no. 48 (Bern, 1931).

62. A. Leyeles, *Rondeaux and Other Poems* (New York: Inzikh, 1926), 76.

63. See, primarily, Fritz Strich, *Deutsche Klassik und Romantik* (Bern, 1954); also Closs, *Die freien Rhythmen in der deutschen Lyrik.*

64. A. Leyeles, *Rondeaux,* 46.

65. E. Grinberg, *Di lange nakht,* 69.

66. Hellenbrecht, *Das Problem der freien Rhythmen,* 11.

67. N. B. Minkov, *Undzer Pyero* (New York, 1927).

68. Leyeles, *A yid oyfn yam,* 220.

69. Used with permission of the estate of H. Leivick; *AYP,* 689 (Copyright © 1986, 2007 Benjamin and Barbara Harshav. All rights reserved. Used with permission of Stanford University Press, www.sup.org).

70. H. Rambaud, "Rhythme et littérature," in *Les rhythmes et la vie* (Paris, 1947), 286.

71. Leyeles, *Rondeaux,* 82.

72. A. Leyeles, *Fabius Lind,* 47.

73. J. Glatshteyn, *Shtralndike yidn* (New York, 1946), 5 f.

74. Closs, *Die freien Rhythmen in der deutschen Lyrik*, 13.

75. S. M. Ginzburg and P. S. Marek, *Evreiskie narodnye pesni v Rossii* [Jewish Folksongs in Russia] (St. Petersburg, 1901), no. 26.

76. A. Leyeles, *Fabius Lind*, 99; see also 105.

CHAPTER 8. FREE RHYTHMS IN YIDDISH FOLKSONGS

1. For a later instance of publishing the lyrics (i.e. the text) without the music, see Adam Bradley and Andrew DuBois, eds., *The Anthology of Rap* (New Haven: Yale University Press, 2010).

2. Cf. August Reissman, *Geschichte des deutschen Liedes* (Berlin, 1874), 51–53.

3. For details, see M. P. Štokmar, *Issledovaniia v oblasti russkogo narodnogo stikhoslozheniia* [Studies on Russian Folk Versification] (Moscow, 1952).

4. On the non-individual relation between melody and text in German folksongs see Hans Mersmann, "Das deutsche Volkslied" [The German Folksong], in *Kulturgeschichte der Musik in Einzeldarstellungen* (Berlin, 1921), 32. The early German lyrics were sung; the distinctive feature of modern folksong, in contrast, is the free filling of syllables. See Andreas Heusler, *Deutsche Versgeschichte (mit Einschluss des altenglischen und altnordischen Stabreimverses)* (Berlin-Leipzig, 1925), 854, 871.

5. Y. L. Cahan (Kahan), *Shtudyes vegn yidisher folksshafung* (New York, 1952), vol. A, p. 48, henceforth cited in this style: Cahan A 48.

6. Heusler, *Deutsche Versgeschichte*, §§872 f.

7. Reissmann (*Geschichte des deutschen Liedes*, 37) believes that the songs with artificial strophe patterns which were popular in German in the sixteenth and seventeenth centuries were derived from the *Minnesang* and *Meistersang*.

8. Cahan A 203 f.

9. Cahan A 201.

10. Cahan A 10.

11. Benjamin Hrushovski [Harshav], "The Typical Strophe of Yiddish Folksong," in *Sefer Dov Sadan*, ed. S. Verses, N. Rotenstreich, and Ch. Shmeruk (Tel Aviv: Ha-Kibbutz Ha-Meuchad, 1977), 111–128.

12. Cahan B 13, B 31; S. M. Ginzburg and P. S. Marek, *Evreiskie narodnye pesni v Rossii* [Jewish Folksongs in Russia] (St. Petersburg, 1901), no. 244, etc.

13. Cahan A 208.

14. For example, Ginzburg and Marek, *Evreiskie narodnye pesni v Rossii*, 1, 5, 6, 7.

15. See Reissmann, *Geschichte des deutschen Liedes*, 43.

16. Sh. Bastomski, *Baym kval: Yidishe folkslider* [At the Source: Yiddish Folksongs] (Vilna, 1923), 188.

17. On the conversion of five-line stanzas to quatrains in another song of Gordon's, see Eleanor Gordon-Mlotek, "The Metamorphosis of Mikhl Gordon's Poem "Di bord" [in Hebrew], *Yivo-bleter*, 35 (1951): 299–311.

18. Cahan B 16.

19. Cf. Heusler, *Deutsche Versgeschichte*, §1218.

20. For an example, see Sh. Lehman, *Ganovim-lider mit melodyes* (Warsaw, 1928), 17; and the Polish source of the song published there, ibid., 209 (notes).

21. Cahan A 16, no. 9.

22. M. Beregovski, *Yidisher muzik-folklor,* vol. 1 (Moscow, 1934), no. 82.

23. Here, incidentally, we have already a folk-like deletion of a metrically compressed syllable.

24. Beregovski, *Yidisher muzik-folklor,* vol. 1, no. 65.

25. Ruth Rubin, *A Treasury of Jewish Folksong* (New York, 1950), 18.

26. See the song in Beregovski, *Yidisher muzik-folklor,* no. 80.

27. Rubin, *Treasury,* 17.

28. Cf. Cahan A 6.

29. Heusler, *Deutsche Versgeschichte,*§874.

30. Cf. Lehman, *Ganovim-lider mit melodyes,* 63.

31. See also Štokmar, *Issledovaniia v oblasti russkogo narodnogo stikhoslozheniia,* 400.

32. Sh. Lehman, "Gazlen-shpil," in *Arkhiv far der yidisher shprakh-visnshaft, literatur-forshung un etnologye* (Warsaw, 1922–1933), 287.

33. Cahan A 90; concerning the *semene* dance, see ibid., 90 f.

34. J. Brutskus, "Two Foreign-Language Counting-Out Rhymes of Jewish Children of Samogitia," *Yivo-bleter,* 26 (1945): 336.

35. Cf., for example, the strong paeonicity of the song about *yisker.* But this was not yet a hard and fast rule, hence the alterations in the a.-s. songs of the poets.

36. See Sh. Katsherginski, *Lider fun getos un lagern* [Songs from Camps and Ghettos] (New York, 1948).

37. Sh. Goldshmid, *Folkslider fun der foterlendisher milkhome* [Folksongs from the Fatherland War (= World War II)] (Moscow, 1944).

APPENDIX A: PERCEPTION, RHYTHMICAL GROUPS, AND THE BIBLE

1. W. Kayser, *Kleine deutsche Versschule* (Bern, 1946), 18.

2. Cf. V. V. Vinogradov, "Poniate sintagmy v sintaksise russkogo jazyka," in *Voprosy sintaksisa sovremennogo russkogo jazyka* (Moscow, 1950); also S. Karcevskij, "Sur la phonologie da la phrase," *Travaux du cercle linguistique de Prague,* 4 (1931): 188–223; and in poetry, see W. Kayser, *Das sprachliche Kunstwerk,* 2nd ed. (Bern, 1951).

3. See Kayser, *Das sprachliche Kunstwerk.*

4. B. Tomaševskij, *O stixe* (Leningrad, 1929).

APPENDIX B: TOWARD A CRITICAL THEORY OF THE STRUCTURES AND FUNCTIONS OF MODERN POETRY

1. The literature in this field is so heterogeneous that I feel the necessity of arguing points which may to some critics seem trivial and to others unconvincing. This is a first, tentative statement of several general aspects, developed in view of a descriptive typology of modern European and American free rhythms, regretfully unsupported here by concrete illustrations. The general concepts here are based on extensive fieldwork, especially with Hebrew and Yiddish poetry—see Chapters 4 and 7.

2. When D. Stauffer (*The Nature of Poetry* [New York, 1946], 204) says that "if free verse had form in any real sense, its form would be detectable," we wonder, on the one hand, why "detectable" should mean falling under presupposed strict numerical rules and, on the other hand, how "detectable" his other terms are: "exact," "intense," "significant," etc. Cf. also Jean Suberville (*Histoire et théorie de la versification française* [Paris, 1956], 158): "il n'y a pas, à proprement parler, de verse sans mesure determine." In the eyes of this dogmatic normativist, it is to a great extent the fault of free verse that the broad public has been estranged from poetry.

3. René Wellek and A. Warren, *Theory of Literature* (1949; New York, 1956), 168.

4. K. Shapiro, *A Bibliography of Modern Prosody* (Baltimore, Md., 1948), 77. This is certainly exaggerated. There are many intelligent and correct observations in the traditional books, and we should admit that a great deal of collected information can be used if it is carefully analyzed and reinterpreted. But sometimes we prefer the laborious task of analyzing anew a vast number of poems because of the questionable reliability of noncritically accumulated facts.

5. J. C. Ransom, "The Strange Music of English Verse," *Kenyon Review,* 18 (1956): 460–477.

6. Cf. W. Kayser, *Das sprachliche Kunstwerk,* 2nd ed. (Bern, 1951).

7. R. Blackmur, "Lord Tennyson's Scissors," in *Form and Value in Modern Poetry* (Garden City, N.Y., 1957), 369.

8. Ibid, 371. These two pronouncements are basically close to Y. Tynjanov's ideas (*Problema stixotvornogo jazyka* [Leningrad, 1924]), expressed in more concrete terms in one of the most interesting modern books on the principles of poetic language.

9. Cf. E. Staiger, who asserts (*Die Kunst der Interpretation* [Zurich, 1955], 391, 16) that the lyric poem is an absolute unity of the meaning of the words and their sounds. But how do we know when such occurs and when not?

10. Blackmur, "Lord Tennyson's Scissors," 383, 388.

11. W. K. Wimsatt, Jr., and C. Brooks, *Literary Criticism, a Short History* (New York, 1957), 750.

12. Kayser, *Das sprachliche Kunstwerk,* 262.

13. Cf. C. Sachs, *Rhythm and Tempo* (New York, 1953), for a parallel problem in music.

14. For some, rhythm was more than a term of poetry. It was, rather, a symbol for dynamic forces in life, which they hoped to echo in their poems. The Russian Symbolist Blok spoke of the "music of the epoch," "the crushing rhythm of the revolution," and the like. The Italian Futurist Marinetti proclaimed that paintings are meant to catch the particular rhythm of every object rather than its outward forms. Kurt Pinthus wrote in his preface to the famous Expressionistic anthology *Menschheitsdämmerung* [The Twilight of Humanity] (Berlin, 1920): "Es kommt darauf an, aus den lärmenden Dissonanzen, den melodischen Harmonien, dem wuchtigen Schreiten der Akkorde, den gebrochensten Halb- und Vierteltönen—die Motive und Themen der wildesten wüstesten Zeit der Weltgeschichte herauszuhören" (The gist of the matter is out of the screaming dissonances, the melodic harmonies, the raging of marching chords, the broken half-tones and quartertones—to hear the motifs and themes of the wildest, most desolate time of world history). But even those who aimed at avoiding "musicality" and at creating a prosaic illusion in

their poems were actually preoccupied with a question of rhythm in its broadest sense, where it is connected with questions of language, meaning, and mimesis.

15. P. M. Jones, *The Background of Modern French Poetry* (Cambridge, England, 1951), 94.

16. T. S. Eliot, "Reflections on Vers Libre," *New Statesman*, March 3, 1917; Eliot, "The Music of Poetry" (lecture). It should be noted that the first statement was written—in 1917, in a mood of polemic—before Eliot's own more daring departures as a poet.

17. A recent bibliography of writings on free rhythms is available only in German: W. Mohr, "Freie Rhythmen," in P. Merker and V. Stammler, *Reallexikon der deutschen Literaturegeschichte*, 2nd ed. (Berlin, 1955); see also H. Hellenbrecht, *Das Problem der freien Rhythmen mit Bezug auf Neitzsche*, Sprache und Dichtung, no. 48 (Bern, 1931). In English, G. Hughes, *Imagism and the Imagists* (Stanford, Calif., and London, 1931), covers the polemical stage of the Imagist movement. But the writings of this period, though of considerable historical interest, have almost no structural value. With the end of the argument, in the 1930s, the entry "free verse" disappeared from American bibliographies of periodicals. A general bibliography of prosody, with valuable annotations, but not complete, is found in Shapiro, *Bibliography of Modern Prosody*. A bibliography of rhythm analyses in modern practical criticism, though much needed, is not available. In M. P. Štokmar, *Bibliografiia rabot po stixosloženiju* (Moscow, 1953), many Russian writings on prosody are listed, and the book is indexed; for criticism and addenda, cf. R. Jakobson, "M. P. Štokmar: Bibliografija rabot po stixosloženiju," *Slavia*, 13 (1934): 416– 431. See also R. Jakobson, "Studies in Comparative Slavic Metrics," *Oxford Slavonic Papers*, 3 (1952): 21–66, on old Slavic metrics; and V. Ehrlich, review of B. Hrushovski [Harshav], "On Free Rhythms in Modern Yiddish Poetry," *Comparative Literature* 8 (1956): 254–255, for some West Slavic studies. In French, H. Morier, *Le rhythme de vers libre symbolist étudié chez Verharen, Henri de Regnier, Vielé-Griffin, et ses relations avec le sens* (Geneva, 1943–1944), contains a small but essential list; Y. LeHir, *Esthétique et structure du vers français d'après le théoriciens du 16ième siècle à nos jours* (Paris, 1956), a strange survey of Slavic prosodic studies over the past five centuries, completes the former. There exists also a vast literature on rhythms in the Bible: for a survey of the main old theories (up to 1905), see W. H. Cobb, *A Criticism of the Systems of Hebrew Meter* (Oxford, 1905); and J. Begrich, "Zur hebräischen Metrik," *Theologische Runsachau*, N.F. 4 (1932): 67–89, contains a good summary of the subsequent twenty-five years. For general problems see the surveys and bibliographies in V. Ehrlich, *Russian Formalism* (The Hague, 1954); Kayser, *Das sprachliche Kunstwerk*; and Wellek and Warren, *Theory of Literature*; for a recent psychological approach see P. Fraisse, *Les structure rythmiques: Étudies psychologique* (Louvain, 1956).

18. A. Closs, *Die freien Rhythmen in der deutschen Lyrik* (Bern, 1947).

19. Review of Closs, "Die Freien Rhythmen . . . ," *Modern Language Notes*, 65 (1950): 127–130.

20. Cf. E. Lachmann, *Hölderlins Hymnen in freien Strophen: Eine metrische Untersuchung* (Frankfurt am Main, 1937); H. Maeder, "Hölderlin und das Wort: Zum Problem der freien Rhythmen in Hölderlins Dichtung," *Trivium* 2 (1944): 42–59; D. Seckel, *Hölderlins Sprachrythmus* (Leipzig, 1937).

21. M. Kommerell, *Gedanken über Gedichte* (Frankfurt am Main, 1943); W. Mohr, "Freie Rhythmen," in Merker and Stammler, *Reallexikon der deutschen Literaturgeschichte;*

G. Müller, "Die Grundformen der deutschen Lyrik," *Von deutscher Art in Sprache und Dichtung,* 5 (1941): 95–135.

22. Yvor Winters, *Primitivism and Decadence* (New York, 1937).

23. In the vast literature on T. S. Eliot there seems to be no really close analysis of the "music" of his verse and its development, except for mechanistic and often uncritical statistics of fifteen poems and passages (Sister M. M. Barry, *An Analysis of the Prosodic Structure of Selected Poems of T. S. Eliot* [dissertation, Catholic University of America, Washington, D.C., 1948] and a simplifying chapter in H. Gardner, *The Art of T. S. Eliot* [London, 1949]).

24. Morier, *Le rhythme de vers libre symbolist;* and L. P. Thomas, *Le vers moderne* (Brussels, 1943). Whether their aesthetic conclusions are well balanced is, of course, a different question.

25. P. Guirard, *Langage et versification d'après l'oeuvre de Paul Valéry* (Paris, 1953).

26. Ehrlich, *Russian Formalism;* Wellek and Warren, *Theory of Literature.*

27. R. Jakobson, *O česškom stixe preimuščestvenno v sopostavlenii s russkim* (= *Sborniki po teorii poetičeskogo jazyka, 5*) (Berlin and Moscow, 1923).

28. Tynjanov, *Problema stixotvornogo jazyka.*

29. O. Brik, "Ritm i sintaksis," *Novyj LEF,* nos. 3–6 (1927): 15–20, 23–29, 32–37, 33–39.

30. B. Tomaševskij, *O stixe* (Leningrad, 1929).

31. In an early attempt (Benjamin Hrushovski [Harshav], "On Free Rhythms in Modern Yiddish Poetry," in *The Field of Yiddish: Studies in Yiddish Language, Folklore, and Literature,* ed. Uriel Weinreich, vol. 1 [New York, 1954], 219–266), I tried to develop methods of structural analysis and a classification of free rhythms, exploring their historical, critical, and linguistic implications in the totality of a relatively little-known body of poetry; cf. Ehrlich, review of Hrushovski, "On Free Rhythms in Modern Yiddish Poetry."

32. This distinction is commonly observed on the continent, though variously emphasized (cf. A. W. de Groot, "Der Rhythmus," *Neophilologus* 17 [1932]: 81–100, 177–197; De Groot, "Zur Grundlegung der allgemeinen Versbaulehrre," *Archives néerlandaises de phonétique expérimentale,* 8–9 [1933]: 68–81; W. Kayser, *Kleine deutsche Versschule* [Bern, 1946]; Kayser, *Das sprachliche Kunstwerk;* Morier, *Le rhythme de vers libre symbolist;* J. Pfeiffer, *Umgang mit Dichtung* [Hamburg, 1936]; Pfeiffer, *Zwischen Dichtung und Philosophie* [Bremen, 1947]; Tomaševskij, *O stixe;* etc.). The fact itself is, of course, known to the most serious critics. For example, when Y. Winters asserts that "*Miltonic* blank verse is one of the greatest metrical inventions in the history of poetry" and that "he invented it for the sake" of "Paradise Lost," he does not mean merely the meter but, in his words, "the total phonetic quality of metrical language," that is, the rhythm.

33. I am far from such absolute dichotomies as were made by the German philosopher L. Klages (*Vom Wesen des Rhythmus* [Zurich, 1931]), where a polar opposition between rhythm and *Takt* (meter) is drawn back to a metaphysical distinction between *Seele* and *Geist* (soul and spirit), to the clear disadvantage of the second. His pupil H. Hellenbrecht writes in his study on free rhythms, "Zur Befreiung gelangt die in den Ketten des Bewusstseins schwingende Seele und befreit wird sie von dem messenden und begrenzenden Prinzip des Geistes" (*Das Problem der freien Rhythmen,* 33), and, accordingly, he disapproves of Goethe's free rhythms for their relative proximity to regular iambs. No

doubt, in most of poetry, meter is the constant organizing factor, around which the local rhythmic configurations as well as the total rhythmic expression are created.

34. The problem has begun to be addressed in Brik, "Ritm i sintaksis"; D. Davie, *Articulate Energy: An Enquiry into the Syntax of English Poetry* (New York, 1958); F. Lockemann, *Das Gedicht und seine Klanggestalt* (Emsdetten, 1952).

35. Blackmur, "Lord Tennyson's Scissors," 373.

36. For example, Robert Graves and Paula Riding (*Contemporary Techniques of Poetry: A Political Analogy* [London, 1925], 24) write: "Metre considered as a set pattern approved by convention will stand for the claims of society as at present organized: the variations on metre will stand for the claims of the individual." We could compile a book of such pronouncements on the "nature" of free rhythms.

37. I refer especially to the recently very influential theories of Heidegger and other phenomenologically minded European critics, such as E. Staiger: *Grundbegriffe der Poetik* (Zurich, 1951); *Die Kunst der Interpretation;* review in *Erasmus,* 6 (1953): 212–213. With a different philosophical background, American critics often did methodically similar things because of a similar movement toward the poem as the central object of observation.

38. The mere knowledge that there are several kinds of rhythmic elements is not enough. Thus Barry (*Analysis of Prosodic Structure*) analyzes several kinds of "cadence" in T. S. Eliot, without trying to understand their concrete interrelations in different types of poems. Despite some valuable details, the discussion leads to nothing but vague generalizations in the summary. (See also the next note.)

39. A most significant case is the following. Barry, in the only existing book on Eliot's prosody (*Analysis of Prosodic Structure*), writes: "An examination of Eliot's poems for the purpose of determining to what extent he uses phrasal cadences reveals that only one combination of this sort can be found running through as many as five poems." She forgets that a "phrasal cadence" is, according to her arbitrary decision, a combination of group cadences which occur in at least 15 percent of the total lines of a poem. So if one occurs in 14 percent (say, in seven subsequent lines out of fifty), it does not exist. Furthermore, one "phrasal cadence" happens to consist of two rising disyllabic groups—two iambs—and that is an analysis which does not distinguish between metric and nonmetric poems. Would we not be able to suspect before the statistics were compiled that a sequence of two iambs may occur in more than one of Eliot's poems? In any case, the whole concept of "phrasal cadence" is misleading, since it is an utterly arbitrary group of syllables, without any consideration of its role in the dynamics of rhythm. In a line like "The dove descending breaks the air" (symbolized: OÓ, OÓO, Ó, OÓ), only the words "descending breaks" form a "cadence" (and are not the first or last words), simply because in the fourth part of "Little Gidding" two adjacent words of this structure happen to occur in more than 15 percent of the lines. Even if the structure were to occur in 100 percent of the lines, what effect would it it have in a poem? That this is a pure iambic line makes no difference to the author; that word boundaries without relation to the meter make no sense, and that grouping without consideration of real phrasal groups does not exist in a poem— none of this is argued by Barry. And then, of course, we discover how few phrases Eliot has—that is, how great the variety of his rhythms is! (A statistical comparison to other

poets is out of the question.) We discover a group like Ó, OÓ in a trochaic poem, and so on. But—what is more important in free rhythms—this exact grouping cannot lead to a perception of repetitions of significantly similar rhythmic groups if they differ in one syllable, a difference which can be unimportant in free rhythms, especially when there is syntactical parallelism or simply in a case of free anacrusis.

40. Staiger, in *Die Kunst der Interpretation,* argues that interpretation of poetry is an art (possibly not the best-chosen term), but that the "art of interpretation" is a science, since it carries all the responsibilities of objective proof and can be dismissed if proved incorrect.

41. We should not be deterred by a rhythm's complexity, since even "simple" elements are simple merely by a convenient illusion. So is stress, according to P. Habermann's recent definition ("Akzent," 16–21, in *Reallexikon der deutschen Literaturgeschichte,* 2nd ed., ed. W. Kohlschmidt and W. Mohr [Berlin, 1955])—"eine sehr Komplexe Verbindung von Tonhöhe, Tonverlauf, Klangfarbe, Stärke, Dauer"—and each of these elements is, probably, as complex in its turn. Therefore, I prefer phenomenology to an atomistic approach.

42. To a considerable extent, Hellenbrecht, Pfeiffer, and many less "rhythmically minded" practical critics are prone to fall into the same dangers; they are usually good in their direct observations but are not concrete and often fail in generalizations if confronted with evidence from wider fields.

43. In Russia, articles on French disputes on free verse, by the French poet R. Ghil, were printed as early as 1903, which influenced English poets (see R. Taupin, *L'influence du symbolism français sur la poésie américaine* [Paris, 1929]), was translated into Russian by the "imagist" Šeršenevič.

44. Wellek and Warren, *Theory of Literature.*

45. Ehrlich, *Russian Formalism,* 194, quoting Tynjanov.

46. V. Pjast, *Sovremennoje stixovedenie* (Leningrad, 1931).

47. Wellek and Warren, *Theory of Literature,* 173.

48. See especially Lockemann, *Das Gedicht und seine Klanggestalt,* 94; and Maeder, "Hölderlin und das Wort."

Publications by Benjamin Harshav (Formerly Hrushovski) on Prosody and Related Fields

E = English; H = Hebrew

BOOKS

American Yiddish Poetry: A Bilingual Anthology. Edited and translated (with Barbara Harshav); with introductions and documents. Los Angeles: University of California Press, 1986; Stanford, CA: Stanford University Press, 2000. [E]

"On Free Rhythms in Modern Yiddish Poetry." In Uriel Weinreich, ed., *The Field of Yiddish: Studies in Yiddish Language, Folklore, and Literature.* Published on the Occasion of the Bicentennial of Columbia University. Vol. 1. New York: Publications of the Linguistic Circle of New York, 1954. Pp. 219–266. [E]

Ritmus Ha-Rakhavut [The Rhythm of Largeness]: *Theory and Practice in Uri-Zvi Grinberg's Expressionist Poetry.* Tel Aviv: Ha-Kibbutz Ha-Meuchad, 1978. [H]

Selected Writings: Studies in Literature and Culture. Jerusalem: Carmel Publishing House; Tel Aviv: Porter Institute for Poetics and Semiotics. [H]

Vol. 1: *Fields and Frames: Studies in the Theory of Literature and Meaning* (including "Do Sounds Have Meaning?"). 2000.

Vol. 2: *The Art of Poetry.* 2000.

Vol. 7. *Meter and Rhythm in Modern Hebrew Poetry.* 2008.

Shirat ha-Tekhiya ha-Ivrit [Poetry of the Hebrew Revival]: A Critical and Historical Anthology. Selected and edited, with textual history, annotations, prosodic analysis of every poem, biographies, and introductions by Benjamin Harshav. 2 vols. Jerusalem: Mosad Bialik; Tel Aviv: Open University, 2000. [H]

Toldot ha-tsurot shel ha-shira ha-ivrit min ha-tanakh ad ha-modernizm [A History of Hebrew Versification from the Bible to Modernism] (including "Hebrew Rhyme: Its Theory and

History in the Last Fifteen Hundred Years" and "The Rivers of Poetry: The Ashke-Sefardi Language in Uri-Zvi Grinberg's *Rehovot Ha-Nahar*"). Ramat Gan: Bar-Ilan University Press, 2008. [H]

STUDIES AND ESSAYS

"The Creation of Accentual Iambs in European Poetry, and Their First Employment in a Yiddish Romance in Italy (1508–09)." In Lucy S. Dawidowicz et al., eds., *For Max Weinreich on His Seventieth Birthday.* The Hague: Mouton, 1964. Pp. 108–146. [E]

"Do Sounds Have Meaning? On the Expressive Aspects of Sound Patterns in Poetry." *Ha-Sifrut*, 1, no. 2 (1968): 410–430. [H]

"The Major Systems of Hebrew Rhyme from the Piyut to the Present: An Essay on Basic Concepts." *Ha-Sifrut*, 2, no. 4 (1971): 721–749. [H]

"The Meaning of Sound Patterns in Poetry: An Interaction Theory." *Poetics Today*, 2, no. 1a (1980): 39–56. [E]

"The Meaning of Sound Patterns in Poetry: An Interaction Theory." In *Explorations in Poetics.* Stanford, CA: Stanford University Press, 2007. [E]

"Neharot Ha-Shir: Ha-Zrimah Ha-Ritmit Be-*Rehovot Ha-Nahar*" [The Rivers of Poetry: The Rhythmical Flow in (U.-Z.Grinberg's book) *Streets of the River*]. In Avidov Lipsker and Tamar Wolf Monson, eds., *Khamishim Shana Le-Rekhovot Ha-Nahar* [Fiftieth Anniversary of *Streets of the River*]: Mivkhar Mekhkarim Ve-Teudot. Ramat Gan: Bar-Ilan University Press, 2006. Pp. 65–85. [H]

"A Note on Hebrew Prosody." In S. Burnshaw, T. Carmi, and E. Spicehandler, eds., *The Modern Hebrew Poem Itself.* New York: Holt, Rinehart and Winston, 1965. Pp. 225–231. [E]

"Note on the Systems of Hebrew Versification." In T. Carmi, ed., *The Penguin Book of Hebrew Verse.* London: Penguin, 1981. Pp. 57–72. [E]

"On Free Rhythms in Modern Poetry." In Thomas A. Sebeok, ed., *Style in Language.* Cambridge, MA: MIT Press; New York: Wiley, 1960. Pp. 173–190. [E]

"Prosody, Hebrew" [Survey of the History of Hebrew Poetic Forms from the Bible to the Present]. *Encyclopaedia Judaica.* Vol. 13 (1972). Pp. 1196–1240. [E]

"The Rhythm of Largeness: Theory and Practice in Uri-Zvi Grinberg's Expressionist Poetry." *Ha-Sifrut*, 1, no.1 (1968): 167–205. [H]

"The Typical Strophe of Yiddish Folksong." In S. Verses, N. Rotenstreich, and Ch. Shmeruk, eds., *Sefer Dov Sadan.* Tel Aviv: Ha-Kibbutz Ha-Meuchad, 1977. Pp. 111–128. [H]

Index of Persons

Index of Topics in
Prosody and Literature

Greek poetry: influence of, on German poetry, 271; metric system in, 4; stress in, 157

grid, 82

haiku, 52

ḥataf, 74, 97

Hebrew poetry. *See* Index of Hebrew Versification and Yiddish Poetry: *Hebrew versification*

hemistich, 11, 47, 74–75

higher poetry, 157

hyperdactyl, 236, 254

iamb, 3, 59, 133, 200

idyll, 67, 136

Introspective trend (*Inzikhizm*), 227, 250. *See also* Index of Hebrew Versification and Yiddish Poetry: Yiddish poets

isochronism, 275

Italian Futurists, 16

Italian poetry: ottava rima in, 172; syllabic meter in, xiii, xv, 186 (*see also* Index of Hebrew Versification and Yiddish Poetry: Hebrew versification in Italy)

line, 47, 265

literary text: basic trait of, 22; interaction of patterns in, 22, 38–39

lower poetry, ix, 157, 162

measure (tact), 219

metaphor, 28, 65, 304, 309, 164, 250–251; Benjamin Harshav on, 318n15; compared with onomatopoeia, 29; frames of reference of, 24; as imagery aspect of poetry, xii; sound-metaphors, 30; two-way interaction in, 23–24

meter: as an abstract pattern, 2, 200, 306–307; basic aspects of, 1–13; compared with rhythm, 200–201, 227, 288, 306–307, 334n32–33; as a construct based, 6;

five kinds of, 3–4, 13, 99, 132–133; and form, xiii; and language, 5; lengths of the line of, 4; as mandatory structure for every poem, xii; multicultural analysis of, 149–150; as an organizing factor, 334n33; as a regular pattern, 2; and rhyme, xii; role of, in poetry, xii; and the rule of correlation, 5–6, 133; as a series of stress and unstressed syllables, 1; and sound, 18–19, 44, 311; and sound orchestration, xii; as a system, xiii, 5; and text, xii, 6, 8

meter, accentual, xiii, 12

meter, accentual-syllabic. *See accentual-syllabic meter*

meter, binary, 3, 13, 99–100, 135

meter, deviant accentual-syllabic, 12, 135. *See also* modern poetry: "ternary net" in

meter, free-accentual, 12

meter, quantitative-syllabic, 12

meter, "scanning," 6, 201

meter, stress, 252–254

meter, syllabic, xiii, 12

meter, ternary, 4, 9, 13, 99–100, 135

meter, word, 12

metonymy, 22, 43, 54

metrical accent, 132; in correlation with language stress, 5; distinguished from language stress, 5, 320n2; symbol of, xx

metrical poem, 165

metrical slack, symbol of, xx, 132

modern poetry: free rhythm in, 152, 297–298, 320n3 (*see also* free rhythms); free verse in, xi; functions of, 302–313; options in, xi; rhythmic devices in, 312; structures of, 302–313; "ternary net" in, 10, 59, 135, 229

New Criticism, 17, 306

onomatopoeia, xiv, 26–28, 32–33; compared with metaphor, 29–30;

Index of Hebrew Versification
and Yiddish Poetry